# THE BARBARIANS

'There were his young barbarians all at play'
Byron, from *Childe Harold*

# THE BARBARIANS

## THE OFFICIAL HISTORY
## OF THE BARBARIAN FOOTBALL CLUB

# NIGEL STARMER-SMITH

**MACDONALD AND JANE'S, LONDON**

Designer: David Fordham
House Editor: Kirsty Nicholson

*The photograph on the back cover shows the Barbarian team that played Devonshire at Exeter on 1 April 1891.* Back row: *G.Young, T.Whittaker, W.P.Carpmael, R.L.Aston, R.T.Duncan, P.F.Hancock, W.H.Manfield.* Middle row: *E.Emley, C.B.Nicholl, P.Christopherson, A.E.Stoddart, D.W.Evans, P.Maud.* On ground: *H.Marshall, C.A.Hooper, F.H.Fox, C.J.Vernon.*

ISBN 0354 085018

First published in 1977 by Macdonald and Jane's Publishers Limited, Paulton House, 8 Shepherdess Walk, London N1 7LW

Photoset, printed and bound by Redwood Burn Limited, Trowbridge & Esher

# CONTENTS

# ACKNOWLEDGEMENTS

I owe my sincere thanks to the many Barbarians whose contributions, both written and verbal, have greatly assisted in the writing of this history. In particular I am grateful to Wilson Shaw, Tom Voyce, Lord Wakefield of Kendal, Haydn Tanner, Noel Murphy senior, Eric Evans, Ronnie Dawson, Stewart Wilson, Noel Murphy junior and John Dawes. I wish to thank also the many officials of clubs that have played against the Barbarians for their assistance in compiling the match records; and the many rugby correspondents whose match reports from 1890 to the present day have been an invaluable source of material. Thanks are also due to Terry McLean, Ian Kirkpatrick and Don Clarke of New Zealand; Basil Medway, Jack Gage, Tjol Lategan, Louis Babrow and 'Tuppy' Owen-Smith of South Africa; Rosaline Fitzgerald, formerly of The Esplanade Hotel, Penarth; and J.V. Greenwood of Bradford RFC, whose research has shed new light on the first Barbarian tour.

I have appreciated, too, the generosity of the present Barbarian Committee in enabling me to have exclusive access to all past records and material relating to the club, and for the guidance which has enabled me to bring this work to fruition. I am especially grateful to the President, Herbert Waddell, who has also kindly provided the foreword.

Amongst the many other Barbarians to whom I am grateful, I wish to single out Andrew 'Jock' Wemyss, and it is to his name that I dedicate this book.

I am indebted also to Kirsty Nicholson and David Fordham, of Macdonald and Jane's, for the generous application of both their patience and professional expertise in the production of this book.

Finally, I owe my greatest debt of gratitude, for many reasons, to my wife, Rosamund.

**N.C.S-S**

The author and publishers wish to acknowledge the generous help afforded by both the *Western Mail and Echo* and Colin Elsey of Colorsport, and for permission to reproduce a selection of their photographs. Thanks also to the *South Wales Argus*, the *Northampton Independent*, and Sport and General.

# FOREWORD

The belief that rugby should be played as an attacking game was firmly held by W.P.Carpmael, the founder of the Barbarians. It was to justify this belief that he formed the club in 1890. Those invited to join him on the short tours that he arranged had not only to share his enthusiasm for hard, clean, attacking rugby, but also to be good company on and off the field.

Carpmael was followed by Emile de Lissa, who had been his Secretary, and in turn the other Presidents were Jack Haigh Smith and Brigadier Glyn Hughes. These three were all as enthusiastic as Tottie Carpmael on the Barbarian idea of rugby, and they strove, with success, to put his vision into practice in the same way as he did himself. It would only be fair to mention at this stage Andrew Wemyss, or Jock Wemyss as he was called, who was our meticulous and devoted Registrar for many years. When you met Barbarians in South Africa, Australia or New Zealand, the first question they asked was 'How is Jock?' He first went on tour in 1924 and was a most enthusiastic Barbarian all his rugby life.

What a wealth of lovable and respected characters the Club has known! The one overriding quality they all seemed to have in abundance was a sense of humour and quick wit that made touring with them fun.

When I was starting my international career, Dan Drysdale, an experienced member of the Scottish side and a Barbarian, told me: 'If ever you are asked to go on tour don't hesitate, accept at once. It is an honour, you will have great fun, you will play against the great Welsh clubs and you'll get to know and like rugby players from all the other countries. It's the best form of rugby in the UK!' When the next year that opportunity came my way every word Dan had said proved to be true. It was tremendous value and I hope it always will be.

This book has been a labour of love by Nigel Starmer-Smith. I have read it with intense interest and I am sure it will be read in a similar way, not only by Barbarians, but by many other rugby players.

As this book goes to print comes the news that, as rugby football's major contribution to help Her Majesty The Queen's Silver Jubilee Appeal Fund, the Barbarians have been invited to play the British Lions on their return from New Zealand. The match is to be played at Twickenham on 10 September 1977 and is unique in that it is the first time that the Lions have played as a team in the UK. It is a great honour for the Barbarian Club and we look forward to a splendid game of attacking rugby, fitting for a royal occasion.

*Herbert Waddell*

**HERBERT WADDELL**
GLASGOW 1977

# INTRODUCTION

A unique club, a unique style, the Barbarians is the most revered rugby touring club in the history of rugby football. From its unpretentious origins as a 'scratch' team raised by 'Tottie' Carpmael to tour the north of England in 1890, the club has grown in the affection and esteem of all rugby people to its present status as the most famous club in the world, with a resolute commitment to attacking rugby. It has changed little over the last eighty-seven years. The Barbarian Football Club is still one of the last remaining bastions of true amateurism in the world of sport.

The Barbarians have no ground, no club-house, no entry fee, no subscription, and virtually no money; the expenses for players and three of the Committee are paid for by the clubs they visit. It is in every sense a touring club, for there are no 'home' matches. But the Barbarians have a 'spiritual' home in South Wales, formerly based on the Esplanade Hotel, Penarth, although the headquarters of the Easter tour is now the Royal Hotel, Cardiff. The traditional warmth of the reception accorded to the Barbarians by the people of South Wales has made Cardiff Arms Park very much a 'home' ground for the big occasions.

There are six annual fixtures, including the cornerstone of Barbarian tradition – the Easter tour of South Wales, when the matches are against Penarth, Cardiff, Swansea and Newport – as well as the Boxing Day game with Leicester and the Mobbs Memorial Match against East Midlands in the spring. In addition the club has been honoured to play, since 1948, every major touring side of the All Blacks, the Springboks, and the Wallabies to visit the British Isles. So far there have been twelve matches, which have produced some of the most memorable and exciting games of rugby ever seen. The club has made occasional overseas tours in recent years, four in all, twice visiting South Africa and twice touring Canada. There have been many other matches too (the Barbarians have played seventy-two different sides altogether), usually to celebrate a special occasion, such as a jubilee or centenary, or to raise money for charity or honour some worthy cause. In this way the Baa-Baas have taken their banner of attractive attacking rugby to all corners of the British Isles. During their long history they have even been known to indulge in such sporting events as cricket and soccer matches, and have competed occasionally in seven-a-side tournaments with notable success, winning the Middlesex Sevens in 1934.

The reason for the name 'Barbarians' is shrouded in mystery. Some have suggested that it is owed to some classical authority who deemed it appropriate to give the club a name.

'dignified by the famous victory of Arminius over Varus and his legions in Germany some two thousand years ago'.

Emile de Lissa, a great Barbarian President, once wrote that he thought it more likely that the word 'Barbarian' was chosen in defiance of those who would style all rugby players as just that!

*Percy Carpmael – a man of vision. He saw the Barbarians as an invitation touring rugby club, with a resolute commitment to playing attacking rugby in an atmosphere of good comradeship and fun.*

*Barbarian Easter Tour, 1931: the very first tour on which the Barbarians won all four matches.*
Back row: *R.J.Henderson, H.S.Mackintosh, L.L.Bedford, J.L.Farrell, J.H.Beattie, W.R.Logan, J.A.Bassett, D.T.Kemp, N.Murphy, A.W.Walker, O.L.Owen.* Middle row: *D.P.Henshaw, J.W.Allan, J.McD.Hodgson, D.St Clair Ford, F.W.S.Malir, R.Bolton, S.J.Huins, J.R.F.Popplewell, R.Burgess, F.Le S.Stone.* Seated: *A.F.Heppenstall, J.J.A.Embleton, A.Wemyss, H.A.Haigh Smith, E.de Lissa, H.L.G.Hughes, D.J.MacMyn, C.R.Hopwood, I.M.B.Stuart.* On ground: *A.Key, E.W.F.deV.Hunt, B.R.Tod, F.L.Williams, J.E.Forrest, J.B.Nelson, S.C.Cravos, C.C.Tanner.*

Membership of the club is by invitation, but there is no discrimination whatsoever by race, colour, or creed. The only criteria considered are that a Barbarian should be a good rugby player and a good sportsman — in the widest sense of that word. Amongst the two thousand or so members of the club are rugby men from the world over, of diverse nationalities and types, but all judged to have been worthy of upholding the Barbarian motto. This, instituted by the Right Reverend W.J.Carey, one of the earliest Barbarians, reads:

'Rugby is a game for gentlemen in all classes, but for no bad sportsmen in any class'.

The club is run (organised would be too strong a word) by its committee, presently made up of Herbert Waddell, the fifth President, Micky Steele-Bodger, the Vice-President, Geoffrey Windsor-Lewis, the Honorary Secretary, and Gordon 'Fergie' Ferguson, the Assistant Honorary Secretary; together with eight other committee members, elected annually. Selection of players is their responsibility, though they never convene to pick a team — for tradition and the club rules both demand that all such business should be conducted by post (and, more recently, by telephone!). Herbert Waddell explains the system:

'When the committee (with representatives in every part of the British Isles) see a man who is good enough for the Barbarians and the right type of man, they write in to the Secretary. They also report on previous Barbarians as to how they have been playing and, finally, if anyone has given years of service to rugby as a player they suggest that he should be asked to play in a game and become a member and give distinction to the Club because of his excellent service to the game.
'The Secretary then consults the President and Vice-President. We

*Barbarian Easter Tour, 1973: the eighth, and most recent, all-conquering Easter tour party.* Back row: *A.G.Ripley, P.M.Davies, R.M.Uttley, R.L.Challis, S.A.McKinney, T.P.David, D.Shedden, G.W.Evans, P.S.Preece, J.D.Gray.* Middle row: *J.S.Spencer, I.R.McGeechan, M.A.Burton, S.J.Smith, R.T.E.Bergiers, J.F.Slattery, M.G.Molloy, P.D.Llewellyn, R.M.Wilkinson, T.A.P.Moore, W.F.Anderson, T.A.Cowell, D.W.Morgan, A.D.Gill, M.J.Cooper, R.A.Codd, A.W.McMaster.* Front row: *D.J.MacMyn, W.R.Willis, C.W.Drummond, A.Wemyss, H.Waddell, H.L.Glyn Hughes, G.Windsor-Lewis, M.R.Steele-Bodger, G.A.Ferguson, R.Higgins, P.G.Yarranton.*

rough out a team and if there are any queries we go back to our informants in the areas and check out with them. The final say is with the President, the Vice-President and the Secretary, but the method works very well and if a man doesn't play in one game, but is good, he can always get in the next time.'

The Barbarian FC is delightfully disorganised in many respects but the end certainly justifies the means. It is a free and easy club, imbued with tradition, though the 'alickadoos' expect a certain standard of courtesy and good behaviour from the playing members. The word 'alickadoo' is the endearing but respectful term used to denote a senior Barbarian member and committee man; by definition, and tradition, he may pontificate, patronise, praise, organise, criticise and participate, but not play — 'all-he-can-do' is talk! The rules are minimal, and during the Easter tour the only ones that the 'alickadoos' ever seem to bother about are that 'players are expected to be in bed by eleven o'clock the night before a match', and that 'players are requested not to play more than nine holes of golf on the morning of a game'!

The overall organisation, or lack of it, is enchanting; for instance, the famous black and white jerseys are kept in a cupboard in 'Fergie' Ferguson's office and the club records are preserved in charming disarray in an old tin trunk and several battered suitcases that belonged to 'Jock' Wemyss. Nor have the Easter traditions changed, though travel arrangements are now more sophisticated and players more independent in that respect — no longer is there the same ritual foregathering for the party at Paddington, and the reserved railway coach to Wales. There is still Herbert Waddell's 'compulsory' Sunday Knockout Golf Tournament, one bag of clubs to each team of four players, taking turn and turn about; the Saturday night revelries; the friendships struck, the pervading atmosphere of relaxation, goodwill and fun. Emile de Lissa once remarked, when he heard Cliff Davies singing *Jerusalem* at one o'clock in the morning, that he had been forty years on tour and never before heard a hymn being sung to a captivated company of Barbarians at that time of day! Such things still happen.

But most significantly of all, the style of rugby that characterises their play has not changed either — the factor which has ensured that the Barbarians have retained their popularity and unique standing. Barbarian policy is to attack from every possible, or even impossible, position — taking the risk even if the odds are against it succeeding. There are never any recriminations. But, with the great strength of the teams opposing the Barbarians, especially in South Wales in the early years, and the overall improvement in standards of club rugby that has been apparent in recent years, it has not always been easy to play 'Barbarian rugby', neither is it easy for a scratch side nowadays. Winning is important, but far from being everything, as Herbert Waddell explains:

> 'We are, of course tremendously keen to win, but we have not got all the inhibitions, national or otherwise, which are inevitably involved in an international match. When we are beaten nobody goes into sackcloth.'

The colours and insignia of the club are known the world over. The jersey has wide horizontal black and white bands with the black monogram on the left breast; a monogram which in the first season, 1890, consisted of a skull and crossbones, with 'BFC' underneath. That was changed a year later to the monogram only that exists today. The tie was introduced in 1895, dark blue and light blue broad stripes with a narrow white line between. Curiously, this was presented to the club by the Blackheathen F.Mitchell, being the colours of the cricket side which he took to the USA earlier that year. The pocket badge of the blazer was originally embroidered with two lambs gambolling with a rugby ball, until in 1930, I.M.B.Stuart drew up the present design — surely the finest of any sporting body. It is made up of two shields, one with the Rose, the Thistle, the Shamrock, and the Prince of Wales' Feathers, emblems of the Four Home Countries, the other with the Silver Fern of New Zealand, the Springbok of South Africa, and the Waratah of Australia. Surmounting the shields are the two lambs, the Baa-Baas, in pursuit of a rugby ball. It is a magnificent emblem, symbolising the worldwide fellowship of the Barbarian Club — a club with a very special character, a remarkable history, and a proud tradition. It is small wonder that the honour of wearing the famous black and white jersey is generally recognised as being second only to that of representing one's country. Who else could have a club song such as this?

> 'For it's a way we have in the Baa-Baas,
> And a jolly good way too,
> For it's a way we have in the Baa-Baas,
> And a rule that we play to;
> For the rugby game, we do not train
> We play it with a will
> For it's a way we have in the Baa-Baas
> And a jolly good way too!

# Chapter 1

# W. P. CARPMAEL AND THE BARBARIAN IDEA

Rugby lovers throughout the world, and Barbarians in particular, owe a great debt of gratitude to William Percy Carpmael. Born in Briscobel, Streatham, in 1853, Percy Carpmael was the founder and first President of the Club, a lover of rugby football not just as a game on the field but for the fun and good fellowship off it.

Percy, or 'Tottie' as he was nicknamed, was the eldest son of the eight children of William Carpmael. He was educated at Christ's College, Finchley, where he was a boarder, and then went to Jesus College, Cambridge as a scholar. On leaving university he joined the business founded by his father — Carpmael and Ransford, chartered patent agents in Chancery Lane. Ultimately he became senior partner in the firm. With relish would he tell of his greatest achievement in the business world — that he had prevailed upon the Board of Trade to pass 'Smith' as a trade-mark!

Like so many of the Victorian sporting breed, Percy Carpmael was a good all-rounder. While at Christ's he walked, threw the weight and the cricket ball and played fives, as well as rugby. At Cambridge he was twice 'aquatic steeplechaser' for the University and rowed in the first Lent Boat. But principally he was a rugby man. At Christ's he was well tutored in the game, for the school produced six Oxford or Cambridge Blues in rugby between 1877 and 1886, including three England internationals — C.H.Coates, H.G.Fuller and C.R.Cleveland. Carpmael won his Blue as a forward in 1885, in the days when the 'Varsity Match was played on the Rectory Field, Blackheath; two of his school team-mates, F.C.Cousins and Cleveland, were in the Oxford side beaten by two tries to nil.

Carpmael's Cambridge days were to be important in relation to the development of the Barbarian club — for although the close links between Blackheath, of which he was a member, and the Baa-Baas are well known it is not always realised that initially the most important connection was with the Universities, and Cambridge in particular.

Of the original members of the Barbarians, fifteen were Cambridge Blues between 1885 and 1891, six of them from the same college as Carpmael, while six more were Oxford University players of the same vintage. In fact that is not particularly surprising, since those were the days when Oxbridge dominated the rugby world, a great proportion of University players then making up the International XVs. The 'Varsity representation in the original fifty Barbarians' membership was substantially greater than that of Blackheath, which accounted for eleven — and seven of those were former University players.

Amongst those first twenty-one University Barbarians were many of the great players of the day: for example, renowned England threequarters like R.L.Aston, Frank Alderson and Percy Christopherson, the centre whose skill at dropping goals was to be a decisive factor in the reduction of their points-scoring value. There were also Leake and Scott, the Cambridge, Harlequin and England half-backs; Sammy Woods, 'Dolly' (P.H.) Morrison, Frank Evershed and R.T.D.Budworth, revered names in the England pack; Scottish international forwards, McGregor and Goodhue; as well as famous administrators like the Oxford captains R.O.B.Lane and Percival Coles, who became the first professional secretary of the RFU in 1904.

William Percy Carpmael, founder of the Barbarian Football Club. A Cambridge Blue and a Blackheath player, Carpmael brought together a group of rugby friends in 1890 for his Southern Nomads tour to the north of England. This 'scratch' team formed the nucleus of the original Barbarian membership.

So even before his Blackheath days, Carpmael was undoubtedly closely involved with many of the leading players of the day. But what prompted him to organise a touring side? It must be remembered that in the eighties and early nineties, rugby tours of more than one game's duration were almost unknown. But there is a vital clue from Carpmael's Cambridge days. One of the earliest ever footballing tours was undertaken in December 1884 by Jesus College, Cambridge, who played four matches in five days in Yorkshire. Percy Carpmael was a member of that team, a successful venture as he recalled:

'We played and beat Leeds, Huddersfield and Bradford, on Friday, Saturday and Monday, and lost on Tuesday to Batley (the Yorkshire cup-holders) by two tries to one. We only had fifteen men (one short the first match) and the celebrations at beating Bradford on their own ground were too much for us. Bradford had beaten the University by 39 points to 3 at Cambridge the month before. We only had one Blue in that year. Alexander, the Welsh international. We challenged the University, who would not play us – good judges!'

No doubt this considerable playing achievement, together with renowned Yorkshire hospitality, made a very favourable impression on the undergraduate. But another pointer to the formulation of the Barbarian idea comes from an after-dinner speech by Alfred Allport – a Blackheath man, contemporary of Carpmael and an original Barbarian – at the first Barbarian reunion dinner at the Royal Adelaide Gallery in the Strand on 17 March, 1928. Allport, by then a sixty-two-year-old surgeon at St Paul's Hospital, proposed the health of the Barbarian Club, and in doing so spoke briefly of the club's origins. He recalled another tour, in 1889, undertaken by Clapham Rovers, who set out at Easter playing five or six matches in the Midlands and Yorkshire during the space of eight days. This ambitious trip was organised by 'Olivey, a Thomas's man,' and Percy Carpmael. It was on a scale which at that time was an undoubted novelty. Allport was himself a member of the party, and he recalled vividly the good time that was had by all:

'We were provided with a saloon carriage which was switched on to and off the various lines and trains we travelled by: there was a piano on board the saloon, and we took with us a member of the Toller family with his fiddle — and in the words of the old song "a very fine fiddler was he". One can say from start to finish it was one long gorgeous mixture of football, music, song and dance — excitement, uproarious fun and humorous incidents that could possibly be crowded at high tension into five days.'

Clearly the success of this venture helped to crystallise a plan in Carpmael's mind for future footballing tours; for it was the following Easter that he organised his own Southern Nomads touring team, to be followed in the same year, 1890, by the first Barbarian tour.

*The Blackheath Team, 1890–91.*
Back row: *A.Allport, P.Coles, A.Spurling, C.B.Nicholl, P.Maud, E.Emley, E.B.Holmes.* Middle row: *J.F.Clyne, G.L.Jeffery, A.E.Stoddart, W.P.Carpmael, P.F.Hancock, P.Christopherson.* Front row: *F.T.D.Aston, F.E.Duckworth, H.J.W.Lovelace, H.Marshall. Eleven of the original Barbarians were members of Blackheath, and thirteen of the team above were elected Barbarians by 1892.*

Allport outlined the character of this ambitious father of the Baa-Baas:

'Percy Carpmael was a man of vision and an extraordinary organiser, who saw things from a perspective that was not apparent to everybody. He recognised that the ordinary football club organisation was not applicable to running tours on any extended scale; firstly, because the work entailed was too great an addition on top of the season's ordinary weekly engagements, but secondly, and chiefly, because the resources of the ordinary club in first-class players was not sufficient to produce the necessary eighteen or twenty men who were able to get away for a tour of three or four, or more

Sammy Woods and Percival Coles, two of the founder members of the Barbarians. Sammy Woods (right), a Cambridge Blue, was capped thirteen times for England as a forward and was an early Barbarian committee member; Percy Coles (above) was captain of Oxford University, and later the first professional Secretary of the Rugby Football Union.

matches. He therefore visualised a club formed for the sole purpose of touring the provinces at holiday times, the membership of which could be drawn not only from anywhere in England, but from Scotland, Wales and Ireland.

'Such a club, he foresaw, would be able to put a very powerful team on the field which would have its own executive officers, with quite sufficient work to do without having it superimposed on the weekday grind of running a club during the whole season.'

This concept was brought to realisation by the work of that one man, Percy Carpmael, who continued to work tirelessly for years to maintain the high renown and position of the club that he founded — even to the extent of writing all the club records in manuscript for each season.

Carpmael was no mean rugby player either; he was a tough, stocky forward, and represented the Barbarians twenty times. He was the first Honorary Secretary and Treasurer of the club, and from his offices at Carpmael and Ransford, 24 Southampton Buildings, Chancery Lane, London WC1, conducted the affairs of the club by post in close liaison with the annually elected membership and committee.

In 1902 he resigned his secretarial duties and Jock Hartley, another fine organiser, took on the secretaryship for a couple of years, before Emile de Lissa became the third to hold that post. The guidance of de Lissa and Carpmael saw the club go from strength to strength in a difficult era until they both resigned their roles as Treasurer and Secretary respectively in 1913, as outlined in a letter to all club members; only for Carpmael to become President and de Lissa to become Treasurer.

As President, Percy Carpmael's involvement with the club was still strong, his fatherly influence and interest continuing until his death in 1936. He never missed a major tour while fit enough to travel and was at Penarth in 1925, complete with characteristic Homburg hat and walking stick, to present the first Barbarian Golf Cup. He was in essence responsible for the establishment of the pattern of the present day Easter tour, including the golf tournament and the traditional festivities at the Esplanade Hotel. He guided the club through difficult years when success in Wales was hard to achieve. His wish of making Barbarian membership classless and ignorant of national boundaries or allegiance was fulfilled, and he left behind him a

*Sadly, Percy Carpmael's final years were tormented by illness. In 1927 he left England for health reasons, to live in the South of France. Until his death in 1936 he kept in close touch with the Barbarians' activities.*

sound and solvent edifice upon which his successors could build. According to his closest surviving relative, his nephew Maurice Carpmael, he was a popular figure, cheerful without being extrovert, never one to talk rugby except in rugby company, and in his administration quietly and thoroughly efficient.

Sadly, the final years of Percy Carpmael's life were tormented by illness. He retired from work in 1925 with ever-encroaching arthritis. In about 1927 he decided for health reasons to leave England and move to Menton in the South of France, where he lived out his final years. Emile de Lissa dutifully kept him informed of Barbarian affairs, and with the aid of English newspapers he kept in touch with rugby at home. Every Easter a telegram would arrive at the Esplanade from the South of France, wishing the Barbarian team good luck. As late as December 1934, a letter from Victoria Park, Menton, to Emile shows his lasting interest:

'I should like to see Unwin, Cranmer, Wooller and Cowey at threequarter versus Leicester.'

Happily, both Cranmer and Wooller *did* play that match, and all four represented the Barbarians that season. Carpmael even wrote from his wheelchair to de Lissa suggesting a first ever overseas tour for the 'Bars', as he called them, to Nice, Turin and Milan.

But those final years were a cruel experience, with arthritis and cancer making his life almost unbearable. As a friend wrote to de Lissa, on visiting Percy Carpmael:

'Every minute of the day is either pain or discomfort for him. It is a most cruel situation and he is a real hero the way he bears it.'

The blessed release that he and his family had longed for came on 27 December, 1936. W.P.Carpmael, aged seventy-three, was laid to rest on the hill above Menton. The following day the Barbarians and Leicester wore black armbands and held a minute's silence before their traditional match. The Barbarians won, twenty points to five – 'Tottie' would have been pleased about that.

# Chapter 2

# FROM OYSTER SUPPER TO FIRST TOUR

'A new rugby touring club is likely to be the outcome of the pleasant Easter trip enjoyed by W.P.Carpmael's fifteen. It was at Huddersfield after the last game of the tour, about the witching hour of the night, that the idea took definite shape, and it was at once carried out by the whole party enthusiastically electing themselves and each other original members of the nascent organization.'

So ran the first paragraph of an article about Percy Carpmael's tour to the North of England in *The Sportsman* of 9 April, 1890. The character of that moment of origin of the Baa-Baas is correct, the setting is not. The opening lines of the original record book of the Barbarian Football Club spell out the location more precisely.

*Barbarian Football Club:*

*It was resolved to form the above club at 2 a.m. on April 9th 1890 at the Alexandra Hotel, Bradford, by the members of a scratch team captained by W. P. Carpmael. This team played the following matches viz:—*

*April 4 Burton      Won 1 goal to 1 try*
*— 5 Moseley     Drawn*
*— 7 Wakefield Trinity Won 2 goals 2 tries to 1 try*
*— 8 Huddersfield  Lost 0 to 1 try*

*The first Annual Meeting was held on 1st 1890 at—*

Carpmael's team had played four matches on their Easter tour, beating Burton, drawing with Moseley, winning against Wakefield Trinity and losing to the newly crowned Yorkshire Cup holders, Huddersfield, one try (one point) to nil. Carpmael's touring side was a genuine scratch team, known variously as 'Carpmael's London team' (at Burton), 'a Blackheath team' (at Moseley), 'W.P.Carpmael's County and International Team' (at Wakefield) and 'The Southern Nomads' (at Huddersfield).

There is one occasion of this northern tour that has become an established part of Barbarian folk-lore, and that is the renowned Oyster Supper. It is almost certain that Carpmael's team was based for that April tour at the Alexandra Hotel, Bradford, and after the match against Huddersfield, the final game, the players returned to their hotel. Having no doubt downed a pint or two, the party went out in high spirits for dinner at a nearby restaurant. Laurie Hickson of Bradford Rugby Club has provided details of that occasion, passed on to him by his father, the late Lieutenant-Colonel Laurie Hickson MC, JP who was actually present at that historic repast — the 'Oyster Supper' that has for so long been a part of the Barbarian legend.

But legends may be built from fact or fiction, and in this case, sad though it is to destroy pleasant illusions, it does seem that the 'Oyster Supper' as such is a myth. Colonel Hickson revealed that in fact this lively company took their meal at Leuchter's Restaurant, No. 7 Darley Street, Bradford, in the New Market Hall on the corner of Darley Street and Kirkgate. This respectable establishment was owned by Charles H. Leuchter until his death in 1895. Later the restaurant became the Café Royal, until in 1906 it was sold to Messrs Kino's, Furriers and Ladies Outfitters. Finally, in 1974, the whole site was demolished and that historically significant corner of Bradford is now taken up by a Littlewoods department store.

This photograph is from the Louis Rothman collection of Victorian photographs by Francis Firth. It shows Leuchter's Restaurant, on the corner of the Market Buildings, 7, Darley Street, Bradford — now the site of a Littlewoods department store. Leuchter's was the setting of the legendary 'Oyster Supper' on 8 April, 1890, at which Percy Carpmael put forward to the members of his Southern Nomads team his ideas for the formation of a new rugby touring club. Later that night Carpmael and his high-spirited rugby disciples formed the Barbarian Football Club, at the Alexandra Hotel in Bradford.

Consider for a moment the likely Yorkshire pronunciation of the German name *Leuchter's* and there is the clue to the legendary 'Oyster' supper — though for the sake of the romantics, it is always conceivable that they did have oysters at Leuchter's! More likely, though, is some slight phonetic distortion of the restaurant's name over the years. But in no way does this detract from the obvious and lasting significance of the occasion. It was a gathering of rugby disciples at supper at the end of a holiday tour under the leadership of 'Tottie' Carpmael, a man devoted to the idea of playing good rugby with top quality players on some of the more distant club grounds of Britain.

Twenty-two players represented the tourists in their four matches, sixteen of them becoming founder members of the Barbarians, the other six of them being substitutes called upon locally during the tour. Carpmael, moreover, had spread his net fairly wide in getting his side together. There was one player each from Middlesex Wanderers, Harlequins, Manchester, St Thomas's Hospital, Dublin University, Rosslyn Park and Lennox, and one each from the Somerset clubs of Wiveliscombe, Castle Cary and Wellington, with two each from Blackheath (including Carpmael himself), Richmond and Moseley. In addition there were the six substitutes, whose club affiliations are not known. Four of the scratch team were internationals: A.Walpole, capped for Ireland in 1888, P.F.Hancock, one of the Somerset trio, an England player of 1886, and W.G.Mitchell and J.H.Rogers who had both won their first England caps earlier in that same season of 1890. It is clear from press reports of the time that these precursors of the Barbarians had already adopted a style of attractive attacking rugby:

'The strength in the team was in its forwards who played well together and brought off some extraordinary passing.

'They gained a brilliant victory over Wakefield by two goals and two tries to a try, but on the Tuesday were defeated in a very fast open game by Huddersfield.'

Quite clearly the Barbarian policy of playing imaginative running rugby was instilled from the outset.

So it needs little imagination to recreate that farewell evening at the end of a highly successful and popular tour: the players, together with friends from the local northern clubs, sitting down together at Leuchter's with plenty of good local ale and food. One can picture too, the dignified figure of Carpmael addressing his friends amidst the euphoria, extolling the virtues of this new idea — rugby touring. His message no doubt fell upon receptive ears; his exhortations, that this delightful experience of rugby playing and fellowship should be repeated, and that the combined efforts of those present could lead to the formation of a touring club whose purpose was to play the game without inhibition, to enjoy rugby in the remoter regions and to share the good company of rugby men everywhere. After dinner, in contented mood, the team returned to the hotel for further festivities, celebration and discussion, culminating at 2am in the resolution to form the Barbarian Football Club. They could scarcely have dreamed of the significance of what they had done.

During the summer months of 1890 Carpmael and his closest associates on the venture, Martin Scott, W.N.Mayne, and Frank Evershed, formulated the first set of rules. There were just five in all, and these were presented to, and passed by, many of those who had been with Carpmael on that momentous occasion in Bradford, together with other invited friends, at the first General Meeting at 5pm on 1 October 1890. The meeting took place at 24 Southampton Buildings, the offices of Carpmael's firm of patent agents in Chancery Lane. There was only one minor alteration made, that future AGM's should be held in September rather than October.

Fifty members were elected for the season 1890–91, as prescribed by the rules, to which a further twelve names were to be added during the season. Percy Carpmael was elected the first Honorary Secretary and Treasurer, with W.N.Mayne as Assistant Secretary; four others were made committee members. Of the fifty original members elected, eleven were Blackheath players, but the other thirty-nine came from twenty different clubs as widely separated as Harlequins and Hartlepool Rovers, Cardiff and Castle Cary, Manchester and Moseley.

### RESULTS:
### H'POOL ROVERS FIXTURES.
#### Season, 1889-90.

| DATE. | NAME OF CLUB. | AT | FOR | | | | AGAINST | | | |
|---|---|---|---|---|---|---|---|---|---|---|
| 1889-90. | | | G | T | M | T | G | T | M | T |
| Sep. 25 | Cardiff Harlequins | home | 1 | — | 6 | | 1 | — | 1 | 2 |
| „ 28 | Percy Park | home | 1 | 2 | 9 | | 1 | — | | 2 |
| Oct. 5 | Northern | home | — | 2 | 4 | | 1 | 5 | | |
| „ 9 | Stockton | away | 14 | 1 | 4 | | | | | |
| „ 12 | Leeds Parish Church | away | — | 1 | 5 | | | | | |
| „ 19 | Sunderland | home | 3 | 2 | 4 | | | 1 | | |
| „ 26 | Durham City | away | | | 4 | | 1 | — | 2 | |
| Nov. 2 | Westoe | away | 1 | 1 | 2 | | 4 | | 1 | |
| „ 18 | North Durham | home | 8 | 6 | 5 | | — | 4 | | |
| „ 23 | York | home | 1 | 2 | 6 | | — | 1 | — | 3 |
| „ 30 | Sunderland | away | — | 1 | 2 | | — | 1 | | |
| Dec. 7 | Westoe—(Not played) | home | | | | | | | | |
| „ 14 | Percy Park | home | — | 3 | 6 | | — | | | 2 |
| „ 21 | Northern | away | 2 | — | 3 | | — | | | |
| „ 26 | Sunderland | home | — | 2 | 3 | | — | | | 2 |
| „ 27 | Ubridge Nomads (Ox) | home | | | | | | | | |
| „ 28 | North Durham | away | 1 | 4 | 4 | | — | | | 1 |
| Jan. 1 | Bury | home | 3 | 1 | 4 | | — | | | 1 |
| „ 2 | York | home | 5 | 7 | 6 | | — | 1 | | 1 |
| „ 4 | Durham City | home | — | 2 | 3 | | | | — | 3 |
| „ 11 | Hull | home | — | 1 | 2 | | | | — | 3 |
| „ 18 | Leeds Parish Church | home | 2 | 1 | 3 | | — | | | |
| Feb. 1 | Hull | away | — | 2 | 1 | | | | — | 3 |
| „ 3 | Clapham Rovers | away | 1 | — | 5 | | — | | | 1 |
| „ 4 | Cambridge University | away | — | 3 | 2 | | 3 | 1 | 3 | |
| „ 12 | Stockton (Not played) | home | | | | | | | | |
| „ 15 | Sunderland | away | 2 | 1 | 2 | | — | | | 4 |
| „ 22 | Northern | home | 2 | 2 | 3 | | — | | | |
| Mar. 1 | Westoe (Cup Tie) | away | 2 | 4 | 8 | | — | | | |
| „ 8 | West h'pool (Cup Tie) | home | 1 | 3 | 7 | | — | | | 1 |
| „ 15 | Tadlow (Cup Tie) | away | 1 | 6 | 9 | | — | | | |
| „ 22 | Barley | home | 2 | 2 | 4 | | — | | | 1 |
| „ 29 | H. Rangers (C.T. Final) | home | 6 | 2 | 9 | | 1 | — | | |
| Apl. 5 | Old Millhilians | home | 3 | 3 | 7 | | — | | | |
| „ 7 | Clapham Rovers | home | 13 | 1 | 6 | | 1 | — | | |
| „ 8 | Belfast Albion | home | — | 4 | 2 | | — | | | |
| „ 12 | Northern (Not played) | away | | | | | | | | |

(†) represents one penalty goal in each case.

---

### ORD'S
### OFFICIAL PROGRAMME.
(B. T. ORD, introducer of the Football Programme in the North.)

## HARTLEPOOL ROVERS
*versus*
## BARBARIANS.

**Friarage Field, H'pool,**

SATURDAY, DEC. 27th, 1890.

**Kick off 2·30 p.m.**

ADMISSION 3D. GRAND STAND
(ENCLOSED) 6D. (UNENCLOSED) 3D.
STAND 1D.

B. T. ORD, PRINTER, HIGH ST., HARTLEPOOL.

---

### H'POOL ROVERS FIXTURES.
#### Season, 1890-91.

| DATE. | NAME OF CLUB. | AT | FOR | | | | AGAINST | | | |
|---|---|---|---|---|---|---|---|---|---|---|
| 1890-91. | | | G | T | M | T | G | T | M | T |
| Sep. 20 | Kendal | away | 1 | 1 | | | 1 | 3 | | 1 |
| „ 27 | York | home | 1 | — | 1 | | — | 3 | | |
| Oct. 4 | Sunderland | away | | | 1 | | 3 | 5 | | |
| „ 11 | Durham City | home | 3 | 2 | 3 | | — | 2 | | 5 |
| „ 18 | Leeds Parish Church | home | | 2 | 2 | | — | | | 2 |
| „ 25 | Tadtoe | home | | 2 | | | — | | | 6 |
| Nov. 1 | Hull | away | 1 | 2 | | | 2 | | | 2 |
| „ 8 | North Durham | home | | | | | | | | |
| „ 15 | | | | | | | | | | |
| „ 22 | Glebholm, Glasgow | home | | | | | | | | |
| „ 29 | Northern (Not played) | home | | | | | | | | |
| Dec. 1 | Cambridge Varsity | away | | 2 | 1 | | 1 | 1 | | |
| „ 13 | Durham City | away | 2 | — | 3 | | 1 | — | 4 | |
| „ 20 | Hull | home | — | 1 | | | — | | | 1 |
| „ 26 | Stanton | away | | | 1 | | 3 | 5 | | 1 |
| Jan. 1 | Aspatria | home | 1 | 1 | 3 | | 3 | — | | 1 |
| „ 2 | Maryport | home | | | | | | | | |
| „ 3 | Warrington | home | | | | | | | | |
| „ 10 | York | away | | | | | | | | |
| „ 17 | Westoe | home | | | | | | | | |
| „ 24 | North Durham | away | | | | | | | | |
| „ 31 | Kendal | home | | | | | | | | |
| Feb. 7 | Northern | home | | | | | | | | |
| „ 14 | Sunderland | home | | | | | | | | |
| „ 21 | Percy Park | away | | | | | | | | |
| „ 28 | | | | | | | | | | |
| Mar. 7 | | | | | | | | | | |
| „ 14 | | | | | | | | | | |
| „ 21 | | | | | | | | | | |
| „ 28 | Swinton | away | | | | | | | | |
| „ 30 | Warrington | away | | | | | | | | |
| Apl. 4 | | | | | | | | | | |
| „ 11 | | | | | | | | | | |

---

Continuing the contacts made through the Southern Nomads, the first ever Barbarian tour was arranged, to the north of England for Christmas. So it was that on 27 December, 1890, the first Barbarian match took place against Hartlepool Rovers – and judging from a diary of that first tour written by an anonymous member of the party, the pattern of future enjoyment on and off the field was set straightaway!

## THE DIARY OF THE BARBARIAN F. C. TOUR.

**BY ONE OF THEM.**

*Xmas 1890*

**December 26.**

5.30 p.m.—Kings Cross Station was enlivened by the presence of P. F. Hancock, S. M. J. Woods, A. E. Stoddart, A. Allport, W. P. Carpmael, E. W. Senior, W. H. Manfield, H. Boucher, A. S. Gedge, T. S. Tregellas, R. B. Sweet-Escott, R. L. Aston, W. H. Carey, R. D. Budworth, P. Maud, and one spectator called "Lupus." An enterprising guard asked why he was so named, we then heard that this keen footballer once ran with the beagles in Somerset; after a time a hare was jumped and this man of panics remarked, "There goes Lupus."

5.45 p.m.—We left King's Cross.

5.50 p.m.—Cards.

10.15.—Arrived at Bradford; found Mayne and A. Rogers. Went to Alexandra Hotel, had supper, and dressed for the dance.

**December 27.**

2 a.m.—Supper.

4 a.m.—Most of the team in bed, but sad to relate one gay man danced until 7.30—this was the only day on which he was down to breakfast.

10 a.m.—Start on a journey to Hartlepool.

10.30 a.m.—Had a most enjoyable wait of half-an-hour at Holbeck—a place noted for its porters. If you want to hear how our secretary was scored off, ask Stoddart.

12.30 p.m.—Melton Mowbray pies and beer. Woods strongly recommends these pies to all players, they should be eaten just before playing. It is reported that since these pies have been made the price of felines has gone up.

2.10 p.m.—Arrived at Hartlepool, three-quarters of an hour late—met by McGregor and Alderson. The joint owners of the canary embraced before an admiring crowd.

2.40 p.m.—Kick-off—had a very fast and interesting game. At half-time we were leading by three goals, condition and the dance then seemed to tell, but we won pretty comfortably by 3-0-1 to 1-1-4. The feature of the match was the passing of McGregor, and the sprint of Allport. I hear that he at once wired to N. Spurling to run him 50 yards. It will be a great race. We had a walking apothecaries' shop, touch judging for us—fortunately for him Carpmael hurt his head, but he, the apothecary judge, then produced lint, bandages, wristlets, &c., &c., and the head was then wonderfully done up by that rising surgeon, Mr. Allport, of Guy's Hospital.

Alderson and Yiend were in good form for the Rovers.

6.50 p.m.—We started by the Harrogate and Leeds express; the feature of the N.E.R. express is that it stops by snow-clad-fields instead of all stations. It is very amusing at first, but after a bit it gets monotonous.

11.15 a.m.—Arrived at Leeds. Several savages were by this time rather good understudies for the desert of Sahara. They climbed out of the saloon which was in a siding, and got to the station—but Leeds is a provincial town, and Gedge is never going to leave London again.

12.10.—We reached Bradford once more.

December 28.

All slept the sleep of the just, got up, had dinner, and went back to bed. One or two rash men who were playing for that insignificant team called the South went for a ten mile walk.

An enterprising interviewer called to-day to see Stoddart. The much paragraphed and photoed one went out to see him; somehow the reporter had vanished, but Budda got an arm-chair !

I may also mention that a hair-singeing establishment was opened with great success in the evening. I ought to have recorded yesterday that a little boy of Hartlepool gave Hancock's height as "six foot and a bally brick." Of course he said the Hartlepool equivalent for bally !

December 29.

6.30 a.m.—The army's breakfast was ready.

7.30 a.m.—The army's breakfast was again got ready.

8.30 a.m.—Ditto.

9.30 a.m.—Ditto.

11.0 a.m.—The army came down—terrible commotion—rush of waiters—awful language of the reserved forces.

11.10 a.m.—The army tackled a kipper and subsided for the day.

1.45. p.m.—The ball was kicked off in the Bradford match. We had Woods, Budworth, Allport, Aston, and Carpmael away but Alderson and Yiend assisted. As we were very hard up for forwards and had any amount of backs we played four three-quarters. We soon got a try which Aldi converted, after this the game got rather energetic. At half-time we led by two goals to one penalty goal. In the second half we had very bad luck, several times what appeared certain tries were just saved, and once Stoddart had a

clear run in but someone in the crowd blew a whistle and he stopped. Bradford got in twice, once because our forwards stopped and appealed. The other try was exceedingly doubtful. Doyle, the back, kicked the ball over our line, Bairstow (three-quarter) and Harrison (forward) rushed up, one kept Boucher off and the other touched down. We claimed confidently for offside, and it seems impossible that it could have been otherwise, as Doyle was knocked over by Alderson and therefore put no one onside.

Anyhow the match was a draw. We should all like to see Hickson captain again. Directly he goes some of the team take to various Northern practices of a doubtful character. Alderson, McGregor, Stoddart, and Senior played very well, the passing being excellent ; all the forwards played hard, Yiend was very good.

4.40 p.m.—We heard that the South had been beaten.

6.0 p.m.—Great rejoicings—Alderson having been elected captain of England.

We then had dinner at the " Talbot," and went to the theatre.

December 30.

10.30 a.m.—The Army had his breakfast.

11.7 a.m.—Just off when the Boots rushed up the platform with No. 18's tooth-brush (he held the brush in his hand). Shouts of Mayne. The little scene reminded us of one of Leech's sketches.

11.8 a.m.—Started for Manchester.

1.10 p.m.—In the middle of lunch and of a great discussion whether there were any songs after the N. v. S. dinner—Budworth and Aston for—Woods and Allport against—a telegram comes putting off the match. Agreed to catch the two o'clock train for London.

6.15 p.m.—Arrived at King's Cross after a pleasant tour. The Army and the Baby have a farewell rag, and we part until the 31st of March at Cardiff.

Barbarians v Devonshire at Exeter, 1 April 1891.
Back row: G.Young, T.Whittaker, W.P.Carpmael, R.L.Aston, R.T.Duncan, P.F.Hancock, W.H.Manfield.
Middle row: E.Emley, C.B.Nicholl, P.Christopherson, A.E.Stoddart (captain), D.W.Evans, P.Maud. Front
row: H.Marshall, C.A.Hooper, F.H.Fox, C.J.Vernon.

The consequence of what was clearly a riotously successful first tour was a further two matches at the end of that season. Thus the long sequence of matches against Cardiff began at Easter 1891, and as has been the case sixty times out of the ninety three matches played, the home side won.

'The game was exceedingly fast and very interesting, and contained many pieces of pretty play. The forwards were fairly well matched, the individual efforts of the Barbarians compensating the better combination of their antagonists. Whittaker played magnificently, and Manfield and Allport did capital scrimmage work. The halves did some good things, and Marshall proved himself a formidable opponent to the Cardiff pair. The best of the threequarters were Hooper and R.L.Aston, though the latter did not appear to relish playing with four threequarters, and seemed out of his element. Pearson was as good as ever for Cardiff, his accurate kicking into touch being the best feature of his all-round play. Ingledew at half played in good style, and made some clever passes. The home forwards showed up well towards the finish, especially Lewis, Mahoney, and Duncan.'

The following day, 1 April, the Barbarians played in Exeter against Devonshire, a stronghold of rugby at that time, in front of a large number of spectators and won by three goals and two tries to nil.

So the seeds of the Easter tour were sown, and the matches in the west were to become an increasingly important part of the Barbarian calendar. From the very outset the Barbarian tour was a tough rugby-playing assignment, as the invitation side pitted themselves against the best club teams in Britain. Already the blueprint for the future was being set and at the end of the season alterations were made to allow all club business to be done by post and to change the club colours from the white to the famous black and white jersey.

# Chapter 3

# NEW FIXTURES AND A NEW RUGBY STYLE

In 1891–92 the Barbarians played seven matches, including the Dublin University side, and Huddersfield, Swinton and Gloucester were the Baa-Baas' opponents for the first time. Each beat the touring side despite the presence of some of the outstanding leading rugby players of the day. The match against Dublin University is of special interest. One can imagine that this fixture was arranged through the good offices of A. Walpole, an original Barbarian member and a Dublin University man, probably helped by the contacts made at international level between Barbarians and University members of the Irish teams. It may be significant, too, that Oxford University had already toured Ireland after the 'Varsity Match of 1886 with a side that included three 'Barbarians-to-be' — Christopherson, Coles and Cousins. Anyway, this was the first of those rare occasions when, so to speak, the Barbarians were 'the home side'. The match was played in early December, 1891, at Blackheath.

Trinity College had been very much the pioneers of rugby in Ireland and their initiatives in the 1870s played a great part in the formation of the Irish Rugby Football Union. The strength of Dublin University rugby is seen in the quality of the side that visited Blackheath. Eight of the students became Irish internationals, including the legendary C.V.Rooke, who won nineteen caps between 1891 and 1897, A.D.Clinch,

*Barbarians v Huddersfield at Huddersfield, 29 December 1891.*
Back row: *W.Sugden, A.Rotherham, P.F.Hancock, C.A.Hooper, C.M.Wells, W.H.Manfield, P.Maud, R.D.Budworth.* Middle row: *D.W.Evans, F.H.R.Alderson, W.P.Carpmael, S.M.J.Woods.* Front row: *A.Allport, F.T.D.Aston, T.A.F.Crow, T.Parker, T.W.P.Storey.*

*Alfred Allport (left) and Percy Christopherson, original members of the club, who both took part in the first tour and represented the Barbarians on frequent occasions in the early years. Both men played for Blackheath and also were capped for England – Allport as a forward, Christopherson as a threequarter.*

A.Q.Bulger, and H.Lindsay. Four of that Dublin University fifteen were to be members of the first Irish Triple Crown Home Championship side of 1894 – W.Sparrow, W.S.Brown, C.V.Rooke and H.Lindsay. So it was no mean achievement then that the Barbarians won by a goal and a try to nil. All the points were scored by W.Nielson, the Scottish-born Cambridge University threequarter, who only thirteen days later was to score a try for his university in their 'Varsity Match win. Eyewitness accounts report that in the game with Dublin University, the Irish were strong up front, though:

'of the Irish rush of which so much has been heard, no good specimen was on view'.

Their passing skills did not compare with the Barbarians, though one report makes the delightful observation:

'Some allowance might be made for the fact that the Blackheath jerseys worn by Aston and Duckworth resembled the colour of the Trinity uniform which may account for the number of numerous passes that fell into the hands of those players'.

The match was refereed by the then secretary of the RFU, George Rowland Hill, who served for twenty-three years as the last of the six honorary secretaries, before his election as president in 1904. A great servant of rugby football, he was the first man to be knighted for his services to the game. Strangely not till 1957 did the Barbarians again play an Irish team.

On the two-match Easter tour of 1892, the Barbarians surprised most observers by beating Cardiff by two goals to nil, and that was achieved despite losing Percy Robertshaw, the famous Bradford player, in the second half. This match is only one of two occasions on which Percy Carpmael is credited with having scored for the Barbarians – and no doubt this stocky hard-working forward thoroughly enjoyed the moment that put the Baa-Baas on the way to their first-ever victory at the Arms Park:

'Ultimately Wells, the Cantab, broke away, and after nearly getting over himself passed to Carpmael, the veteran scoring between the posts.'

The scarcely flattering term 'veteran' was clearly as beloved of journalists then as it is now, and it should quickly be added that Carpmael was still turning out for the Barbarians six years later!

The sight of the home side being beaten by this scratch fifteen was clearly not to the liking of the Arms Park crowd, who seemed to vent their spleen on the referee —

'the crowd now assumed a disrespectful attitude towards the referee who could not see exactly "eye to eye" with them'.

But for all that it was a thrilling game:

'Excitement was now intense but the home side rose to the occasion and re-lieved their lines. Again did the visitors try their hands at passing and again did they lose ground.'

No wonder the Baa-Baas have been ever-welcomed in Cardiff!

It is significant that press reports of these early matches highlight the passing tactics of the Barbarians, for this style of play was very much an innovation:

'On resuming the Barbarians adopted passing tactics but they lost valuable yards thereby.'                                         *(v Cardiff in 1892)*

'But their (Dublin University) ideas of modern tactics . . . are quite rudimen-tary, and when, in imitation of their opponents, they did take to passing, it did more harm than good.'          *(v Dublin University in 1891)*

'In the second half the visiting pack did not give Devon a chance, whilst the passing of the backs completely bewildered them.'   *(v Devonshire in 1891)*

The 'Barbarian style', now a description of a type of rugby football in its own right, is the consequence of many happenings in the rugby world coincident with the founding of the club. In 1877 rugby football changed from twenty to fifteen aside, and naturally the possibilities of movement of the ball accordingly increased with only thirty as opposed to forty players on the field. Nevertheless rugby remained a game with a predominance of kick and rush, dribbling, and general rough and tumble which had characterised its early years of development.

No individual had a greater rôle in changing the style of play than Harry Vassall of Oxford University, Blackheath and England. While captain of the University in 1881–82, he saw the advantages to be gained by advancing one of the two full-backs to make a third threequarter, and then of moving the ball away from the nine-man scrummage to the open spaces elsewhere in the field of play. Until his innovation it had been customary for there to be two full-backs and only two three-quarters. The success of Oxford's innovation took some time to rub off on the game as a whole; even passing from one half-back to the other was frowned upon until the early nineties. But the Barbarians, with a large proportion of University Blues, proved to be the ideal disciples of this more entertaining passing game.

The Baa-Baas in fact took things a stage further, and from their foundation played one full-back, four threequarters, two halves and only eight forwards — whereas it is worth pointing out that not until the 'Varsity Match of 1893, nor until Wales introduced a similar line-up against England in that same year, was this prac-tice adopted at the highest level.

The emphasis on running, passing and scoring tries was helped, too, by the gradual changes in the scoring system. Until 1886 matches were decided by a

# Barbarian Football Club.

*The first annual fixture card, for the season 1891–92. The Barbarians' only victory was against Cardiff, one of only two occasions on which Cardiff have failed to score any points against the Baa-Baas.*

majority of goals; only when goals were equal, or no goals were scored, did tries come into the reckoning. But then points-scoring was introduced, and the try, initially worth one point, was upgraded to two in 1891, and then to three in 1893. Allied to this was the advent of the penalty kick, which amongst other things helped to curb off-side tactics. So the sum total of these factors was that the Barbarians' style became the new vogue. Indeed not only did it thrive on these changes in the game, but it played a significant part in the game's development towards a more open pattern of play.

\*      \*      \*

There were some remarkable characters in these first years, apart from W.P.Carpmael himself. They included some renowned England internationals; Randolph Aston who scored thirty tries on the first ever British Isles team missionary tour to South Africa in 1891; Alfred Allport, a fiery forward and later a distinguished surgeon at St Paul's Hospital; Fred Alderson, a threequarter with a dreaded hand-off, who captained England on his first international appearance; and the legendary Australian Sammy Woods, capped for England at rugby and for Australia at cricket. There was Frank Evershed, who was an international forward with remarkable try-scoring ability and no mean cricketer either, and Percy Christopherson, another England international who, with his father and nine brothers, made up a cricket eleven against Blackheath. From Wales came R.B.Sweet-Escott, the international from Cardiff, while G.McGregor was thirteen times capped for Scotland. Andrew Stoddart, the Barbarians' first captain, was one of the greatest double internationals of all time – an outstanding batsman in partnership with W.G.Grace, and in rugby a great threequarter. Dr Howard Marshall was another with a rare distinction. He was capped only once, against Wales in 1893 when he scored all three of England's tries; surely the unluckiest of all England's 'one-cap wonders'!

At this time the sportsman was often an all-rounder, for specialisation was much less pronounced than it is today. The demands in terms of fitness, training and preparation were relatively small, so the 'natural' games player could successfully compete in several sports.

The presence of many all-rounders in the Barbarian ranks has something to do with the unique sporting encounter that took place between the Baa-Baas and that other cherished domain of amateur sport, the Corinthians in 1892. Indeed in a letter of 1932 to the Barbarian President, Emile de Lissa, N. Lane Jackson of the Corinthians suggested that a long chat he had had with Percy Carpmael at the Sport's Club all about the origins and ideals of the Corinthians had a significant bearing on Carpmael's ideas on the foundation of his rugby club. This may or may not be so. What is certain is that Carpmael himself had been a member of the Corinthian club and had played soccer for them to the extent of representing them in the final of the London Senior Cup. That factor together with the existence of athletes of diverse

*Dr Howard Marshall, a Barbarian committee member, an 1891 'British Lion', and captain of Blackheath in 1893 – the same year in which he won his one and only cap for England, in the international against Wales. He scored all three of England's tries!*

talents in both clubs was the reason for the challenge issued by the Corinthians for a triangular contest to take place. It was to consist of association and rugby football matches and athletics, with a cricket match to be played at a later date, and all in aid of charity. So on Boat Race Day, 9 April 1892, and on Monday 11 April, the events took place. Not surprisingly it was thought that the two football games would be farcical, with six of the Corinthians being soccer internationals and eight international Barbarians in the rugby match. But the matches were well contested and by no means predictable in their results! As the magazine *Pastime* reported:

'The Barbarians soon showed that they were well up in the association rules, and beyond occasionally pushing an opponent or holding him off with the arm, they made few mistakes. They were, however, quite unable to cope with the pace and combination of their experienced rivals, who won easily by six goals to love.'

But what shocks were in store in the rugby, as the talented Corinthians beat the Barbarians at their own game, fourteen points to twelve . . .

'This surprising result may be accounted for partly by the extraordinary speed and energy shown by the winners towards the end of the game and partly by the carelessness of the Barbarians, who after neglecting their opportunities and allowing the game to become a loose scramble, were unable, from exhaustion, to retrieve the day. They lost much, too, by their courteous indulgence in not claiming penalties for breaches of the rules, especially for off-side forward play and picking up in the scrummage.'

Outstanding for the Corinthians on the wing was one C.B.Fry! Indeed that renowned Test cricketer certainly had a busy weekend. Not only did he take part to good effect in the soccer, at which he was an international, and the rugby, at which only injury deprived him of an Oxford Blue, but he also helped the Corinthians to victory in the athletics sports, by winning the long jump, as befitted the holder of the world record in that event. The athletics in fact proved an exciting contest, with the outcome undecided until the ninth and final event when F.M.Ingram of the Corinthians won the mile in 4 minutes 34 seconds. Such was the appreciation of the weekend's proceedings that a witness to the events was prompted to write to the editor of *The Sportsman* newspaper.

'Those who did not witness the good sport on both days, accompanied by the two novel football matches, missed the greatest amusement in sport of the season. The rugby match was enjoyed so intensely that apart from the spectators screaming with laughter during the game, most of them laughed on their way home, and I may add that the unique manner in which the Corinthians played and beat the Barbarians at the latter's own game will never be forgotten'.

Not until the cricket match on 30 April did the Barbarians salvage some honour. Even C.B.Fry, with twenty-five runs and two wickets, failed to prevent a Barbarian victory by four wickets. But the Barbarian eleven included some truly versatile players; John le Fleming was not only a rugby international, AAA 120 yards hurdles champion and ice-skater of note, but also a Kent cricketer; Cyril Wells, an England international half-back, was an outstanding batsman, who excelled as an all-round cricketer for Surrey and later Middlesex, and he bowled Fry in this match; Frank Evershed, ten times capped as a forward for England (though not a 'Blue' while up at Oxford), was for five years a county cricketer for Derbyshire. Contrast this with the rarity nowadays of an M.J.K.Smith! These encounters with the Corinthians proved, if further evidence were needed, that these original Barbarians were a breed of real sporting men.

The following seasons of the nineties saw some significant changes on the Barbarian calendar. Most notably, despite the strong early ties, Bradford, Swinton and Huddersfield disappeared from the fixture list, to be replaced by Newport and Hartlepool Rovers on a regular basis, and South Shields, Percy Park and Old Dunelmians in the north-east, for varying durations. Bath and West of England in the west country were amongst several one-off matches. These changes were not without reason. The early nineties were a restless and traumatic period of rugby history, culminating in the crisis of 1893 and 'the great schism'. Professionalism of a kind was taking over in the flourishing rugby towns of Yorkshire and Lancashire. Illicit payments, inducements to players, and remuneration for broken time gradually came to the notice of the Rugby Union. The outcome is well-known and documented elsewhere. In brief it can be said that efforts on the part of a body of northern clubs to legalise payment for loss of money through playing rugby football in work-

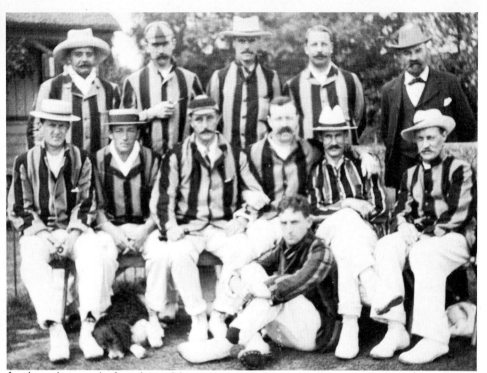

*A unique photograph of a unique cricket team — the Barbarian XI who played against the Corinthians at Queen's Club on 30 April, 1892. Cricket was the only game in which the Baa-Baas beat the Corinthians, in a challenge sporting encounter in aid of charity. Thanks to an innings of 55 not out by John le Fleming, Percy Carpmael's XI won by four wickets.*

ing hours failed. Thanks to the notable efforts of William Cail, president of the Rugby Football Union, Rowland Hill (Honorary Secretary) and others, such as the great Yorkshire administrator, Reverend Frank Marshall and H.E.Steed of Lennox, the RFU rejected the motion, 'that players be allowed compensation for *bona fide* loss of time' and carried an amendment to it:

'That this Meeting, believing that the above principle is contrary to the true interest of the game and its spirit, declines to sanction the same'.

I mention this milestone in the annals of amateur sport because of the momentous influence it was to have on the future of the Barbarians. Amongst those clubs to break away were Bradford, Huddersfield, Leeds, Swinton and Wakefield Trinity, all of whom had at some time or other received Barbarian (or Southern Nomads) teams. So, sadly, these early ties were broken — though in the case of Bradford, where an amateur part of the original club managed to survive, they were gloriously restored in 1965 (albeit this time at Lidget Green, not at the original Park Avenue ground), when the Barbarians returned to play their first-ever opponents, Hartlepool Rovers, and Bradford, in their seventy-fifth anniversary season.

New laws were drafted to ensure that professionalism was driven out of the game, which acted as the final spur for the secession from the RFU of many leading clubs in the north of England. Twenty-two of them banded together as founder members of the Northern Football Union — the body that within a few years declared for unrestricted professionalism. The effect on amateur rugby football within Yorkshire and Lancashire, in particular, was dramatic, not fully indicated by the establishment of a new Union by twenty-two clubs, but more apparent from the fact that while there were 481 clubs in membership of the RFU in 1893, by 1896 that total had dropped to 383.

So therein lies the background to the changing fixture list of the next decade. The match against Rovers, who had been the first club ever to play the Barbarians, was re-established on a regular basis for each year until 1902 – not without some prompting, no doubt, from Frank Alderson, a Rover himself, a great friend of Carpmael, an England international, and committee member of the Baa-Baas from 1892–1904. There were other influences from within the membership of Hartlepool Rovers, amongst them an original Barbarian member, W.Yiend, and, also of that decade, old Barbarians such as F.C.Lohden, E.C.Carter and Arthur Murrell who captained the Rovers against the Barbarians in their last match of that sequence in 1902. There was too that most famous of all Hartlepool Rovers, R.F.'Bob' Oakes, elected a Barbarian 1896–97, who received just about every playing and administrative honour the game has to offer.

The enjoyment of these annual encounters with the Rovers is well recorded in match reports of the day. The game of 1893 was watched by a crowd of some 7,000 and the rugby was invariably closely contested –

'Yiend started for the Rovers, and Lamphers returned, McDougall getting the ball, passed to Alderson, who was only stopped close to the line. Fine interchanges led to more scrummaging and Alderson then unsuccessfully dropped for goal, the Rovers having slightly the best of exchanges. Eventually Mansfield ran in for the Barbarians, Wilson converting. The Rovers now invaded, and Hodgson narrowly missed a couple of tries. After failing a drop-kick, he scored for the home team but the angle was too acute for Alderson's excellent effort at goal to prove successful. Brilliant passing by the Barbarians enabled them to score again, Wilson again doing the needful. By fast play and good dribbling, McDougall kicked well down and Yiend following up crossed the visitors line, Alderson converting.'

There was a narrow win in the end for the Barbarians, ten points to seven.

In the programme of the match when the Barbarians revisited the New Friarage during their 75th anniversary season, Fred Theaker's report of the 1901 match was reprinted:

'The feature of the season was a visit from the Barbarians, comprising of players drawn from English, Scottish and Welsh clubs including A.E.Stoddart, R.L.Aston, Gregor McGregor and S.M.J.Woods and after a well-contested game, the visitors won by three goals and one try to one goal and one try. It was a splendid exposition and one of the best matches I have ever seen and, as an object lesson, it ought to have been witnessed by all other players, and probably some of them learned how happily the rules could be put into operation and as long as the Barbarians and Rovers can meet and show the same skill, the games will be delightful to watch. . . . The Barbarians did not make the mistake of playing the game of individuals but as a team gave an exhibition worthy of the game.'

In the long term the most significant new fixture to find a place on the Barbarian Calendar was Newport. Initially the fixture was played as part of the Christmas tour, the day following the Cardiff Boxing Day encounter. However, in the very first year the match was played at the end of the season, 4 April 1893, as it had been cancelled on 27 December on account of frost. In those years, Newport were all-conquering. Under T.C.Graham's captaincy they had enjoyed an invincible season in 1891–92, winning twenty-nine and drawing four of their thirty-three matches –

five hundred and thirty-five points for and only twenty-five against! In the thirteen seasons from that unbeaten year, up to the first Barbarian victory against Newport in December, 1904, the Black-and-Ambers won two hundred and ninety-two of their three hundred and seventy-two matches. No wonder the Barbarians were in for a lean spell at Rodney Parade. Indeed, judging from a contemporary report, their strength at that time may account for what seemed a certain reluctance on Newport's part for the first fixture to take place.

'In glorious weather and in the presence of a fair crowd of onlookers the teams met to try conclusions at Newport this afternoon. It will be remembered that the contest was previously fixed to take place on 27 December last, but owing to the hard condition of the ground it did not come off. Since that time the Barbarians had expressed their willingness to play the match and, the Newport men acquiescing, the tussle was accordingly brought off today.'

*Philip Maud, later Brigadier-General Maud, CMG, CBE, who, together with Frank Stout and M.P. Atkinson, holds the record of twenty-four appearances for the Barbarians.*

In the Barbarians' team, captained by Carpmael, seven current, or future, internationals took the field, six of them from England – Hooper, Lohden, Maud, Finlinson, Carey and Poole – and one Welshman, C.B.Nicholl. But Newport, despite the absence through injury of the renowned Wallace Watts and fellow international F.C.Dauncey, had an even more formidable line-up, including a pack which has been hailed by many as the greatest of all time, five of whom were in the first-ever Welsh Triple Crown side earlier that season. There were nine internationals in the team that met the Barbarians: in the backs, Arthur Gould, twenty-seven caps between 1885 and 1897; Bert Gould, three caps between 1892 and 1893; and Arthur Boucher, thirteen caps between 1892 and 1897. At half-back were Percy Phillips, six caps between 1892 and 1894, and Fred Parfitt, nine caps between 1893 and 1896. In the forwards the team captain, Tom Graham, had twelve caps between 1890 and 1895, and was also captain of Wales. Jim Hannan had nineteen caps between 1888 and 1895, T.Pook, one cap in 1895, and H.Packer, seven caps between 1891 and 1897.

*Frederick Lohden (left) was elected a Barbarian member in 1892, and played in the first-ever match against Newport on 4 April, 1893, which the Barbarians lost 8 points to 3. F.H.Maturin (right) played in the Barbarian XV, captained by 'Tottie' Carpmael, which lost to Bedford at Goldington Road 7 points to 3.*

Yet despite this formidable array of home talent on that first occasion, the Barbarians were apparently unlucky to lose by two dropped goals (eight points) to a try (three points in Wales, though still only two points elsewhere).

'Newport gave a very poor display, and were lucky in winning at all. Forward they did not exhibit that dash which at one time characterised their play. Behind they appeared to be all at sea, and gained very little ground by their passing.'

For the Barbarians, F.C.Lohden and P.Maud of Blackheath and C.B.Nicholl were prominent in the forward battle, while the London Scottish half-backs R.S.Baiss and R.F.Easterbrook gave the celebrated Newport pair a lot of trouble. The Baa-Baas centres, Latter and Conway Rees, came close to scoring on several occasions, but in the end all the visitors could muster was an early try by their captain, Percy Carpmael. Yet this was a noble effort, especially when you consider that five of the party had travelled overnight from Huddersfield, where they had been playing the previous day. Remember too that those were not the days of Inter-City and motorways!

With the establishment of the Cardiff and Newport fixtures, the present-day pattern was beginning to take shape. In the first few years these two matches formed a Christmas tour, to be succeeded in 1896 by the placing of the games over the Easter holiday. But these were far from being the only fixtures of these years and in the nineties the Barbarians roamed far and wide.

In 1894, in what may have been a challenge match, six thousand spectators saw Bedford, unbeaten in twenty-four matches, as the *Bedford Standard* related:

'retire with their proud record still unbroken at Goldington Road with their most creditable victory of the season by a dropped goal and a try to one try'.

It was one of those occasions that litter Barbarian history, when a well-drilled team proved more than the equal of a star-studded scratch fifteen, that at Bedford included Wells, Finlinson, Todd, Field, Maturin and one, no doubt very excited, substitute, F.A.Cory, a pupil at Bedford Grammar School.

Big crowds saw the Baa-Baas in action at Carlisle and Rockliff, and the next season ten thousand greeted the visitors at Rodney Parade. South Shields and Percy Park strengthened the weakened Northern Alliance, with fixtures against Bath and the West of England a new feature of the west country tours. The first game of 1896 against a West of England combination, made up largely of Bristol players, provides a rare and most un-Barbarianlike scoreline – a nil-nil draw!

In contrast, the opening match of 1897 saw the Barbarians register their biggest win of their history thus far, thirty-five points to nil against Liverpool. Maybe the margin of this victory owes something to the fact that this was to be the farewell appearance in Barbarian colours of their founder Percy Carpmael. It was his twentieth game for his club, and while the previous nineteen had been as a forward, on this occasion he was the full-back. Seven tries were scored, including two each by Leslie-Jones and Wallis, but the three remaining scorers are not recorded. It would be nice to think that one of those might have been the perfect moment in W.P.Carpmael's swansong.

This overwhelming success was followed by victories in successive days over Hartlepool Rovers, Old Dunelmians and Percy Park, to give the Baa-Baas an unbeaten Christmas Durham tour – a considerable achievement, especially for J.F.Byrne, the Moseley and England full-back, who played in all four matches.

There were matches, too, against Exeter, which ended the Christmas Tour of 1898, Birkenhead Park, when the fixture with Hartlepool Rovers was cancelled as the Rovers were engaged in a cup-tie, and both the Park and Gloucester (the following season) beat the Barbarians on their only encounter. But two of the most remarkable occasions came during the final seasons of the decade. On 15 February 1899 the Baa-Baas entertained at the Rectory Field the Stade Français, the first of the big French clubs, and beat them thirty-three-nil. It was one of the earliest Anglo-French matches, some time in advance of the entry of France into the international arena of 1906, though one player of that Stade XV, H.Amand, on the wing was to play in France's first international season, against New Zealand.

In 1900 the overseas influence continued when the Barbarians this time demolished Le Havre by forty-one points to three, though for some reason each side fielded only fourteen men (one well knows what can happen on tour!). One of the Frenchmen, with the Gallic name of E.W.Lewis, was to play for France in their first match with England. To these successes could be added a victory over Cardiff, at Easter 1900, by twenty-seven points to twelve, which was to remain the greatest number of points scored at the Arms Park by the Barbarians until the forty-nil win of 1957. That Cardiff side of 1900 included as captain the twenty-four times capped Welsh international legend E.Gwyn Nicholls, as well as many great names – Percy Bush, Selwyn Biggs and Dobson, Blake and Neil in the pack.

So apart from the continued reversals at Newport, these were heady days for the Barbarians. None of those who were present at their original meeting in Bradford could have anticipated the unique touring club's immediate popularity. The crowds that supported the fixtures in the north, midlands, the west country and Wales were as large as those for international matches – enthralled, no doubt, by the adventurous rugby style. Newspapers brought the attention of a wider public to some epic encounters. Most significantly of all perhaps, the club had already attracted the cream of British rugby players into its fold. Carpmael's conception of a touring team had enticed the highest calibre of player from the start. The original membership included a large proportion of internationals – nineteen English, one Irish, two Scottish and two Welsh.

The annual membership had continued to elect to the club fellow players and sporting gentlemen of a kind that would continue as disciples of good rugby and good fellowship on tour. This can be gauged, too, from the fact that the twenty-one

# UN GRAND MATCH DE FOOTBALL-RUGBY

Hier, au Bois de Boulogne, sur le terrain du Polo, les Barbarians, une formidable
sélection de joueurs anglais, ont battu, par 17 points à o, l'équipe première du Racing
Club de France, qui s'est bien défendue.

The Barbarian XV that defeated Racing Club de France in 1908 — the first ever overseas match that
they played.
Back row: F.Hutchinson, G.V.Kyrke, J.R.Upson, F.T.Turner, J.M.Mackenzie, J.L.Fisher, R.P.G.Begbie,
F.Burges Watson, R.D.Cox, R.A.Gibbs, Emile de Lissa. Front row: P.J.Monaghan, Cecil Dixon,
J.E.C.Partridge, J.C.Wilson, P.F.MacEvedy, F.W.Hinings.

man missionary touring party to South Africa (sometimes called the 1891 British
Lions — though properly styled the English tour to Cape Colony) included fourteen
Barbarians, of whom W.G.Mitchell, J.Hammond and R.L.Aston, all original members, played in every one of the twenty matches — with Aston scoring a Lions'
record of thirty tries. Similarly, despite the presence of ten Irishmen, of whom few
were Baa-Baas in the early years, there were twelve Barbarians in the 1896 British
Lions party. It is doubtful whether these early forebears of a great tradition could
have anticipated that all thirty-two players of the 1974 Lions tour would be Barbarian members!

So by the turn of the century, the club was firmly on its feet, already enjoying a
reputation as a provider of all that was most exciting in rugby football. But the twentieth century was to be ushered in by one of the most significant seasons in Barbarian
history, at the beginning of a new era.

# Chapter 4

# THE EASTER TOUR OF WALES

The season of 1900–01 brought with it the first of the four-match Easter tours of Wales. Cardiff had been a fixture from the outset, and Newport since 1893. Then in 1901, Penarth and Swansea first appeared on the Easter itinerary, to make up the quartet of clubs that have entertained the Barbarians annually, with very occasional intermissions, ever since.

Why Penarth? Well not really because of the prowess of its rugby club at that time, which flourished but was never of the class of the major Welsh teams. Rather it was because Penarth was ideal as a Barbarian headquarters, for if the Baa-Baas can ever be deemed to have had a home, that was it. Penarth in late Victorian days was a delightful and highly respectable resort of seaview villas and promenade guest-houses on the Bristol Channel. A few miles from Cardiff, and only sixteen from Newport, it represented the base point for the Barbarian tour party. Apart from its proximity to the match grounds, there was bracing sea air, a relaxing holiday atmosphere and a desirable relative isolation for the players to enjoy. But above all there was The Esplanade. This seafront hotel, together with its sympathetic staff, played a greater part in Barbarian history and folk-lore than any other single factor in the seventy years between 1901 and 1971.

*The Esplanade Hotel, Penarth, the 'headquarters' of the Barbarian tour of South Wales until 1971. The 'Esp', and its tolerant staff, will be fondly remembered by the many hundreds of Barbarians who enjoyed there the friendliness and hospitality which was such an important part of the Easter Tour.*

Suffice to say at this point that the choice of The Esplanade as a touring head-quarters was not only the happiest chance but also the principal reason for the inclusion of the local club, Penarth, in the fixtures, as a reciprocation for the generosity of Penarth people towards the Baa-Baas, which has continued ever since.

The traditional Good Friday encounter with Penarth has not only proved the source of many friendships and the highlight of the local club's season with a tremendous depth of loyal, local support, but something of a valuable 'pipe-opener' for the tourists in preparation for the tougher encounters to come. Not that one should in any way be patronising about the Penarth v Barbarians game, as the shock result every few years continues to prove. Few people realise, too, that in the early years Penarth certainly held their own with the illustrious visitors, including a hat-trick of wins between 1904 and 1906.

In addition to the institution of The Esplanade, the other factor that guaranteed the contentedness of the Baa-Baas in Penarth was the association that developed with the Penarth Golf Club. Since Easter 1901 to the present day, the Penarth Golf Club has allowed members on tour to play over their glorious links whenever they wish to do so. Barbarians also have the use of their clubhouse and even the sacrifice of their members' sets of clubs. Such a wonderfully generous gesture has made the compulsory golf tournament a major part of the Barbarian legend and, in the eyes of certain 'alickadoos', almost of equal importance to the encounters on the rugby field!

In 1924–25, in recognition of the generosity of the host club, the ninety-five Barbarian members subscribed a total of £52 17s to a 95-ounce perpetual silver cup, called the Barbarian Challenge Cup, to be competed for annually. On Good Friday, 16 April, 1925, Percy Carpmael made the presentation of the new trophy to G.H.P.Redford, captain of the Glamorgan Golf Club, with these words:

'Sportsmen — I say sportsmen advisedly, because people who have stood Barbarian golf for twenty years are sportsmen of the first degree. We are not often golfers really, but gardeners. We are presenting this cup to the Penarth Club because they have stood our golf for so many years, and coming up the drive I thought of an appropriate rule which might be embodied in those governing the play for the Cup.

'It is this, "No one must leave the green until the score has been properly settled". If the problem is a big one then all the players must sit down on the green and discuss the matter over a bottle of Worthington. I think on the Penarth links the bottle will be found in the hole. I have the greatest pleasure in handing over to such a fine body of sportsmen this cup which has been subscribed by many past and present players, some of whom are at the moment as far away as India and Shanghai.'

The reply by the club captain was equally apt:

'There is an old proverb which says "Never trust a Greek when he is bearing gifts", but of course it is quite unnecessary to say this because we are not dealing with Greeks, but Barbarians.'

The Barbarians were made eligible to compete for the cup, and in those first years of the competition the 'real' golfers did so. In fact in the very first competition for the Barbarian Cup of 1925, appropriately the result was a tie between local member W.H.Guest, and the Scotland and Barbarian player, J.C.Dykes, who each scored a net 73, off handicaps of 14 and 9 respectively. Eighth, with a net 78, was one H.L.G. Hughes!

At the same time as Penarth became a new fixture of the Easter tour, so too did the match with Swansea. This new fixture came about in the same year that Emile de Lissa first became a Barbarian 'supporter'. It was a late addition to the 1901 Barbarian season, so late in fact that it was not printed on the annual club membership card for 1900–01. The scheduled Easter tour for that year was to include only the two matches, Newport and Cardiff. But the increasing realisation that it was impractical to combine both the north of England and Wales in one tour, made the inclusion of Swansea, the premier Welsh club of that time, a logical step. Yet it was a bold move, since Swansea were well-nigh unbeatable. In the season of 1900–01, prior to the first Barbarian match, they had won twenty-seven and drawn two of their thirty-one games; it was also the year in which Swansea's W.J.Bancroft made his thirty-third and final appearance at full-back for Wales, while Dick Jones and Dickie Owen made their international half-back debuts.

Certainly the Barbarians were putting their collective head on the block. Victories over Cardiff were already hard to come by; Newport, as already mentioned, were proving invincible; and from that first game on 9 April 1901 until 2 April 1923, the Barbarians did not beat Swansea. But neither did any other English, Scottish or Irish club beat Swansea at home for twenty years up to 1919. Whether it was the excesses of the Sunday Golf Tournament or the new-found jollifications at The Esplanade which took their toll in the lean years of the early 1900s is hard to say! What is certain is that this was an exceptional period in Welsh club rugby – the era of Welsh Triple Crowns in 1900, 1902, 1905, 1908, 1909 and 1911, and of many great names.

It was indeed a tough tour schedule to play against teams of such talent. Cardiff could boast Gwyn Nicholls, Percy Bush, Cecil Biggs and H.B.Winfield, Sweet-Escott, Blake, Neill, S.L.Williams, Rhys Gabe and Reggie Gibbs; Newport had George Llewellyn Lloyd, Lou Phillips, Tommy Vile and Walter Martin, and Fred Birt,

*Percy Carpmael (seated) presents the Barbarian Challenge Cup to G.H.P.Redford of Penarth Golf Club, on Good Friday 1925. Since then, under the driving influence of Herbert Waddell, the compulsory Sunday Golf Tournament has flourished.*

*Barbarians v Devonport Albion, 14 April 1903*
Back row: *A.F.Roberts, N.W.Godfrey, H.R.Elliott, A.Brettargh, E.W.Dillon, B.A.Hill, J.G.Graham, R.G.Bingham.* Middle row: *D.R.Bedell-Sivright, G.Fraser, W.P.Scott, R.T.Skrimshire, B.C.Hartley, F.M.Stout, J.E.Franks.* Front row: *E.W.Elliott, T.A.Gibson, F.Wood, A.Brown.*

in the backs; George Boots, Jehoida Hodges and Harry Uzzell amongst the pack. In Swansea these were the days of Jack Bancroft, Dickie Owen, Danny Rees and Dick Jones, W.J.Trew, George Davies, W.W.Joseph, Fred Scrines, D.J.Thomas, W.Parker and Syd Bevan and Reverend Alban Davies. There were all these and more. Even Penarth, who held their own, could boast Louis Dyke before he played for Cardiff.

This is not to suggest that there was any shortage of talent in Barbarian ranks, with 'Darkie' Bedell-Sivright and Munro of Scotland, the Stouts of Gloucester, Adrian Stoop, G.V.Carey, J.G.G.Birkett and Sivree of Harlequins, Unwin and Vassall of Blackheath, Coffey, Beatty, Hinton and Brown of Ireland, as well as A.F.Harding and some of the aforementioned Welshmen, when not engaged with their own clubs. But there were few victories for the Baa-Baas in this period. As a correspondent of 1907 put it:

'I don't see how a scratch side, however good, can hope to get the better of Swansea or Cardiff (and one may as well include Newport here) unless the locals happen to have a very off-day — the general team combination and the forward packing are so good.'

As if to tempt fate still further, the Barbarians persisted with both Christmas and Easter tours in the west, playing Cardiff and Newport regularly twice a season. Conversely, the matches in the north and north-east gradually diminished in number as did the earlier close personal contacts with these northern clubs, with men such as F.H.R.Alderson and Bob Oakes of Hartlepool and the Robertshaws of Bradford.

So the north of England matches, which had initiated the Barbarian touring tradition, ceased in 1902 with the games against Hartlepool Rovers and West Hartlepool. How appropriate that the final match (until 1965!) against Hartlepool Rovers, who had been the Barbarian Football Club's first ever opponents, should have been refereed by that famous original Barbarian and Rover, Frank Alderson, with the result a three-all draw.

*Two of Cardiff's most illustrious captains: Gwyn Nicholls (left) and Percy Bush. Gwyn Nicholls, the 'prince' of centres, formed with Rhys Gabe one of Cardiff and Wales's most successful threequarter pairings ever. He was captain of Cardiff between 1898 and 1901, and again in the season 1903–04. On Boxing Day 1903, Gwyn Nicholls led Cardiff to a record victory over the Barbarians, 41–3; of nine tries, three were scored by Nicholls. This victory was not to be avenged until 1957, when the Baa-Baas won 40–0. Percy Bush was another outstanding captain of Cardiff in three of the four seasons between 1905 and 1909. In 1905–06 he led Cardiff to thirty-one victories and only one defeat – that by New Zealand – and both Nicholls (captain) and Bush (his first cap) were in the Wales XV that brought the All Blacks their only defeat.*

Perhaps the most significant factor which may account for the cessation of these north country matches was a practical one. By the early 1900s there was no doubt that the Welsh tour, centred on Penarth, was there to stay. South Wales offered then, as it does now, easy accessibility by rail from London, huge crowds for the games, satisfactory match guarantees to cover expenses and the highest quality rugby. But in 1902 the Baa-Baas over-ambitiously tried to combine the west, Wales and the north into one Easter tour. Imagine the administrative problems and exhausting schedule for a touring party which in those days numbered twenty or so, compared with the present group of thirty or more. Over Easter 1902, the tourists played Penarth on 28 March, Devonport Albion on 31 March, Swansea on 1 April, Cardiff on 2 April, Hartlepool Rovers on 5 April and West Hartlepool on 7 April. The indefatigable E.M.Harrison of Guy's Hospital played in all six games! No doubt his vocation enabled him to look after himself better than most – but clearly such an itinerary was impracticable. The upshot was that the growing rugby strength of the west country beckoned as a more convenient alternative to the north of England.

So began the inclusion of both Devonport Albion and Plymouth, and later Exeter and Cheltenham, in the Barbarian calendar. But, as in Wales, the power of west country rugby did not make these easy matches for the tourists, who won nine and lost eight up to World War I, failing to beat Plymouth on each of the three occasions. The Barbarians, on a supposedly carefree tour, were pitting themselves against the strongest clubs in Britain, frequently playing five matches in six days. The results testify to the enormity of the task.

| | | |
|---|---|---|
| 1901–02 | Played 8 | Lost 6 Drawn 1 |
| 1902–03 | Played 6 | Lost 3 |
| 1903–04 | Played 7 | Lost 7 (on 26 December, Cardiff won 41–3) |
| 1904–05 | Played 7 | Lost 5 (for the first time beating Newport 10–6) |
| 1905–06 | Played 6 | Lost 6 (Cardiff winning 38–0) |
| 1906–07 | Played 5 | Lost 2 (Cardiff winning 35–0) |
| 1907–08 | Played 7 | Lost 4 |
| 1908–09 | Played 5 | Lost 3 |
| 1909–10 | Played 7 | Lost 4 (Cardiff won 30–0, ten tries to nil!) |
| 1910–11 | Played 7 | Lost 5 |
| 1911–12 | Played 7 | Lost 6 |
| 1912–13 | Played 6 | Lost 5 |
| 1913–14 | Played 7 | Lost 5 |

# Chapter 5

# THE BARBARIAN CALENDAR COMPLETED

There was one additional and lasting innovation during the pre-war years. In 1909 the Barbarians played Leicester as the third and final match of the Christmas tour which is now the only surviving game of that earlier Barbarian tradition.

Under the guidance of Tom Crumbie, the club's Honorary Secretary from 1898, Leicester had come through to the forefront of British rugby at this time. In 1906, for instance, there were five Leicester men playing for England. Leicester was always an invitation side and Crumbie brought players from far and wide. I say brought, and not bought, because Crumbie's policy of inviting people from outside the local area had something to do with allegations of professionalism at the club in 1908. These allegations were put before a Rugby Union enquiry on 14 January, 1908, in particular maintaining that three players, all British Lions of 1908 — F.Jackson, T.W.Smith and S.Matthews — 'had received money from the Northern Union, and that the services of A.L.Kewney, T.Hogarth, E.J.Jackett and F.Jackson had been obtained for the Leicester club in violation of the laws on professionalism'. Happily the findings of the inquisition declared the club and its players innocent of all charges.

> 'Your committee is strongly of the opinion that the allegations against the Leicester club are largely due to the fact that the club, having a strong team with a good match list, attracts players who are unable to get such good football in other localities, but that, however undesirable this may be, the players have not benefited pecuniarly thereby'.
>
> signed T.C.Pring, Arthur Hartley, F.Hugh Fox. 30 January, 1909

I mention all this so that the significance can be appreciated of the gesture made to the club by the Barbarians, in agreeing to the new fixture a fortnight *before* the sitting of the court of enquiry. Clearly the Baa-Baas had no doubts as to Leicester's innocence of the impending charges. No wonder the relationship between the Tigers and the Barbarians has remained so close.

That the match was introduced at all owes much to the efforts of both Crumbie and W.C.Wilson, a former Richmond player who, on joining the Leicestershire Regiment, became a member of the local club, the Tigers. Walter Wilson was himself an England international at centre in 1907, the same year in which he was elected to the Barbarians. Prior to the first match with Leicester he had been on five Barbarian tours, and in the 1909–1910 season was elected to the committee. In that position, and as a popular fellow, he was able to press for the introduction of the new fixture. It was most appropriate therefore that Wilson was captain of the Barbarians for the opening match on 29 December 1909. Before a crowd of more than ten thousand and amidst some tricky conditions, he scored a try in a nine-all draw.

> 'The play was in Leicester's 25 when Lloyd intercepted a pass and wisely ran straight. Seeing that he must be tackled, he had recourse to a short punt. That kick Wilson followed up and though hotly pursued by Jackett, he kicked the ball and raced after it. He repeated the manoeuvre successfully and in the end his pace told. It was a capital try which he scored, after travelling some seventy yards.'

Walter Wilson – Richmond, Leicester, Barbarians, and England. Wilson and Leicester's secretary, Tom Crumbie, were instrumental in bringing about the annual fixture between the Barbarians and Leicester, and Wilson was appropriately the Baa-Baas' captain for the first-ever match with the Tigers in December 1909. It was drawn nine points all.

And the tailpiece of that *Daily Telegraph* report is appropriate to this passage of Barbarian history:

'With this game, the Christmas tour of the Barbarians came to an end. They failed, it is true, to win a match, but the large crowds which assembled at Cardiff, Newport and Leicester testified to their reputation and their popularity, and whether they win or lose they are known to be good to watch. They are frankly a scratch side but they are deservedly one of the greatest institutions of English Rugby Football, all the same.'

No wonder they were popular; although the Welsh may find it easy to be generous in victory, there's no doubting the sincerity of some contemporary press comments!

'It was early observable that the visitors were quite a class team and they commenced a display of passing such as few visiting teams have given at Swansea . . . the exhibition was a treat.' *(Swansea, 1 April, 1902)*

'The Barbarians seem destined to play an important part in the great development of rugby. The tour which ended this week was successful in introducing to South Wales and the West of England, not only a great standard of skill, but showing to these localities the glorious spirit of chivalry in which real rugby can be played . . . The Barbarians left behind them a fine impression of the highest principles of the game.' *(Easter Tour 1907)*

But not every game was a glorious spectacle!

'The play was disappointing and the score did not show the trend of it. The many informalities were a reflection on Welsh football, putting the ball in the scrummage unfairly being the most grievous fault.' *(Cardiff 1907)*

'The match was for the most part slow. There were fast movements but play rarely reached brilliance. Penarth as a combination did not do credit to their form, which in back play is usually far above that seen in this match. The Barbarians, on the other hand, were a team of units, otherwise a huge score would have been piled up by them.' *(Penarth 1909)*

But, all in all, by the time of World War I, under the guidance of their founder, Percy Carpmael, the Barbarians were already an institution. Their popularity brought record attendances at club grounds wherever they played — ten thousand at Plymouth and Penarth, Bradford and Birkenhead, and in 1914 over twenty thousand at the Arms Park. The organising efficiency of Emile de Lissa and his shrewd diplomacy

*Edgar Mobbs, one of the most renowned of all Barbarians — a great rugby player, a true sportsman, and an inspiring leader, both on the rugby field and in battle. Tragically, Lieutenant-Colonel Mobbs was killed at Passchaendale in July, 1917. But his name lives on in the annual Mobbs Memorial Match between the Barbarians and the East Midlands.*

had been invaluable as he took over much of the administration and selection from Carpmael in his years as Honorary Secretary from 1905. There was a wealth of ability, enthusiasm and contacts in the ranks of the committee; members such as W.N.Mayne, Carpmael's first right hand man in the 1890s, Frank Evershed and Alderson, C.B.Nicholl, A.E.Stoddart and S.M.J.Woods, Maud, Byrne, P.C.Tarbutt and Unwin. Also very much in evidence were B.C.Hartley, who took over secretarial duties between 1902 and 1905, and Lyon, Wilson and E.R.Mobbs.

If one judges the merits of these men by the results they achieved with their infant club (and that does not mean on the field of play) then their successors owe an overwhelming debt of gratitude to these Barbarian 'alickadoos'. The future of the Barbarians was assured by the time World War I broke out, not least because within their ranks were the men to safeguard the club's future. On 21 March 1913, at Penarth, the Barbarians did not distinguish themselves on the field of play, losing by eight points to three. But in that Barbarian fifteen playing alongside each other in the pack, and both in the black and white jerseys for the first time, were H.A.Haigh-Smith and H.L.G.Hughes. Thank goodness that, despite the result, they were invited to play again!

No one needs reminding of the horrors of World War I, but the fact that sixty-three Barbarian members were killed out of just over two hundred on active service, represents an appalling sacrifice. Yet, ironically, the Barbarians did more than their share in helping both the war effort and recruitment. In September 1914, the new Secretary, T.R.Treloar, sent out the annual printed letter to the club members.

'Dear Sir,
It has been decided to proceed with the Annual Election as usual. However there is no intention of playing any matches this season, unless the war should be over in time to allow the fixtures as arranged, to be carried out.'

But despite the cancellation of existing fixtures, Treloar and the committee were not to be daunted. The efforts of one man in particular lay behind the resounding success of the six matches played in the 1914–15 season – Edgar Mobbs.

Mobbs, a Northampton player, had been elected a Barbarian in 1911, having already been capped for England seven times in 1909 and 1910. His first match on the Easter tour of 1912, against Cardiff, though lost 16–9, was one of his best.

'The hero of the game was Mobbs, the Old International, whose fine play for England on the same ground will long be remembered. He knows the game through and through, and his determined bursts could not fail to elicit admiring cheers, whilst he gave an excellent lesson in handing-off.'

And again . . .

'Mobbs was head and shoulders the best of their threequarters. Built on generous lines, he was terribly hard to hold and did what we rarely see nowadays – handed off beautifully.'

That hand-off was to become his hallmark. The following season, Mobbs was elected to the committee, a man as popular off the field of play as he was fearsome on it. He was that rare thing, a natural leader by example, as his war-time experiences were to show. His organisation of the War Service matches typified both his rugby and patriotic enthusiasm. While based at Shoreham, he raised and captained a camp team against the Baa-Baas in aid of Lady Jellicoe's North Sea Fleet Fund. He led the Barbarians against Leicester (T.H.Crumbie's XV) on both 2 January and 27 March, 1915, to encourage local recruiting and to aid Patriotic Funds and Leicester Royal Infirmary.

He then led the Barbarians against RAMC, Crookham, at Richmond Old Deer Park, in aid of the British Red Cross, and on 17 April, 1915, he captained the Barbarians (or England, as the team had been billed) against Wales at Cardiff Arms Park. On only one other occasion have the Barbarians played another of the home countries' fifteens, when they met a Scottish fifteen in Edinburgh in 1970, in aid of the Commonwealth Games.

*The first of the six war service charitable and recruiting matches. Emile de Lissa and Edgar Mobbs brought together teams made up of players who were engaged in naval or military service, and, as the appalling number of Barbarians and other players killed in action would indicate, rugby men were in the forefront when it came to responding to Lord Kitchener's call.*

*Sat. Dec. 19ᵗʰ 1914*

**Official Programme.**　　　　**Price One Penny,**

# GOLDSTONE GROUND HOVE.

# Great Rugby Match

—— IN AID OF ——

# "NORTH SEA FLEET"

**Under the Patronage of**

**Lady Jellicoe and General Sir J. Ramsay.**

## Shoreham Camp v. Barbarians (Service Team)

### BARBARIANS (Black & White.)

**FULL BACK.**

J. L. Urquhart ~~Pte. G. W. Somerset~~ (Yorkshire).

**THREE-QUARTER BACKS.**

LIEUT. G. G. ZIEGLER. ~~LIEUT.~~ ~~(Cumberland.)~~ ~~SⁿᵈLIEUT. G. A. VAUGHAN~~
~~(South~~ ~~and Richmond.)~~ ~~(Cumberland.)~~

**HALF-BACKS.**

*PTE. H. COVERDALE. 　　PTE. L. R. BROSTER.
(Blackheath and England).　(Guy's Hospital and Offord).

**FORWARDS**

*LIEUT. H. C. HARRISON. LIEUT. J. B. ROSHER. *CORPL. IAN PENDER. ~~Pte. H. Hoyer~~
(United Service and England), 　(Rosslyn Park).　(London Scottish & Scotland).　(Leicester).

PTE. M. P. ATKINSON,　　　　　PTE. C. KIDMAN.　　　PTE. T. HOPKINS.
(London Hospital).　　　　　　(Guy's Hospital).　　　(Leicester).

**KICK-OFF** 2.30 P.M.

O

**FORWARDS**

PTE. E. W. MANN.　~~Corpl. W. Pilkington.~~　CPL. J. H. MARTYN.　CPL. W. Bookman
(Northampton)　　(Northampton).　　　　(Rosslyn Park).　　(Northampton).
CPL. L. SKIMPTON.　CPL. L. DUNBRIDGE.　LIEUT. H. GRIERSON.　CPL. J. J. LAWSON.
(Northampton).　　(Stroud).　　　　　(Rosslyn Park).　　(Gloucester).

**HALF-BACKS.**

CPL. H. WILLETT　　　　LIEUT. B. H. HOLLOWAY.
(East Midlands).　　　(Cambridge University).

**THREE-QUARTER BACKS.**

PTE. J. GILLHAM. LIEUT. C. H. MARTYN. *LIEUT. E. R. MOBBS (Capt.) CORPL. E. G. BUTCHER.
(Bedford).　　(East Midlands).　(Northampton and England).　(Devonshire).

**BACK.**

LIEUT. R. GURNEY (Bedford).

### SHOREHAM CAMP (Blue and White)

• INTERNATIONALS

[P.T.O.

*The Barbarian Service XV, styled 'England' and captained by Edgar Mobbs, that had the distinction of beating Wales at Cardiff Arms Park in April 1915 by 26 points to 10. Emile de Lissa suggested that the only way in which he could account for this remarkable result was that fourteen of the Barbarians were 'extra fit' as a result of training for active service.*

The match at Cardiff had a sensational outcome with the Barbarians crushing Wales 26–10. The strength of Welsh rugby has been alluded to before – and the fifteen captained by the intrepid Reverend Alban Davies of Swansea included thirteen Welsh internationals, nine of them in the 1914 Welsh fifteen. Yet, in the best Barbarian tradition, on foregathering at Paddington the Baa-Baas found they were a forward short. By chance J.G.G.Birkett happened to be on the train to Wales to watch the match. The problem was solved – the Barbarians played seven forwards and eight backs . . .

'And it happened that the famous Harlequin played as well as ever he did. His speed was surprising, his dash overpowering, and what tackling he did was delightfully characteristic. The reappearance of Birkett was quite a feature of the match, but he was only one of a completely successful three-quarter line. I do not recall having seen Minch and Quinn, the Irishmen, playing so well. In defence and attack they were capital, venturesome, and, so I thought, yards faster than when I have seen them playing for their country. Then there was Edgar Mobbs – big, dashing, enthusiastic, and the best of captains, and Butcher, the clever young man of Devon. I am sure they are free to confess, however, that they owed much to Higgins, the Old Edwardian fly-half, whose play at any other time would have won for him his country's cap.'

The Barbarian fifteen overwhelmed the opposition – and:

'though fighting with great vigour forward right to the end, the Welsh team was beaten as it had never been beaten before in modern times. The Reverend Alban Davies, now a chaplain in the Welsh Regiment, strove hard to get his forwards going as they played a year ago, but how those seven Barbarian forwards managed to hold the Welsh eight and to get the ball as well was one of those mysteries of the game. Even the admirable Clem Lewis found that the Barbarians carried too many guns for his game. The Welsh team were so outplayed that at one time R.F.Williams, the full-back exclaimed, "What has happened?"'

But the crowd was not left to be stirred merely by the fine rugby. The band of the Third Battalion of the Welsh Regiment played national airs before the game, the Mackintosh of Mackintosh sent the pipers and drums of the Cameron Highlanders to the parade, the recruiting sergeants were busy talking to apparent eligibles, and at half-time several of the officers addressed the company on the terraces. Adding to this the fact that every player of the Barbarian fifteen belonged to the 'new Army', it was not surprising that the recruiting officers of the various regiments were more than pleased with the day's results.

Indeed, rugby men were in the van when it came to signing on for service. Blackheath, as ever closely involved with the Barbarians, minuted a resolution in August, 1914 —

'It is the duty of every able-bodied man of enlistable age to offer personal war service to his King and Country, and that every Rugby footballer of the present day comes within the scope of Lord Kitchener's appeal.'

*Barbarian matches to encourage local recruiting and to raise 'patriotic funds' were also held at Leicester in 1915, with Edgar Mobbs again the Barbarian captain.*

**Vision of E. R. Mobbs and his Corps at the Front.**

*Reproduced from the " Northampton Independent."*

*A postcard sent from Lieutenant E.R.Mobbs in September 1914 while stationed at Shoreham Camp, to Emile de Lissa. The cartoon taken from the* Northampton Independent *shows Edgar Mobbs leading his Corps in battle and scattering the German defence – translating his renowned hand off, which was the outstanding hallmark of his play as a centre-threequarter, from the rugby field to the field of battle!*

More was the pity, one is tempted to add; since Mobbs, then Lieutenant-Colonel Edgar Robert Mobbs DSO, was killed in action on 31 July 1917 at Passchaendale, a month short of his thirty-fifth birthday.

E.H.D.Sewell, in his book *The Rugby Football Internationals Roll of Honour*, published in 1919, recalls that over and above Mobbs's outstanding playing contribution to his club Northampton, to England and the Barbarians, each of whom he captained in his career:

'He had a beautiful disposition for games, being the possessor of a perfect temper, a burning hatred of all things mean and unsporting, and a heart of gold. Full of fun, he was the life and soul of every team he toured with.'

Following his death, his Brigadier wrote to his parents:

'He had an extraordinary influence over all his men, who would have done anything for him, and he died leading them in one of the most gallant attacks that any battalion has ever made.'

At the outset of the war Edgar Mobbs had been refused a commission on the grounds of his age – thirty-two. But not to be daunted he signed on as a private, and through sheer enthusiasm and the strength of his charismatic personality raised his own corps of two hundred and sixty-four men as 'D' Company of the 7th Northants Regiment. His men, who numbered over four hundred in the end, included many

*The scene in Northampton's Market Square in 1921 when Lord Lilford unveiled a memorial to Edgar Mobbs. Thousands of people, including eighty-five surviving members of Mobbs 'D' Company, came to pay tribute to the memory of a great hero. At the foot of the twenty-foot high stone pedestal is a life-size bust of Mobbs with an inscription which includes these words '. . . erected by subscriptions of admirers the world over to the memory of a great and gallant sportsman'.*

rugby men, amongst them E.R.Butcher, the Devon captain, Corporal H.Willett, Bedford's captain (both elected Barbarians in 1915), as well apparently as the whole of Long Buckby village rugby team, and nine of the East Midlands fifteen. These men, spurred on by their beloved leader, lined up on the Barrack Square, Northampton, on 14 September 1914 for their departure for Shoreham Camp, and ultimately went on to successive operations in the front line. In July 1921 just eighty-five surviving members of 'D' Company returned amidst a massive throng of people to the market square to pay tribute to their hero. There Lord Lilford unveiled a twenty-foot high Portland stone pedestal, surmounted by a bronze figure, symbolising glory to the dead. At the foot of this memorial to Mobbs is a life-size bust of him with a poignant inscription that includes these words:

'. . . erected by subscriptions of admirers the world over to the memory of a great and gallant sportsman'.

Amongst the many wreaths placed at the foot was one from the Barbarians, who had already paid a more lasting tribute to one of their greatest members. On 10 February, 1921 at Franklins Gardens, Northampton, the first Mobbs Memorial Match was played between the Barbarians and the East Midlands — two sides for whom Mobbs had given great service — and the proceeds were donated to the promotion of rugby football in the district. At the dinner following the match, J.B.Minahan, Honorary Secretary of East Midlands, expressed his hope that it would be possible to make the fixture an annual one. No doubt such thoughts were already in the mind of Emile de Lissa, who in his speech referred to Edgar Mobbs as his . . .

'greatest friend — a better fellow for playing the game, and for teaching others to play it, never lived'.

Except during World War II, the Mobbs Memorial Match has been played every year since. It continues as a fitting tribute to an outstanding Barbarian, representing, one would like to feel, all those members who gave their lives in the two World Wars.

Thus the sixth and last of the regular annual Barbarian matches came into being, despite, incidentally, a strange incident that occurred during the first game. After only sixty-eight minutes on the field the referee, Adrian Stoop, blew his whistle for no-side. As D.R.Gent reported:

'the men rapidly made their way to the dressing-rooms and it was not until the spectators on the unreserved stands began to protest, that Mr Stoop realized anything was wrong. Much perturbed, he immediately requested the players to take the field again although Luck, the Saints' forward, was already in the bath and others were stripped and about to join him, they readily assented, but naturally there was a little delay, and ten minutes passed before the game was again in progress.'

At the 'final' whistle the score was 18–8 to the Baa-Baas, but the ultimate scoreline was 21–14 — no doubt the last ten minutes made it all worthwhile!

So in that unusual manner, the now traditional pattern of the Barbarian calendar was established. That same season of 1920–21 saw the last full Christmas tour to Wales. To raise a touring party of true Barbarian calibre for two tours a season was becoming an ever-increasing problem for the committee. One presumes that the marriage of the then Honorary Secretary, Lawrence Merriam, during that same year, was not in itself of undue significance in respect of the changes in the Barbarian calendar! But the matches against Cardiff on 27 December 1920, and Newport the next day, were the final Christmas games in Wales, and the official programme of the Cardiff match (as well-produced then as it is currently) anticipated this:

'Latterly our friends (the Baa-Baas) have found it difficult to get a truly representative side together to tour during the Christmas festivities, and for this reason it is well on the cards that this will be their last appearance on any (Welsh) ground during the festive season.'

Thus it proved to be. The defeat at the hands of Newport by thirty-nine points to nil on the following day may well have been the last straw! What is certain is that since that year the traditional Barbarian itinerary has been Leicester on Boxing Day, the East Midlands on the first Thursday in March and the four Welsh clubs — Penarth, Cardiff, Swansea and Newport — on the Easter tour.

# Chapter 6

# THE BARBARIANS IN WALES

The four matches in South Wales have become the cornerstone of Barbarian tradition since the inception of a four-match Easter tour in its present form in 1901. The familiar quartet of Easter matches, however, did not become a *regular* occurrence until a few years after World War I, for a number of reasons. Between 1901 and 1925, the tour fixtures as we know them today were only completed three times, in 1901, 1903 and 1922. In 1902, and between 1904 and 1920, the Newport match was played as part of the Christmas tour, which also included Cardiff. Although the Newport match reverted to Eastertide in 1922, relations between the Barbarians and the 'Usksiders' were suspended for two seasons, in 1923 and 1924, in the same way that matches were not played with Swansea in 1906 and 1907. But from 1925 onwards, apart from the years of World War II, the sequence of the four matches has continued uninterrupted.

The 1976 Easter tour is the only occasion on which the Barbarians have lost all four matches in South Wales, and in fact it also represents the longest sequence of defeats ever in Wales on Easter tour. The Baa-Baas did lose to Penarth, Cardiff and Swansea in 1913, 1914 and 1920, years in which Newport was not played. In addition the Barbarians lost all their Easter tour matches in 1904, against Penarth, Cardiff, Swansea, Devonport Albion and Plymouth, and again in 1906, losing to Penarth, Cardiff, Devonport Albion, and Plymouth.

The Barbarians have on four tours lost to Cardiff, Swansea and Newport in succession, while beating only Penarth — in 1922, 1925, 1938, 1956.

## ALL-CONQUERING EASTER TOURS

|      | Penarth | Cardiff | Swansea | Newport |
|------|---------|---------|---------|---------|
| 1931 | 9–0     | 11–9    | 21–3    | 18–9    |
| 1932 | 22–16   | 14–8    | 12–8    | 9–6     |
| 1933 | 24–7    | 17–13   | 20–7    | 21–9    |
| 1934 | 16–3    | 14–9    | 12–6    | 11–6    |
| 1935 | 16–3    | 20–5    | 16–3    | 23–3    |
| 1949 | 14–11   | 6–5     | 10–3    | 6–5     |
| 1970 | 42–6    | 30–28   | 24–8    | 22–3    |
| 1973 | 23–6    | 16–6    | 35–9    | 60–15   |

## UNDEFEATED EASTER TOURS

|      | Penarth | Cardiff | Swansea | Newport |
|------|---------|---------|---------|---------|
| 1955 | 3–3     | 6–3     | 6–3     | 14–14   |
| 1959 | 6–6     | 21–0    | 18–11   | 15–5    |

## EASTER TOURS WITHOUT A WIN

|      | Penarth | Cardiff | Swansea | Newport |
|------|---------|---------|---------|---------|
| 1976 | 30–36   | 28–29   | 25–37   | 0–43    |

## LONGEST SEQUENCE OF VICTORIES IN WALES ON EASTER TOUR

Twenty-one wins, between 3 April 1931 (v Penarth) and 10 April 1936 (v Penarth) inclusive. Newport and District were also defeated in October 1933.

OFFICIAL

PROGRAMME

PRICE

THREEPENCE

## PENARTH RUGBY FOOTBALL CLUB

# PENARTH v. BARBARIANS
### GOOD FRIDAY, 15th APRIL, 1960

Easter 1960 brings us our usual welcome visitors and we are delighted to have them. "Grandstand" and inclement weather have played havoc with our gates this year, so once more we look forward to a bumper gate and the filling of a sadly depleted exchequer.

For the first time ever the home side fields two Barbarians against their illustrious visitors and it would not be amiss to write how much the Penarth Club appreciate the invitations to their players.

That we shall have an "out of the book" game goes without saying and it only remains to wish the Barbarians a most successful and enjoyable tour.

The Welsh Sevens are due at Cardiff on the afternoon of April 30th. Stand Tickets, 5/- each, can be obtained from the Club Secretary.

We are once more indepted to Col. W. R. Crawshay, D.S.O., for the services of the 6th Bn. Welch Rgt. Band.

## BARBARIANS v PENARTH 1901–1976

Of the six regular Barbarian fixtures, it is not surprising that the Baa-Baas have been most consistently successful against Penarth. In fact it is greatly to the credit of the home club that they have beaten the illustrious visitors ten times in their sixty-five encounters, and it is the occasional shock result, such as those of 1971 and 1976, that helps to keep the fixture very much alive.

Apart from the great hospitality that the Barbarians have enjoyed over seventy-five years from the club and the people at this small seaside resort outside Cardiff, the game has been invaluable in itself as a 'pipe-opener' for the visitors on Good Friday, in preparation for the tougher fixtures with the three major South Wales clubs that follow. Indeed, that alone is an excellent reason for the continuation of the fixture, for another, more difficult, match at the start of the tour would be an absurd task for the Barbarians to face. Even as things stand the match has, as often as not, proved to be a well-fought contest, with Penarth on occasion raising their game to unaccustomed heights for this peak of their season. Playing like men inspired they have sometimes taken advantage of Barbarian sides that have regarded the outcome as a foregone conclusion, or else Penarth have quite simply proved to be the better side on the day.

## SUMMARY OF MATCHES

**Played: 65   Won: 51   Lost: 10   Drawn: 4**
**Points for: 1145   Points against: 468**

Average points for Barbarians per match: 17.6
Average points for Penarth per match: 7.2
Total tries for Barbarians: 243
Average Barbarian tries per game: 3.7

| First win: | 1901 | 14–4 |
|---|---|---|
| First Penarth win: | 1904 | 4–5 |
| Biggest win: | 1974 | 73–10 (13T, 9C, 1PG) to (2T, 2C) |
| Biggest defeat: | 1976 | 30–36 (6T, 3C) to (7T, 4C) |

Longest run of victories: 1922–1954 inclusive (27 matches)
Longest run of defeats: 1912–1920 inclusive ( 4 matches)
Most tries for a Barbarian player in one match: C.B.Holmes (5T 1947)
Most tries for a Penarth player in one match: G. Klombies (2T 1913), T. Johnson (2T 1920), D. Hicks (2T 1921), T. Smith (2T 1950), D. John (2T 1976), M. Chinnock (2T 1976)

Most points for a Barbarian in a match: A. M. Jorden 21 (9C, 1PG) in 1974
Most points for a Penarth player in a match: D. John 16 (2T, 4C) in 1976

## MEMORABLE MOMENTS AND MATCHES

Penarth has always enjoyed a huge 'gate' for the annual Barbarian match. In 1907 it exceeded everyone's expectations, even the Treasurer's, as ten thousand flocked to see the great visitors' side, led by Adrian Stoop. The extra stands for five hundred were filled, the Cardiff City Band entertained the gathering throng for an hour preceding the match, and all awaited a grand game, in the knowledge, too, that the home team's ground record was at stake. A try by the big Harlequin winger Lambert was exceeded by a try by Purnell with a superb conversion by Ralph Thomas to put Penarth 5–3 ahead at half-time. Imagine the excitement!

Penarth had been playing an extra back and only seven forwards in the first half, but understandably they were 'overweighted' in front and finding that the policy of playing a 'rover' did not pay, Jenkins (full-back) was sent into the pack in the second half as 'forward'. One of the South Walian rugby scribes wrote at the time:

> '... once A.D.Stoop broke away cleverly for the Barbarians, but he was grandly tackled by Kirby, and after two narrow shaves J.F.Williams scored near the post.'

The try was converted to put the Baa-Baas three points ahead. Penarth went great guns after this, Davies and Shattock almost scored and Louis Dyke missed, by a whisker, a drop-goal attempt. But Stoop at fly-half was in control.

> 'Flemmer, Stoop, Vassal, Smidt and Lambert brought off a grand bout of passing for the visitors, but Lambert, when looking desperately dangerous, was magnificently tackled by Ralph Thomas.'

Penarth countered time and again but the Barbarians held out, thanks largely to their hero, W.P.Hinton, the Irish full-back, 'who never made a mistake and was like a rock in defence'. For Penarth the press singled out R.C.Thomas, L.M.Dyke, F.Davies, R.Kirby, L.S.Thomas and Hutchings as best. Needless to say, the crowd was even bigger the following year.

In 1912, in heavy going and drizzling rain, Penarth scored their third victory in nine years, albeit by the narrowest of margins. Nil-nil at half-time, Penarth's persistent efforts were rewarded by a try by Crossman which proved sufficient for a home-team victory. This was one of only two occasions in their history that the Barbarians failed to score any points at Penarth. It was also the first of four successive wins for the 'Seasiders', so that by 1920 Penarth had won six of fifteen encounters.

*The Barbarian XV which beat Penarth 8–0 in 1938. This game will be remembered for the spectacular try scored by the Russian prince, winger Alexander Obolensky.* Back row: R.V.Reynolds, H.C.Lyddon, A.E.Allan, F.M.McRae, A.Obolensky, H.A.Haigh Smith. Middle row: C.L.Melville, P.Cranmer, R.M.Grieve (captain), G.T.Dancer, G.Roberts, A.A.Brown. Front row: T.A.Kemp, B.C.Gadney, C.V.Boyle.

A persistent feature of Penarth play was, and still is, relentless and ruthless tackling, and never more so than in the glorious drawn game of 1921, as seen through the eyes of the rugby correspondent of *The Observer*:

'The tourists opened up the game at every opportunity and a long period of Penarth pressure was abruptly ended when King rounded off a movement initiated in the home half by scoring. The international converted. Penarth returned to the attack and Hicks scored after pretty play. Just before the interval Garnett whipped the ball out smartly to J.E.Davies, who dropped a neat goal, thus enabling the Seasiders to cross over with the slender lead of two points.'

In the second half J.C.Seager and A.T.Young, the Barbarian half-backs, excelled, Seager scoring a try –

'but in the concluding stages Penarth rallied and Hicks pulled the game out of the fire by scoring after a thrilling dribble along the touchline.'

So a great reputation for exciting matches between the two clubs developed. As Philip Trevor wrote in *The Daily Telegraph* in 1923:

'Good Friday is always a great day in Penarth, for that's the day when Emile de Lissa takes there year after year his team of all the talents.'

In that year the outstanding figure in a nineteen points to five victory was T. Lawton, being groomed by the Barbarians as the fly-half successor to the England captain W.J.A.Davies.

'He took the ball superbly and distributed it with rare judgement and ability. Many of his openings were brilliant, and four of the tries came from movements which he initiated.'

Fifty points and twelve tries in the game of 1926 tells of a feast of running rugby and a festival occasion for Penarth as reported by the *Penarth Times*:

'A brilliant sunshine poured down on what closely resembled a miniature Ascot. Magnificent dresses were to be seen everywhere, whilst the gentlemen, not to be outdone by the ladies, made a brave show with their plus-fours and sandies. Truly it was a gala day for Penarth, and a sight which should have made the Treasurer and the Secretary rub their hands together right handsomely. The game itself proved one of the most thrilling and interesting contests yet played on the Recreation Ground, with plenty of good scoring, and the play so even in the first threequarters of the play that no one could safely foretell what the final result would be. The Baa-Baas' supporters clustered on the steps of the Grandstand and entertained the crowd with the famous Baa-Baas' song whenever the spirit moved them, and good-humoured enthusiasm prevailed throughout the whole afternoon.'

In the Barbarian side that won thirty-three points to seventeen were Mark Sugden, Ian Stuart and Jack Gage of Ireland and renowned English players E.Coley, W.E.Tucker and Glyn Hughes, but Penarth had their own hero, Jack Bassett. The following year it was the legendary Welsh full-back who was:

'chiefly responsible for holding up the Barbarian attack, and it is safe to say that if he had tackled and kicked in Welsh trial matches as he did on Good Friday, he would have been first choice for the International side this season. Four times he brought Cussen to earth, when it seemed the Irish "cap" must score.'

*The opening match, at the Recreation Ground, Penarth, of the first all-conquering Barbarian Easter tour since 1935. The Barbarians, with Barney Mullan as captain, beat Penarth 14–11 in this 1949 match.*

And if a yardstick for comparison was needed that day, W.E.Crawford was Bassett's opposite number.

A succession of great names graced the Recreation Ground turf in the vintage Barbarian years of the next decade, such as Dan Drysdale, Carl Aarvold, C.C.Tanner and R.S.Spong, Kendrew, Jenkins and Harry Lind, Jack Heaton and Hal Sever. But perhaps one of the greatest memories was left by that young prince of the rugby field Alexander Obolensky, in 1938. His spectacular try in an unspectacular game was one of those brilliant moments that characterised his tragically brief career. J.P.Jordan, the renowned rugby writer, recorded it thus:

'Catching a drop-out by Peter Cranmer, he flashed away in brilliant style down the right wing. By clever changes of pace he beat man after man to end up a glorious run behind the posts after covering threequarters of the length of the field.'

That score secured the Barbarians seventeenth successive victory, but success was not always to remain so sure. In 1955 Penarth, with a try by B. Griffiths held out for a draw, three points all, in the opening game of a tour in which the Baa-Baas were to beat both Cardiff and Swansea and draw with Newport. In 1958 the margin of Barbarian victory was only a single point and the following year honour was served at six points all against a Barbarian team that included Arthur Smith, Jim Roberts, Bev Risman, S.R.Smith, Geoff Windsor-Lewis, Wright, Godwin and Millar, Haydn Mainwaring and Clem Thomas –

'Penarth played with tremendous fire. They failed in the set scrum against a good shove and Godwin, but made up for it elsewhere, particularly in the line-out, where Price, Jones and Petersen, out-jumped Hughes, Kemp and Ellis.'

Templeman, the irrepressible Penarth scrum-half, dropped a goal in the last quarter, and Vizard the fly-half put Coombes in for the equalising try. A fine effort, that thrilled the uninhibited crowd.

*In 1970, again an all-conquering tour, the Barbarians beat Penarth 42–6. Keith Fielding, shown here sprinting for the line, scored a hat-trick of tries.*

In 1960 Penarth achieved their first victory over the Barbarians for forty years, by ten points to eight, led this time by that same effervescent scrum-half Brian Templeman. In 1961 he scored thirteen points in a magnificent exhibition of open rugby that brought about a remarkable recovery from twenty-three points to eight down, to a final losing margin for Penarth of twenty-six points to twenty-two.

The next ten years, as if by way of reaction, saw the Barbarians make amends for the 1960 lapse with a string of convincing wins. But Penarth, as ever, continue to show their ability to upset the greatest odds by sheer determination and inspired performances on the day. Victory came their way in 1971, but the Barbarians countered in 1973 by recording their biggest ever score in a match with thirteen tries and a total of seventy-three points in celebration of Herbert Waddell's fifty years of Barbarian membership. But who would have believed that in a game of sixty-six points in 1976, Penarth would yet again assert themselves, as a delirious crowd roared on Lynn Baxter's fifteen to a deserved victory by six points? It was indeed a splendid way for Penarth to celebrate the seventy-fifth anniversary of the first ever fixture between these clubs.

## BARBARIANS v PENARTH

| YEAR | SCORE | CAPTAINS BARBARIANS/ PENARTH | SCORERS FOR | AGAINST |
|------|-------|------------------------------|-------------|---------|
| 1901 | 14–4 | | P. W. Stout (1T) J. G. Graham (1T) E. W. Elliot (1T) J. G. Graham (1PG, 1C) | H. Jones (1DG) |
| 1902 | 11–0 | E. C. Galloway *C. Warburton* | A. F. King-Stephens (3T) W. B. Odgers (1C) | |
| 1903 | 3–0 | J. G. Franks | T. Simpson (1T) | |
| 1904 | 4–5 | B. C. Hartley | S. F. Coopper (1DG) | R. C. Thomas (1T) R. A. Gibbs (1C) |
| 1905 | 5–8 | | N. W. Godfrey (1T) A. F. Harding (1C) | E. Williams (1T) W. M. Llewellyn (1T) J. C. M. Dyke (1C) |
| 1906 | 0–5 | A. F. Harding | | F. Davies (1T) J. C. M. Dyke (1C) |
| 1907 | 8–5 | A. D. Stoop | D. Lambert (1T) J. F. Williams (1T) G. D. Roberts (1C) | A. Purnell (1T) R. C. Thomas (1C) |
| 1908 | 3–0 | J. E. C. Partridge | G. D. Roberts (1T) | |
| 1909 | 8–3 | G. D. Roberts | H. Martin (1T) H. H. Vassall (1T) J. C. M. Dyke (1C) | R. Jellings (1T) |
| 1910 | 10–10 | G. D. Roberts | G. D. Roberts (1GM) H. H. Vassall (1DG) D. Lambert (1PG) | W. Shepherd (1T) G. Heslop (1T) H. Shepherd (2C) |
| 1911 | 13–6 | W. S. D. Craven | H. Whitehead (1T) G. D. Campbell (1T) W. S. D. Craven (1T) F. le S. Stone (2C) | E. Hamilton (1T) F. Davies (1T) |
| 1912 | 0–3 | R. Honey | | T. Crossman (1T) |
| 1913 | 3–8 | J. M. B. Scott | T. H. Vile (1PG) | G. Klombies (2T) W. Roberts (1C) |
| 1914 | 3–8 | R. H. Williams *A. Bryant* | T. H. Vile (1 PG) | C. McIver (1T) T. Crossman (1T) W. Roberts (1C) |
| 1915–1919 | | WAR YEARS | | |
| 1920 | 10–12 | H. L. G. Hughes *T. Crossman* | A. F. Blakiston (1T) E. F. van der Riet (1T) C. F. G. T. Hallaran (2C) | T. Johnson (2T) J. Williams (1T) P. O'Brien (1T) |

| YEAR | SCORE | CAPTAINS BARBARIANS/ PENARTH | SCORERS FOR | AGAINST |
|---|---|---|---|---|
| 1921 | 10–10 | E. F. van der Riet<br>*J. Hill* | Q. E. M. A. King (1T, 2C)<br>J. C. Seager (1T) | D. Hicks (2T)<br>D. E. Davies (1DG) |
| 1922 | 8–6 | T. H. Vile<br>*C. McIver* | T. G. Wallis (2T)<br>T. Lawton (1C) | T. Crossman (1T)<br>L. Box (1T) |
| 1923 | 19–5 | T. Lawton<br>*M. Vyvyan* | T. Lawton (1T)<br>H. L. G. Hughes (1T)<br>J. C. Seager (1T)<br>J. C. Hubbard (1T)<br>H. P. Jacob (1T)<br>T. Lawton (2C) | S. Crole (1T)<br>H. Norman (1C) |
| 1924 | 11–9 | D. Drysdale | R. L. Raymond (2T)<br>W. E. Crawford (1C)<br>E. J. Massey (1T) | E. J. Scott (1T)<br>M. Vyvyan (1T)<br>S. Hinam (1T) |
| 1925 | 22–11 | W. E. Crawford<br>*M. Vyvyan* | E. Coley (2T)<br>G. V. Palmer (1T)<br>R. G. Hopkins (1T)<br>G. Fellows-Smith (1T)<br>E. E. E. Cass (1T)<br>R. H. B. Bettington (1C)<br>W. E. Crawford (1C) | A. Lloyd (1T)<br>T. N. Payne (1T)<br>S. Phillips (1T)<br>W. Evans (1C) |
| 1926 | 33–17 | I. M. B. Stuart | S. J. Huins (2T)<br>J. H. Gage (1T)<br>W. E. Tucker (1T)<br>G. Fellows-Smith (1T)<br>C. L. Steyn (1T)<br>J. M. Durr (1T, 6C) | H. Norman (1T)<br>T. Richards (1T)<br>A. Lloyd (1T)<br>T. Morgan (1T)<br>M. Evans (1T)<br>A. Lloyd (1C) |
| 1927 | 8–3 | P. S. Douty<br>*T. N. Payne* | T. C. Barber (1T)<br>D. Turquand-Young (1T)<br>K. J. Stark (1C) | M. Jacobs (1T) |
| 1928 | 9–7 | A. R. Aslett | C. D. Aarvold (1T)<br>T. C. Barber (1T)<br>T. E. Priest (1T) | J. H. Ellerway (1T)<br>E. Price (1DG) |
| 1929 | 18–6 | I. M. B. Stuart<br>*I. McPherson* | I. C. Bendall (1T)<br>E. G. Taylor (1T)<br>G. A. McIlwaine (1T)<br>W. M. Simmers (1T, 1DG)<br>W. H. Wood (1C) | E. Price (1T)<br>J. H. John (1T) |
| 1930 | 24–9 | W. H. Wood<br>*I. McPherson* | W. H. Wood (2T)<br>F. S. Kendall (1T)<br>F. W. S. Malir (1T)<br>I. M. B. Stuart (1T)<br>E. Coley (1T)<br>J. W. Allan (3C) | D. Davies (1T)<br>C. Cameron (1T)<br>T. Lee (1PG) |

| | | CAPTAINS | SCORERS | |
|---|---|---|---|---|
| YEAR | SCORE | BARBARIANS/<br>PENARTH | FOR | AGAINST |
| 1931 | 9–0 | A. F. Heppenstall<br>*J. A. Bassett* | A. Key (1T)<br>L. L. Bedford (1T, 1PG) | |
| 1932 | 22–16 | H. Rew<br>*G. Jones* | D. St. Clair Ford (2T)<br>A. C. Harrison (1T)<br>E. Mercer (1T)<br>F. L. Williams (1T)<br>A. Key (1T)<br>H. Rew (2C) | W. Rees (1T)<br>A. White (1T)<br>J. Maddocks (1T)<br>J. O'Brien (1T)<br>T. Lee (2C) |
| 1933 | 24–7 | P. C. Hordern<br>*A. G. Clark* | P. C. Alexander (1T)<br>P. C. Hordern (1T)<br>F. L. Williams (1T)<br>P. C. Minns (1T)<br>E. Coley (1T)<br>C. P. B. Goldson (1T)<br>C. G. Gosling (3C) | W. C. Goodman (1T)<br>M. Hopkins (1DG) |
| 1934 | 16–3 | J. W. Allan<br>*A. G. Clark* | P. C. Hordern (1T)<br>J. I. Rees (1T)<br>G. W. C. Meikle (1T)<br>J. Dicks (1T)<br>V. G. J. Jenkins (2C) | W. Goodman (1T) |
| 1935 | 16–3 | H. Lind<br>*J. J. Davies* | H. S. Sever (2T)<br>R. Willsher (1T)<br>D. A. Thom (1T)<br>V. G. J. Jenkins (1DG) | W. Baker (1T) |
| 1936 | 25–3 | B. C. Gadney<br>*J. Daly* | E. J. Unwin (3T)<br>R. C. S. Dick (1T)<br>R. J. L. Hammond (1T)<br>P. C. Hordern (1T)<br>J. R. Evans (1C)<br>M. McG. Cooper (1T)<br>J. I. Rees (1C) | J. Daly (1T) |
| 1937 | 33–8 | H. B. Toft<br>*H. Weston* | P. L. Candler (3T)<br>J. G. Rogers (1T)<br>R. H. Dryden (1T)<br>A. G. Cridlan (1T)<br>G. W. Parker (3C, 2PG)<br>H. Lind (1GM) | R. A. Matthews (1T)<br>H. Weston (1PG, 1C) |
| 1938 | 8–0 | R. M. Grieve<br>*J. C. Shepherd* | A. Obolensky (1T)<br>C. L. Melville (1T)<br>P. Cranmer (1C) | |
| 1939 | 30–11 | R. Leyland<br>*R. F. Trott* | D. G. Cobden (2T)<br>W. C. W. Murdoch (2T)<br>R. Willsher (1T)<br>R. Leyland (1T)<br>W. M. Penman (6C) | P. Manley (1T)<br>W. E. Jones (2DG) |

| YEAR | SCORE | CAPTAINS BARBARIANS/ PENARTH | SCORERS FOR | AGAINST |
|------|-------|------|------|------|
| 1940–1945 | | WAR YEARS | | |
| 1946 | 27–6 | R. J. L. Hammond *L. Morgan* | J. S. R. Innes (3T) I. Preece (2T) W. A. Meates (2T) C. J. Murphy (3C) | E. R. Knapp (1T) A. C. Jones (1PG) |
| 1947 | 36–10 | H. Tanner *E. Barratt* | C. B. Holmes (5T) M. F. Turner (2T) C. W. R. Andrew (1T) R. F. Trott (3C) C. W. R. Andrew (1C, 1DG) | T. L. Lloyd (1T) J. Warman (1T) D. Evans (1DG) |
| 1948 | 12–7 | R. W. F. Sampson *J. Heslop* | D. D. Mackenzie (1T) C. W. R. Andrew (3PG) | N. T. Fryer (1DG) R. Holbrow (1PG) |
| 1949 | 14–11 | B. Mullan *J. Gibson* | G. H. Sullivan (1T) J. A. R. Macphail (1T) D. B. Vaughan (1T) V. G. Roberts (1T) B. Mullan (1C) | R. Davies (1T) D. Evans (2DG, 1C) |
| 1950 | 17–11 | Glyn Davies *D. W. Evans* | D. W. Swarbrick (2T) B. J. Brennan (2T) G. Williams (1C) D. F. White (1PG) | T. Smith (2T) W. Tillyard (1T) D. W. Evans (1C) |
| 1951 | 16–0 | V. G. Roberts *G. S. Davies* | M. C. Thomas (1T, 1DG) J. V. Smith (1T) B. Lewis Jones (2C, 1PG) | |
| 1952 | 36–3 | M. J. Berridge | F. G. Griffiths (2T) B. L. Jones (1T) B. M. Gray (1T) W. C. Woodgate (1T) J. A. Boothman (1T) B. L. Jones (5C, 2PG) J. E. Nelson (1C) | T. Smith (1T) |
| 1953 | 13–3 | B. L. Williams *T. Smith* | J. D. Robins (2C, 1PG) E. E. Woodgate (2T) | A. Baker (1T) |
| 1954 | 15–0 | I. King *K. Bush* | B. M. Gray (1T) M. C. Thomas (1T) I. King (3C) L. P. MacLachlan (1T) | |
| 1955 | 3–3 | I. King *K. Bush* | R. C. Bazley (1T) | B. Griffiths (1T) |
| 1956 | 9–3 | K. J. Jones *D. Hughes* | R. K. G. MacEwen (1T) R. W. T. Chisholm (1T) M. C. Thomas (1PG) | B. Templeman (1T) |

| | | CAPTAINS | SCORERS | |
|---|---|---|---|---|
| *YEAR* | *SCORE* | BARBARIANS/ *PENARTH* | *FOR* | *AGAINST* |
| 1957 | 28–15 | C. I. Morgan *T. Smith* | G. M. Griffiths (2T) G. T. Wells (2T) A. C. Pedlow (1T) M. A. Pearey (1T) H. J. Mainwaring (5C) | B. Templeman (1T) H. Davies (1T) P. Donovan (1T) K. Bush (3C) |
| 1958 | 6–5 | J. T. Greenwood *T. Smith* | A. A. Mulligan (1T) H. J. Mainwaring (1PG) | H. Griffiths (1T) R. Payne (1C) |
| 1959 | 6–6 | R. C. C. Thomas *H. Jacobs* | A. B. W. Risman (1T) D. C. Glass (1T) | S. Coombes (1T) B. Templeman (1DG) |
| 1960 | 8–10 | A. Robson *B. Templeman* | A. Robson (1T) G. Windsor-Lewis (1T) H. J. Mainwaring (1C) | D. Walkey (1T) K. Roberts (1T) B. Templeman (2C) |
| 1961 | 26–22 | D. C. Manley *D. Vizard* | R. H. Thomson (2T) A. C. B. Hurst (3T) O. Grieveson (1PG, 4C) | P. Turnbull (1T) D. Mainder (1T) P. Donovan (1T) B. Templeman (3PG, 2C) |
| 1962 | 39–3 | A. A. Mulligan *J. Price* | D. A. Stanford (2T) J. B. Steven (2T) P. Thorning (2T) D. Nash (1T) J. E. Owen (1T) H. J. C. Brown (1T) D. C. Coley (1T) J. G. Willcox (1C) D. Nash (2C) R. A. W. Sharp (1DG) | D. Jones (1PG) |
| 1963 | 13–0 | P. G. Yarranton *E. Jones* | J. W. Telfer (1T) D. P. Rogers (1T) J. Roberts (1T) J. G. Willcox (2C) | |
| 1964 | 24–3 | M. S. Phillips *E. Jones* | J. W. Macdonald (1T, 1C) B. C. Henderson (1T) D. P. Rogers (1T) M. S. Phillips (1T) S. A. Morris (2PG, 2C) | A. Jenkins (1PG) |
| 1965 | 26–13 | S. J. S. Clarke *A. Jenkins* | T. Kiernan (2T, 4C) W. J. Hunter (1T) D. W. A. Rosser (1T) R. B. Taylor (1T) A. W. Hancock (1T) | J. Hughes (1T) M. Welch (1T) A. Wielding (1DG) A. Jenkins (2C) |
| 1966 | 12–8 | J. G. Willcox *B. Evans* | F. B. K. Bresnihan (1T) M. K. Flynn (1T, 1DG) W. R. Hunter (1T) | E. Davies (1T) M. Welch (1T) A. Rayer (1C) |
| 1967 | 13–0 | K. P. Andrews *F. Wilson* | B. Capaldi (2T) D. L. Powell (1T) A. Hickie (2C) | |

| YEAR | SCORE | CAPTAINS BARBARIANS/ PENARTH | SCORERS FOR | AGAINST |
|------|-------|------|-----|---------|
| 1968 | 19–5 | D. Rutherford<br>*C. Prescott* | K. C. Plummer (2T)<br>R. J. Arneil (1T)<br>M. Grimshaw (1T)<br>D. Rutherford (1PG, 2C) | G. Lock (1T, 1C) |
| 1969 | 45–9 | W. G. Hullin<br>*A. Jones* | C. D. Saville (3T)<br>C. M. Telfer (2T)<br>D. H. Prout (2T)<br>W. Lauder (2T)<br>M. N. Grimshaw (1T)<br>C. S. Wardlow (1T)<br>W. Lauder (4C)<br>W. G. Macdonald (2C) | P. Codd (3PG) |
| 1970 | 42–6 | N. C. Starmer-Smith<br>*A. Jones* | K. J. Fielding (3T)<br>N. C. Starmer-Smith (2T)<br>J. N. M. Frame (2T)<br>P. J. Dixon (1T)<br>B. J. O'Driscoll (6C, 1PT)<br>C. M. Telfer (1DG) | A. Watts (1T)<br>A. Jones (1T) |
| 1971 | 12–15 | W. G. Hullin<br>*B. Mort* | M. P. Bulpitt (1T)<br>W. G. Hullin (1T, 2PG) | R. B. Taylor (1T)<br>P. Cosh (1T)<br>W. Carter (3PG) |
| 1972 | 41–17 | J. S. Spencer<br>*J. H. Williams* | L. G. Dick (3T)<br>G. W. Evans (2T)<br>A. Neary (1T)<br>A. M. Jorden (3PG, 4C) | J. H. Williams (1T)<br>B. Davies (1T)<br>A. Taine (1T)<br>W. Carter (1PG, 1C) |
| 1973 | 23–6 | J. S. Spencer<br>*A. Stamp* | P. M. Davies (2T)<br>A. G. Ripley (1T)<br>S. A. McKinney (1T)<br>R. A. Codd (1PG, 2C) | S. Sidford (1T)<br>P. Marsh (1C) |
| 1974 | 73–10 | D. J. Duckham<br>*P. Griffiths* | R. T. E. Bergiers (3T)<br>K. Smith (3T)<br>D. J. Duckham (2T)<br>W. Lauder (1T)<br>R. E. Wilkinson (1T)<br>L. G. Dick (2T)<br>J. M. Broderick (1T)<br>A. M. Jorden (9C, 1PG) | P. Griffiths (1T)<br>P. Helmore (1T)<br>P. Marsh (2C) |
| 1975 | 21–11 | J. S. Spencer<br>*L. D. Baxter* | D. Robinson (1T)<br>J. S. Spencer (1T)<br>W. N. Bennett (3C, 1PG)<br>D. I. Bell (1T) | J. Parsons (1T)<br>P. Helmore (1T)<br>P. Marsh (1PG) |
| 1976 | 30–36 | P. Bennett<br>*L. D. Baxter* | C. Kent (1T)<br>C. F. W. Rees (1T)<br>J. J. Williams (2T)<br>D. B. Williams (1T)<br>D. A. Cooke (1T)<br>A. R. Irvine (3C) | D. John (2T)<br>M. Chinnock (2T)<br>S. Phillips (1T)<br>J. Davies (1T)<br>A. Stamp (1T)<br>D. John (4C) |

# OFFICIAL PROGRAMME

## CARDIFF RUGBY FOOTBALL CLUB.

Cardiff Arms Park.

# BARBARIANS

v.

# CARDIFF.

SATURDAY, April 15th, 1911.

R. A. GIBBS, Capt.     J. PUGSLEY, Vice-Capt.
Photos by A. & G. Taylor, Cardiff.

## Theatre Royal

To-night—" **The Power of the King.**"

Next Week—

**ITALIAN GRAND OPERA Co**

# HEATH'S FOR MUSIC

76, QUEEN STREET, CARDIFF          NAT. TEL. 2199

## THE WEEK'S GOSSIP.

What a bright galaxy of talent the secretary of the Barbarians has at his command again this time ! Last season it will be recalled, a strong team drew with Penarth on Good Friday, and then trounced us in no unmistakable manner on the Saturday—the score being 2 goals 2 tries to a goal.

To use the historic words of Harry Tate, they will beat us again this time *I don't think.* Adrian Stoop, Birkett, Lindsay and Lambert will not represent the Baa-baas to-day, but they will sport the Harlequin's colours on Monday.

A sensational score was contributed by the backs last Easter. Frank Stoop intercepted a pass from Wyndham Jones, and then gave to big John Birkett who covered half the length of the field without encountering any opposition.

Mr. J. Games, the referee, gave the visitors a try for fouling by Reardon. No referee is infallible, and this was one of the mistakes made that day, for shoulder to shoulder charging when two players run for the ball is quite legitimate.

The form of Cardiff against Leicester was very gratifying. To those who saw the debacle at Gloucester, the two teams did not seem one and the same. It is to be hoped that the best humour will be shown from now to the end.

After the defeat of Swansea last Saturday, the display of a weak Cardiff team against Bridgend was as happy as could reasonably be expected. Rogers, the out-side half, dropped another goal, this being the 30th from his foot this season. It looks as if he can easily out-Bush Bush.

We shall not see Louis Dyke, the pluckiest of the plucky, in the team again this year I am afraid. He has not yet recovered from his illness.

LOOSEHEAD.

# HEATH'S FOR TUNING

76, QUEEN STREET, CARDIFF          NAT. TEL. 2199

## BARBARIANS v CARDIFF 1891–1976

Of the long-standing fixtures of the Easter tour, Cardiff have been marginally the most successful, winning almost two-thirds of their ninety-three matches. This remarkable record is even more creditable since, on account of the availability of Barbarian players, the Baa-Baas have tended to put their strongest combination out at the Arms Park. The very fact that, on average, more than twenty-one points have been scored in each match, indicates to some extent the quality of entertainment that the match has engendered.

Since the first ever fixture between the clubs on 31 March 1891, Cardiff has been at the hub of the Barbarian tour, spanning a period of eighty-five years with a fixture played every season, apart from during the war years. In the early days, matches were on occasion played at Christmas as in 1892, 1893 and 1894. Such was their popularity and success that from 1898 until 1920, Cardiff and the Barbarians met at both Christmas and Easter – despite the fact that the Baa-Baas were able to win only four of the thirty-four matches played in that period. Since then the balance of results has been just about even, with a sequence of matches that has produced some of the finest games of rugby ever witnessed at the Arms Park, never more so than in recent years.

## SUMMARY OF MATCHES

**Played: 93   Won: 29   Lost: 60   Drawn: 4**
**Points for: 742   Points against: 1245**

Average points for Barbarians per game: 7.9
Average points for Cardiff per game: 13.4

Total tries for Barbarians: 162
Average Barbarian tries per game: 1.7

First win:         March 1892 (10–0)
First Cardiff win: March 1891 (3–7)
Biggest win:       1957 (40–0) (10T, 5C)
Biggest defeat:    December 1903 (3–41) (9T, 5C, 1DG)
                   1906 (0–38) (9T, 4C, 1PG)

Longest run of victories: 1931–1935 inclusive (5 matches)
Longest run of defeats: December 1910-December 1920 inclusive (11 matches)
Most tries for a Barbarian in one match: L. D. Bailey 4 (April 1900)
Most tries for a Cardiff player in one match: J. L. Williams 5 (April 1906)
Most points for a Barbarian in one match: A. R. Irvine 16 (1T, 2PG, 3C) 1976
Most points for a Cardiff player in one match: H. V. P. Huzzey 17 (2T, 4C, 1PG) 1897

## MEMORABLE MATCHES AND MOMENTS

The first encounter of 1891 has already been described and the game of 1892 was significant for two reasons. It was the first Barbarian victory and the only occasion until 1957 that Cardiff failed to score!

'It was a good game and hardly won. The truth must be told (reluctantly, it seems!). The Barbarians were just a little better than the home lot but there was very little in it. At forward and half they compared very favourably, but their threequarters, although good individually, did not combine as well as Cardiff. Johnstone at back was very good. Hubbard and Robertshaw were the pick of the threes, although the former was well looked after by Pearson.

Darcy Thompson kicked very well, but Biggs did nothing (which is scarcely surprising since he didn't play!). Wells was the most effective of the halves, although Marshall played a sound game. Nicholl, Carpmael, Allport and Jeffrey were the best of a heavy and hard-working pack. Rooney did very well for Cardiff at back, never being at a loss, and Pearson and Cosslett put in some grand work at threequarters.'

A converted try by Carpmael gave the Barbarians a half-time lead:

'although the spectators began to audibly express their opinion of the referee in terms explicit rather than complimentary'.

In the second half Cardiff's efforts were to no avail, although R.Davies did manage to cross the line only for a foot in touch to be signalled. Just on the call of time Wells scored for the Barbarians, 'who had taken the aggressive again'. Johnstone converted and the visitors won by two goals to nil.

But such victories were to be gained rarely, and even a Barbarian team of 'exceptional strength' in 1902 was soundly beaten nineteen points to six in a match refereed by A.J.Gould. The Barbarians included nine England internationals, F.M.Stout, T.A.Gibson, B.A.Hill, G.Fraser, and B.C.Hartley in the pack, Kendall and Hulme the half-backs, R.Forrest, A.G.Brettargh, in the threes, as well as the Newport and Welsh international Skrimshire and two Irish caps Franks and Harvey. But Cardiff, under H.B.Winfield, were themselves a powerful team in those days, with the legendary Gwyn Nicholls, Wayne Morgan, 'Wax' Williams, and the Biggs family.

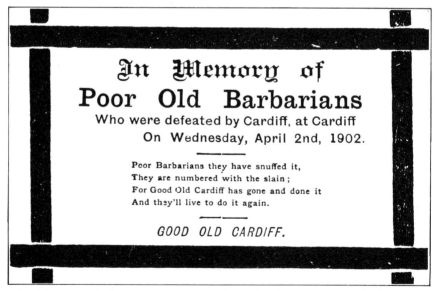

In Memory of
# Poor Old Barbarians
### Who were defeated by Cardiff, at Cardiff
### On Wednesday, April 2nd, 1902.

Poor Barbarians they have snuffed it,
They are numbered with the slain ;
For Good Old Cardiff has gone and done it
And they'll live to do it again.

*GOOD OLD CARDIFF.*

*Understandable sympathy from Cardiff, expressed in 1902 – the year in which the Barbarians were beaten for the tenth time in fourteen matches. On this occasion Walter Winfield led the Cardiff XV.*

There was plenty of good rugby in those early years but the games were not always without controversial incident. The match of Easter 1907 was extensively reported. 'Foul Play Alleged' ran one headline. 'Unpleasant Incident' led another. It seems that tempers frayed on a scorching day. It was so hot that Gwyn Nicholls, for one, appeared to be considerably affected, for during the interval he went into the press box and had a cold water bandage applied to his head and the game was resumed without him! Anyway, referee J.Games of Abercarn had a lean time of it and gave some dubious decisions. Early on, a pass which appeared forward between Reggie Gibbs and Nicholls brought a try:

'then from the half-way W.Neill, who was playing a great game, opened out the play again and fine passing and inter-passing between Nicholls and Gibbs — in which once more there was a forward transfer — resulted in Nicholls racing in at such an angle that Gibbs was able to place a goal. There were shouts from the crowd of "Play the game, referee".'

A vigorous protest was made by the Barbarians against allowing the second try, not on account of the forward pass, but because of an alleged foul by Ralph Thomas. They averred that:

'Thomas so obstructed Macevedy that he was unable to get at Nicholls'.

A.D.Stoop, in the hearing of pressmen and spectators alike, called the foul 'filthy', and later charges were made against the Cardiff club and players for foul play. The Barbarian touch judge (probably Emile de Lissa) complained, too, of the tactics of R.J.David:

'I am surprised at the Cardiff Club playing him. Why don't they play a gentleman?'

To which Percy Bush, the famous Cardiff captain and a long-standing friend of the Barbarians, made an amusing riposte:

'When an inside-half is spoken of as free from vice and blemish, then, indeed, is the New Utopia at hand.'

The Barbarian Easter Tour Party of 1909.
Back row: P.R.Nelson, J.C.Parke, D.F.Smith, S.N.Cronje, J.Mehaffey, H.J.S.Morton, H.West, G.D.Roberts, C.T. te Water, H.Martin, W.C.Wilson, A.A.Adams, R.H.M.Hands. Middle row: J.Ross, J.Muir Mackenzie, H.H.Vassall, J.J.Coffey, E. de Lissa, W.P.Carpmael, F.O.B.Wilson, D.G.Schulze, E.J.B.Tagg, C.A.Bolton. Front row: G.M.Chapman, J.M.McKeand, G.V.Carey, R.H.Williamson, A.C.Palmer, J.H.Bruce-Lockhart, F.N.Smartt, B.B.Bennetts.

By Christmas the hubbub had died down and the Barbarians were as welcome as ever, as shown by the notes of 'Blind-side' in the Cardiff programme:

'Although they call themselves Baa-Baas, it will pay Cardiff not to hold them too sheep. Vassall is going into the English Fifteen this season, so are Lambert and Birkett. LAMB-ert is essentially a Baa-Baa and a fine player. Keep both eyes on him. Vassall's name belies him. He is no-one's slave, but is quite good enough for a first-class Welsh side . . . There need be no fear about the forwards, for strong as is the pack used by our uncivilised friends, it will not come near our own ruck for skill and honest work. Cardiff should win by ten or twelve points.'

In fact Rhys Gabe's team won eleven points to five, and once more the twenty thousand crowd went home satisfied.

More often than not in the early years of the Barbarian tour Swansea was the Saturday match and Cardiff Easter Monday, and for both clubs it was invariably the finale to the home season. How sensible! Easter Monday 1909 brought a crowd of twenty-five thousand to the Arms Park:

'The Baa-baas have brought down this time the very strongest team they have ever mustered. In fact, they are more than mustard hot. If Cardiff manage to get the better of them then indeed may they be proclaimed not only the Champions of Wales, but the Champions of the British Isles for the Barbarian side, including as it does, such men as Schulze, Parke, Poulton-Palmer, Coffey, Williamson, Bedell-Sivright, to mention only a few of the stars, is a stronger side by far than any International team of the season. It looks rather as if the Blue and Black fold are sheep before the shearers, but the men are all determined that they will honour their skipper and make him Captain of the Champions for the third time, so the result needn't be worried about. Percy Bush's many friends and enemies will deeply sympathize with him, we feel sure, in the trouble which is about to overtake him. He is to be married on 23rd of June; gentlemen and ladies only! This does not mean that he will give up football because if it had not been for the intervention of his bride-elect he would have finished football four years ago, even before he was captain, but SHE commanded and of course he obeyed!'

Well, 'Blind-Side's' optimism was indeed justified; the scoreline was twenty-two points to nil, and Percy was able to enjoy his wedding all the more! Nor had the Barbarians seen the best of this great Cardiff side. In the rain and quagmire of the Arms Park of Christmas 1909 Cardiff were to give what must surely rank as one of their best performances ever in beating the Barbarians by ten tries (all unconverted) to nil. One of the Blackheath Barbarians on tour described the slaughter:

'The way that Spiller and Dyke, the Cardiff centres, handled and passed the ball was truly wonderful; Bush and Morgan (the halves) excelled in dribbling, one try by the former was magnificent; he took the ball at his feet through the whole side and scored under the posts. Half the tries came from dribbling; the other half from passing, so that Cardiff was great whichever the style it practised. The Barbarians could not move at all; they turned only to flounder in the mud. It is a mystery to me how these Welshmen can do so well when their grounds are literally a morass. W.C.Wilson did a lot of saving; Nicholas and Palmer did as well as anyone could expect in the circumstances but Joubert, the South African, seemed lost in the mud; our full-back (G.R.Maxwell-Dove) will not soon forget his first experience of Welsh football. Our forwards after the first few minutes could not manage to find any sort of game . . . It soon became almost impossible to mark which were Welshmen and which Barbarians; the whole thirty looked like mud figures, but the hospitality of the Cardiff people in the evening rid us of the depressed feelings set up by a bad failure.'

But the Barbarians have always been a club to bounce back and at Easter 1911 it seems that, but for some injudicious refereeing by Mr Scholfield of Bridgend, T.Smyth's Barbarian side that included twelve internationals might well have won.

*One of the finest Barbarian sides to take the field – the Barbarians versus Cardiff, Easter 1924. The Baa-Baas won, 23–18.*
*Standing: D.Marsden-Jones, W.Idris Jones, A.E.Beith, A.T.Voyce, R.Y.Crichton, R.L.Raymond, I.S.Smith. Sitting: A.F.Blakiston, A.Wemyss, J.C.R.Buchanan, A.C.Wallace, G.G.Aitken. On ground: H.Waddell, A.T.Young. (T.Wallace played but missed the photograph!)*
*Beith was the only non-international in the side. It was Herbert Waddell's first game for the Barbarians and the team included three of the famous Oxford and Scotland threequarter line – Smith, Aitken, and Wallace – as well as the 'veteran' 'Jock' Wemyss, the Scottish international, who was capped both before and after World War I, despite losing an eye in between.*

In 1913 and 1919 it was again that characteristic ankle-deep mud and slime that thwarted Barbarian hopes. The latter game was described as more a trial of endurance than normal skill, the referee cutting the length of the game short with Cardiff leading six points to three.

In 1921 the supporters of the Baa-Baas were much in evidence with 'toy "baa-baas", tin whistles and kindred "musical" instruments which considerably enlivened proceedings', and were heard with great effect when the tourist side took an early lead through A.M.David the centre, in an exhibition of hard straight running that brought a brilliant try. This time even the wiles of Clem Lewis, Johnson and Sloan, who ran eighty yards for a try, could not stem the Barbarian tide, and the tourists scored their first victory over Cardiff in thirteen matches. So that although Clem Lewis hit back with a brilliant hat-trick of tries for victory the following season, the one-sided sequence of results over a long period was never to be repeated.

Some outstanding matches followed, but in 1925 there was apparently little of the holiday spirit at Cardiff Arms Park. Despite a thrilling first sixty minutes to the match that had brought eight tries, the remaining minutes were inglorious to say the least. Trevor Nicholas, the Cardiff wing, was heavily tackled by Burton, his opposite number and a Richmond player. Nicholas held the ball on the ground after the tackle and Burton tried to kick it, or the man. In any event he succeeded only in connecting with the player and not the leather and that did not do Nicholas much good. While he staggered in pain, some incensed spectators rushed on to the Park, clamouring for Burton to be summarily dismissed. The referee, one Moses, with the united efforts of players and policemen, cleared the pitch, but when play resumed it had lost its earlier friendliness. Mr Moses issued cautions and appeals but within a few minutes Marsden-Jones of London Welsh, a former Swansea and Cardiff player and Welsh international playing for the Barbarians, was knocked out with a blow in the mouth from Frank Stephens, the Cardiff forward, benefiting no doubt from his experiences as both a policeman and amateur boxer. Stephens was promptly ordered off and at the end of the game the referee was escorted from the field by a bodyguard of players and police protecting him from the hooligan element in the hostile crowd. It was an unfortunate incident, following on as it did a particularly vicious game between Cardiff and Newport the preceding week. Marsden-Jones commented afterwards that he had no recollection as to what happened but he knew there was something wrong when he found himself alone under the shower-bath in the dressing-room! As for Stephens, he left for home after changing, declining the well-intentioned invitations by some of the Barbarian party for him to join them at dinner. Inevitably the press had a field day.

In pleasant contrast, 1927 brought a glorious game of rugby, when Cardiff with eight Welsh caps under W.J.Delahay beat the first all-international Barbarian Fifteen, that included Herbert Waddell as captain, J.B.Nelson, Dan Drysdale, Jack Gage, Aslett, Ganly and Windsor Lewis, Ireland, Stark, the McVickers, Eyres, and MacMyn. It was:

'a continuous succession of thrills. Play alternated between one end and the other in bewildering fashion, and if anything, there were too many brilliant incidents, for before the onlookers had time to appreciate one movement another equally thrilling came along. As they left the field the spectators probably felt very much like a small boy who had eaten too many good things.'

But for all the brilliant backs on the field that Cardiff victory, sixteen points to eight, was determined by the home pack led by Idris Richards. But as *The Times* commented:

'the Barbarians had their usual consolation in defeat ... they played the game of rugby as it ought to be played ...'

Perhaps the crowning moment was the second try by Jack Gage:

'Aslett sent him away by a perfectly timed pass but even so, Gage had to run quite sixty yards down the touch-line, slip three opponents who had dashed across to cut him off, and finally run right through Males' tackle before he could get the touch-down. A better try can rarely have been seen at the Arms Park.'

The Barbarians' invincible years of the early thirties were brought to a halt by Cardiff in 1936 – these were the rival fifteens:

**Barbarians:** V.G.J.Jenkins; C.V.Boyle, P.Cranmer, W.Wooller, K.C.Fyfe; W.R.Logan (capt), R.W.Shaw; R.J.Longland, C.R.A.Graves, C.E.St J.Beamish, S.J.Deering, J.Russell, R.Alexandar, D.L.K.Milman, R.J.L.Hammond.

**Cardiff:** T.Stone (capt); Arthur Bassett, J.J.Davies, Duncan Brown, G.L.Porter; J.E.Bowcott, A.H.Jones; J.Regan, J.D.Jones, Harry Rees, L.M.Spence, V.R.Osmond, Gwyn Williams, Eddie Watkins, K.Street.

**Referee:** A.E.Freethy (Neath).

## BARBARIANS

Full Back : *D. Drysdale (A) or *W. E. Crawford  →l.w Wind
(Heriots and Scotland)        (Lansdowne and Ireland)

Right Wing :              Right Centre :              Left Centre :              Left Wing :
*J. H. Gage (B)        *A. R. Aslett (C)        *J. B. Ganly (D)        *D. J. Cussen (E)
(Queen's Univ., Belfast & Ireland)    (Army and England)    (Monkston and Ireland)    (St. Mary's Hospital & Ireland)

Inside Half : *J. B. Nelson (F)        Outside Half : *H. Waddell, Capt. (G)
(Glasgow Acads. and Scotland)                    (Glasgow Acads. and Scotland)

Forwards : *J. C. H. Ireland (H)    *J. G. Gilchrist (I)    *K. J. Stark (K)    *J. McVicker (L)
(Glasgow High School & Scotland)  (Glasgow Acads. & Scotland)  (Old Alleynians & England)  (Belfast Coll. & Ireland)

*H. McVicker (M)    *D. J. MacMyn (N)    *T. O. Pike (O)    *W. C. T. Eyres (P)
(Army & Ireland)    (London Scots. & Scotland)    (Lansdowne & Ireland)    (Navy & England)

Possible Change : *H. W. Stevenson for Gilchrist ;
(Glasgow Acads. & Scotland)

Referee
Mr. JACK WETTER,
Newport.

THE ROATH FURNISHING Co.
BRANCHES EVERYWHERE

Kick-off 3.30 p.m.

Forwards from *Idris Richards (H)    *Tom Lewis (J)    R. Barrell (K)    *J. Burns (L)
W. Watkins (N)    K. P. Turnbull (O)    E. Spillane (P)    P. Bunce (Q)    Trevor Arnott (R)

Inside Half : *W. J. Delahay, Capt. (F)        Outside Half : *Gwyn Richards (G)    H.

Left Wing :              Left Centre :              Right Centre :              Right Wing :
*John Roberts (B)    D. E. Davies (C)    *B. R. Turnbull (D)    Llew. Williams (E)

Full Back : *B. O. Male (A)

* W J Ould

Corresponding result last season :
Cardiff 8 pts. ; Barbarians—4 pts

**CARDIFF** 8 Internats.        * Denotes Internationals.

*The teams for the Cardiff match of 1927 in which Cardiff, under W.J.Delahay beat the first all-international Barbarian team, captained by Herbert Waddell, 16 points to 8.*

It seemed impossible the Barbarians could be beaten with seven of the best internationals behind the scrum and five of the season's great Irish pack. But the Cardiff players were equal to their daunting task; Regan outhooked Graves; Bowcott and Jones unsettled Logan and Shaw, while Wooller and Cranmer could only once pierce the Cardiff defence. Bassett intercepted a Cranmer pass for the first try, which was the only scoring till fifteen minutes from the end. Then Shaw fed Cranmer who, in turn, sent Wooller sailing down field for a spectacular try to level the scores. It was A.H. Jones who became the Cardiff hero and the Baa-Baas' *bête-noir* (black sheep?) by superbly dropping a goal to clinch the game for Cardiff.

The following season there was only one team in it as Wilfred Wooller, back this time in Cardiff colours, inspired the Black and Blues' victory, scoring thirteen of his side's sixteen points. But he had to share the crowd's adulation that day with the groundsman's dog. Trained by a local cricketer, T.Preece, the animal came on at half-time and gave a stunning exhibition of dribbling by the nose, crowning his efforts by getting hold of the ball by the lace and scoring a try between the posts!

The Barbarian victory of 1939 is best remembered by the threatening runs of the two wingers, Alex Obolensky and New Zealander D.G.Cobden. On this occasion it was Cobden in particular who was the scorer of a spectacular try. What a tragic co-incidence that both these brilliant young players should have been killed within a year of this match while serving in the RAF. But just as Obolensky's try against the Third All Blacks in 1936 will always be recalled, so those fortunate enough to witness Cobden's great moment against Cardiff will forever recall it. Early in the second half, and deep in his own territory, the burly winger gathered a perfect pass from Hammond who stooped, gathered and swept the ball out in one movement. Cobden then went striding along the touch-line, checking his pace to hand-off three coverers in succession, before beating the full-back on the outside to score in classic wing-threequarter style.

Two fellow New Zealanders, E.G.Boggs and W.A.Meates, tourists with the New Zealand Armed Forces' side, were honoured as Barbarians at Cardiff in the first postwar match of 1946, when two sides brimming with internationals produced a brilliant spectacle. On this occasion it was the genius of Haydn Tanner which sparked a one-point Barbarian win in the face of a mighty Cardiff side that included Jackie Matthews, Bleddyn Williams, Frank Trott and Billy Cleaver. But scorelines do not tell all, for Cardiff played for all but two minutes of the match without Selwyn Evans, their winger, who injured his shoulder at the start.

But the names of Tanner, Trott, Tamplin and Cleaver, Bleddyn Williams, Jack Matthews, Cliff Morgan, Rex Willis, Maldwyn James, Gareth Griffiths, and others of that great era were to become recurrent thorns in the flesh of Barbarian sides at the Arms Park, just as each of them in turn was to become famous as a Barbarian playing member too. There was the confrontation between Hardy and Shuttleworth, Morgan and Willis in 1951 with the honours and the game going to the Cardiff men; in 1953, the captain's example of Sid Judd tireless in the loose with his side one man short through another early injury, but aided by the match-winning ability of Cliff Morgan, Lloyd and B.L., the Williams brothers, Griffiths, and C.D.Williams — more than enough to counter the waning strength of Dr J. Matthews who, no longer a Cardiff first fifteen player, had donned the black and white jersey. There was the 1954 game, when the Barbarians, before a crowd of over 35,000, were pitted against exactly the same Cardiff side of Bleddyn Williams that had just beaten the All Blacks. It was certainly one of those occasions when the teamwork and understanding of a top-class club side clearly wrought havoc amongst the incohesive touring fifteen — the Barbarians, under Clem Thomas of Swansea, failed to 'click'. Two tries by Bleddyn Williams, another by Sid Judd, two conversions and a penalty added up to Cardiff's third biggest win post-war.

But the Barbarians did not have long to wait for revenge. In 1957 hundreds of home supporters left the ground well before the end of the game rather than witness any more of the annihilation of their team. Ten tries to none and five conversions to nil reads the bare statistic, a Barbarian record at Cardiff. Cardiff, it must be said, were without the services of Wells, Morgan and Griffiths who were on the Barbarian tour themselves, yet strangely ended up playing for neither side on that Saturday. But with Terry Davies, Tony O'Reilly, Arthur Smith, Peter Thompson, the uncapped R.R.Winn, D.G.S.Baker, and Andy Mulligan making a scintillating back division, thriving on the service of a dominant pack, it is doubtful if any Cardiff combination could have significantly affected the outcome. The forward combination was scarcely less impressive: Jacobs, Evans, Hastings, R.H.Williams and Marques, P.G.D.Robbins, J.R.G.Stephens, and A.Robson. This was one of the occasions when the Baa-Baas not only had the class, but also were able to produce the teamwork. The ever-lengthening stride of skipper Arthur Smith was seen at its most impressive in scoring a hat-trick of tries. O'Reilly and Thompson scored two apiece, with Hastings and Mulligan accounting for the rest. The Barbarians were jubilant, poor Cardiff were stunned in suffering their heaviest-ever defeat. In 1959 another fluent Barbarian victory was achieved, this time inspired by Andy Mulligan and a brilliant back row performance by Murphy, Ashcroft and Robbins. But the attempt to play the traditional Barbarian-style open running rugby, without first gaining the initiative up front, lay behind the convincing defeats of 1962 and 1964. Nor in truth was the 1962 Barbarian side of equal strength to previous years. Two years later insufficient regard was paid to the fact that John MacDonald was injured and left the field for good towards the end of the first half, while Mike Gibson retired hurt in the second. In the days of J.P.O'Shea, Howard Norris, W.J.Thomas, Dai Hayward and Keith Rowlands, it was a mammoth task for any forward combination to hold Cardiff up front.

In October of 1964 the Barbarians were once more at Cardiff, to play one of the rare matches that the club has played at night, on the occasion of the opening, or rather switching on, of Cardiff's new lights. The Baa-Baas' victory was undistinguished, save for one moment which Herbert Waddell recalls as one of the most memorable Barbarian tries:

'C.P.Simpson came into the line, and made an extra man, passed beautifully to Chisholm, who went through pretty fast and got in a quick, flat pass to Shackleton who drew the full-back (Drew was also his name) and passed to Flynn, who passed to Stuart Watkins who scored. Done at colossal pace. Sixty yards. All running dead straight. Loud applause for five minutes by the crowd.'

Cardiff again reached the heights in 1967. A workmanlike pack was still spear-headed by Norris, Thomas and O'Shea but a polished back division had Gerald Davies, Maurice Richards, D.Ken Jones, Keri Jones and Bill Hullin. The efforts of the Barbarian pack, led by Noel Murphy, foundered when once more (and a recurring theme this), P.J.Thorne was injured and Tom Bedford dropped out to the threes. Keri Jones scored the two Cardiff tries.

It took Gareth Edwards and Barry John to create a new points-scoring record for Cardiff against the Barbarians on 1 April 1972, when they won forty-three points to ten. Yet if these players provided the catalyst, the raw material was fashioned from the gallant efforts of a seven-man pack, since Roger Lane played centre, and very well too, after John Regan was hurt. Lasting memories will be some delightful unorthodox play from Wayne Lewis, the two tries for hooker Gary Davies, a storming game by Mervyn John and the partnership of Edwards and Barry John. It was a tough initiation for Frenchman Pierre Villepreux into Barbarian ranks.

And so to the immediate past, games marred undoubtedly by a sickening sequence of injuries to Barbarian players in those absurd pre-replacement days. But there are happier recollections of a magnificent try by Dave Duckham at his classical best in 1974 with a Barbarian team captained that day by John Spencer, who, along with Duckham, excelled until he was injured. In 1975 Brynmor Williams left his mark on the match, and P.L.Jones's try-scoring effort was a sheer delight to the crowd. But 1976 may well be regarded as the most remarkable game of all ninety-three — certainly no game has ever witnessed a greater transformation in fortunes. Early in the second-half the Barbarians were leading twenty-four points to nil and the outcome of the match looked entirely predictable, even, perhaps, set for a record Barbarian win. The first half had seen tries scored by Andy Irvine, resulting from swift handling in a counter-attack, and by Mike Biggar, after a clever darting run by Alan Lawson: and after the interval it was Biggar who set up a try for Tony Neary. Added to this were three conversions and a penalty by Andy Irvine. Thus a seemingly invincible lead had been achieved, fashioned from a surfeit of possession for the Barba-

John Spencer, of
Cambridge
University,
Headingley, England,
and the British Lions,
scoring a try against
Cardiff. Spencer has
had the distinction of
captaining the
Barbarians on four
Easter tours, and he
also led the Baa-Baas
against Penarth and
Cardiff on the
invincible tour of
1973.

rians and a plethora of Cardiff errors. It may have been the fear of total humiliation that prompted a transformation in Cardiff ranks. The forwards began to win some ball, Gareth Edwards scored a try and the atmosphere began to change. David McKay countered with a try for the Baa-Baas, but there was a new confidence in young Gareth Davies, the Cardiff fly-half who instigated the moves that led to tries in quick succession for Chris Camilleri and John Davies. Allan Phillips, the hooker, added a fourth try, Gerald Davies a fifth, and with the score 26–28, still in favour of the Barbarians, Gareth Edwards produced the winning drop-goal from a rucked ball to give the ecstatic home crowd a fairy-tale victory. Cardiff had scored twenty-three points in fifteen minutes and the Barbarians, with fourteen internationals, must have wondered what kind of supernatural force had brought about such a turn of events. It was certainly one of the most extraordinary games in a glorious history of matches between the two clubs.

# BARBARIANS v CARDIFF

| YEAR | SCORE | CAPTAINS BARBARIANS/ CARDIFF | SCORERS FOR | AGAINST |
|---|---|---|---|---|
| 1891 | 3–7 | W. P. Carpmael D. W. Evans | H. Marshall (1T & ?C) | F. N. Jones (1T) A. Lewis (1T) D. W. Evans (1DG) T. W. Pearson (1C) |
| 1892 | 10–0 | D. W. Evans | W. P. Carpmael (1T) C. M. Wells (1T) A. S. Johnston (2C) | |
| Dec 1892 | 3–12 | T. W. Pearson | C. B. Nicholl (1T) | T. W. Pearson (3T) E. P. Biggs (1T) |
| Dec 1893 | 3–14 | N. H. Biggs | P. F. Hancock (1T) | N. H. Biggs (2T, 1C) T. W. Pearson (2T) |
| Dec 1894 | 9–6 | R. B. Sweet- Escott | E. M. Baker (2T) J. Conway-Rees (1T) | E. Gwyn-Nicholls (1T) T. W. Pearson (1T) |
| 1896 | 3–16 | J. E. Elliott | G. C. Robinson (1T) | H. V. P. Huzzey (3T) W. Phillips (1T) Wat. Davies (2C) |
| 1897 | 5–26 | J. E. Elliott | T. L. Hendry (1T) ?E. F. Fookes or (1C) F. H. R. Alderson | H. V. P. Huzzey (2T) W. Jones (2T) J. Blake (1T) H. V. P. Huzzey (4C, 1PG) |
| 1898 | 0–6 | S. Biggs | | F. Cornish (1T) H. V. P. Huzzey (1T) |
| Dec 1898 | 3–29 | S. Biggs | T. P. Thomas (1T) | H. V. P. Huzzey (2T) W. Jones (2T) G. Dobson (1T) C. Sweet-Escott (1T) H. V. P. Huzzey (4C, 1PG) |
| Dec 1899 | 3–27 | H. V. P. Huzzey | F. M. Stout or (1PG) R. T. Skrimshire | A. M. Ricketts (2T) F. J. Box (1T) I. P. Jones (1T) G. Dobson (1T) J. Blake (1T) F. Hine (1T) H. B. Winfield (3C) |

| | | CAPTAINS | SCORERS | |
| | | BARBARIANS/ | | |
| YEAR | SCORE | CARDIFF | FOR | AGAINST |
|------|-------|----------|-----|---------|
| 1900 | 27–12 | P. C. Tarbutt<br>*E. Gwyn-Nicholls* | J. G. Franks (1C)<br>L. D. Bailey (4T)<br>R. Forrest (2T)<br>G. R. Gibson (1T)<br>F. W. H. Weaver (2C) | J. Wheeler (1T)<br>E. Gwyn Nicholls (2T)<br>F. J. Box (1T) |
| 1901 | 6–6 | *E. Gwyn Nicholls* | W. N. G. Douglas (1T)<br>E. W. Elliot (1T) | W. Williams (1T)<br>C. Kestrell (1T) |
| Dec<br>1901 | 0–9 | *D. L. Bowen* | | C. F. Biggs (2T)<br>W. Williams (1T) |
| 1902 | 6–19 | R. T. Skrimshire<br>*H. B. Winfield* | F. C. Hulme (1T)<br>R. Forrest (1T) | C. Stranaghan (1T)<br>W. R. Jenkins (1T)<br>W. Jones (2T)<br>H. Hutchings (1T)<br>H. B. Winfield (2C) |
| Dec<br>1902 | 0–6 | *H. B. Winfield* | | P. F. Bush (1T)<br>C. F. Biggs (1T) |
| 1903 | 10–4 | F. M. Stout<br>*H. B. Winfield* | R. T. Skrimshire (1T)<br>E. Watkins-Baker (1T)<br>J. G. Franks (2C) | C. F. Biggs (1FG) |
| Dec<br>1903 | 3–41 | B. C. Hartley<br>*E. Gwyn Nicholls* | H. W. Bacchus (1T) | R. T. Gabe (2T)<br>P. F. Bush (2T)<br>E. Gwyn Nicholls (3T)<br>A. B. Timms (1T)<br>A. Spackman (1T)<br>H. B. Winfield (5C)<br>A. B. Timms (1DG) |
| 1904 | 0–8 | B. C. Hartley<br>*E. Gwyn Nicholls* | | C. F. Biggs (1T)<br>P. F. Bush (1T)<br>P. F. Bush (1C) |
| Dec<br>1904 | 5–27 | *C. F. Biggs* | C. H. Milton (1T)<br>H. F. P. Hearson (1C) | C. F. Biggs (2T)<br>R. T. Gabe (2T)<br>J. L. Williams (1T)<br>W. H. Gunstone (1T)<br>R. A. Gibbs (3C)<br>C. F. Biggs (1PG) |
| 1905 | 8–5 | F. M. Stout<br>*W. Neill* | S. F. Coopper (1T)<br>A. Brettargh (1T)<br>W. L. Y. Rogers (1C) | J. L. Williams (1T)<br>H. B. Winfield (1C) |

| YEAR | SCORE | CAPTAINS BARBARIANS/ CARDIFF | SCORERS FOR | AGAINST |
|------|-------|------------------------------|-------------|---------|
| Dec 1905 | 0–15 | C. E. L. Hammond<br>*? W. Neill* | | R. T. Gabe (1T)<br>E. Gwyn Nicholls (1T)<br>D. Westacott (1T)<br>H. B. Winfield (3C) |
| 1906 | 0–38 | F. M. Stout<br>*P. F. Bush* | | J. L. Williams (5T)<br>C. F. Biggs (2T)<br>E. Rumbelow (1T)<br>E. Gwyn Nicholls (1T)<br>F. Wood (2C)<br>P. F. Bush (2C, 1PG) |
| Dec 1906 | 0–35 | A. F. Harding | | J. L. Williams (3T)<br>C. F. Biggs (2T)<br>R. A. Gibbs (2T)<br>E. Gwyn Nicholls (1T)<br>L. George (1T)<br>H. B. Winfield (4C) |
| 1907 | 0–17 | D. R. Bedell-Sivright<br>*P. F. Bush* | | E. Gwyn Nicholls (2T)<br>R. C. Thomas (1T)<br>R. A. Gibbs (2C)<br>P. F. Bush (1DG) |
| Dec 1907 | 5–11 | S. F. Coopper<br>*R. T. Gabe* | A. C. Palmer (1T, 1C) | R. A. Gibbs (1T)<br>J. L. Williams (1T)<br>J. Casey (1T)<br>H. B. Winfield (1C) |
| 1908 | 5–6 | J. J. Coffey<br>*J. Brown* | W. C. Wilson (1T)<br>G. D. Roberts (1C) | G. Northmore (1T)<br>W. A. Jones (1T) |
| Dec 1908 | 3–6 | S. F. Coopper<br>*F. Smith* | A. C. Palmer (1T) | J. Brown (1T)<br>F. Gaccon (1T) |
| 1909 | 0–22 | J. J. Coffey<br>*P. F. Bush* | | W. L. Morgan (1T)<br>W. Spiller (2T)<br>J. L. Williams (1T)<br>P. F. Bush (3C)<br>L. M. Dyke (1DG) |
| Dec 1909 | 0–30 | W. C. Wilson<br>*J. L. Williams* | | R. A. Gibbs (4T)<br>J. L. Williams (2T)<br>W. Spiller (2T)<br>W. L. Morgan (1T)<br>P. F. Bush (1T) |

| YEAR | SCORE | CAPTAINS BARBARIANS/ CARDIFF | SCORERS FOR | AGAINST |
|---|---|---|---|---|
| 1910 | 16–5 | A. D. Stoop<br>*J. L. Williams* | J. G. G. Birkett (2T)<br>H. E. Ward (1T)<br>D. Lambert (1PT)<br>D. Lambert (1C)<br>G. D. Roberts (1C) | W. J. Jenkins (1T)<br>L. M. Dyke (1C) |
| Dec 1910 | 3–16 | W. C. Wilson<br>*R. A. Gibbs* | H. J. S. Morton (1T) | J. L. Williams (1T)<br>L. M. Dyke (1T)<br>R. A. Gibbs (2T)<br>L. M. Dyke (2C) |
| 1911 | 8–15 | T. Smyth<br>*R. A. Gibbs* | A. D. Roberts (1T)<br>B. B. Bennetts (1T)<br>G. H. D'O. Lyon (1C) | J. Pugsley (1T)<br>W. Spiller (1T)<br>J. M. C. Lewis (1DG)<br>R. A. Gibbs (1PG, 1C) |
| Dec 1911 | 0–19 | T. Smyth<br>*L. M. Dyke* | | W. Spiller (1T)<br>L. M. Dyke (1T)<br>E. Davies (1T)<br>J. M. C. Lewis (1T)<br>W. J. Jenkins (1T)<br>L. M. Dyke (1C)<br>J. Powell (1C) |
| 1912 | 9–16 | W. S. D. Craven<br>*L. M. Dyke* | E. R. Mobbs (1T)<br>W. S. D. Craven (1T)<br>W. P. Hinton (1PG) | E. Davies (1T)<br>J. Powell (1T)<br>W. Spiller (1T)<br>W. J. Jenkins (1T)<br>L. M. Dyke (2C) |
| Dec 1912 | 5–18 | W. S. D. Craven<br>*W. Spiller* | W. S. D. Craven (1T)<br>A. A. Adams (1C) | W. Spiller (2T)<br>T. Evans (1T)<br>R. F. Williams (1T)<br>J. Rogers (3C) |
| 1913 | 0–10 | J. M. B. Scott<br>*W. J. Jenkins* | | M. Griffiths (1T)<br>F. Rogers (1T)<br>J. M. C. Lewis (2C) |
| Dec 1913 | 3–20 | A. R. V. Jackson<br>*R. F. Williams* | M. P. Atkinson (1T) | W. Spiller (1T)<br>A. Baker (1T)<br>W. H. Thomas (1T)<br>T. Evans (1T)<br>W. L. Ferrier (1T)<br>J. M. C. Lewis (1T, 1C) |
| 1914 | 5–6 | A. R. V. Jackson<br>*W. J. Jenkins* | H. J. Pemberton (1T)<br>M. P. Atkinson (1C) | W. P. Thomas (1T)<br>A. Lewis (1T) |

| YEAR | SCORE | CAPTAINS BARBARIANS/ CARDIFF | SCORERS FOR | AGAINST |
|---|---|---|---|---|
| Dec 1919 | 3–6 | H. L. G. Hughes<br>*W. Powell* | R. P. Dalton (1T) | C. Bryant (1T)<br>W. J. Jenkins (1T) |
| 1920 | 6–12 | M. P. Atkinson<br>*W. J. Jenkins* | C. Adams (1T)<br>M. G. Thomas (1T) | R. Cornish (3T)<br>C. Bryant (1T) |
| Dec 1920 | 5–6 | A. F. Blakiston<br>*J. M. C. Lewis* | T. E. Morel (1T)<br>A. B. Blake (1C) | F. Cravos (1T)<br>T. Johnson (1PG) |
| 1921 | 10–5 | M. P. Atkinson<br>*J. M. C. Lewis* | A. M. David (1T)<br>A. T. Sloan (1T)<br>M. P. Atkinson (2C) | T. Johnson (1PT)<br>J. Sullivan (1C) |
| 1922 | 3–28 | M. P. Atkinson<br>*R. A. Cornish* | W. E. Crawford (1PG) | J. M. C. Lewis (3T)<br>T. Johnson (3T)<br>J. Powell (2T)<br>T. Wallace (2C) |
| 1923 | 20–14 | M. P. Atkinson<br>*T. Wallace* | J. L. F. Steele (3T)<br>M. P. Atkinson (2T)<br>E. McLaren (1T)<br>D. Drysdale (1C) | D. E. Davies (1T)<br>G. Rees (1T)<br>D. G. Davies (1T)<br>T. Wallace (1PG, 1C) |
| 1924 | 23–18 | J. C. R. Buchanan<br>*I. Richards* | H. Waddell (1T)<br>I. S. Smith (1T)<br>J. C. R. Buchanan (1T)<br>A. T. Voyce (1T)<br>T. Wallace (4C)<br>A. C. Wallace (1T) | M. Regan (2T)<br>T. Johnson (1T)<br>W. J. Ould (1T)<br>B. O. Male (3C) |
| 1925 | 21–25 | A. Wemyss<br>*I. Richards* | J. M. Durr (2T)<br>R. M. Kinnear (1T)<br>G. V. Palmer (1T)<br>H. C. Burton (1T)<br>D. Drysdale (3C) | S. Hinam (2T)<br>R. A. Cornish (1T)<br>J. Brown (1T)<br>D. Herily (1T)<br>P. Rayer (1T)<br>J. Burns (1T)<br>B. O. Male (2C) |
| 1926 | 4–8 | W. E. Crawford<br>*D. E. Davies* | A. R. Aslett (1DG) | M. O'Regan (1T)<br>D. E. Davies (1T)<br>B. O. Male (1C) |
| 1927 | 8–16 | H. Waddell<br>*W. J. Delahay* | J. H. Gage (2T)<br>H. Waddell (1C) | W. J. Ould (1T)<br>R. Barrell (1T)<br>B. R. Turnbull (1T)<br>B. O. Male (2C, 1PG) |
| 1928 | 9–3 | J. C. Dykes<br>*K. P. Turnbull* | S. R. Whitfield (1T)<br>W. B. J. Sheehan (1DG)<br>J. C. Dykes (1C) | G. Jones (1T) |

| | | CAPTAINS | SCORERS | |
|---|---|---|---|---|
| YEAR | SCORE | BARBARIANS/ CARDIFF | FOR | AGAINST |
| 1929 | 3–16 | T. G. P. Crick *B. O. Male* | T. G. P. Crick (1T) | G. Davies (1T) H. Poole (1T) H. Brothers (1T) J. Roberts (1T) B. O. Male (2C) |
| 1930 | 9–11 | Windsor H. Lewis *S. C. Cravos* | Windsor H. Lewis (1T) Windsor H. Lewis (1DG) J. W. Allan (1C) | J. Roberts (1T) I. Issac (1T) R. Barrell (1T) T. Stone (1C) |
| 1931 | 11–9 | C. R. Hopwood *B. R. Turnbull* | C. C. Tanner (1T) A. W. Walker (1T) D. P. Henshaw (1T) J. W. Allan (1C) | R. W. Boon (1T) J. Roberts (1T) G. Jones (1T) |
| 1932 | 14–8 | C. D. Aarvold *H. M. Bowcott* | J. E. Forrest (1T) B. R. Tod (1T) M. P. Crowe (1T) E. W. F. de V. Hunt (1T) B. H. Black (1C) | G. Jones (1T) H. Bowcott (1PG) T. Stone (1C) |
| 1933 | 17–13 | A. Key *T. Lewis* | W. Elliot (3T) W. McC. Ross (1T) H. Lind (1T) D. A. Kendrew (1C) | R. G. Jones (1T) A. Skym (1T) R. Barrell (1T) T. Stone (2C) |
| 1934 | 14–9 | N. Murphy *T. Stone* | R. W. Shaw (2T) W. R. Logan (1T) P. Cranmer (1PG) R. W. Shaw (1C) | Lewis Rees (1T) W. Reardon (1T) R. W. Boon (1T) |
| 1935 | 20–5 | J. A. E. Siggins *A. Skym* | P. Cranmer (2T) W. Wooller (1T) R. Leyland (1T) R. W. Shaw (1T) J. E. Forrest (1T) J. A. E. Siggins (1C) | J. D. Jones (1T) D. Brown (1C) |
| 1936 | 3–7 | W. R. Logan *T. Stone* | W. Wooller (1T) | A. Bassett (1T) A. H. Jones (1DG) |
| 1937 | 3–16 | H. G. Owen-Smith *L. M. Spence* | J. A. E. Siggins (1T) | W. Wooller (2T, 2C, 1PG) H. M. Hughes (1T) |
| 1938 | 8–8 | J. A. Waters *H. Rees* | R. U. Reynolds (1T) V. G. J. Jenkins (1PG, 1C) | E. R. Knapp (1T) W. Wooller (1PG, 1C) |
| 1939 | 11–6 | D. J. Macrae *W. Wooller* | R. J. L. Hammond (1T) D. G. Cobden (1T) J. R. Spear (1T) D. J. Macrae (1C) | L. Arnold (1T) W. Wooller (1PG) |

| YEAR | SCORE | CAPTAINS BARBARIANS/ CARDIFF | SCORERS FOR | AGAINST |
|---|---|---|---|---|
| 1940 | 8–16 | E. C. Davey<br>W. Wooiler | T. A. Kemp (1T)<br>E. J. Unwin (1T)<br>V. G. J. Jenkins (1C) | G. Hale (1T)<br>R. C. Gillard (1T)<br>W. Wooller (1PG, 2C)<br>D. Brown (1PG) |
| 1941–1945 | | WAR YEARS | | |
| 1946 | 10–9 | H. Tanner<br>J. Matthews | H. Tanner (1T)<br>W. A. Meates (1T)<br>R. H. Lloyd-Davies (1DG) | J. Matthews (1T, 1DG)<br>M. James (1C) |
| 1947 | 0–3 | J. O. Newton-Thompson<br>J. Matthews | | W. E. Tamplin (1PG) |
| 1948 | 3–13 | W. C. W. Murdoch<br>H. Tanner | B. Mullan (1PG) | W. B. Cleaver (1T)<br>J. Matthews (1T)<br>R. Roberts (2C, 1PG) |
| 1949 | 6–5 | B. H. Travers<br>B. L. Williams | M. F. Lane (1T)<br>J. W. Kyle (1T) | J. D. Nelson (1T)<br>S. Judd (1C) |
| 1950 | 8–6 | J. A. Gwilliam<br>R. F. Trott | B. Lewis-Jones (2T, 1C) | T. Cook (1T)<br>W. E. Tamplin (1PG) |
| 1951 | 3–13 | J. E. Nelson<br>W. E. Tamplin | D. McKibbin (1PG) | H. Morris (1T)<br>J. R. Phillips (1T)<br>W. E. Tamplin (2C,1PG) |
| 1952 | 3–6 | D. W. Shuttle-worth<br>J. Matthews | I. King (1DG) | H. Morris (1T)<br>S. Judd (1T) |
| 1953 | 0–14 | D. T. Wilkins<br>S. Judd | | G. M. Griffiths (2T)<br>C. D. Williams (1T)<br>W. E. Tamplin (1PG, 1C) |
| 1954 | 0–16 | R. C. C. Thomas<br>B. L. Williams | | B. L. Williams (2T)<br>S. Judd (1T)<br>J. Llewellyn (1C)<br>G. Rowlands (1PG, 1C) |
| 1955 | 6–3 | R. H. Thompson<br>B. L. Williams | P. H. Ryan (1T)<br>M. Regan (1T) | J. Llewellyn (1PG) |
| 1956 | 6–6 | J. A. O'Meara<br>M. L. Collins | P. H. Thompson (1T)<br>G. D. Owen (1PG) | C. L. Davies (1T)<br>G. Rowlands (1DG) |

|  |  | CAPTAINS | SCORERS | |
|---|---|---|---|---|
| YEAR | SCORE | BARBARIANS/<br>CARDIFF | FOR | AGAINST |
| 1957 | 40–0 | A. R. Smith<br>*P. Goodfellow* | A. R. Smith (3T, 1C)<br>A. J. F. O'Reilly (2T)<br>P. H. Thompson (2T)<br>G. W. Hastings (1T)<br>R. R. Winn (1T)<br>A. A. Mulligan (1T)<br>D. G. S. Baker (2C)<br>T. E. Davies (2C) | |
| 1958 | 6–14 | M. C. Thomas<br>*C. D. Williams* | P. H. Thompson (1T)<br>A. R. Smith (1PG) | D. J. Hayward (1T)<br>G. M. Griffiths (1T)<br>C. Williams (1T)<br>A. Priday (1C, 1PG) |
| 1959 | 21–0 | A. A. Mulligan<br>*C. D. Williams* | W. M. Patterson (2T)<br>J. R. C. Young (1T)<br>A. A. Mulligan (1T)<br>G. W. Hastings (3C, 1PG) | |
| 1960 | 10–10 | P. T. Wright<br>*G. T. Wells* | W. G. D. Morgan (1T)<br>J. Roberts (1T)<br>D. Rutherford (2C) | M. Roberts (2T)<br>A. J. Priday (2C) |
| 1961 | 19–11 | A. J. F. O'Reilly<br>*A. J. Priday* | R. C. Cowan (3T)<br>D. M. D. Rollo (1T)<br>A. J. F. O'Reilly (1T)<br>T. J. Kiernan (2C) | E. Williams (2T)<br>R. Glastonbury (1T)<br>A. J. Priday (1C) |
| 1962 | 0–10 | K. J. F. Scotland<br>*L. H. Williams* | | H. M. Roberts (1T)<br>C. O. Williams (1T)<br>A. J. Priday (2C) |
| 1963 | 12–3 | M. G. Culliton<br>*D. J. Hayward* | A. J. F. O'Reilly (2T)<br>D. Rutherford (2PG) | A. J. Priday (1PG) |
| 1964 | 3–21 | M. P. Weston<br>*D. J. Hayward* | T. J. Kiernan (1PG) | C. Howe (2T)<br>H. Norris (1T)<br>P. Thomas (1T)<br>A. J. Priday (3C, 1PG) |
| Oct<br>1964 | 12–8 | A. R. Dawson<br>*H. M. Roberts* | A. J. Hastie (1T)<br>S. J. Watkins (1T)<br>J. A. P. Shackleton (1T)<br>C. P. Simpson (1T) | M. Richards (1T)<br>A. Drew (1PG, 1C) |
| 1965 | 14–11 | D. P. Rogers<br>*C. H. Norris* | A. J. Hinshelwood (2T)<br>G. P. Frankcom (1T)<br>C. M. H. Gibson (1DG)<br>D. Rutherford (1C) | J. H. Williams (2T)<br>J. P. O'Shea (1T)<br>A. J. Priday (1C) |
| 1966 | 3–16 | D. P. Rogers<br>*K. A. Rowlands* | J. M. Dee (1T) | T. McCarthy (2T)<br>A. R. Pender (1T)<br>K. A. Rowlands (1T)<br>R. Bassett (2C) |

| | | CAPTAINS | SCORERS | |
|---|---|---|---|---|
| YEAR | SCORE | BARBARIANS/ CARDIFF | FOR | AGAINST |
| 1967 | 5–11 | N. A. A. Murphy<br>W. Hullin | W. H. Raybould (1T)<br>R. W. Hosen (1C) | Keri Jones (2T)<br>D. Gethin (1PG, 1C) |
| 1968 | 11–16 | D. P. Rogers<br>W. Hullin | J. Gachassin (1T, 1DG)<br>R. J. Arneil (1T)<br>C. Lacaze (1C) | A. D. Williams (2T)<br>I. M. Lewis (1T)<br>L. Jones (1T)<br>D. Gethin (2C) |
| 1969 | 16–20 | J. R. H. Green-wood<br>C. H. Norris | A. T. A. Duggan (2T)<br>C. S. Wardlow (1T)<br>B. J. McGann (1DG, 1C)<br>B. J. O'Driscoll (1C) | M. C. R. Richards (2T)<br>C. H. Norris (1T)<br>D. Gethin (2PG, 1C)<br>B. John (1PG) |
| 1970 | 30–28 | R. M. Young<br>J. P. O'Shea | M. P. Bulpitt (2T)<br>J. S. Spencer (1T)<br>J. F. Slattery (1T)<br>A. M. Jorden (3PG, 3C)<br>P. Bennett (1DG) | M. John (1T)<br>A. A. Finlayson (1T)<br>R. Williams (4PG, 2C, 1DG)<br>G. O. Edwards (1DG) |
| 1971 | 11–9 | D. Williams<br>J. Hickey | D. E. J. Watt (1T)<br>P. J. Dixon (1T)<br>P. A. Rossborough (1PG, 1C) | J. Bevan (1T)<br>G. O. Edwards (2PG) |
| 1972 | 10–43 | D. J. Lloyd<br>R. Beard | W. C. C. Steele (1T)<br>P. Villepreux (2PG) | Gary Davies (2T)<br>L. D. Baxter (1T)<br>J. Bevan (1T)<br>G. O. Edwards (1T)<br>I. Robinson (1T)<br>W. Lewis (1T)<br>B. John (1PG, 6C) |
| 1973 | 16–6 | M. G. Molloy<br>G. Wallace | J. F. Slattery (1T)<br>A. D. Gill (1T)<br>G. W. Evans (1T)<br>R. A. Codd (2C) | K. James (1DG)<br>L. Davies (1DG) |
| 1974 | 9–11 | J. S. Spencer<br>G. Davies | D. J. Duckham (1T)<br>I. McRae (1PG)<br>W. H. Hare (1C) | G. Davies (1T)<br>K. James (1T, 1PG) |
| 1975 | 19–24 | A. G. B. Old<br>M. John | K. Smith (1T)<br>A. J. Morley (1T)<br>A. R. Irvine (3PG, 1C) | J. Davies (1T)<br>G. Davies (1T, 2C)<br>B. D. Williams (1T)<br>I. Robinson (1T)<br>P. L. Jones (1T) |
| 1976 | 28–29 | I. R. McGeechan<br>T. G. R. Davies | A. R. Irvine (1T, 2PG, 3C)<br>M. A. Biggar (1T)<br>A. Neary (1T)<br>D. McKay (1T) | G. O. Edwards (1T, 1DG)<br>J. Davies (1T)<br>C. Camilleri (1T)<br>A. Phillips (1T)<br>T. G. R. Davies (1T)<br>G. Davies (3C) |

# Swansea Rugby Football Club

### SEASON 1923—1924.

ST. HELEN'S GROUND, SWANSEA.
MONDAY, APRIL 21st, 1924,

## Swansea v. Barbarians

Kick-off 3-0 p.m.

# OFFICIAL PROGRAMME

**(With the Compliments of the Rugby Committee)**

Printed by the Swansea Printers Limited, and published by the Bart Cronin
Advertising Agency, High-street Arcade, Swansea.

## BARBARIANS v SWANSEA 1901–1976

Of the three major Welsh clubs that the Barbarians encounter annually, Swansea is the only one to have lost more matches than they have won. That is in spite of the fact that the 'All-Whites' were victorious in the first fourteen matches played against the touring side. Between the wars the Barbarians had the greater share of victories, and since 1946 the Baa-Baas have also won the lion's share. Yet the last ten years in particular have not only produced a series of high scoring matches but several very close results, indicative of the excitement of the rugby enjoyed by the huge Bank Holiday crowds.

Since 1901 St Helen's has been the venue for the traditional Easter Monday game, although in some of the early years, as already mentioned, the Swansea match was on the Saturday with Cardiff versus the Barbarians on the Monday. But the pattern has now long been established that the Harlequins and the Barbarians play Swansea and Cardiff in reverse order over Easter, so that the South Wales rugby fraternity can nearly always enjoy superb entertainment over the whole holiday period.

## SUMMARY OF MATCHES

**Played: 63    Won: 33    Lost: 29    Drawn: 1**
**Points for: 702    Points against: 686**

Average points for Barbarians per game: 11.1
Average points for Swansea per game: 10.8
Total tries for Barbarians: 140
Average Barbarian tries per game: 2.2

First win:              1923 (23–0)
First Swansea win:      1901 (0–11)
Biggest win:            1973 (35–9) (6T, 4C, 1PG)
Biggest defeat:         1903 (0–28) (5T, 5C, 1PG)

Longest run of victories: 1930–1937 inclusive (8 matches)
Longest run of defeats: 1901–1922 inclusive (15 matches)
Most tries for a Barbarian in one match: T. C. Barber (4T 1927)
Most tries for a Swansea player in one match: D. Rees (3T 1905), G. Jones (3T 1976)
Most points for a Barbarian in one match: C. Lacaze 13(3PG, 2C) 1968
Most points for a Swansea player in one match: W. J. Bancroft 13(5C, 1PG) 1903

## MEMORABLE MATCHES AND MOMENTS

When the Barbarians first set foot on St Helen's on Easter Monday, 9 April 1901, Swansea were embarking upon the greatest period in their rugby history. It was a golden era lasting until the Great War that produced players of immortal fame: Dickie Owen and Dick Jones at half-back; Danny Rees, W.J.Trew, 'Gennie' Gordon in the threes; W.J., and later Jack, Bancroft at full back, Fred Scrines, Will Joseph and the two Dai Davies – identified as 'Mumbles' Davies and 'Port Tennant' Davies. The Barbarians initiation into Swansea rugby was a true baptism of fire – and the 'All Whites' won eleven to nil, with tries by Danny Rees, 'General' Gordon and Jowett, plus one conversion by Peter Lockman. Nor was this against a weak Barbarian side with Skrimshire, Brettargh, Beamish, Forrest and Boyd, and nine internationals in all. One of the Barbarians is recorded as saying after the game:

> 'I wouldn't like to play against Swansea very often, why, it is harder chasing them than following the hounds, and the forwards are all as strong as blacksmiths.'

*The first ever Barbarian team to play against Swansea, at St Helen's, 9 April 1901.*
Back row: *F.M.Stout, N.S.Cox, T.A.Gibson, E.W.Elliott, C.A.Boyd, W.N.G.Douglas, G.Fraser, W.P.Carpmael, R.O.Schwarz.* Middle row: *B.C.Hartley, R.Forrest, R.T.Skrimshire (captain), T.P.H.Beamish, H.W.Dudgeon, J.G.Franks.* Front row: *S.G.Wood, A.Brettargh, H.H.Corley, A.Brown, T.Drysdale.*

Small wonder, then, that Swansea won all but two of their thirty-two games that season!

The following April it was seventeen points to nil despite the fact that 'the visitors were quite a class team, and they commenced a display of passing such as few visiting teams have given at Swansea'. Seventeen points became twenty-eight in 1903 (a season in which Swansea lost only four matches), with five tries, all converted by W.J.Bancroft. A year later it was twenty-three to nil, with the Welsh club suffering only one defeat and one draw in thirty-one matches that year. W.J.Trew, Danny Rees and the diminutive five foot one inch, and nine stone twelve pounds, Dickie Owen, were Swansea's outstanding performers. But in 1904–05, under the captaincy of Frank Gordon, it was a brilliant pack of forwards that laid down the foundations for their invincible season. The Barbarians in losing twenty-six points to six that year at least scored their first points against Swansea, through tries by the great Cardiff player A.F.Harding and F.M.Stout of Gloucester.

Yet, disregarding the sequence of heavy defeats, the Barbarians continued to captivate the St Helen's crowds, although it might seem that tactically the visitors may have been playing into Swansea's hands! In 1909:

'the generous disposition of the Barbarians to play a fine open game enabled Swansea to provide a capital spectacle ... For the Barbarians, Schulze (at full back) was very valuable, Palmer, Parke and Vassall were excellent threequarters; the halves were not in it with Owen and Jones, but in McKenzie, Cronje and F.Wilson they had at least three fine forwards.'

But in those days three good forwards were not enough to take on the Swansea pack in which Edgar Morgan, Ike Williams and Hayward were outstanding. Gradually the Barbarians came at least within striking distance of a victory. In 1913, fifteen thousand saw Swansea, who had already beaten South Africa that season, defeat the Barbarians eight points to nil:

> 'but practically everybody on leaving the ground asked how the Baa-Baas were so many points behind when they had such a great portion of the game . . . they went all out for a win, and gave the leather plenty of air, passing prettily, but the defence was as safe and steady as a rock. One beautiful bout of passing by the visitors saw Bancroft splendidly pull up Watson, whilst Tom Williams later bundled over Pillman after Watson had intercepted some Swansea passing. The homesters have to thank Oswald Jenkins for obtaining the only try of the match, and he deserves full credit for his capital dribble and excellent pick-up before he transferred to the Reverend Alban Davies who had simply to run over for the points.'

Swansea ended that season with only two defeats.

There was little to commend the match of 1922. Swansea's golden era was over, and with Rowe Harding beginning to make his mark, the All-Whites were rebuilding a side. But for the Baa-Baas, the significance of that game lies in the result – a nil-nil draw and the first time the tourists had held their own at St Helen's. It was a result largely credited to D.J.Malan, their scrum-half. So the way was prepared for Easter 1923. Given confidence by victories over Penarth and Cardiff, on 2 April the Barbarians crushed Swansea by four goals and a try (twenty-three points) to nil.

*The earliest action photograph of a match between the Barbarians and Swansea, 22 April 1905. This was the fifth in a sequence of fourteen matches won by Swansea. The Barbarians in the action are, from left to right, Hearson (with the ball), Munro, Stoop, Butcher (waiting for the pass), Newbold (over Butcher's shoulder), unknown player, Jimmie Ross, Dillon and another unknown player.*

The Barbarians 'warming up' for their match with Swansea in 1909! From left to right, J.S.Wilson, F.N.Smartt, J.C.Parke, D.G.Schulze, H.J.S.Morton, C.A.Bolton, C. te Water, H.H.Vassall, F.O.B.Wilson.

'The visitors thoroughly deserved their big win, but Swansea had hard lines in failing to score on at least half-a-dozen occasions, partly through lack of finish to their movements and partly through the magnificent display at full-back of Drysdale, the Scottish international. The Visitors' backs showed wonderful understanding, and their passing was clean and pretty to watch.'

The bogey had been laid, but the change in fortunes was short-lived. A year later, even a back-division that included the formidable Scottish combination of Drysdale, Aitken, Wallace, Smith and Waddell and the English scrum-half A.T.Young, with Buchanan, Blakiston, Wemyss and Marsden-Jones in the pack, could not contain Rowe Harding's young Swansea side — even though the home team were reduced to thirteen fit players for the last quarter of an hour. What is more, during those fifteen minutes Joe Jones sprinted in with the winning try.

Another brilliant individual try, this time a long, swerving run by Ian Smith, showed the talent of the Barbarian backs in 1925, but once again the Swansea forwards ruled the day and were the cornerstone of yet another victory. Incidentally, that was the first season in which the 'All-Whites' wore an all-white strip, for, despite their nickname, until 1925 blue shorts had always been worn.

By the late twenties the Swansea stranglehold had been broken. In 1927 The Times correspondent wrote:

'Swansea rugby has deteriorated sadly since the great and glorious days of twenty years ago ... In the home of F.Scrines, perhaps the first of all wingers, no adventurer, even of the second class, has been produced recently to make things more difficult for the opposing backs.'

Mark Sugden, the brilliant Dublin University scrum-half, and Herbert Waddell schemed the Barbarian victory; Reverend O.Fulljames of Rosslyn Park carved gaps in midfield and apparently his unselfishness when close to the goal-line 'helped Barber to score four tries'! That was a Barbarian try-scoring record against Swansea for T.C.Barber, aided by the reverend gentleman and his outstanding fellow centre, R.F.Kelly.

The year 1930 brought the start of a sequence of eight successive victories over Swansea that was to include the vintage years of all-conquering Barbarian seasons between 1931 and 1935. But by 1938 the tourists had a new combination at St Helen's to reckon with – 'Tanner and Davies Show the Barbarians How' ran the

*Barbarians v Swansea 1933. This was the fourth in the Baa-Baas' longest run of victories against Swansea, eight matches won between 1933 and 1937, during a sequence of twenty-one consecutive victories in South Wales.* Back row: P.C.Alexander, P.C.Hordern, W.H.Weston, H.Rew, T.G.P.Crick, M.J.Dunne, D.A.Kendrew, W.McC.Ross, J.A.E.Siggins, P.C.Minns. Front row: F.L.Williams, C.P.B.Goldson, K.C.Fyfe, H.Lind, C.G.Gosling.

headline of a report of Easter 1938. That brilliant half-back partnership of Willie Davies and Haydn Tanner was to bring the Baa-Baas to heel in successive years. In 1938, Tanner and Davies outplayed their opposite numbers Giles and Torrens, while W.T.H.Davies's gliding runs were responsible for two spectacular tries. South African Louis Babrow and D.J.Macrae, of whom much had been expected for the Barbarians, were outplayed by the Swansea centres, and Obolensky on the wing, by all accounts the one danger man on the visitors' side, received but a single reasonable chance. Present day history does indeed have its roots in the past!

But that day, Davies was at his most brilliant, as *The Times* noted:

'There was a touch of genius about everything Davies did, whether it was cutting out openings in midfield or punting across field or getting back to cover his defence. One noted that it was Davies alone who foiled the best Barbarian move in the match – a pass from Giles, which sent A.Obolensky on a 50-yard run down the right touch-line.'

The following year produced almost a repeat performance in that the Swansea half-backs again called the tune. W.T.H.Davies was once more the outstanding player on the field, and in the Swansea centre Claude Davey and Ron Williams tackled magnificently. *The Daily Telegraph* reported:

'Macrae crashed away monotonously but was invariably grassed and Leyland, too often watching the man instead of keeping his eye on the ball, rarely took his passes.'

One must admit to a certain sympathy with the Barbarian centre in opposition to that impenetrable Swansea defence. As a result, though, Obolensky and S. Williams on the wing never received the ball. Moreover this game was apparently not played in holiday spirit:

'The Swansea front row set about countering H.B.Toft's acknowledged hooking mastery with vigorous methods, crashing into the set scrums with the fire of stags in the rutting season. The Barbarians refused to be drawn into the butting contest and there were times when both front rows (Teden, Toft, and Sampson, for the Baa-Baas, E.D.Price, E.Morgan and L.Davies for Swansea) stood up facing each other scowling or laughing according to temperament . . . The forwards crashed about and the scrum swung round and round, waltzing in slow time to an unheard tune called "Killing a grand game" . . . Poor holiday fare on the whole, but redeemed by W.H.Davies, a really great player.'

Critics of the modern game, please note!

The first post-war match, in 1946, was a unique affair. The touring Kiwis, the New Zealand Armed Forces side, provided six of the players for the Easter Monday game. The All-Whites included three as guests, H.E.Cook at full-back, R.L.Dobson at centre and Charlie Saxton, the Kiwis' captain, who was courteously made Swansea captain for the day. The Baa-Baas included Freddy Allen, J.B.Smith and R.D.B.Johnston, and although the outstanding player on the field was the guest Swansea full-back, H.E.Cook, the fourteen international players in the Barbarian side began that day an unbeaten sequence of ten matches at St Helen's.

The Irish Grand Slam triumph of 1948 was reflected in the selection of the party for the Easter tour that year, and at Swansea, the home team was confronted by ten of that season's Irish team. Colm Callan, a vigorous second-row forward from Clontarf, was the Barbarian captain, with a pack that included all but the hooker, Karl Mullen, of the Irish eight that clinched the Grand Slam at Ravenhill against Wales a fortnight earlier: Bill McKay, Jim McCarthy and Des O'Brien; Jimmy Nelson, A.A.McConnell, and John Daly, the man who scored the winning try against Wales, who was playing at Swansea his last match for the Barbarians. In addition, at half-back were Ernie Strathdee and Jack Kyle, with Bertie O'Hanlon on the wing. With Spray of Newport and three Scots, Charlie Drummond, W.C.W.Murdoch and R.W.F.Sampson making up the fifteen, it was indeed a unique Barbarian team, with no English player included.

Before a crowd of seventeen thousand, that Barbarian combination became the first club side to beat the All-Whites on their own ground that season, though the touring Wallabies had previously won an exciting match at St Helen's in December. Under the captaincy of Glyn Davies, the Swansea full-back (who had taken over as skipper at the start of the season when Rees Williams signed for League club Batley), the home team put up a brave show against the Barbarians. But the exceptional power of the Irish pack coupled with the good form shown by Drummond, Spray, Mackenzie and O'Hanlon in the backs in a thoroughly entertaining game, brought a Barbarian victory by three tries and a penalty to a try by Swansea winger L.G.Shaw.

It was a much more cosmopolitan side that produced a spectacular display at St

Helen's in April, 1953 to win 18–8. Above all it was a triumphant Barbarian debut for Gareth Griffiths, wing for Cardiff and Wales, but centre threequarter on this occasion, who scored a sparkling hat-trick of tries. Ian King, who was capped for England the following season, led the Barbarians that day at full-back and set an example for his team – by joining in the threequarter attacking movements – a rare occurrence even in the fifties. His side included seven Englishmen, three Irishmen, three Welshmen and one Scot. Especially interesting was the presence amongst them of R.C.C.Thomas, alongside J.Mc.G. Kendall-Carpenter of England and W.E.Bell of Ireland in the back-row. Clem Thomas, an outstanding Swansea player over many years, but with Coventry for that particular season, thus had the rare opportunity of representing the Barbarians against his own club.

For Swansea, the two newcomers to the club made a big impression. One was Ken Richards, a nineteen-year-old, who scored a magnificent try as a centre against the Barbarians, a player who later with Cardiff and then Bridgend became one of Wales's most talented fly-halves. The other was the new number eight forward, Haydn Mainwaring, who was to show remarkable versatility and skill as a forward of many positions, as a threequarter – and finally as a powerful, fifteen-stone, uncapped full-back for the Barbarians against Avril Malan's Springboks in 1961. His talents were recognised by Wales for the match against France later that season.

Mainwaring was still in the team in those vintage years of Swansea rugby that brought victories over the Barbarians in 1960 and 1961. It was a side of all round talent that included Bryan Richards, Norman Gale, Dewi Bebb, John Faull, John Leleu and John Hopkins. But none of those players was in the All-Whites side when the uncapped S.A.Morris of Newton Abbot, and Scottish scrum-half, Alex Hastie, starred in the Barbarian victory in 1964.

Two years later, with thirty players unavailable for the Easter tour because of the ensuing British Lions tour, the second-half inspiration of Ian Robertson of Watsonians, with an all-Irish threequarter line outside him, resulted in a game of six tries, four to two in favour of the Barbarians. Significantly, this was the start of the continuing sequence of high-scoring Easter Monday games, for only once since then have there been fewer than four tries scored in the match. Noel Murphy's team scored six of the nine tries in 1967, Clive Rowlands's Swansea team scored four of the seven in 1968, though the Barbarians won that game thanks to the sixteen points contributed by the French pair, Jean Gachassin and Claude Lacaze. André Campaes, the winger, was another Gallic visitor to St Helen's the following year, with two of the Barbarian tries to his credit.

Yet in a sequence of high-scoring matches in recent years at Swansea, perhaps none has proved more exciting than 1972. On that occasion the All-Whites played with only fourteen men for all but fifteen minutes of the first half. Alan Meredith, their scrum-half, was injured and Colin Davies moved up from full-back to take his place, made his first appearance at the base of the scrum and played magnificently. With four tries apiece, Swansea clinched the match four minutes from time with a penalty goal by David Protheroe.

The 1976 game was remarkable for the fact that it produced a record sixty-two points, and a third Swansea victory in six years. Although seven tries (including a hat-trick by Gerwyn James) in any circumstances is a creditable performance against the Barbarians, it was not the thrilling match that the scoreline 37–25 would seem to indicate. Swansea's victory owed much to the fact that McKay and Shedden, the Baa-Baas wings, were both injured; and thanks to the Rugby Union's delay in introducing substitutes at club level until the following season, the Barbarians played over half the match with just thirteen fit men.

## BARBARIANS v SWANSEA

| YEAR | SCORE | CAPTAINS BARBARIANS/ SWANSEA | SCORERS FOR | AGAINST |
|---|---|---|---|---|
| 1901 | 0–11 | R. T. Skrimshire | | D. Rees (1T) F. Gordon (1T) F. Jowett (1T) P. Lockman (1C) |
| 1902 | 0–17 | R. T. Skrimshire *F. J. Gordon* | | D. Rees (1T) A. E. Freear (1T) R. Jones (1T) F. Gordon (1T) S. Bevan (1T) P. Lockman (1C) |
| 1903 | 0–28 | *F. J. Gordon* | | F. Scrines (1T) W. J. Trew (1T) F. Gordon (1T) D. Rees (1T) W. J. Bancroft (5C,1PG) A. Smith (1T) |
| 1904 | 0–23 | W. L. Y. Rogers *W. Parker* | | W. Arnold (2T) R. Jones (1T) W. J. Trew (1T) W. Joseph (1T) S. Bevan (1T) D. Rees (1T) G. Davies (1C) |
| 1905 | 6–26 | *F. Gordon* | A. F. Harding (1T) F. M. Stout (1T) | D. Rees (3T) F. Gordon (2T) F. Jowett (1T) R. M. Owen (2C) J. Bancroft (2C) |
| 1906–1907 | | *No fixture* | | |
| 1908 | 0–12 | J. J. Coffey *W. J. Trew* | | H. Toft (1T) R. M. Owen (1T) R. Jones (1T) I. Morgan (1T) |
| 1909 | 5–19 | J. M. Mackenzie | S. N. Cronje (1T) J. C. Parke (1C) | E. Morgan (1T) B. R. Lewis (1T) I. Morgan (2T) R. M. Owen (1T) J. Bancroft (1C) P. Hopkins (1C) |
| 1910 | 0–11 | A. D. Stoop *W. J. Trew* | | W. J. Rapsey (1T) D. Davies (1T) J. Bancroft (1PG, 1C) |
| 1911 | 8–18 | T. Smyth *? R. M. Owen* | L. B. Stringer (1T) C. H. Pillman (1T) G. H. D'O. Lyon (1C) | H. Lewis (1T) W. S. Goff (1T) P. Hopkins (1T, 3C) I. Morgan (1T) |

| YEAR | SCORE | CAPTAINS BARBARIANS/ SWANSEA | SCORERS FOR | AGAINST |
|---|---|---|---|---|
| 1912 | 8–12 | E. R. Mobbs<br>*R. M. Owen* | D. O. H. Tripp (1T)<br>W. P. Hinton (1PG, 1C) | J. A. Davies (1T)<br>S. Jerram (1T)<br>H. Evans (1T)<br>A. Waters (1T) |
| 1913 | 0–8 | J. M. B. Scott | | J. A. Davies (1T)<br>J. Bancroft (1PG, 1C) |
| 1914 | 9–17 | G. J. C. Smyth<br>*D. J. Thomas* | H. J. Pemberton (1T)<br>M. P. Atkinson (1C)<br>H. L. Higgins (1DG) | Owen Jenkins (1T)<br>G. Evans (1T)<br>C. B. Davies (1T)<br>Oswald Jenkins (2C)<br>T. Williams (1DG) |
| 1920 | 3–14 | H. L. G. Hughes | H. J. White (1T) | W. Bowen (2T)<br>D. J. John (1T)<br>E. Davies (1PG, 1C) |
| 1921 | 3–11 | M. P. Atkinson | A. T. Sloan (1T) | W. Bowen (1T)<br>T. Davies (1DG)<br>W. Bowen (1DG) |
| 1922 | 0–0 | N. Clarke<br>*R. Huxtable* | | |
| 1923 | 23–0 | D. Marsden-Jones<br>*G. E. Beynon* | C. F. G. T. Hallaran (1T)<br>H. P. Jacob (1T)<br>G. G. Aitken (1T)<br>J. C. Hubbard (1T)<br>G. W. C. Parker (1T)<br>T. Lawton (4C) | |
| 1924 | 9–11 | A. T. Young<br>*R. Harding* | G. G. Aitken (1T)<br>I. S. Smith (1T)<br>J. L. F. Steele (1T) | R. Harding (1T)<br>J. Jones (1T)<br>E. Rees (1T)<br>A. Lewis (1C) |
| 1925 | 8–16 | W. Idris-Jones<br>*R. Harding* | E. Coley (1T)<br>I. S. Smith (1T)<br>R. H. B. Bettington (1C) | D. Burns (2T)<br>A. Parker (1T)<br>T. Mabbett (1T)<br>D. Parker (1C)<br>D. M. Bertram (1C) |
| 1926 | 11–17 | D. J. MacMyn | S. R. Whitfield (1T)<br>J. M. Durr (1T)<br>G. Fellows-Smith (1T)<br>E. W. Crawford (1C) | B. Barter (1T)<br>D. Hopkins (1T)<br>L. Howells (1T)<br>D. Parker (2PG)<br>B. Barker (1C) |
| 1927 | 27–9 | D. J. MacMyn<br>*D. S. Parker* | T. C. Barber (4T)<br>R. F. Kelly (1T)<br>M. Sugden (1T)<br>J. A. Ross (1T)<br>H. Waddell (2C)<br>W. E. Crawford (1C) | T. Hopkins (1T)<br>E. Hopkins (1T)<br>W. G. Morgan (1GM) |

| YEAR | SCORE | CAPTAINS BARBARIANS/ SWANSEA | SCORERS FOR | AGAINST |
|---|---|---|---|---|
| 1928 | 6–3 | H. G. Periton *D. S. Parker* | E. Priest (1T) J. C. Dykes (1PG) | D. P. Manley (1T) |
| 1929 | 6–16 | W. A. V. Thomas *Rowe Harding* | E. G. Taylor (1T) L. M. Stuart (1PG) | W. G. Thomas (1T) D. P. Manley (1T) D. Parker (2PG, 2C) |
| 1930 | 6–5 | L. M. Stuart *W. R. Jones* | M. A. McCanlis (1PT) D. Crichton-Miller (1T) | W. Davies (1T) W. J. Trew (1C) |
| 1931 | 21–3 | J. B. Nelson *W. R. Jones* | D. T. Kemp (1T) G. E. S. Williams (1T) F. W. S. Malir (1T) J. E. Forrest (1T) L. L. Bedford (1T, 1DG) J. W. Allan (1C) | R. Bateman (1T) |
| 1932 | 12–8 | C. D. Aarvold *J. Rees* | M. P. Crowe (1T) E. W. F. de V. Hunt (1T) C. D. Aarvold (1DG) J. W. Allan (1C) | G. Jones (1T) Idwal Rees (1PG, 1C) |
| 1933 | 20–7 | D. A. Kendrew *T. B. Day* | H. Lind (2T) P. C. Minns (1T) P. C. Alexander (1T) J. A. E. Siggins (4C) | R. R. Morris (1T, 1DG) |
| 1934 | 12–6 | Watcyn G. Thomas *T. B. Day* | B. T. V. Cowey (1T) R. W. Shaw (1PG, 1C) G. W. C. Meikle (1DG) | E. G. Davies (1T) G. Davies (1PG) |
| 1935 | 16–3 | J. A. Beattie *D. Thomas* | H. S. Sever (2T) K. W. Marshall (1T) J. E. Forrest (1T) R. W. Shaw (2C) | D. Thomas (1T) |
| 1936 | 19–8 | K. C. Fyfe *E. Long* | K. C. Fyfe (3T) E. J. Unwin (2T) V. G. J. Jenkins (2C) | E. Long (2T, 1C) |
| 1937 | 10–3 | H. S. Sever *R. Williams* | D. J. Macrae (2T) S. I. Howard-Jones (2C) | G. Jenkins (1PG) |
| 1938 | 7–14 | V. G. J. Jenkins *H. Payne* | J. D. Torrens (1DG) V. G. J. Jenkins (1PG) | H. M. Powell (2T) J. D. Hunt (1T) I. Davies (1T) E. Long (1C) |
| 1939 | 3–12 | R.J.L. Hammond *W. E. Harris* | D. J. Macrae (1PG) | T. Sullivan (1T) H. M. Powell (1T) W. T. H. Davies (1T) H. Davies (1PG) |
| 1940– 1945 | | WAR YEARS | | |

| YEAR | SCORE | CAPTAINS BARBARIANS/ SWANSEA | SCORERS FOR | AGAINST |
|------|-------|------------------------------|-------------|---------|
| 1946 | 11–6 | C. R. Bruce<br>C. K. Saxton | P. H. Davies (2T)<br>C. P. Callan (1T)<br>J. B. Smith (1C) | L. Davies (1T)<br>G. Addenbrooke (1T) |
| 1947 | 7–6 | C. R. Bruce<br>D. L. Davies | C. R. Bruce (1T)<br>S. C. Newman (1DG) | T. Briggs (2T) |
| 1948 | 12–3 | C. P. Callan<br>D. G. Davies | K. A. N. Spray (1T)<br>D. D. Mackenzie (1T)<br>J. W. McKay (1T)<br>W. C. W. Murdoch (1PG) | L. J. Shaw (1T) |
| 1949 | 10–3 | J. W. Kyle<br>Bryn Evans | W. D. McKee (1T)<br>G. A. Wilson (1T)<br>W. B. Holmes (2C) | L. Blyth (1T) |
| 1950 | 11–11 | J. A. Gwilliam<br>Alun G. Thomas | B. Lewis-Jones (1T)<br>J. V. Smith (1T)<br>B. Lewis-Jones (1PG, 1C) | G. Jeffreys (1T)<br>R. C. C. Thomas (1T)<br>L. Davies (1PG, 1C) |
| 1951 | 17–9 | T. Gray<br>Bryn Evans | D. M. Scott (1T)<br>R. C. Taylor (1T)<br>V. G. Roberts (1T)<br>J. V. Smith (1T)<br>J. D. Robins (1PG, 1C) | B. Edwards (2T)<br>W. D. Johnson (1T) |
| 1952 | 18–0 | E. R. John<br>R. Sutton | M. C. Thomas (2T)<br>R. C. Bazley (2T)<br>I. King (3C) | |
| 1953 | 18–8 | I. King<br>W. D. Johnson | G. M. Griffiths (3T)<br>B. M. Gray (1T)<br>I. King (3C) | W. D. Johnson (1T)<br>K. Richards (1T, 1C) |
| 1954 | 16–6 | R. V. Stirling<br>W. D. Johnson | A. G. Thomas (1T)<br>C. E. Winn (1T)<br>J. E. Williams (1T)<br>I. King (2C, 1PG) | T. Williams (1T)<br>H. D. Phillips (1T) |
| 1955 | 6–3 | R. H. Thompson<br>R. C. C. Thomas | P. H. Ryan (1T)<br>A. R. Smith (1T) | K. Williams (1PG) |
| 1956 | 0–8 | N. J. Henderson<br>W. O. G. Williams | | W. P. C. Davies (1T)<br>A. Prosser-Harries (1PG, 1C) |
| 1957 | 10–15 | G. W. D. Hastings<br>T. Williams | G. M. Griffiths (1T)<br>P. H. Thompson (1T)<br>T. E. Davies (2C) | B. Ford (1T)<br>B. Richards (1T)<br>G. Davies (1T)<br>A. Prosser-Harries (3C) |
| 1958 | 6–5 | C. R. Jacobs<br>R. C. C. Thomas | A. R. Smith (1PG)<br>W. R. Evans (1T) | R. H. Lloyd (1T)<br>D. Parkhouse (1C) |

| YEAR | SCORE | CAPTAINS BARBARIANS/ SWANSEA | SCORERS FOR | AGAINST |
|---|---|---|---|---|
| 1959 | 18–11 | A. R. Dawson<br>*B. Richards* | M. S. Phillips (1T)<br>A. R. Smith (1T)<br>K. J. F. Scotland (1T)<br>A. B. W. Risman (1PG, 3C) | J. Hopkins (1T)<br>D. Parkhouse (1PG, 1C)<br>B. Richards (1DG) |
| 1960 | 0–16 | A. R. Dawson<br>*G. Morris* | | D. I. Bebb (1T)<br>B. Richards (1T)<br>M. Evans (1T)<br>H. J. Mainwaring (1PG, 2C) |
| 1961 | 0–8 | N. S. Bruce<br>*D. I. Bebb* | | G. Lewis (1T)<br>W. O. Williams (1T)<br>B. Richards (1C) |
| 1962 | 13–9 | S. R. Smith<br>*G. Lewis* | J. B. Steven (1T)<br>J. E. Owen (1T)<br>R. A. W. Sharp (1DG)<br>K. J. F. Scotland (2C) | J. Clifford (1T)<br>D. Bebb (1T)<br>J. Faull (1PG) |
| 1963 | 11–9 | J. G. Willcox<br>*D. I. Bebb* | J. G. Willcox (1T, 2PG, 1C) | Gwyn Thomas (1T)<br>Gareth Thomas (1PG)<br>M. Evans (1T) |
| 1964 | 14–9 | M. J. Campbell-Lamerton<br>*W. Jenkins* | A. J. Hastie (1T)<br>R. J. C. Glasgow (1T)<br>T. J. Brophy (1T)<br>S. A. Morris (1PG, 1C) | Geoff Thomas (1T)<br>Gareth Thomas (1PG)<br>D. Parkhouse (1DG) |
| 1965 | 8–9 | T. J. Kiernan<br>*D. I. Bebb* | S. J. S. Clarke (1T)<br>T. J. Kiernan (1PG, 1C) | W. Upton (1T)<br>I. Jones (1PG)<br>E. Lewis (1DG) |
| 1966 | 18–8 | S. J. S. Clarke<br>*M. Evans* | P. J. C. King (1T)<br>W. R. Hunter (1T)<br>I. Robertson (1T)<br>J. R. H. Greenwood (1T)<br>J. E. Willcox (3C) | G. Morgan (1T)<br>N. Thomas (1T)<br>S. Ferguson (1C) |
| 1967 | 26–16 | N. A. A. Murphy<br>*S. Davies* | K. Bradshaw (2T)<br>R. E. Webb (2T)<br>R. D. A. Pickering (1T)<br>A. C. B. Hurst (1T)<br>K. Bradshaw (4C) | D. Weaver (2T)<br>D. I. Bebb (1T)<br>S. Ferguson (1PG, 2C) |
| 1968 | 22–16 | K. P. Andrews<br>*C. Rowlands* | G. Edwards (1T)<br>J. Gachassin (1T)<br>I. Duckworth (1T)<br>C. Lacaze (3PG, 2C) | G. Atherton (2T)<br>W. Lewis (1T)<br>D. Rogers (1T)<br>S. Ferguson (2C) |

| YEAR | SCORE | CAPTAINS BARBARIANS/ SWANSEA | SCORERS FOR | AGAINST |
|---|---|---|---|---|
| 1969 | 28–11 | N. Suddon<br>*C. Dyer* | A. Campaes (2T)<br>W. Lauder (2T)<br>C. M. Telfer (1DG)<br>D. T. Deans (1T)<br>J. P. O'Shea (1T)<br>W. G. Macdonald (1T, 1C)<br>B. J. McGann (1C) | R. Davies (1T)<br>C. Dyer (1T)<br>R. Blyth (1PG, 1C) |
| 1970 | 24–8 | R. M. Young<br>*S. Davies* | J. F. Slattery (2T)<br>P. J. Dixon (1T)<br>B. J. O'Driscoll (3C, 1PG)<br>P. Bennett (2DG) | G. Rees (1T)<br>S. Davies (1T)<br>D. Morgan (1C) |
| 1971 | 6–8 | A. J. Lewis<br>*S. Davies* | T. G. Elliot (1T)<br>J. G. Webster (1T) | S. Davies (2T)<br>D. Lewis (1C) |
| 1972 | 25–27 | A. M. Jorden<br>*P. Llewellyn* | L. G. Dick (2T)<br>A. G. B. Old (1T)<br>R. Smith (1T)<br>A. M. Jorden (1PG, 3C) | M. James (1T)<br>A. Rees (1T)<br>M. Davies (1T)<br>D. Cole (1T)<br>D. Prothero (1PG, 4C) |
| 1973 | 35–9 | M. G. Molloy<br>*T. M. Davies* | T. P. David (2T)<br>R. T. E. Bergiers (1T)<br>A. D. Gill (1T)<br>D. W. Morgan (1T)<br>D. M. Barry (1T)<br>A. H. Ensor (4C, 1PG) | T. M. Davies (1T)<br>R. Beynon (1PG, 1C) |
| 1974 | 16–12 | D. L. Powell<br>*R. Dyer* | A. J. Morley (2T)<br>P. J. Squires (1T)<br>W. H. Hare (2C) | A. Mages (1T)<br>W. R. Blyth (2PG, 1C) |
| 1975 | 13–12 | A. G. B. Old<br>*T. M. Davies* | W. Beaumont (1T)<br>A. G. B. Old (3PG) | D. Richards (1T)<br>W. R. Blyth (2PG, 1C) |
| 1976 | 25–37 | D. M. Rollitt<br>*N. Webb* | J. S. Spencer (1T)<br>A. J. Tomes (1T)<br>M. A. Biggar (1T)<br>K. M. Bushell (1T)<br>I. R. McGeechan (3C, 1PG) | G. Jones (3T)<br>R. Davies (1T)<br>W. R. Blyth (1T)<br>A. Meredith (1T)<br>B. Evans (1T)<br>D. Richards (1DG)<br>J. Rees (3C) |

*Official Programme* - .. - **3d**.

**Newport Rugby**  **Football Club**

# BARBARIANS

v.

# NEWPORT

TUESDAY, 31st MARCH, 1959.    Kick-off 3.30 p.m.

# BARBARIANS v NEWPORT 1893–1976

Of the 69 matches played against Newport at Rodney Parade, the Barbarians have won only one-third, a fact which in itself testifies to the outstanding strength of the Black-and-Ambers' rugby over eighty-three seasons. As with Cardiff, in the early years of the fixture the Barbarians met Newport at both Christmas and Easter; but despite playing twice a season the tourists did not record a victory at Rodney Parade until December 1904, in the fourteenth match of the series. Furthermore, that first surprise win was to be a drop in the ocean, for the Barbarians proceeded to lose the following ten encounters to establish the remarkable record of one win against Newport in the first twenty-four games! Since 1926, however, the honours have been evenly divided, despite the frequent problem for the Barbarians' Committee of raising a fully-fit fifteen for this final match of the Easter tour. The traditional Tuesday game continues to provide some splendid rugby for the knowledgeable 'Usksiders' and the 'foreigners' to enjoy.

## SUMMARY OF MATCHES

**Played: 69   Won: 23   Lost: 44   Drawn: 2**
**Points for: 591   Points against: 862**

Average points for Barbarians per game: 8.6
Average points for Newport per game: 12.5
Total tries for Barbarians: 125
Average Barbarian tries per game: 1.8

First win:            1904 (10–6)
First Newport win:   April 1893 (3–8)
Biggest win:         1973 60–15 (12T, 6C)
Biggest defeat:      1976 0–43 (8T, 4C, 1PG)
                     (n.b. 1920 0–39 (9T, 2DG, 2C)

Longest run of victories: 1931–1935 inclusive (5 matches) followed by draw 1936; 1969–1973 inclusive (5 matches)
Longest run of defeats: April 1893–1904 inclusive (13 matches)
Most tries for a Barbarian in one match: J. Heaton (3T 1935), M. R. Wade (3T 1959), J. R. H. Greenwood (3T 1967), J. S. Spencer (3T 1973)
Most tries for a Newport player in one match: T. W. Pearson (3T April 1896), R. T. Skrimshire (3T April 1898), H. G. Alexander (3T 1898), W. J. Martin (3T 1910), R. C. S. Plummer (3T 1919)
Most points for a Barbarian in one game: W. N. Bennett 14(1T, 5C) 1975
Most points for a Newport player in one game: L. Davies 15(1T, 4C, 1PG) 1976

## MEMORABLE MOMENTS AND MATCHES

When Percy Carpmael led the Barbarians from the field at Rodney Parade for the first time in April 1893 he was probably grievously disappointed at losing by eight points to three.

> 'It was a most stubbornly-contested game throughout, and although the Londoners were defeated they were not by any means disgraced. They played a fine dashing game, and there can be no denying the fact that taken all through, they had the best of the argument, and more especially was this noticeable in the second half, when they were continually pinning the homesters to their 25. The pace was a fast one, and this seemed to tell on the Newport men, who were very much off-colour, but not so with their opponents, who were as fresh as ever when the game concluded.'

Lohden, Nicholl and Maud were the pick of the forwards:

> 'being exceptionally clever in the open, and in the tight scrums, heeling the ball admirably out to their halves Easterbrook and Baiss, who both gave the Newport pack a lot of trouble.'

But Carpmael's try was the only Barbarian score in reply to two drop goals by wing threequarter Fred Cooper. Not until the turn of the century were the Barbarians to come that close again. The first year of the fixture at Rodney Parade coincided with the third season of a golden age in Newport rugby; when the Black-and-Ambers provided five players in the pack of the Welsh Triple Crown team of 1893, as well as the half-backs Fred Parfitt and Percy Phillips. At the same time Tom Graham established his reputation as Newport's finest-ever captain, only to be succeeded by others of almost equal greatness — Arthur Gould, the centre who was eighteen times captain of Wales, Arthur Boucher, an outstanding forward and leader, and George Llewellyn Lloyd who, in his first three seasons of captaincy, led Newport to just seven defeats in eighty-nine games!

In the first thirteen matches the Barbarians scored a total of only thirty-four points, failing to score at all on six occasions. Nor could this be explained by a short-age of international players in those unsuccessful teams; Alderson, Wells, Sammy Woods, C.B.Nicholl, Lohden, Bulger, Maud, Skrimshire, Schwarz, Unwin, and a whole host of outstanding individuals fell before the might of Newport. The fact was that Newport in those years would almost certainly have accounted for any national team, in a period of success which no other club has really surpassed.

The game of December 1904 brought to an end Newport's sequence of victories, albeit fleetingly. H.F.P.Hearson's two conversions of tries by A.R.Thompson and S.F.Coopper were the deciding factor, in reply to two tries by the home side, but, barring their captain, Jehoida Hodges, and George Boots, the great names of Newport in the nineties had gone. Yet this proved to be but a brief interlude of Barbarian success. In 1907 Hodges and Charlie Pritchard, the captain, both for-wards, appropriately scored two of Newport's three tries in a match dominated by the home pack. Their efforts were considerably helped by the fact that the Barbarian centre, W.C.Wilson, was injured early on, gamely swapped positions with a forward, and hobbled along until the final whistle!

One of the most humbling of defeats for the Baa-Baas came in 1910, when the Newport men scored five tries to win 21–0 with as weak a team as anyone could recall the Black-and-Ambers putting into the field. More than half the regular first fif-teen were unable to play, and since the Newport Seconds were away on tour, the captain Tommy Vile had to call on players from the third side and from Pill Wander-ers to make up the numbers. It was the third match in another long spell of defeats for the Barbarians at Rodney Parade, only this time the scourge of the tourists was not Gould, Hannan, Boucher or Lloyd, but the great half-back pairing of Walter Martin and Tommy Vile. Even the elevation of Vile to the ranks of international ref-eree in the immediate post-war years did not bring a respite for the tourists. In 1919 Martin had a new partner in Jack Wetter, and it was Wetter who stole the show against a team composed largely of players from the Services and London Hospitals. As *The Times* reported:

> 'Unfortunately fifteen good players do not necessarily make a good team, and this was the case with the Barbarians on Saturday. They did not seem to understand each other's methods and at least two of the tries scored against them were due to a complete lack of understanding between the members of the defence.'

Such weaknesses were inevitably exploited by a team that had not lost a match that season, and the veteran winger R.C.S.Plummer, who had first played against the Barbarians in 1907, scored a magnificent hat-trick of tries. Five tries were scored by Newport that day, to be followed by nine the following year, a total that has never been exceeded. It was no mean achievement for the Barbarians, therefore, that in 1922, with only six minutes of the match remaining, the score was six points all. The Barbarian half-backs A.T.Young, the England scrum-half, and his partner J.C.Seager of Blackheath had been outstanding, as Colonel Philip Trevor reported:

'What made their performance the more creditable was the fact that they were not playing in rear of winning forwards . . . again and again did Young and Seager evoke the applause of the large crowd and admirably did they work together. Young certainly treated Seager generously and Seager duly shared his practical appreciation of the treatment.'

But Newport's forwards outlasted their opponents and in those final minutes set up three tries, the last one of all being especially popular since it was scored by Melville Baker, an old Welsh international winger of 1909, playing his first game for Newport since returning from an eight-year sojourn in South Africa.

In 1925, twenty-one years after their last victory over Newport, it looked as though the Barbarians finally had a side capable of stemming the tide of defeats. It included Irish internationals Ernie Crawford, the legendary full-back, and J.R.Wheeler at fly-half, Scottish internationals J.C.R.Buchanan, Ian Smith, and the indestructible 'Jock' Wemyss, as well as Marsden-Jones of Cardiff and Wales, and one H.L.Glyn Hughes. As the *Western Mail* reported:

'For the first quarter of an hour the Barbarians played with a dash and resource that was bewildering, and were much too fast for the home side – Hughes intercepted well in some loose play and ran in with the first try, which Wheeler converted. A few minutes later Wheeler came into the picture with a fine corkscrew run which beat half-a-dozen opponents, to put J.Durr of Guy's in with a try, which Wheeler converted.'

But that ten-point lead was not enough, Newport's pack out-scrummaged the Barbarians who, yet again, seemed unable to last the pace, and the home team ran in three tries to win 15–10.

However, the close-fought game had given the Barbarians a scent of victory at Rodney Parade; the way was now paved for the following year. Wisely, by 1926 the Barbarians had enlarged their touring party to thirty players, so that the Barbarian team that took the field against Newport on 6 April of that year was not as battle-worn as some of those that had preceded it. In R.H.Bettington's side were five internationals, three of them Irish, including the South African Jack Gage on the wing, Ian Stuart and D.J.Cussen, together with A.R.Aslett and A.T.Young of England. The first Barbarian victory in twenty-two years at Newport was largely attributable to the pack, who, in unprecedented fashion, won all phases of the forward battle. Bettington kicked a long penalty, to put the Baa-Baas in front, but Newport retaliated with a converted try by Hathway. Then, just before half-time, the Barbarians countered with what was to prove to be the winning score. A loose Newport clearance was seized on by the visitors on the half-way line. Aslett, the Richmond centre, carved his way through the disorganised defence, linked with the Watsonian, R.F.Kelly, who in turn sent in E.Coley of Northampton for a glorious try. A thrilling second half, with only one point separating the teams, was dominated by the Barbarian forwards, with Young and E.E.Cass at half-back helping to keep the Black-and-Ambers at bay, aided by some magnificent all-round defensive tackling. It must have been a sweet sound for the Barbarians when Captain Burge blew for full-time, and an occasion for rejoicing over the victory by six points to five.

That game marked a watershed in the long history of matches against Newport, for from 1926 onwards the number of successes and failures between the clubs have been almost the same, with a remarkable frequency of very close results. For a time, though, the Barbarians took the upper hand in that glorious era of unbeaten tours in the early thirties. But during the Easter of 1937 when Emile de Lissa became President on the death of Percy Carpmael, the Baa-Baas lost to Newport for the first time in seven seasons. Eleven internationals in the tourists' fifteen took the field on a glorious spring day on a well-sanded pitch — the legacy of a phenomenally wet winter. The fact that Newport only scored seven points was largely due to the brilliance of 'Tuppy' Owen-Smith at full-back, a South African Barbarian playing in his last match before returning home, whose defensive play quickly made him a hero of the crowd. But Owen-Smith apart, it was a weary lack-lustre performance by the Baa-Baas that allowed Newport to win. Their hero was Jim Hawkins who scored all the points with a drop goal and a try, a scrum-half who but for Haydn Tanner would surely have been capped. Moreover with internationals Bill Everson, Tommy Rees and John Evans this was no weak Black-and-Ambers' side.

*Barbarians v Newport 1933. Another invincible Barbarian team, in the third of five consecutive unbeaten Easter tours in South Wales.*
Back row: *P.C.Alexander, W.Elliot, S.R.Couchman, P.C.Hordern, H.Rew, W.H.Weston, J.A.E.Siggins, M.J.Dunne, V.G.J.Jenkins, D.I.Brown.* Front row: *V.J.Pike, L.A.Booth, R.W.Boon, A.Key (absent, Watcyn G.Thomas).*

Jim Hawkins was captain of the Newport side that beat New Zealander Freddy Allen's Barbarians in the immediate post-World War II season. It was an exciting last fifteen minutes which saw Allen himself inspire a Barbarian recovery from 11–0 down, making a try for his Kiwi partner W.A.Meates, and another for Scottish centre W.H.Munro in the dying minutes. But if that game had a thrilling finish, none was more dramatic than that of 1955. This Easter tour preceded the memorable British Lions' tour of South Africa, and thoroughly disappointing Barbarian displays against Cardiff and Swansea had provoked depressing forebodings as to the likely outcome of the Lions' chances against the Springboks.

Much of the cream of British rugby was included in the Barbarian touring party. Fourteen internationals were in the side that could only draw 3–3 with Penarth; there were fourteen caps too, in the side that gave a dull performance at the Arms Park, winning 6–3, and the scoreline was the same at Swansea. Amongst these players were in fact twelve of the eventual Lions' party – in the backs Angus Cameron, Arthur Smith, Gareth Griffiths, Tony O'Reilly, Alun Thomas, and Johnny Williams; in the forwards Hugh McLeod, Bryn Meredith, Reg Higgins, W.O.G.Williams, J.T.Greenwood and the Lions' captain, Robin Thompson. Add to that illustrious list Dennis Shuttleworth, Eric Evans, Martin Regan, P.H.Ryan, Peter Yarranton, R.C.Bazley and Ian King, of England; J.W.Y.Kemp, Ian McGregor and A.Robson of Scotland; Garfield Owen the Welsh full-back and Noel Henderson of Ireland, all internationals, and the general apprehension as to the forthcoming tour can be understood.

But as J.B.G.Thomas of the *Western Mail*, who has been as close as any reporter to the unpredictable vagaries of talented Barbarian teams, stated at the time:

'The fine match at Newport which ended the 1955 Barbarian tour did much to restore faith in the British team.'

There were thirteen internationals under Reg Higgins's captaincy on that Easter Tuesday, and he clearly instilled into his side some renewed vitality. At half-time the Baa-Baas led Malcolm Thomas's Newport fifteen by eight points to three, thanks to a penalty and then a try by Alun Thomas, converted from wide out by Angus Cameron. Garfield Owen, who had earlier played as full back for the Baa-Baas against Penarth and Swansea, now kicked a penalty for his own club Newport, before Thomas sent in Gray, the uncapped Richmond winger, for a Barbarian try to increase their lead. Bazley scored another to put them further ahead at fourteen points to six. Then came the dramatic finale. Despite an earlier shoulder injury the Newport fly-half dropped for goal – and it was one of those occasions when a drop goal attempt can become the perfect cross-kick. Ken Jones, after three superb runs in the first half, ultimately reaped his just reward. He followed the mis-kick at great speed and beat Cameron for the touch-down with a spectacular drive for a try which was converted by Owen – fourteen points to eleven. With ten minutes remaining Burnett finally left the fray and Malcolm Thomas moved up to fly-half. Then in the fading moments Onllwyn Brace, who had been the inspiration of Newport at the base of the scrum, put his partner away from a set scrum, thrust his way through the Barbarian defence and dived through a tackle for the equalising try – fourteen points all. The outcome of the match hung on the conversion, which was not a difficult one, but Owen missed; the final whistle blew and in a memorable encounter justice had been served.

Three years later the Barbarians again saved their best performance of the tour for the final match, in which their play was described by *The Times* as a display of:

'. . . dazzling criss-cross patterns that gave the crowd much pleasure, and at times had them on their feet in the wildest exhilaration'.

But even the brilliant running of a back division that included Arthur Smith and Pedlow on the wings, Gordon Waddell and Andy Mulligan at half-back, Ken Scotland and Mick English, was not sufficient to win the day. It was in fact a glorious swansong for Wales's most capped rugby player of the time, K.J.Jones, who appeared that day on his own club ground for the last time. At the end of the game in which he produced some of his characteristic powerful bursts on the wing, he was borne off on the shoulders of a host of his enthusiastic supporters. But it was the other Newport wing, Roy Burnett, who was the 'man of the match' with two brilliant tries that sparked a famous victory for the home team. That victory also owed

The fifteen that rounded off the unbeaten tour of 1955 by drawing fourteen-all with Newport.
Back row: D.W.Swarbrick, A.J.F.O'Reilly, A.Robson, P.G.Yarranton, W.O.G.Williams, J.W.Y.Kemp,
B.M.Gray, D.C.Joynson (referee). Middle row: R.C.Bazley, H.F.McLeod, R.Higgins (captain), E.Evans,
J.Ritchie. Front row: A.G.Thomas, A.Cameron, D.W.Shuttleworth, G.M.Griffiths.

much to the solid scrummaging of the pack in opposition to such revered set-piece
specialists as Mulcahy, McLeod and Evans.

In 1959 the Barbarians produced one of their finest performances to beat Newport and so end their tour unbeaten with three wins, and a draw against Penarth.
This victory, against Brian Jones's fifteen, was all the more meritorious, though
sadly marred, on account of the injury to the Baa-Baas captain of the day, Peter
Robbins, the brilliant England back-row forward. In leading a counter-attack just
before half-time, he fell over Hartstill, the Newport full-back who had gone down on
the ball, landed awkwardly and broke his leg. It was an injury which prevented him
from touring with the British Lions to Australia and New Zealand that summer, for
which tour he had already been selected. The Barbarians showed tremendous spirit
in overcoming this set-back, the fourteen players rising to the challenge. The Barbarians eventually won fifteen points to five, thanks to a splendid understanding
between the Cambridge University half-backs, S.R.Smith and Gordon Waddell,
Mike Wade, a fellow Cantabrian in the centre who three times carved his way
through the defence to score a try, and the speed of both John Young and Jim
Roberts on the wings. But the greatest plaudits were reserved for the seven-man
pack, in which Bert Godwin gave a masterly hooking display, and Vic Harding, Alan
Ashcroft and Haydn Mainwaring worked like Trojans against the superior odds.
Wade's final try of his hat-trick ten minutes from time brought the game to an
emotional climax, with the Barbarian supporters singing the team song It's a way we
have in the Baa-Baas followed by a tumultuous ovation from the crowd for their
team's efforts at the end of a thrilling display.

Under the captaincy of Haydn Mainwaring the Barbarians' win of 1960 was yet
another in a sequence of truly exciting matches. A narrow victory by eleven points to

*The team that beat Newport in the final game of the all-conquering Easter tour of 1970.*
Back row: *B.Butler, M.P.Bulpitt, A.L.Bucknall, P.J.Hayward, C.S.Wardlow, M.J.Leadbetter, P.J.Larter, M.C.Hipwell, A.Williams, G.A.Ferguson (touch-judge).* Front row: *A.Jorden, I.McLauchlan, J.V.Pullin, J.S.Spencer, C.M.Telfer, N.C.Starmer-Smith.*

nine was sufficient to take away Newport's unbeaten home record for the season. Again it was achieved by fourteen men, since Dewi Bebb was injured and left the field early in the second half. The Barbarians' hero was Templeman at scrum-half, who had plotted the Baa-Baas downfall only four days earlier at Penarth, but now set the tourists on the road to victory with a drop-goal to which was added a try by Bebb and another by Andy Hurst after a long solo run.

After three successive victories by the Black-and-Ambers, the Barbarians returned in 1964 to produce a rousing finish to that Easter tour. With only twenty minutes of the match remaining, they trailed 3–0. David Watkins, the Newport and Wales fly-half, had tantalised and tormented the opposition for threequarters of the game, but quite suddenly the whole pattern changed. From loose play Tom Kiernan joined a threequarter move to set up a try for Brian Henderson, which opened the floodgates for four more tries. Bob Taylor burst through from a line-out to score and he made another try for Jim Telfer. Taylor it was, too, who set the threes away again for Peter Cook to touch down for a further two tries. Kiernan rounded off a splendid afternoon with four conversions from his carefully measured kicks. So from tottering on the brink of defeat, the Barbarians had recovered to astound both Newport players and spectators alike, as well as themselves, with twenty-three points in twenty minutes.

A lasting memory of 1972 at Rodney Parade is of the *coup de grâce* inflicted by that most popular of all French rugby players, Pierre Villepreux of Stade Toulousain. It seemed the match was lost for the Barbarians, for with six minutes remaining they were still two points behind. But then Billy Steele on the wing switched the direction of a Barbarian attack to link with the other threequarters. Villepreux raced into the line, passed on to Roy Mathias who in turn fed back inside to Arthur Lewis, before

Lewis passed back to Villepreux, who just found enough room to score the winning try. For the French full-back it was a joyous moment which atoned for two missed kicks at goal. After that game, which followed the end of his international career, he mused on a match of free-running attacking rugby in Wales:

*'Je désespérais de faire un jour au Pays de Galles un match en attaque. Je pensais qu'ils auraient gardé de moi l'image d'un buteur. Vraiment je suis heureux.'*

Villepreux, who had taken to the Baa-Baas as much as they had taken to him, summed up his enjoyment of Barbarian rugby very succinctly,

*'Tout d'abord on est libre'.*

But of all the matches between the Barbarians and Newport none could have had a more appropriate ending than the one on 24 April 1973. It came at the end of an outstanding tour in which the Baa-Baas were unbeaten throughout, in a year which marked the sixtieth anniversary of the club President's (Brigadier Glyn Hughes) first ever Barbarian Easter in Wales. In achieving the 'grand slam' for only the third time in post-war years, the Barbarians succeeded in beating Newport by sixty points to fifteen to record their biggest ever margin of victory to that time, and to inflict on the home club their heaviest defeat. Under the captaincy of John Spencer, one of the most popular and successful of latter-day Baa-Baas, the tourists gave a dazzling exhibition of idealised Barbarian rugby. Spencer revelled in the occasion with three tries, and there were two each for Tim Cowell, Geoff Evans and Peter Preece, with one apiece for Martin Cooper, Terry Moore and Tony Ensor. But the perfect scoreline was contrived by John Gray, who, rather than convert the twelfth and final try by his team captain, deliberately hooked the attempt to ensure that the final total remained at exactly sixty as a delightful tribute to 'Hughie' from the players.

Yet Newport are not a club to be subdued for long, and the following season, in 1974, the Black-and-Ambers won by three tries to nil, only for the Barbarians to retaliate with nine tries to one in 1975, with Spencer once again amongst the scorers. There must have been extra satisfaction, therefore, for Newport captain Colin Smart in transforming a massive deficit into an overwhelming victory over the Barbarians within the space of a year. In 1976 Newport trounced the visitors 43–0, including eight tries in that total, shared between seven players, amongst them Smart himself. Long may the excitement, high scoring and unpredictability of the matches of the last ten years continue!

# BARBARIANS v NEWPORT

| YEAR | SCORE | CAPTAINS BARBARIANS/ NEWPORT | SCORERS FOR | AGAINST |
|------|-------|------|------|---------|
| 1893 | 3–8 | W. P. Carpmael T. C. Graham | W. P. Carpmael (1T) | F. W. Cooper (2DG) |
| Dec 1893 | 0–19 | A. J. Gould | | W. L. Thomas (2T) W. H. Watts (2T) A. J. Gould (1T, 2C) |
| Dec 1894 | 3–19 | A. J. Gould | C. B. Nicholl (1T) | W. Parsons (2T) T. Pook (1T) A. J. Gould (1T) M. Hannan (1T) T. England (2C) |
| 1896 | 6–24 | A. W. Boucher | R. O'H. Livesay (1T) E. M. Baker (1T) | T. W. Pearson (3T) A. J. Gould (1T) W. H. Watts (1T) T. Saunders (1T) A. W. Boucher (3C) |
| Dec 1896 | 0–16 | A. W. Boucher | | W. Watts (1T) A. W. Boucher (1T) H. Packer (1T) A. J. Gould (1T) A. W. Boucher (2C) |
| 1897 | 0–19 | A. W. Boucher | | F. W. Davies (1T) F. H. Dauncey (1T) T. W. Pearson (1T) A. Sawtell (1T) J. Jenkins (1T) A. W. Boucher (2C) |
| 1898 | 0–21 | F. H. Dauncey | | R. T. Skrimshire (3T) G. Ll. Lloyd (1T, 2C) T. W. Pearson (1T) F. H. Dauncey (1C) |
| Dec 1898 | 0–16 | A. W. Boucher | | H. G. Alexander (3T) T. Jones (1T) A. W. Boucher (2C) |
| 1900 | 10–15 | G. Boots | C. S. Edgar (1T) R. T. Cumberledge (1T) J. G. Franks (2C) | F. W. Huggett (1T) J. J. Hodges (1T) T. W. Pearson (1T) E. Thomas (1T) D. G. Harris (1T) |
| 1901 | 3–9 | G. Ll. Lloyd | B. C. Hartley (1T) | M. Price (1T) T. Beard (1T) T. W. Pearson (1T) |

| | | CAPTAINS | SCORERS | |
|---|---|---|---|---|
| YEAR | SCORE | BARBARIANS/ NEWPORT | FOR | AGAINST |
| Dec 1901 | 0–4 | G. Ll. Lloyd | | C. E. Lewis (1DG) |
| 1902 | 4–20 | G. Boots | R. T. Skrimshire (1DG) | T. W. Pearson (2T) E. Thomas (1T) T. H. Vile (1T) G. Boots (2C) T. W. Pearson (1DG) |
| 1903 | 5–17 | B. C. Hartley G. Boots | R. G. Bingham (1T) E. Wayne-Morgan (1C) | W. M. Llewellyn (1T) G. Boots (1T) C. C. Pritchard (1T) C. E. Lewis (2C, 1DG) |
| Dec 1904 | 10–6 | J. J. Hodges | A. R. Thompson (1T) S. F. Coopper (1T) H. F. P. Hearson (2C) | J. E. C. Partridge (1T) H. Wetter (1T) |
| Dec 1905 | 3–11 | C. E. L. Hammond C. M. Pritchard | H. C. Jackson (1T) | A. Davies (2T) C. E. Lewis (1T) R. B. Griffiths (1C) |
| Dec 1906 | | | Cancelled owing to frost | |
| Dec 1907 | 0–12 | S. F. Coopper C. M. Pritchard | | R. C. S. Plummer (1T) J. J. Hodges (1T) C. M. Pritchard (1T) F. W. Birt (1GM) |
| Dec 1908 | | | Cancelled owing to frost | |
| Dec 1909 | 8–19 | F. O'B. Wilson T. H. Vile | C. H. Medlock (1T) E. G. Ede (1T) S. Joubert (1C) | W. J. Martin (2T) R. C. S. Plummer (1T) T. H. Vile (1T) J. P. Jones (1T) F. W. Birt (2C) |
| Dec 1911 | 6–15 | W. S. D. Craven T. H. Vile | H. W. Thomas (1T) J. H. D. Watson (1T) | R. C. Hicks (2T) J. R. M'Gregor (2T) R. C. S. Plummer (1T) |
| Dec 1910 | 0–21 | W. C. Wilson T. H. Vile | | W. J. Martin (3T) A. P. Coldrick (1T) G. L. Hirst (1T) W. Webb (1DG) G. Boots (1C) |

| YEAR | SCORE | CAPTAINS BARBARIANS/ NEWPORT | SCORERS FOR | AGAINST |
|---|---|---|---|---|
| Dec 1913 | 0–14 | A. R. V. Jackson *W. J. Martin* | | G. L. Hirst (2T) J. Wetter (1T) R. Dibble (1T) F. W. Birt (1C) |
| 1914– 1918 | | WAR YEARS | | |
| Dec 1919 | 0–19 | L. G. Thomas | | R. C. S. Plummer (3T) N. C. McPherson (1T) J. Shea (1T, 1C) E. D. G. Hammett (1C) |
| Dec 1920 | 0–39 | F. Bekker | | J. Rees (2T) E. D. G. Hammett (2T) J. Shea (2T) J. Whitfield (2T) H. Uzzell (1T) J. Shea (1DG) F. W. Birt (2C) E. D. G. Hammett (1DG) |
| 1922 | 6–15 | B. S. Cumberlege *N. C. Macpherson* | G. W. C. Parker (1T) T. Lawton (1T) | W. Radford (2T) J. Whitfield (1T) A. M. Baker (1T) A. Stock (1T) |
| 1923– 1924 | | *No matches* | | |
| 1925 | 10–15 | J. R. Wheeler *R. Edwards* | H. L. G. Hughes (1T) J. M. Durr (1T) J. R. Wheeler (2C) | A. Stock (2T) J. Collins (1T) J. Wetter (3C) |
| 1926 | 6–5 | R. H. Bettington *H. J. Davies* | E. Coley (1T) R. H. B. Bettington (1PG) | R. Hathway (1T) W. A. Everson (1C) |
| 1927 | 8–9 | J. H. Gage *W. J. Roche* | J. B. Ganly (1T) J. H. Gage (1T) D. Drysdale (1C) | H. M'Gregor (1T) W. C. Morgan (1T) W. A. Everson (1PG) |
| 1928 | 0–17 | D. Turquand-Young *V. M. Griffiths* | | J. C. Morley (2T) C. J. Jerman (1T) R. Hathway (1T) W. H. Lewis (1PG) T. Babington (1C) |
| 1929 | 4–3 | J. M. Bannerman *V. M. Griffiths* | E.W.F. de V.Hunt (1DG) | W. A. Everson (1PG) |
| 1930 | 13–23 | D. Bradley *W. A. Everson* | E. Coley (2T) A. G. Johnson (1T) C. J. Hanrahan (2C) | D. E. Hughes (1T) K. Watkins (1T) A. C. Lyle (1T) R. Green (1T) W. A. Everson (2C, 1PG) R. Carter (1DG) |

| YEAR | SCORE | CAPTAINS BARBARIANS/ NEWPORT | SCORERS FOR | AGAINST |
|---|---|---|---|---|
| 1931 | 18–9 | J. J. A. Embleton<br>*W. A. Everson* | J. J. A. Embleton (1T)<br>D. P. Henshaw (1T)<br>W. R. Logan (1T)<br>C. C. Tanner (1T)<br>J. W. Allan (3C) | J. C. Morley (1T)<br>A. G. Martin (1T)<br>W. A. Everson (1PG) |
| 1932 | 9–6 | D. St. Clair Ford<br>*P. C. Hordern* | B. H. Black (1T, 1PG)<br>A. C. Harrison (1T) | A. J. Berry (1T)<br>J. F. C. Swallow (1T) |
| 1933 | 21–9 | P. C. Hordern<br>*A. R. Ralph* | S. R. Couchman (1T)<br>V. G. J. Jenkins (1T)<br>R. W. Boon (1T)<br>P. C. Alexander (1T)<br>J. A. E. Siggins (1PG, 1C)<br>W. Elliot (1DG) | H. Jones (1T)<br>J. F. C. Swallow (1DG)<br>W. A. Everson (1C) |
| 1934 | 11–6 | H. Rew<br>*W. A. Everson* | P. Cranmer (1T)<br>Idwal Rees (1T)<br>J. Dicks (1T)<br>J. W. Allan (1C) | F. C. Emms (1T)<br>R. L. Jones (1T) |
| 1935 | 23–3 | M. J. Dunne<br>*E. J. Shiner* | J. Heaton (3T)<br>V. G. J. Jenkins (4C)<br>R. J. L. Hammond (1T)<br>P. Cranmer (1T) | J. R. Evans (1PG) |
| 1936 | 11–11 | J. Idwal Rees<br>*J. R. Evans* | J. I. Rees (1T)<br>R. C. S. Dick (1T)<br>S. J. B. Deering (1T)<br>K. C. Fyfe (1C) | F. Cheshire (1T)<br>J. T. Knowles (1T)<br>W. H. Hopkins (1T)<br>W. S. G. Legge (1C) |
| 1937 | 3–7 | M. McG. Cooper<br>*J. R. Evans* | M. McG. Cooper (1T) | J. C. Hawkins (1T, 1DG) |
| 1938 | 0–8 | C. R. A. Graves<br>*V. J. Law* | | G. Williams (1T)<br>T. G. Thomas (1T)<br>R. F. Allen (1C) |
| 1939 | 9–6 | L. Babrow<br>*V. J. Law* | J. W. S. Irwin (1T)<br>H. R. McKibbin (1DG)<br>W. M. Penman (1C) | J. T. Knowles (1T)<br>W. S. G. Legge (1PG) |
| 1940–1945 | | WAR YEARS | | |
| 1946 | 6–11 | F. R. Allen<br>*J. C. Hawkins* | W. H. Munro (1T)<br>W. A. Meates (1T) | A. H. Rowland (1T)<br>M. Chatwin (1T)<br>D. R. Morgan (1PG, 1C) |
| 1947 | 19–3 | M. R. Steele-<br>Bodger<br>*J. H. Bale* | H. Tanner (1T)<br>W. H. Munro (1T)<br>B. L. Williams (1T)<br>M. F. Turner (1T)<br>F. H. Coutts (2C, 1PG) | A. H. Rowland (1T) |
| 1948 | 3–5 | B. L. Williams<br>*Gwili Jenkins* | H. H. Campbell (1T) | W. H. Thomas (1T)<br>G. Jenkins (1C) |
| 1949 | 6–5 | B. H. Travers<br>*P. Davies* | W. B. Holmes (1DG, 1PG) | R. Burnett (1PT)<br>P. Davies (1C) |

| YEAR | SCORE | CAPTAINS BARBARIANS/ NEWPORT | SCORERS FOR | AGAINST |
|------|-------|------------------------------|-------------|---------|
| 1950 | 8–14 | Glyn Davies<br>*L. E. T. Jones* | J. V. Smith (1T)<br>B. Lewis Jones (1PG, 1C) | A. H. Rowland (1T)<br>S. Kimpton (1T)<br>T. Sterry (1T)<br>L. Davies (1T)<br>B. Edwards (1C) |
| 1951 | 6–13 | J. R. G. Stevens<br>*K. J. Jones* | J. M. Williams (2T) | R. T. Evans (1T)<br>G. Ross (1T)<br>R. D. Owen (1T)<br>B. Edwards (2C) |
| 1952 | 3–8 | G. Williams<br>*R. Burnett* | G. Williams (1DG) | B. Williams (1T)<br>L. Davies (1T)<br>M. C. Thomas (1C) |
| 1953 | 8–6 | J. Matthews<br>*R. Burnett* | C. J. Saunders (1T)<br>J. D. Robins (1PG, 1C) | K. J. Jones (1T)<br>R. D. Burnett (1DG) |
| 1954 | 3–14 | B. M. Gray<br>*K. J. Jones* | V. Evans (1PG) | J. Lane (1T)<br>B. Jones (1C)<br>R. Sheppard (1T)<br>D. O. Brace (1DG)<br>D. A. G. Ackerman (1T) |
| 1955 | 14–14 | R. Higgins<br>*M. C. Thomas* | A. G. Thomas (1T)<br>B. M. Gray (1T)<br>R. C. Bazley (1T)<br>A. Cameron (1C)<br>A. G. Thomas (1PG) | J. Phillips (1T)<br>K. J. Jones (1T)<br>M. C. Thomas (1T)<br>G. D. Owen (1PG, 1C) |
| 1956 | 3–14 | E. Evans<br>*M. C. Thomas* | P. H. Thompson (1T) | D. Greenslade (1T)<br>M. C. Thomas (1T)<br>C. Evans (1T)<br>N. Morgan (1PG, 1C) |
| 1957 | 8–5 | V. G. Roberts<br>*M. C. Thomas* | A. R. Smith (1T)<br>R. R. Winn (1T)<br>H. J. Mainwaring (1C) | R. Burnett (1T)<br>N. Morgan (1C) |
| 1958 | 8–13 | E. Evans<br>*L. H. Jenkins* | A. C. Pedlow (1T)<br>A. A. Mulligan (1T)<br>K. J. F. Scotland (1C) | R. Burnett (2T)<br>B. V. Meredith (1T)<br>N. Morgan (2C) |
| 1959 | 15–5 | P. G. D. Robbins<br>*B. J. Jones* | M. R. Wade (3T)<br>G. W. Hastings (3C) | J. Anderson (1T)<br>G. Evans (1C) |
| 1960 | 11–9 | H. J. Mainwaring<br>*B. J. Jones* | D. I. Bebb (1T)<br>A. C. B. Hurst (1T)<br>B. Templeman (1DG)<br>H. J. Mainwaring (1C) | B. Jones (1T)<br>N. Morgan (2PG) |
| 1961 | 0–6 | W. R. Evans<br>*G. Davidge* | | B. V. Meredith (1T)<br>J. Anderson (1T) |
| 1962 | 8–17 | A. A. Mulligan<br>*B. V. Meredith* | T. O. Grant (1T)<br>J. N. Blake (1DG)<br>K. J. F. Scotland (1C) | P. Rees (2T)<br>B. Thomas (1T)<br>N. Morgan (2PG, 1C) |

| | | CAPTAINS | SCORERS | |
| | | BARBARIANS/ | | |
| YEAR | SCORE | NEWPORT | FOR | AGAINST |
|---|---|---|---|---|
| 1963 | 15–16 | C. R. Jacobs<br>*G. Davidge* | J. Roberts (1T)<br>P. Ford (1T)<br>D. R. R. Morgan (1T)<br>D. Rutherford (3C) | D. Perrott (2T)<br>J. Anderson (1T)<br>J. Uzzell (1DG)<br>R. Cheney (2C) |
| 1964 | 23–3 | D. P. Rogers<br>*B. Price* | P. W. Cook (2T)<br>B. C. Henderson (1T)<br>J. W. Telfer (1T)<br>R. B. Taylor (1T)<br>T. J. Kiernan (4C) | P. M. Rees (1T) |
| 1965 | 8–9 | A. M. Davis<br>*W. R. Prosser* | A. J. Hinshelwood (1T)<br>T. J. Brophy (1T)<br>D. Rutherford (1C) | P. M. Rees (1T)<br>D. Perrott (1T)<br>R. Cheney (1PG) |
| 1966 | 3–13 | W. J. Hunter<br>*A. Thomas* | K. Bradshaw (1PG) | V. Perrins (1T)<br>J. Anthony (2C, 1PG) |
| 1967 | 15–6 | T. P. Bedford<br>*G. R. Britton* | J. R. H. Greenwood (3T)<br>M. P. Weston (3C) | M. Webber (1T)<br>B. J. Jones (1PG) |
| 1968 | 11–26 | C. Lacaze<br>*M. Webber* | M. N. Grimshaw (1T)<br>I. Duckworth (1T)<br>C. Lacaze (1PG, 1C) | D. Cornwall (2T)<br>J. Davies (1T)<br>J. Watkins (1T)<br>P. Rees (1T)<br>J. Anthony (4C, 1PG) |
| 1969 | 16–3 | W. G. Hullin<br>*J. Anthony* | B. J. O'Driscoll (1T)<br>M. L. Hipwell (1T)<br>I. S. Gallacher (1T)<br>B. J. O'Driscoll (1PG, 2C) | J. J. Jeffrey (1T) |
| 1970 | 22–3 | J. V. Pullin<br>*J. Anthony* | C. S. Wardlow (2T)<br>N. C. Starmer-Smith (1T)<br>M. P. Bulpitt (1T)<br>A. D. Williams (1T)<br>C. M. Telfer (1DG)<br>A. M. Jorden (2C) | J. Anthony (1T) |
| 1971 | 16–11 | K. E. Fairbrother<br>*K. Poole* | W. C. C. Steele (2T)<br>I. G. McRae (1T)<br>P. A. Rossborough (1PG,<br>2C) | I. Taylor (1T)<br>G. Fuller (1T)<br>A. Hearne (1T)<br>L. Daniel (1C) |
| 1972 | 14–12 | D. J. Lloyd<br>*K. Poole* | N. A. MacEwen (1T)<br>R. Hopkins (1T)<br>P. Villepreux (1T, 1C) | G. Evans (1T)<br>J. Anthony (2PG, 1C) |
| 1973 | 60–15 | J. S. Spencer<br>*G. Evans* | J. S. Spencer (3T)<br>T. A. Cowell (2T)<br>G. W. Evans (2T)<br>P. S. Preece (2T)<br>M. J. Cooper (1T, 1C)<br>T. A. P. Moore (1T)<br>A. H. Ensor (1T, 1C)<br>J. D. Gray (3C)<br>S. McKinney (1C) | K. Poole (1T)<br>R. Williams (3PG, 1C) |

| | | CAPTAINS | SCORERS | |
| | | BARBARIANS/ | | |
| YEAR | SCORE | NEWPORT | FOR | AGAINST |
|---|---|---|---|---|
| 1974 | 0–16 | D. L. Powell<br>*G. Evans* | | C. Jenkins (1T)<br>G. Evans (1T)<br>D. Hadden (1T)<br>A. Hearne (2C) |
| 1975 | 46–9 | J. S. Spencer<br>*G. Evans* | L. G. Dick (2T)<br>J. S. Spencer (2T)<br>P. J. Squires (1T)<br>G. Richards (1T)<br>A. R. Trickey (1T)<br>H. W. Jenkins (1T)<br>W. N. Bennett (1T, 5C) | J. J. Jeffrey (1T)<br>R. Morgan (1PG, 1C) |
| 1976 | 0–43 | A. Neary<br>*C. Smart* | | J. Martin (2T)<br>C. Smart (1T)<br>Geoff Evans (1T)<br>Gareth Evans (1T)<br>L. Davies (1T, 4C, 1PG)<br>D. Burcher (1T)<br>T. O'Gorman (1T) |

# Chapter 7

# BAA~BAAS AT PLAY

To talk of great tries, memorable matches, wins, losses, and a host of historical facts and figures is to tell only half the story. The Barbarian tradition is founded equally upon the enjoyment of rugby fellowship and friendships off the field as much as for the rugby itself. From the hilarity of the first Barbarian tour of the north in 1890, to the present-day pleasures of the more-organised visits to South Wales, the emphasis throughout the club's history has always been on enjoyment. This is not to imply that the rugby is approached in a casual way — but rather that the pressures and tensions surrounding, for instance, international matches, are absent; that the manner and style of play is almost as important as the result; and that away from the rugby field there is a relaxing and friendly atmosphere in which players and committee members, from different clubs and countries, may enjoy each other's company. That the Barbarians have continued to maintain the unique character of the club reflects chiefly upon many great personalities who have been its leaders, and a host of outstanding sportsmen who have become its members — all of them of the kind which rugby, perhaps more than other sports, seems to produce.

*Left: The Barbarian mascot of Easter 1911 being reluctantly put out to grass by, from the left, H.Whitehead, C.H.Pillman, G.D.Roberts, J.M.B.Scott and L.B.Stringer. Above: Barbarians at leisure with the locals in 1904.*

The club owes its success and its standing in no small measure, too, to the happy associations built up with the rugby people of the north initially, later the Midlands, and always, South Wales — to the friendliest ties with the inhabitants of Penarth, its golf club, and a remarkable hotel and its staff, the Esplanade on the Promenade.

To mention the 'Esp' is to evoke a hundred and one memories for any Barbarian who has experienced an Easter tour in Wales, between 1901 and 1971. Sadly, with the sale of the hotel in 1971, the Baa-Baas were reluctantly forced to move. Since then they have been happily accommodated at the Royal Hotel, Cardiff — and with the creation of a Barbarians Room in the hotel, decorated in the club colours, the Baa-Baas have a new 'home'. But for a long time to come only one place will be remembered as the Barbarian HQ — the beloved Esplanade. The stories of the 'goings-on' at this sedate, red-brick, Gothic-style building at the bottom of the hill, opposite the pier on the sea-front, are legion.

In the early years, the 'Esp' underwent many changes in its proprietorship and management, having both managers and manageresses. As Emile de Lissa mentioned in his publication of the records of the Barbarian Football Club in 1933:

> 'Some of the latter have been overcome and distracted beyond words, by the noise, perpetual singing, and general merriment. Urgent appeals and threats of expulsion of some or all, and so forth, have occasionally occurred, but as assistance has always been forthcoming by those in charge of the party, in quelling and smoothing over all and sundry disturbances and riots, peace has ultimately reigned and invariably, when leaving, a cordial welcome has been extended to the next Easter visit.'

*The Barbarians at play! Outside the Penarth Golf Club in 1908, in the early years of the Sunday golfing revelries. From left to right, W.C.Wilson, F.J.V.Hopley, J.G.G.Birkett, J.J.Coffey and J.S.Stranaghan.*

*A formidable trio of Barbarian forwards waiting to embark from Paddington on the journey to South Wales and the west country in March, 1907: 'Darkie' Bedell-Sivright and M.R.Dickson of Scotland flank the England international, and future QC, 'Khaki' Roberts.*

The head waiter, Webber, or 'Fritz', was an institution for many years, and the head waitress, 'Peggy', was another who helped tend and care for the youngest Barbarian lambs! De Lissa continued:

'All extras, which are not included in the general bill are collected from individuals by her, and she sees that she gets cash on the spot. In recent years, ''egg and bacon'' suppers are an institution with those not in bed, and this is one of Peggy's charges; but no supper is forthcoming without previous payment!'

Emile recalled, too, the 'B' (for Barbarian) Band – 'Tarzan' David, Frank Stone, Rex Hellier, Hugh Duncan and Glyn Hughes, who performed with an unlikely combination of instruments – a ukelele, penny whistles, cymbals, mouth organ and the hotel gong. An unbearable noise ensued, but, with practice, this unmusical gathering ventured to serenade the assembled company on the tour of 1921, with 'Barbarian songs and marches'. They had the audacity, too, to impose their cacophony upon the unsuspecting crowds at the games that Easter.

Those earliest years at the Esplanade can now be recalled by only a very few living Barbarians. For instance, Lord Wakefield of Kendal, then Wavell Wakefield, first played in a Baa-Baas match in 1916, but as with many others before and since, his Easter commitments to his club, the Harlequins, prevented him from joining the Baa-Baas on tour. It is seldom remembered, too, that in those days when England played France in Paris the fixture was on Easter Monday. But Tom Voyce, the great

George Fraser of Richmond, and England, earnestly scanning the distant fairway in 1905, but looking rather more optimistic about his drive than many of his Barbarian successors who have 'gardened' their way round the delightful course of Penarth Golf Club.

Gloucester and England forward, although declining for similar reasons the invitation to play over Easter on many occasions, did, for the first time, take part in the tour of 1923–24:

'What times we had; we used to dance round the table after the soup was served. I never saw one bowl spilled – we were a "gentle lot" – good with our feet! . . . On the Saturday night, after the 23 points to 18 victory over Cardiff, Arthur Blakiston and I were somehow locked in our bedroom at the Esplanade up on the third floor. Outside, to the next room, is a ledge, no more than three inches wide, and J.C.R.Buchanan suddenly appeared negotiating his way along it! "Blakie" and I grabbed him. There's no doubt that had he been sober he could not have done it. Next morning, we were amazed, when viewing Buchanan's achievement in daylight, that such a feat was possible – so was Buchanan! . . . I was much amused to learn what happened on Monday, too. My name was down in the Swansea programme for the match, but I had to return to Gloucester. The match at Swansea was not very old when the referee suddenly blew his whistle. "Offside Voyce!" he said. There was an immediate outburst of laughter from all the players – who, of course, knew I wasn't playing! Referee's prejudice, if ever there were!'

Herbert Waddell was witness to one of the most often recounted pranks that have passed into Barbarian folklore. There was one occasion when Miss Davis, as manageress, had found good reason to become annoyed with some members of the touring party, and had taken them to task over the matter. The culprits decided to seek redress. As a result of certain nocturnal happenings, the following morning various items of underwear belonging to the aforementioned Miss Davis were to be seen proudly flying from the hotel's flagstaff, much to the amusement not only of the hotel's inmates, but also to most of the inhabitants of Penarth. Then there was the Easter tour when a huge canvas banner with the announcement 'Opening Easter Monday' was displayed over the entrance to the pier across the road, to announce the forthcoming arrival of a variety show. The opportunity was irresistible and, following the activities of various Barbarians working under the cover of night, the dawn revealed the imminent opening of the Esplanade Hotel! As Jack Gage, the re-

*Three great Barbarians taking the sea air on the Marine Promenade at Penarth in 1906 — Percy Carpmael, Emile de Lissa, in his first year as Honorary Secretary, and W.S.D.Craven, who played for the Baa-Baas on fifteen occasions, and was a committee member. Perhaps, too, they were recuperating at the end of a season in which the Barbarians lost all six matches!*

nowned Irish and South African threequarter of the twenties recalled, reminiscing on his Barbarian experiences:

'These were wonderful years — no running water, but basins and jugs, usually to be found brimming full of beer, not $H_2O$. No rules, of which I'm aware, about early bedtime before a match. Great characters, Jammie Clinch, Mark Sugden and Ernie Crawford amongst the Irish — Crawford of the witty tongue, whose war injury meant he would always attempt the tackle on one side of his body only. There was Turquand Young, a favourite with the girls, when they were about, which was seldom. Herbert Waddell, too, a noisy character, "Horsey" Browne, a terrific athlete, and J.B.Nelson. The spontaneous Saturday night party — a worrying time for "Haigho" — the assembly in a nearby pub, and the occasional road sign to recall our trip. There was Ian Stuart, "Ginger" we called him, and he gave as much trouble as anyone, and I recall his pre-match team talk, "We'll play the usual game, boys!" But, above all, there was this great spirit of friendship amongst ourselves and with our Welsh hosts — they really loved the Baa-Baas.'

Another, and very significant, factor that made the Esplanade such an ideal home was the cheapness of the account which was rendered to the Barbarians for accommodation. In the season of 1908–09, the Christmas account was £24.15s.8d, all inclusive; at Easter, £119.13s.2d. With the expense guarantees from the Welsh clubs being nothing more than modest, this was a continuing advantage, to add to the many others of the Esplanade Hotel. Nor did the terms ever become anything but generous and fair throughout the seventy years' association with the hotel. Certainly, it was significant in guaranteeing the close association that developed with the 'Esp', but the happiest chance of all which ensured the continuation of Penarth as the Baa-Baas' home, was the arrival, in 1931, of Mr and Mrs King and family, as proprietors and managers of the Esplanade. Mary and Alfred, daughter 'Rosie' (Rosaline) and Aunt Kate were the most adored of hosts and quickly became a part of the Barbarian family. But they took over the hotel at a time when rugby players were exceptionally boisterous. It was just as well, therefore, that they always gave the Baa-Baas the free run of the Esplanade, and made sure that no unsuspecting guest, in search of a quiet Easter week-end, was accommodated at

*Fun and games at the Esplanade in 1908: pyjama-clad Barbarians enjoy a late breakfast on the hotel terrace.*
Back row: *H.H.Vassall, J.M.Mackenzie, J.M.McKeand, E.J.B.Tagg (behind), D.F.Smith, F.N.Smartt (behind), J.C.Parke.* In front: *G.M.Sharman, H.Martin, P.R.Nelson.*

the same time. Rosie, now Rosaline Fitzgerald, who 'survived' forty years of Barbarian tours, recalls the first years vividly and admits to being almost frightened to start with!

On that very first tour of 1931, Crichton-Miller had brought his bagpipes; when Peggy, the waitress, called the Baa-Baas into the dining-room for dinner, the piper led the way, in full flow. Straight across the room he swept, Barbarians following behind, through the door, out on to the terrace, down the steps and off up the hill . . . dinner was very late that night. On another occasion, stirring music filled the air, and the assembled company were so inspired by their own martial rhythm that tablecloths were rent asunder in time to the music. Having, as always, paid for whatever damage had been done, 'Haigho' suggested to Mrs King that in advance of the next tour, paper tablecloths might be a wise innovation. But even paper tablecloths have a place in Barbarian legend. At the Saturday night gathering of Easter 1947, as Jock Wemyss recalled, the renowned Australian B.H.'Jika' Travers, who won six caps as a forward for England, was, in the early hours of the morning:

'. . . vehemently delivering his views on back-row defence. After he had drawn every detail on a tablecloth in the dining room, coats were off, furniture removed to the side and a demonstration given in the lounge. Now, on the Monday, "Jika" was leading the pack against Swansea when what he had so forthrightly declared could not happen actually did so! From a scrum near our left corner and about five yards out, the All Whites got the ball and scored. When the players came over to the stand side for the restart and "Jika" was within hearing range, the Baa-Baas in the stand roared in unison, "Why didn't you bring your blinking tablecloth?"'

The Irish contribution to the 'social side' of things has always been notorious. Surely everyone will have heard of Noel Murphy senior, Jimmy Farrell and the cow? Noel, a cattle-dealer from Cork, tells the story quite modestly:

'Jimmy and I were taking a stroll on the Promenade before going to bed when we saw, to our great astonishment, a cow, yes, a real live cow — taking her constitutional on the self-same Promenade. Thinking to spring something on the boys, we drove the cow back to the hotel and stalled her in the hall. Up to this time the cow took it all quietly but, possibly excited by the unexpected splendour of her new surroundings she started to bellow at the top of her voice . . .'

(and as Herbert Waddell suggests, did one or two more things besides . . .)

'The effect was dramatic. Most of the boys, apparently, had never before heard of a cow mooing like a foghorn — at least, not at such close quarters. It caused almost panic amongst the assembled Barbarians, who decided that it must be something from Outer Space!'

Then there was Mickey Dunne from Lansdowne. There was also the Marina, the pier entertainment and dance-hall across the road from the 'Esp' which always opened its doors to the Baa-Baas on Saturday night after dinner. On this occasion,

*Francis le Strange Stone and E.G.Ede. In 1911 Stone was capped once for England as a forward, and both he and Ede, a scrum-half, played in the match against Penarth in 1911, the only victory in South Wales that season. Ede was one of sixty-four Barbarians who were killed in World War I.*

the Marina would not let Dunne into the dance, quite understandably, since it was an evening dress affair. However, he was allowed on to the balcony to observe proceedings, but observing was not really good enough for the Irishman. He leapt down on to the floor and, to cut short a long story, which may have been embellished in the telling, spent the night elsewhere under police protection.

Wilson Shaw is another with recollections of police activity and the Saturday night hop – though the two items were not interconnected:

'There was great friendliness from all the local people in Penarth, who never objected to some occasional horseplay at the dance. The setting off of fireworks and the riding of a bicycle, all on the dance floor, were accepted in the spirit in which these actions were done. I used to conduct the Dance Band, for several years in succession. In retrospect, I cannot understand this as I was timber-toned and couldn't play a musical instrument. It is quite amazing what beer can do!'

As for the notorious incident concerning the removal of the policeman's helmet, the past-President of the Scottish Rugby Union (who many contend played some of his most brilliant rugby as stand-off in the Barbarian jersey, especially when in partnership with Ross Logan) has agreed to turn Queen's Evidence . . .

'I must plead guilty to this, it happened when the constable's arms were pinned to his side by Watcyn Thomas. This was not a very popular action, at least as far as Emile de Lissa and Haigh-Smith were concerned. An early return home to Scotland was only narrowly avoided. However the unfortunate constable was completely mollified by the presentation of a Barbarian book and a few pints of beer in the Esplanade Hotel!'

*Four sets of gold clubs amongst six players, something unheard of in the years since Herbert Waddell instituted the Sunday Knockout Golf Tournament at the Penarth Club! From left to right, F.N.Smartt, S.N.Cronje, H.Martin, D.F.Smith, G.M.Chapman, and P.R.Nelson, about to sally forth.*

*An Anglo-Scottish partnership: J.H.McKeand of Edinburgh Academicals and C. te Water of Richmond.*

The high-jinks and fun of Penarth have been the experience of every touring party to spend an Easter there. Together with the longest serving alickadoos, Mrs Fitzgerald, who took over as manageress from her mother in later years, has happy memories of so many likeable Barbarians that came to the Esplanade. Peter Cranmer, the big England centre, was often to the fore, whether parading through the town with a billboard, or jumping in a carefree mood from a ground floor window to the pavement, ignoring the twelve-foot abyss that lay between. His fall, broken by a fortuitously placed cupboard, did not do his ankle, nor, in the longer term, his rugby career much good. The luckless Cranmer on another occasion fell down and split his lip, whereupon his fellow Barbarians, on a vote, decided that stitches were advisable and summoned Dr Hughes from the snug bar to perform the ceremony in the early hours of the morning. Happily, anaesthetics were not deemed necessary. Happily too, the owner of the baby's pram which was requisitioned and used as a means of Barbarian transport along the promenade by this self-same centre threequarter was quite content to receive the money for a new one.

Less fortunate was Gavin Young, of an earlier vintage, who after the match at the Arms Park was first out of the changing rooms to the bus. Since no one else was ready to leave, he took a short stroll round the block to pass the time. In the meantime the players arrived, realised that Young was missing and promptly told the

*'Barbarians are expected to be in bed by 11 o'clock the day before a match — but surely that meant at night, not in the morning! Left, two England internationals, G.D.Roberts and A.C.Palmer; right, F.N.Stuart, J.C.Parke, and E.J.B.Tagg enjoy a pyjama party at the 'Esp'.*

driver to depart for Penarth forthwith. A coatless and kitless Blackheathen arrived at the Esplanade some while later!

Milk and orange-juice may in recent years have replaced jugs of ale to some extent, as players increasingly tend to be more concerned over match fitness, diet and preparation. But seldom at the Esplanade did anyone shun the offer of early morning, or late night, bacon and eggs or sandwiches. At one time, the afore-mentioned Peter Cranmer was the chef on late night duty, and though his aptitude for his self-inflicted role may be called into question, no one could doubt his enthusi-asm or unselfishness in performing his duties. Eggs were at times scattered on the downstairs kitchen floor, but there was Cranmer scooping them up, presenting his tasty fare to all and sundry, but with the kitchen becoming increasingly crowded, the harried cook was forced on one occasion to eat his supper in the neighbouring coal-house, perched on a pile of coal. His clothes were not therefore exactly in an ideal condition for the golf tournament the following day. But perhaps the greatest dis-penser of bacon and eggs was Charles Hopwood, who apart from being one of the most distinguished of Barbarian members, was also one of the most amusing. Three dozen eggs put under his bed every night was the standard requirement of the staff, and in expert fashion he would take charge of the traditional fry-up in the still room. One Easter, 'Aunt Kate' was woken by him in the early morning hours with a request for the dining room key, as it had been locked, together with all the cutlery, as a pre-caution against possible intruders! Although knives and forks were eventually forth-coming, for the rest of the tour Charlie continued to use the carving knife and crumb tray which he had already requisitioned as being the only implements with which to distribute the victuals.

The tolerance and understanding of the staff of the Esplanade is evident throughout the course of Barbarian history, though one of my favourite stories con-cerns the night after the dramatic Barbarian victory over Avril Malan's Springboks.

Dr.  Barbarian Football Club  Cr

Receipts ~ Payments account from Sept. 1908 to Sept. 1909

| | £. s. d | | £. s. d |
|---|---|---|---|
| Balance brought forward from Sept. 1908 | 197. 11. 11 | Players travelling expenses. Xmas £10. 9. 8 Easter 44. 18. 2 | 55 . 7. 10 |
| Dec. 08 and apl 09 By Cheques Received from Cardiff Swansea Newport Penarth ~ Cheltenham | 241. 3. 9 | Printing and stationery | 3. 5. 11 |
| | | Postage ~ wires | 4. 18. 9 |
| | | Subscription to Rugby Union do. to Norman Biggs Memorial fund | 1. 1. - 5. - |
| April 1909 By cheques received from P.R. Nelson ~ J. Ross Hotel a/c ~ Rly, tickets | 8. 10. 5 | Great Western Rly. a/c. Xmas £15. 11. 1 Easter 32. 2. - | 13. 1 |
| April 1909 Received from D.F. Schulz for new jersey | 7. 6 | Hotel accounts Esplanade Hotel £24. 15. 8. Penarth. Xmas do. do. 119. 13. 2. Easter Bath Cheltenham 5. 11. 7. Hotel Xmas. Metropole Hotel 6. 10. 6. Swansea Easter Royal Hotel 3. 12. 6 160. 3. 5 Cardiff Xmas | |
| | | Luncheon Cheltenham 3. 4. 6 Dinners on trains Xmas £2. 19. 6. Easter 3. 12. - 6. 11. 6 | |
| | | Petty Expenditure - washing jerseys luggage porterage, cabs, hotel, ground. men ~ porters tips Xmas £7. 1. 10. Easter 6. 5. 1 13. 7. 1 | |
| | | Petty Expss. paid by Hon. Sec. | 1. 10. 9 |
| | | G. Lewis Jersey account | 4. 15. - |
| | | Balance carried forward | 145. 9. 9 |
| | £447. 13. 7 | | £447. 13. 7 |

The Barbarian Accounts for the season 1908–09. The Baa-Baas have depended upon the match guarantees for their opponents on tour to remain solvent, and the extraordinarily generous terms of the Esplanade Hotel are evidenced by the charges for accommodation in these accounts. They always remained so, too, until the hotel's closure in 1971.

The hero of the day, Haydn Mainwaring, would not let the Springbok head out of his sight. He had sole charge of the hand-carved trophy. The head returned with him to Penarth, but as bed-time approached, there was the difficult problem for Mainwaring as to where he could safely entrust it for the night. Mrs King happened to be ill in bed with phlebitis, so the burly Welshman thought nowhere could be safer to stow the animal head than under her bed. Her reaction to this suggestion, at some unearthly hour of the night, was along these lines:

'If you think I'm going to sleep with that thing underneath me . . .'

It was in gratitude for her kindness over many years as manageress that Mrs King was presented on her retirement with a magnificent silver salver inscribed with the many names of the contributing Barbarians.

The eleven o'clock curfew for players taking part in the game the next day, chats and reminiscences with the alickadoos in the snug bar, sing-songs, boisterous dinners, pranks and japes, all have helped to build up the wealth of Barbarian tradition. And it still continues. Perhaps, though, there may be a less carefree attitude

BARBARIAN FOOTBALL CLUB

·

## 1st. REUNION DINNER

⊕

A. ALLPORT, Esq., M.R.C.S., L.R.C.P.

— Chairman —

❀

held at

**The Royal Adelaide Gallery,**

(A. Oddenino, Managing Director)

**King William Street, Strand, W.C.2.**

on

SATURDAY, MARCH 17th, 1928.

Left: *The First Reunion Dinner of the club on 17 March 1928, at which one of the original members of the Barbarians, Alfred Allport, by then a distinguished surgeon, shed light on the earliest days of the Baa-Baas when proposing the health of the club, to which Emile de Lissa replied.* Above: *Peter Cranmer, sixteen times capped as a centre for England. He was a renowned Barbarian who played through some of the vintage unbeaten seasons in the mid-thirties.*

amongst the young players of today. Some might deem them more responsible. Nevertheless, the Saturday night after-dinner entertainment under Peter Yarranton's cheerful guidance and organisation, with each new Barbarian tour member having to provide a variety act, can be quite hilarious. Picture three broad-accented northerners singing *Three Little Maids from School*, burly Welsh props going through a soft-shoe-shuffle routine, or an Irish second row forward dressed in drag — and you can understand how readily the camaraderie between players is built up. The beer-drinking may be less these days, but the fun, enjoyment and growth of friendship has not diminished. Added to all this, there is still the Sunday Golf Tournament.

The freedom of the course on Easter Sunday that is offered to all Barbarians by the Glamorgan Golf Club at Penarth is a most treasured aspect of the Barbarian tour. Although the playing of golf in the early years was a voluntary matter, it is now 'compulsory' for all to take part. In fact more time and discussion revolves around the organisation of the golf tournament than probably for the rest of Barbarian affairs put together! It is a matter even of considerable importance to certain of the Barbarian alickadoos, who were prompted initially by the enthusiasm of Herbert Waddell (never one to take such matters as golf lightly). Each team is made up of players of supposedly varying ability. They play on a knockout basis for the winners' tankards, and the sweepstake which always makes up the bar 'kitty' afterwards. Herbert Waddell is the organiser, and his allocation of golf players, or non-players, to each team — supposedly to make every four- or five-man squad of equal strength — is a constant source of dispute!

I remember Pat Orr, when travelling down to Wales on his first Barbarian tour, being earnestly interrogated by Herbert, in the way that he questioned all new-

*Nursemaids and children!*

comers on the train journey: 'Orr, now I suppose you are a scratch golfer?' 'Yes, as a matter of fact, I am', replied Pat, in all innocence. The remark was recorded by the then vice-President, and to no one's surprise Orr's name duly appeared in Mr Waddell's team when the lists for the Sunday tournament were published on the Barbarian noticeboard in the Esplanade. It did not need more than one air-shot by Orr at the first tee on Sunday for the misunderstanding between Pat Orr's meaning of the word 'scratch' and, the interpretation put on it by his team captain, to be quickly revealed. Herbert Waddell now asks newcomers if they possess a set of clubs — a safer question by far!

It has always been a day of perfect relaxation, for some. The golf may be as serious or as frivolous as one may wish it to be, although it must be said that this does rather depend upon the person that happens to be the team leader. Gordon 'Fergie' Ferguson, the ever-popular Barbarian assistant secretary, has endured the most frustrating results in recent years; and Micky Steele-Bodger is often confronted with the task of trying to make a silk purse out of a sow's ear (as far as the talent that Herbert Waddell has assigned to him is concerned) — though, as Noel Murphy junior will avow, there have been times when he has managed to do just that. Murphy was once in 'Bodger's' team of left-handers when they won the tournament. The next day the Irishman, a non-golfer, was with the Vice-President when they drove past a golf club. 'Micky, look!' said Noel. 'There's somebody playing our game!'

Above: *A Victorian pose at Easter 1938.*
Standing: *A.E.Allan, P.Cranmer, R.M.Grieve, G.T.Dancer, C.L.Melville, B.C.Gadney, J.P.Jordan, G.E.Jones.* Seated: *H.C.Lyddon.* On ground: *P.L.Duff, F.M.McCrae, T.A.Kemp.*
Right: *The 'B' Band on parade at Cardiff Arms Park in 1933. And the man in the middle on the euphonium? H.L.G.Hughes!*

In fact, when one considers the 'serious' approach to the game of, for example, Geoff Windsor-Lewis, Vic Roberts, Peter Yarranton, Rex Willis and the other 'team' captains of recent years, it is not surprising that every one enjoys their day's golf as much as they do! My personal golfing recollection will always be of the year in which Mike Weston, Roger Hosen and I were nobly skippered by 'Jock' Wemyss. We won the tankards that day; though our golf was not up to much, that's for sure. But the carefully-timed quip, and the last minute tip, offered by Jock Wemyss to our opponents, together with his own great ability to retrieve from the impossible positions into which the rest of his team had placed him, more than made up for our collective deficiencies.

The traditions of the Easter tour will, one hopes, not diminish but grow. The unique character of the Barbarian club owes as much to the intermingling, communication and growth of friendship amongst all its members as it does to its

Above: *Two of the most dearly loved Barbarian 'alickadoos' – Charlie Hopwood and 'Jock' Wemyss, both of whom gave invaluable service to the club, and whose names will forever be associated with the Baa-Baas.* Right: *A card from the incorrigible Irishman, Tom Reid, who left his Barbarian scarf behind at the Esplanade in 1957 a few days before he was to depart with the Barbarians on the Canadian Tour: hence the reference to 'Injun Squaws'!*

reputation for playing open and enthusiastic rugby football. As one of the greatest and most popular Barbarian tourists, Eric Evans, summarises the essence of feeling:

'The Barbarians bring together all the nationalities, and people from so many different walks of life and, as I look back now, of course I realise that that was, and still is, the very secret of the success of the Baa-Baas. The richness of this pattern of selection inevitably leads to a richness of play, not only on the field but off it as well.'

It was Brian Henderson, the Scottish centre threequarter, who, on the tour of 1965, wittily expressed some of the character of the Barbarian Easter ritual in the following song:

### THE BAA-BAAS IN WALES
#### (to the tune of *Messing about on the River*)
##### By Brian Henderson

When Easter comes round the Baa-Baas are found
Just messing about playing Rugger,
We dance and we drink and say what we think
For training we don't give a buggah,
We play the game well and bad sportsmen avoid
But if we get beaten we're bloody annoyed,
Now here are some tales of the Baa-Baas in Wales
Just messing about playing Rugger.

There's all sort of lads, some single, some dads,
Who're all gathered here to play Rugger.
We've nothing to lose for the Alickadoos
Know nothing at all about Rugger.
There's Hughie and Herbert and Micky Steele-B,
With Geoff, Jock and Fergie to add to these three.
They always ensure a bloody good tour
Just messing about playing Rugger.

Of the Alickadoos there's Hughie Glyn Hughes
A man who is greatly admired,
He's been coming here for 50 odd years
And many a chap has inspired.
We know Hughie's said to be kind and humane
But one word of warning if golf is your game
It's a cardinal sin if Hughie don't win
You'll never be back playing Rugger.

Then of course there's Jock Wemyss whose knowledge of teams
Is accurate down to the letter,
It's often expressed he's one of the best,
But we know a bloody sight better.
We'll never forget back in 1,9,2,4
Old Jock missed the kick to convert Ian Smith's score,
'Twas a bloody good try for a chap with one eye,
But the book says the kick was a sitter

For one day in six we take up golf sticks,
No messing about playing Rugger;
Club members that day just stay home and pray,
That we'll soon be back playing Rugger.
We hack, duff and gouge, it's a shocking disgrace,
We don't replace turf so they returf the place,
But in the clubhouse at night we set things aright,
By singing them songs about Rugger.

On the Saturday night the lads all get tight,
And at the Marina foregather,
But the Alickadoos just stay on the booze
And work themselves into a lather.
Let's not forget Herbert a player of fame,
We're almost convinced he invented the game
But while he stays in and wallows in gin,
The lads are out chasing the other.

# Chapter 8

# THE MIDLANDS CONNECTION

## BARBARIANS v LEICESTER 1900–1976

Following the cessation of the north-country tour in the early nineteen hundreds, Leicester has been the only club in England to have a regular fixture with the Barbarians. From the first game in 1909, when the match with the 'Tigers' was added to the two-match tour in South Wales, the Barbarians' visit to Welford Road has become the rugby showpiece of the Christmas Festival. As with the Mobbs Memorial Match, it has also enabled the clubs which have their own Easter tours to provide players to represent the Barbarians.

The first game was played in conditions hardly conducive to open rugby, but both teams contrived to play attractive football in the mud, setting a precedent for the continuing tradition of high-scoring and entertaining rugby. Many a player has been able to catch the selector's eye in this fixture, coming as it does in advance of the home international season; and this is just one of the reasons why the Baa-Baas have managed to raise such strong teams during the Christmas holiday, though the home team have never been overawed by the calibre of their opponents. Above all the match between Leicester and the Barbarians has succeeded in providing, for the players and the many Midlands rugby followers alike, rugby for pure enjoyment, and for those on the pitch or watching through the Christmas cigar-smoke haze of the stands, it is a great afternoon out.

## SUMMARY OF MATCHES

**Played: 59   Won: 31   Lost: 23   Drawn: 5**
**Points for: 795   Points against: 588**

Average points for Barbarians per game: 13.5
Average points for Leicester per game: 9.9

Total tries for Barbarians: 185
Average Barbarian tries per game: 3.15

First win:           February 1914 (5–3)
First Leicester win:  1910 (3–29)
Biggest win:         1974 43–4 (9T, 2C, 1P)
Biggest defeat:       1910 3–29 (7T, 4C)

Longest run of victories: 1952–1957 inclusive (6 matches)
Longest run of defeats: 1924–1927 inclusive (4 matches)

Most tries by a Barbarian in one match: P. H. Thompson (5T 1956), D. J. Duckham (5T 1969)
Most tries by a Leicester player in one match: P. W. Lawrie (3T 1910), G. W. C. Meikle (3T 1933), J. Quick (3T 1965), R. Barker (3T 1971)
Most points by a Barbarian in one match: P. H. Thompson 15(5T) 1956, D. J. Duckham 15(5T) 1969
Most points by a Leicester player in one match: G.W.C.Meikle 13 (3T, 1DG) 1933

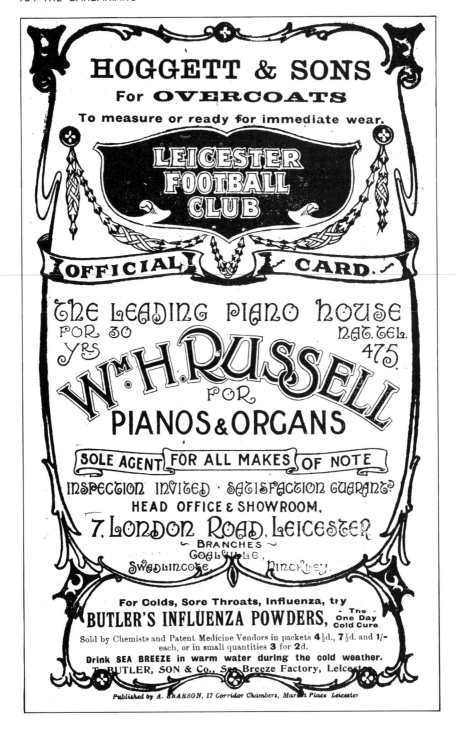

## MEMORABLE MOMENTS AND MATCHES

Conditions were hardly auspicious for the first game between the two clubs. The Christmas tour of 1909 was beset by problems caused by inclement weather. At Cardiff, on 27 December, the Arms Park had been literally under water, though that merely served as an excuse for Cardiff to show their versatility in scoring ten tries. At Newport, the following day, conditions were again atrocious. But while there had been heavy rain in South Wales, in Leicester the more serious problem was the threat of frost, which the Leicester club had shrewdly anticipated by putting down straw. Heavy frost indeed descended to compound the groundsmen's misery, but no sooner had the straw been removed, and the already-saturated turf begun to thaw, than torrential rain fell; so that although on the afternoon of the match the weather was fine, conditions underfoot were not. Yet both teams' players contributed equally to a thoroughly entertaining display, with the match being drawn with three tries to either side. As Major Philip Trevor reported:

'Both packs lasted finely and not a man in either side shirked the extreme-ly hard work which had to be done. Good as all were, one noticed the ex-cellence of Wodehouse, Jenkins and Hands in the Barbarian pack; while Penny, Gimson and Burdett were nearly always in the van of the Leicester rushes. The game, although very hard, was clean and sportsmanlike, and it was extremely well controlled by Mr A.O.Jones.'

That same local referee had the distinction of officiating in the succeeding four matches, and not until the last of those, in 1914, did the Barbarians record their first victory; though one may safely assume the two facts are in no way connected!

However 'The Tiger', rugby writer of the *Leicester Mail* did criticise the same ref-eree in the match of 1912 for giving too many penalties, complaining that Mr Jones 'is such a stickler for terminological exactitudes'. But nevertheless the referee's strict interpretation of the laws did not prevent Leicester from giving another impressive performance, to secure their fourth win in a row, while playing, incidentally, their fourth match in five days. The Tigers were exceptionally strong at this time, always had a powerful pack and regularly fielded four or five England players; on this oc-casion their captain Percy Lawrie, F.N.Tarr, F.M.Taylor and G.Ward. Thus, despite the presence in the Barbarian back division of Edgar Mobbs and the Welsh half-back pair of Newport's Tommy Vile and Swansea's H.W.Thomas (who had the previous season played together against South Africa), Leicester were too strong up front. Taylor and Wood were judged to have held their own with their illustrious half-back opponents and the Tigers scored four tries, including two by Lawrie — though in scoring eleven points the Barbarians registered the highest number of points of any team at Welford Road up to that point in the season.

On account of heavy snow which had caused the match to be postponed, the Barbarians had to wait until February of 1914 to score their first win at Leicester. There was a crowd of over five thousand for the Monday afternoon when the Black-heathen W.S.D.Craven led the Barbarians to victory, with a team that once more in-cluded Tommy Vile, this time playing at stand-off half, as well as two late replacements, provided by the Leicester club, H.S.B.Lawrie and Steve Farmer. Ironi-cally, it was Farmer who was to score the winning try against his own club:

'Early in the second half, after one of the many clever openings by Vile, he gave to Farmer, and the latter feinted at the critical moment and then made a grand dash for the line, scoring a very brilliant try.'

Millett, later to be capped by England at full-back, added the conversion to give the Barbarians victory by two points, a win 'deserved on account of the visitors' extra dash and combination.' The Tigers only score was a try by W.Dalby, one of three

The programme for the match between Leicester and the Barbarians on 23 February 1914, a game re-arranged in place of the one that had been abandoned because of snow the previous December. W.S.D.Craven led the Barbarians to victory by one goal to a try.

players in the Leicester pack to be killed during the war. Despite the outbreak of hostilities, the energy and patriotism of both Tom Crumbie, on Leicester's behalf, and Edgar Mobbs for the Barbarians, resulted in the playing of matches between the clubs in both January and March 1915 to aid recruiting and to raise funds for charity.

Lack of match practice may have accounted for some dismal performances in the Christmas tour of the post-war season of 1919. Defeats at Cardiff and Newport were followed by the humiliation of five tries being scored against the Barbarians by a Leicester side that played with only fourteen men for half of the match. Teddy Haslemere and E.C.Crooks on the wings were outstanding for the Tigers, with the halves A.Bates and G.W.('Pedlar') Wood also in excellent form. But in an exciting game of kick and rush in the mud of the following Christmas, the conversion by J.Wilkinson, the Leicester full-back, of F.M.Taylor's second try gave the Tigers a thrilling two-point victory. However the continued lack of success and the problems of raising a good enough side for the three matches over Christmas determined that this should be the last of the winter tours. From 1921 until the present day, Leicester has remained the only Barbarian fixture at Christmas-time.

Difficult playing conditions have, understandably, been an intermittent feature of the matches with Leicester. In 1922 sharp frost reduced Welford Road to a quagmire, producing a game which, as Philip Trevor of *The Daily Telegraph* reported, was scarcely recognisable as normal rugby football, though, to begin with, both sides did attempt to pick up and carry the ball in their hands:

'Their efforts to do so certainly amused the section of the crowd which finds simple pleasure in the simple folly of the circus clown. Often did a player who fell slide ten or a dozen yards; nor did this miniature tobogganning pay the man who was forced to indulge in it. Very soon was the handling game abandoned. Belief in the efficacy of the flying kick is banned at rugby football as rank heresy. Yesterday at Leicester players frequently found salvation through heresy . . . We have heard of forwards becoming backs when a game is opened up; yesterday backs joined forwards in dribbling, or perhaps one should say kicking rushes. To referee such a game as was seen was something of a fine art, and though Mr A.E. Freethy was compelled to do a good deal of whistling, he administered the advantage rule most judiciously.'

A.F.Blakiston, the Northampton and England forward, seemed to revel in the terrible conditions. His extra speed in a foot rush through the mud brought him a try, though, with four minutes of the match remaining, a wild miskick on the Barbarian goal-line planted the ball in Frank Taylor's arms for the equalising score, and a fair and reasonable result. But it was certainly a pity that the crowd did not have a chance to see the running and handling brilliance of the internationals A.C.Wallace, George Aitken and H.H.Forsayth of Scotland, H.P.Jacob and E.J.Massey of England, who were in the Barbarian back division that day.

Bernard Gadney, a famous Leicester 'Tiger' and Barbarian, who was capped fourteen times for England at scrum-half between 1932 and 1938.

The early 1920s were outstanding years for Leicester rugby, culminating in the remarkable achievement of supplying the whole of the Leicestershire side that won the County Championship in 1925. Harold Day, A.M.Smallwood, 'Tim' Taylor, Wavell Wakefield, E.J.Massey, H.L.Price, E.Myers, R.A.Buckingham and Doug Prentice, all won England caps, J.C.R.Buchanan and J.R.Lawrie represented Scotland, George Beamish and R.Collopy, Ireland, and C.W.Jones, Wales. Interestingly, these talented players used a different formation in club matches from their contemporaries, lining up with eight backs and seven forwards, including two halves, two five-eighths and only three threequarters. A highly successful pattern it proved to be, with the seven man pack as often as not being able to hold their opponents in the set-piece, especially against the Barbarians.

Between 1924 and 1927, Leicester won four consecutive matches, their longest sequence of victories over the Baa-Baas.

A sawdust-strewn playing surface in 1924 could not diminish the heaviness of the turf and the Tigers, no doubt well-familiarised with the unpleasant conditions over the Christmas period, won handsomely by four tries to two. Nor was it insignificant that Leicester's team included seven current or future internationals under the leadership of H.L.V.Day, who incidentally, was to score a total of thirty-one points against the Barbarians between 1921 and 1927. But even without Day, in 1926, Leicester were yet again too good for the Baa-Baas, though, in a hotly contested game, the Christmas spirit seemed for once to be lacking. According to Frank Mitchell of the *Morning Post*:

> 'At times the game was so hard as to seem to be rough, there being one instance of a player being most unnecessarily kicked when on the ground in the open. This is not rugby football. Referees are constantly in receipt of various notices as to small points that matter little, but they might well be instructed to do their duty in the matter of rough play.'

That comment may sound familiar but it was written fifty years ago! The Barbarians had to wait until 1928 for the tide to turn, but even then the game was almost half-an-hour old before the visitors took the lead. In fact it was the second of the six Barbarian tries that made the newspaper headlines the following day, highlighting the extraordinary occurrence of a full-back scoring a try — something new even in the annals of Barbarian rugby. Dan Drysdale, the renowned Scottish international, was credited with introducing seven-a-side rugby tactics into the fifteen-man-a-side game:

> 'After Laird of Harlequins and Sladen, United Services, had done the initial manoeuvring, the ball went to W.J.Taylor, who, however, was marked by Farndon. There was space to spare on Taylor's left, and observing the fact, Drysdale moved up and supplied the necessary help at the right time . . . and did it so effectively that he became the odd-man out, complete and untouchable.'

Drysdale's try was a splendid precedent for later Barbarians to emulate in more recent years. Memorable, too, was the performance of Wavell Wakefield, by this time a Harlequin playing against his former club:

> . . . as a great runner for the line, still without an equal at forward, and with few superiors among the backs'.

The Barbarians went to Leicester in 1933 with a winning sequence of eleven matches behind them and five victories in a row against the Tigers. There was an additional interest in the Boxing Day match on this occasion, since the four England selectors were present, affording especially close scrutiny to three guest players for Leicester — Bob Gerrard of Bath, and the two Meikles, G.W.C. and S.S.C., of Waterloo, who reinforced the Tigers' threequarter-line. So the game was a virtual 'trial' to precede the final England trial. It was these players, together with the accomplished half-back pairing of the two Northampton 'cast-offs', now with Leicester — B.C.Gadney, the England scrum-half and Charles Slow — that produced a convincing win for Leicester.

A huge crowd rose to the home team's performance in opposition to a Barbarians' side that included twelve internationals. There was an exceptionally strong Scottish representation in the team, with K.C.Fyfe and H.Lind in the threes, K.L.T. Jackson and W.R.Logan at half-back with J.A.Waters and Jock Beattie in the pack. But the player that was to leave his mark on the game was the 'Leicester' centre, G.W.C.Meikle. For him the match was a personal triumph. Howard Marshall takes up the story midway through the first half:

'Yard by yard the Barbarians were driven back, and then suddenly the ball came out to G.W.C.Meikle, who leapt into his stride, swung inwards past Owen-Smith, and hurled himself over the line as Lind tackled. A fine try, but Lind scored an equally fine one for the Barbarians a few minutes later. Crabtree began the movement by breaking through, and Lind went left-handed, sold the dummy perfectly and jinked inwards through a barn-door gap to touch down near the posts. This was lively football, and very soon Gerrard ran strongly, found Slow up with him, and Slow sent G.W.C. Meikle storming over the line for his second try. By this time Meikle was a great favourite with the crowd, and when, just before half-time, he dropped a superb goal from long range, the cheering was immense. Leicester were thus leading by three points at the interval and they kept up a tremendous pace. Gerrard intercepted and nearly sent Slow in, and soon afterwards Gadney broke clear from a loose maul and slung a long pass to G.W.C.Meikle who scored again.'

A brilliant final flourish by Fyfe brought a spectacular Barbarian try, but it was to be a sparkling success for Leicester and in particular for Meikle. England's selectors duly awarded him his first cap later that season and both he and his already-capped brother became regular Leicester players.

*Tommy Kemp's Barbarian XV that trounced Leicester 29 points to nil, on 27 December 1949 – the second largest victory up to that time.*
Standing: *P.F.Cooper (referee), T.G.P.Crick, H.L.G.Hughes, I.J.Botting, P.B.C.Moore, M.B.Hofmeyr, H.D.Small, G.R.D'A.Hosking, A.N.Vintcent, B.Boobbyer, F.D.Prentice, J.P.Hyde, C.R.Hopwood, H.A.Haigh-Smith. Sitting: Haydn Thomas, J.McG.K.Kendall-Carpenter, M.R.Steele-Bodger, T.A.Kemp (captain), T.W.Price, J.H.Steeds, C.B. van Ryneveld, D.W.Swarbrick (touch-judge).*

Rain and mud returned to dominate play in the following two years, which were in the midst of the Barbarians' invincible years, though Leicester were enjoying some vintage seasons too. In 1934, in a Barbarian team of fifteen internationals, Wilson Shaw excelled:

> ... time after time he drew forth rounds of applause from the large and knowledgeable crowd with his fielding, his pace off the mark and his clever tactics.'

It was Shaw (taking a pass from Logan on Leicester's twenty-five, with a sudden break and a short kick ahead) who won the game with a brilliant solo try, to clinch victory by six points to five. A year later it was closer still. For the only time in the history of fixtures between the clubs, the result was a nil-nil draw as both teams floundered in the morass that was Welford Road. It was tragic that the elements should have been so cruel, for not only did the Barbarians select outstanding sides for these games, but Leicester had a fifteen of equal talent. Apart from Gadney and Slow there were fellow internationals Leyland, R.J.Barr, Auty, R.A.Buckingham, the Meikles and Alex Obolensky in the backs, D.A.Kendrew, the Beamishes, Tom Berry, Greaves, Hodgson and Nicholson in a formidable pack. Indeed, as *The Times* reported in 1935:

> ... it spoke volumes for the skill and keenness of all the players that in spite of innumerable flounderings and mistakes, their efforts in most cases bore the closest examination. It was surprising the way that players like J.R.Auty and Prince Alexander Obolensky, for example, served Leicester as runners. For the Barbarians it was often amazing to see Peter Cranmer pick up and break away with a slimy ball as if conditions were flawless. Wilf Wooller, now a famous character, was less steady but equally lively for all the extra handicap of long legs; while there was a finish about the inevitably cramped play of J.E.Forrest and K.C.Fyfe on the wings that drew more than one round of applause.'

But conditions triumphed and neither side could score a point.

The fact that the Boxing Day fixture has usually preceded the final England trial may help to account for some repeatedly outstanding performances by current or future English caps in the match. But in 1937 there was added incentive for B.C.Gadney and J.R.Auty to dazzle the crowd with brilliant play. With typical Barbarian 'feeling' the two half-backs, by this time playing for Headingley, were invited to return to play at Welford Road. Auty's dummy and side-step were seen at their most hypnotic as he scored three of the eight tries in the Barbarians' biggest-ever victory against Leicester up to that time. Auty and Gadney excelled, and the two 'probable' England centres, Peter Cranmer and F.M.McRae, with a try each, also bemused the defence in 'spasms of brilliance'.

With the outbreak of war, normal fixtures ceased, but thanks to the extraordinary efforts of J.E.Thorneloe, the long serving secretary, and of C.R.Nunn and Doug Norman, Leicester continued as a centre for rugby football during the war years. Eric Thorneloe, like his predecessor Tom Crumbie, managed to organise 'Midland' and 'J.E.Thorneloe' Fifteens and they met the Barbarians in Service Charity Matches on no less than seven occasions. Some outstanding Barbarians took the field in those matches: Tommy Kemp, Louis Babrow, R.H.Guest, Haydn Tanner, H.C.Lyddon and E.J.Unwin, Robin Prescott, Ray Longland and Jack Heaton and many more, who helped to keep the Barbarian spirit alive during those difficult years.

The post-war years, far from seeing any diminution in the popularity of the Christmas fixture, brought huge crowds to Welford Road. In 1948, seventeen thousand people, the largest attendance ever for a club match with Leicester, saw the

**BARBARIANS   V   J. E. THORNELOE'S XV**

In aid of Lord Wigram's Sportsmen's Committee of the Red Cross.

Saturday 27th December, 1941.                                KICK-OFF 3-0 p.m.

**BARBARIANS.**

1  Major G. W. PARKER (Gloucester and England)
2  Lt. E. D. H. WILLIAMS (Cambridge Unv. and Army)
3  Lt. J. GRAHAM-JONES (St. Mary's Hospital and Army)
4  W. MASTERS (Metropolitan Police)
5  Sub. Lt. G. HOLLIS, R.N. (Oxford University)
6  Serg. HAYDEN TANNER (Army and Wales)
7  Cadet L. BRUCE LOCKHART (Cambridge Unv. Army and Scotland)
8  Capt. R. E. PRESCOTT (Army and England)
9  Sqdn. Ldr. C. G. GILLTHORPE (R.A.F. and England)
10 Capt. W. E. N. DAVIS, (Army and Wales)
11 Pay.-Lt. H. C. LYDDON R.N. (Royal Navy)
12 R. HALL (Barts. Hospital)
14 Pay.-Lt. J. K. WATKINS R.N. (Royal Navy and England)
15 M. R. MULLINS (Guys Hospital)
16 Lt. A. W. B. BUCHANAN (London Scottish and Army)

**J. E. THORNELOE'S XV.**

O.  L. G. STEVENSON (HINCKLEY) (17)
     R. WOODWARD (ATHLESTON ST. JAMES)
N.  M. HARDING (Newport) (18)
M.  F. G. EDWARDS (Leicester and England) (19) K. BIGGER (EDINBURGH WANDERERS)
L.  R. RANKIN (N.S.W. and Australia) (20)
K.  C. B. HOLMES (Manchester) (21)
J.  G. A. WALKER (R.A.F. and England) (22)
I.  J. PARSONS (Cambridge Unv. and Leicester) (23)
A.  J. H. STEEDS (Cambridge Unv. and Middx. Hospital) (24)
B.  R. SAMPSON (London Scottish and Scotland) (25) S. PRATT X.
C.  T. G. DANCER (Bedford and England) (26) O. RYDINGS (RUGBY)
D.  P. C. PHILLIPS (Oxford Unv. and Blackheath) (27)
E.  B. H. HAMILTON (London Scottish) (28) TR BOURKE (DERBY)
F.  J. T. W. BERRY (Leicester and England) Captain (29)
G.  J. P. JERWOOD (Leicester) (30)
H.  W. FALLOWFIELD (Northampton) (31)

RE BARRADELL (Leicestershire Society)

Referee : Squadron Leader C. H. GADNEY.

Official   Programme                    **Price 1ᴰ·**

The Barbarians and the Leicester secretary, J.E.Thorneloe, managed to keep rugby football going during the war years. This programme was for the first of six games between the Barbarians and J.E.Thorneloe's XV, with proceeds in aid of charity. The Baa-Baas won, with tries by Williams and Tanner, and one conversion by Parker, to a try by C.B.Holmes.

Tigers win for the first time since 1938. It was a dramatic last-minute victory. The hero for the home crowd was the giant forward and captain, H.P.Jerwood, a survivor of the pre-war Leicester fifteen. The Barbarians fielded a side of fourteen internationals plus G.A.Wilson, the Oxford captain, and were favourites to win. Jerwood, for Leicester, opened with a penalty, but the Baa-Baas countered with a try by J.V.Smith, set up for him by Lew Cannell and L.F.Oakley, and a second by prop forward D.Keller of Guy's, after a powerful breakaway in the loose by Brian Vaughan. But the Tigers' pack was not to be disheartened and their persistent efforts were rewarded, with scores by both the second row. First Lacey charged his way through for a try from ten yards out, and with the score at 8–6, and only seconds of the match remaining, Jerwood rounded off a tremendous forward assault to bring Leicester victory by one point, and send the record crowd home satisfied. That win by Leicester was to be the Barbarians' only defeat of the season.

In 1952, the Barbarians more than made amends. When Haigh-Smith wrote on 30 December to his fellow and much-loved 'alickadoo', Jock Wemyss, who had not been able to come down from Scotland, he described the game as:

'. . . one of the best I have ever seen. It was extraordinary how few passes were dropped, and all movements were carried out at top speed. Your boys (the Scotsmen, N.G.Davidson of Hawick and A.F.Dorward of Gala, the half-backs) look a good couple and ought to be very useful to us in the future. Davidson has lovely hands which is half the battle for a stand-off half.'

L.B.Cannell and Jeff Butterfield, the Northampton centres, excelled, each scoring a try with a third coming from another player from the Saints, Don White.

Three years later, the game was again hailed as one in the best Barbarian tradition, and small wonder, since the Barbarian team was largely comprised of players from the great Lions touring team of the summer. It was fitting that this particular game should have been such a fine example of Barbarian rugby, since, as a formal prelude to this match, the teams and seventeen thousand spectators stood for two minutes bare-headed and in silence as a tribute to Emile de Lissa and Jack Haigh-Smith, who had both died since the end of the last season. It was appropriate too that the Barbarians' fifteen must rank as one of the finest ever to play at Welford Road: D.G.S.Baker; A.J.F.O'Reilly; W.P.C.Davies, G.Wells, A.R.Smith; A.Thomas, J.E.Williams; C.C.Meredith, R.Roe, W.O.G.Williams, R.H.Thompson, R.H.Williams, J.T.Greenwood, T.E.Reid and R.C.C.Thomas. These players provided a wonderful exhibition of running rugby on a playing surface and in weather conditions far removed from those in which they had entertained the crowds at Ellis Park and Newlands. Once again there was continuous rain and a treacherous pitch, but nevertheless the ball reached the wings remarkably often, and Tony O'Reilly scored two tries. His first was typical of the adventurous style that characterises Barbarian play. Smith threw a high ball into the line, Rhys Williams caught it and from scrum-half Johnny Williams the ball moved swiftly down the line from Thomas to Wells to Davies and finally to O'Reilly. He, gathering the ball with his left hand, accelerated, rounded his man and scored a classical winger's try.

O'Reilly's strong running crowned with a five-yard dive brought his second try and he, too, was responsible for the third, when he darted up the blind side, and on being held flipped an inside pass to Robin Roe for the hooker to go over. It was appropriate that the 'front row union' should have been amongst the points, since Meredith, Roe and Williams had been very much in evidence in the loose, in addition to being their usual dominant selves in the set-piece! Let it not be thought, however, that Leicester were outclassed for, despite the absence through injury of their captain John Elders, Chawner, Ashurst, Konig and acting-skipper Tom Bleasdale, led a spirited forward battle. There were many compliments paid also to the young Wyggeston Grammar School boy, Mike Wade, in the centre — seven years before he was capped for England.

It would be fair to say that seldom have Leicester been overwhelmed at forward and that many of the Barbarians' victories are rather attributable to superiority in the backs, where the problems of organisation and 'settling-down' for a scratch unit are perhaps not quite so manifest. That was certainly true of 1957's encounter. Tom Bleasdale, Leicester's captain for the third time, in a run of what was to be five successive matches against the Barbarians, led his pack to a grand all-round display that day, in opposition to the formidable array of forward strength that included Marques, Jacobs, Dawson, Prosser, and Faull. But at half-back S.R.Smith and Horrocks-Taylor outclassed their opponents, and provided a plentiful supply of passes with which Malcolm Phillips and C.A.H.Davies could feed those hungry wingers, Peter Thompson and O'Reilly. Seven tries in all were scored by the visitors, whose running in the backs left Leicester mesmerised. Rumour has it that it was a Leicester back-row forward who in this game first made memorable the 'Horrocks-Taylor joke'; in trying to tackle his man, the elusive long-legged fly-half, he lunged fearlessly forward — 'but Horrocks went one way, Taylor the other, and all I got was the hyphen!' For Peter Thompson, captain that day, it was a triumphant return a year after he had himself scored five tries — to equal the record set by C.B.Holmes in 1947 at Penarth, for most tries by a Barbarian in one game.

But 1957 was the last in a run of six wins for the Barbarians, followed by Leicester victories in 1958, 1963 and 1964. Again in 1965 the Tigers thrilled their loyal supporters with a win that was engineered by their back-row trio, Small, Quick, and the team captain, David Matthews. It was an especially memorable game for John Quick, the number eight, who scored three tries. Yet as befitted a jubilee occasion, it was the Barbarians who provided the brilliance in 1969. They celebrated the fiftieth

*The programme for the Golden Jubilee Match, the fiftieth game between the two clubs, on 27 December 1969. The Baa-Baas won 35 points to nil, with nine tries scored (and not one penalty goal within the total) in a brilliant exhibition of fifteen-man rugby.*

match between these two clubs with a thirty-five points to nil victory, made more remarkable by dint of the fact that there was not a single penalty goal within that total. Nine Barbarian tries had the crowd baying for more, with David Duckham and John Spencer giving one of their classic demonstrations of attacking centre-threequarter play. Spencer's unselfishness and creative ability helped his England partner, Duckham, to use his acceleration, pace and sense of timing to snap up a record-equalling five tries.

Victories for Leicester quickly redressed any imbalance of results. In 1971 the Barbarians were in danger of being well and truly savaged by the Tigers as Leicester ran up a twenty-point lead through a hat-trick of tries by the talented local winger, Bob Barker. But scores resulting from the determined running of both Jeremy Janion and Rodney Webb pulled back most of the leeway. The following season it was that great servant of Leicester, and most resourceful of scrum-halves, John Allen, who was the key figure in his team's victory. Nor was the Leicester pack prepared to play second fiddle, for despite the constant threat up front posed by Bob Wilkinson, Derek Quinnell, Andy Ripley and Fergus Slattery, the play of Bob Rowell and Eric Bann, Peter Wheeler and Gary Adey did much to neutralise their efforts.

*David Duckham passing to his centre partner, John Spencer, in the Jubilee Match at Leicester in 1969. The two England threequarters gave a classic demonstration of attacking play, which brought Duckham a Barbarian record-equalling five tries.*

Four tries to two at the final whistle was a fair reflection of the superiority of Leicester's disciplined and enterprising play in a thoroughly entertaining match.

But that missing authority and composure was there in abundance for the Barbarians in 1974, bringing nine tries (including two each for Peter Preece, David Duckham and Roger Blyth) and a record win in the series by forty-three points to four. All the more credit therefore to Leicester, that they made the Barbarians fight the whole way for victory the following year. The Baa-Baas committee had selected a side of exceptional strength under the captaincy of Mike Gibson, in preparation for the forthcoming match with the touring Australians. The back division of Edwards, Bennett, Tikoisuva, Gibson, Gravell, Duckham and J.P.R.Williams was an impressive line-up of talent. It was a typically touching gesture that the popular Fijian, Bosco Tikoisuva, should have been included. Not only was he one of that exuberant and uninhibited Fijian touring side that had humbled the Barbarians at Gosforth in 1970, but, since returning to England, he had brought his exciting and effervescent style of play to the Harlequins, with great success at fly-half for that club. But Leicester did not allow either him or his illustrious Barbarian colleagues to have free reign. Led by the example of their captain, Bob Rowell, Leicester's determination kept the Barbarians within bounds, in particular never allowing them to dominate up front.

The brave Leicester win of 1976 epitomises the reason for the continuing success and popularity of this unique fixture. It stems from the ability of the Leicester Tigers to provide formidable opposition for even the most talented combination of players in Barbarian colours, without in any way attempting to spoil the tradition of the match as a very special Christmas rugby entertainment. The balance of results, the exciting finishes to so many of the matches, and the great number of tries scored by either side, testify to that.

## BARBARIANS v LEICESTER

| YEAR | SCORE | CAPTAINS BARBARIANS/ LEICESTER | SCORERS FOR | AGAINST |
|---|---|---|---|---|
| 1909 | 9–9 | W. C. Wilson J. R. Watson | N. A. Wodehouse (1PT) R. H. M. Hands (1T) W. C. Wilson (1T) | J. C. Burdett (1T) G. Greasley (1T) K. B. Wood (1T) |
| 1910 | 3–29 | | W. S. D. Craven (1T) | P. W. Lawrie (3T) F. N. Tarr (1T) G. W. Wood (1T) G. Greasley (1T) C. Gimson (3C) R. Jackett (1T, 1C) |
| 1911 | 6–13 | R. Honey P. W. Lawrie | M. E. Neale (2T) | G. Hopkins (1T) R. Jackett (1T) J. C. Burdett (1T) W. J. Allen (2C) |
| 1912 | 11–15 | E. R. Mobbs P. W. Lawrie | W. P. Geen (1T) J. H. D. Watson (1PG, 1C) J. H. D. Watson (1T) | P. W. Lawrie (2T) G. W. Wood (1T) O. J. Hargrave (1T) J. W. Bream (1PG) |
| Feb 1914 | 5–3 | W. S. D. Craven P. W. Lawrie | S. Farmer (1T) H. Millett (1C) | W. Dalby (1T) |
| Jan 1915 | 6–21 | E. R. Mobbs | E. G. Butcher (1T) E. R. Mobbs (1T) | K. Pearce (2T) G. Wood (2T) W. J. Allen (1T) P. W. Lawrie (2C) H. Lawrie (1C) |
| Mar 1915 | 3–3 | E. R. Mobbs | G. E. Kidman (1T) | A. V. Manton (1T) |
| 1919 | 6–17 | H. C. Harrison | S. W. Harris (2T) | E. Haslemere (1T) W. C. Hicks (1T) A. Bates (1T) G. W. Wood (1T) A. Crooks (1T) E. G. Butcher (1C) |
| 1920 | 6–8 | S. Cook P. W. Lawrie | A. F. Blakiston (1T) W. D. Doherty (1T) | F. M. Taylor (2T) J. Wilkinson (1C) |
| 1921 | 10–28 | M. P. Atkinson G. Ward | H. W. H. Considine (2T) M. P. Atkinson (2C) | C. W. Cross (1T) W. C. Hicks (1T) J. Wilkinson (1T, 1DG) H. L. V. Day (1T, 3C) N. Coates (1T) R. H. C. Usher (1T) |
| 1922 | 3–3 | G. S. Conway | A. F. Blakiston (1T) | F. Taylor (1T) |
| 1923 | 5–3 | A. F. Blakiston W. W. Wakefield | R. Briggs (1T) W. F. Gaisford (1C) | H. L. V. Day (1PG) |
| 1924 | 6–16 | P. H. Lawless H. L. V. Day | A. C. Wallace (2T) | F. D. Prentice (2T) J. R. Lawrie (1T) A. M. Smallwood (1T) H. L. V. Day (2C) |

| YEAR | SCORE | CAPTAINS BARBARIANS/ LEICESTER | SCORERS FOR | AGAINST |
|------|-------|-----------------------|-------------|---------|
| 1925 | 9–14 | F. W. R. Douglas *H. L. V. Day* | A. F. Blakiston (1T) W. W. Wakefield (1T) D. Turquand-Young (1T) | W. E. Farndon (2T) C. E. A. Flewitt (1T) H. L. V. Day (1T, 1C) |
| 1926 | 8–13 | A. R. Aslett | C. S. Barlow (1T, 1C) W. E. Tucker (1T) | C. E. A. Flewitt (2T) H. D. Greenlees (1T) F. D. Prentice (2C) |
| 1927 | 13–16 | H. G. Periton | H. G. Periton (3T) R. T. Foulds (1C) K. A. Sellar (1C) | H. L. V. Day (2T, 2C) F. D. Prentice (1T) E. A. Sweatman (1T) |
| 1928 | 24–8 | *F. D. Prentice* | W. J. Taylor (2T) D. Drysdale (1T, 3C) H. Rew (1T) D. Turquand-Young (1T) G. M. Sladen (1T) | J. H. F. Edmiston (1T) R. V. M. Odbert (1T) F. D. Prentice (1C) |
| 1929 | 21–14 | E. Coley *F. D. Prentice* | H. Wilkinson (1T) W. W. Wakefield (1T) A. F. Heppenstall (1T) J. S. R. Reeve (1T) J. C. Hubbard (3C, 1PG) | J. R. H. Polt (2T) C. H. Williams (1T) F. D. Prentice (1C, 1PG) |
| 1930 | 13–6 | H. C. C. Laird *H. D. Greenlees* | R. C. Brumwell (1T) J. S. R. Reeve (1T) A. Key (1T) W. E. Henley (2C) | R. A. Buckingham (1T) F. D. Prentice (1PG) |
| 1931 | 14–13 | A. L. Novis | E. de V. Hunt (1T, 1C) A. R. Ramsay (1T) A. L. Novis (1T) A. C. Harrison (1T) | H. A. Constantine (1T) H. D. Greenlees (1T, 2C) B. C. Gadney (1T) |
| 1932 | 22–10 | E.W.F.de V.Hunt *D. J. Norman* | E. W. F. de V. Hunt (2T) P. W. P. Brook (1T) W. B. Welsh (1T) R. Rowand (1T) C. L. Troop (2C) J. W. Allan (1PG) | L. W. Burton (1T) P. E. Dunkley (1T) J. H. F. Edmiston (1DG) |
| 1933 | 10–21 | Watcyn G. Thomas *B. C. Gadney* | H. Lind (1T, 1DG) K. C. Fyfe (1T) | G. W. C. Meikle (3T, 1DG) R. A. Gerrard (1T) M. P. Crowe (1T, 1C) |
| 1934 | 6–5 | W. R. Logan *B. C. Gadney* | L. A. Booth (1T) R. W. Shaw (1T) | J. T. W. Berry (1T) R. A. Buckingham (1C) |
| 1935 | 0–0 | J. E. Forrest *B. C. Gadney* | | |
| 1936 | 20–5 | *R. J. Barr* | P. L. Candler (2T) J. A. Waters (1T) A. G. Butler (1T) M. McG. Cooper (2C) H. G. Owen-Smith (1C) E. C. Davey (1C) | W. M. Adams (1T) N. A. York (1C) |

| YEAR | SCORE | CAPTAINS BARBARIANS/ LEICESTER | SCORERS FOR | AGAINST |
|------|-------|-------------------------------|-------------|---------|
| 1937 | 34–0 | P. Cranmer<br>*R. J. Barr* | J. R. Auty (3T)<br>P. Cranmer (1T)<br>F. M. McRae (1T)<br>J. A. Waters (1T)<br>J. A. Macdonald (1T)<br>C. L. Melville (1T, 5C) | |
| 1938 | 6–8 | K. C. Fyfe<br>*J. T. W. Berry* | J. Ellis (1T)<br>A. Obolensky (1T) | F. G. Edwards (2T)<br>S. F. Herbert (1C) |
| 1939–1944 | | WAR YEARS | *(though Barbarians did play service charity matches at Leicester against Midlands XVs raised by Leicester Secretary J. E. Thornloe)* | |
| 1945 | 3–0 | D. J. B. Johnston<br>*J. T. W. Berry* | P. R. G. Graham (1T) | |
| 1946 | 8–3 | J. Mycock<br>*J. T. W. Berry* | D. J. W. Bridge (1T)<br>M. R. Steele-Bodger (1T)<br>D. B. Vaughan (1C) | F. G. Edwards (1T) |
| 1947 | 15–10 | M. R. Steele-Bodger<br>*H. P. Jerwood* | D. D. Mackenzie (3T)<br>S. C. Newman (2C)<br>T. Gray (1C) | A. C. Towell (1T)<br>H. P. Jerwood (1T)<br>E. Watkins (2C) |
| 1948 | 8–9 | K. D. Mullen<br>*H. P. Jerwood* | J. V. Smith (1T)<br>D. H. Keller (1T)<br>W. B. Holmes (1C) | H. P. Jerwood (1T, 1PG)<br>E. C. Lacey (1T) |
| 1949 | 29–0 | T. A. Kemp<br>*A. C. Towell* | T. A. Kemp (1T)<br>H. D. Small (1T)<br>G. R. d'A. Hoskins (1T)<br>P. B. C. Moore (1T)<br>W. H. Thomas (1T)<br>M. B. Hofymeyr (4C, 2PG) | |
| 1950 | 13–13 | M. B. Hofmeyr<br>*W. K. T. Moore* | W. I. D. Elliot (1T)<br>C. E. Winn (1T)<br>J. McG. Kendall-Carpenter (1T)<br>M. B. Hofmeyr (2C) | H. W. Sibson (1T)<br>C. G. S. Lawrence (1T)<br>H. G. Thomas (1T)<br>J. P. Morris (2C) |
| 1951 | 8–13 | J. A. Gwilliam<br>*W. K. T. Moore* | B. Boobbyer (1T)<br>J. A. Gwilliam (1T)<br>M. C. Thomas (1C) | H. W. Sibson (1T)<br>H. Thomas (1T)<br>R. H. Smith (1T)<br>G. H. Cullen (2C) |
| 1952 | 22–9 | A. F. Dorward<br>*W. K. T. Moore* | L. B. Cannell (1T)<br>J. Butterfield (1T)<br>D. J. White (1T)<br>D. A. Barker (1T)<br>I. King (2C, 2PG) | C. G. S. Lawrence (1T)<br>M. R. Channer (1PG, 1DG) |
| 1953 | 39–11 | D. F. White<br>*J. M. Jenkins* | K. J. Jones (3T)<br>J. Butterfield (2T)<br>W. P. C. Davies (2T)<br>B. M. Gray (1T)<br>S. Judd (1T)<br>I. King (6C) | A. D. Ashurst (1T)<br>D. St G. Hazell (1T, 1PG, 1C) |

| YEAR | SCORE | CAPTAINS BARBARIANS/ LEICESTER | SCORERS FOR | AGAINST |
|---|---|---|---|---|
| 1954 | 22–13 | E. Evans J. M. Jenkins | P. H. Ryan (1T) F. D. Sykes (1T) R. H. Thompson (1T) B. M. Gray (1T) R. Higgins (1T) P. G. Johnstone (2C) D. McKibbin (1PG) | J. Elders (1T) M. R. Channer (1T) D. St. G. Hazell (2C, 1PG) |
| 1955 | 12–3 | R. H. Thompson T. H. Bleasdale | A. J. F. O'Reilly (2T) R. Roe (1T) A. R. Smith (1PG) | P. Konig (1T) |
| 1956 | 23–6 | C. I. Morgan T. H. Bleasdale | P. H. Thompson (5T) J. W. Clements (1T) A. J. F. O'Reilly (1T) T. E. Davies (1C) | C. G. Martin (2PG) |
| 1957 | 25–6 | P. H. Thompson T. H. Bleasdale | A. J. F. O'Reilly (3T) P. H. Thompson (1T) R. H. Davies (1T) T. R. Prosser (1T) M. S. Phillips (1T) J. Faull (2C) | C. G. Martin (2PG) |
| 1958 | 3–9 | A. R. Dawson T. H. Bleasdale | G. Windsor-Lewis (1T) | C. Shepherd (1T) D. J. Matthews (1T) L. H. Jenkins (1T) |
| 1959 | 7–9 | B. V. Meredith T. H. Bleasdale | M. S. Phillips (2T) A. R. Smith (1T) B. V. Meredith (1T) N. H. Morgan (1PG, 1C) | C. G. Martin (1T) M. N. Gavins (2PG) |
| 1960 | 14–5 | A. R. Dawson C. G. Martin | H. J. Morgan (2T) R. C. Cowan (1T) J. Roberts (1T) A. B. W. Risman (1C) | M. Freer (1T) M. N. Gavins (1C) |
| March 1962 | 5–3 | H. J. Morgan C. G. Martin | K. A. Rowlands (1T) J. G. Willcox (1C) | K. J. F. Scotland (1PG) |
| March 1963 | 9–16 | J. Roberts C. G. Martin | D. R. R. Morgan (1T) N. S. Bruce (1T) B. Price (1T) | D. W. Bird (1T) M. J. Dymond (1T) M. R. Wade (1T) D. J. Matthews (1T) C. G. Martin (2C) |
| Dec 1963 | 13–6 | J. G. Willcox M. R. Wade | J. Roberts (1T) S. J. Watkins (1T) C. M. H. Gibson (1T) J. G. Willcox (2C) | C. G. Martin (2PG) |
| 1964 | 11–12 | P. E. Judd M. J. Harrison | B. C. Henderson (1T) P. W. Cook (1T) S. J. Purdy (1PG, 1C) | D. W. Bird (1T) D. J. Matthews (1T) C. G. Martin (2PG) |
| 1965 | 10–14 | K. A. Rowlands D. J. Matthews | E. L. Rudd (1T) A. W. Hancock (1T) D. Rutherford (2C) | J. Quick (3T) K. Chilton (1PG, 1C) |

| YEAR | SCORE | CAPTAINS BARBARIANS/ LEICESTER | SCORERS FOR | AGAINST |
|------|-------|------------------------------|-------------|---------|
| 1966 | 3–14 | M. J. Campbell-Lamerton *D. J. Matthews* | S. J. Watkins (1T) | D. W. Bird (1T) K. P. Andrews (1T) M. J. Harrison (1T) M. Brownhill (1T) J. Allen (1C) |
| 1967 | 15–6 | D. Rutherford *D. J. Matthews* | P. J. Thorne (2T) D. Rutherford (3PG) | P. G. S. Pulfrey (1T) D. J. Matthews (1PG) |
| 1968 | 19–11 | R. B. Taylor *G. G. Willars* | A. K. Morgan (1T) M. A. Smith (1T) D. J. Duckham (1T) A. F. McHarg (1T) B. J. O'Driscoll (1PG, 2C) | D. J. Matthews (2T) R. V. Grove (1T) E. Bann (1C) |
| 1969 | 35–0 | A. M. Davis *K. P. Andrews* | D. J. Duckham (5T) K. J. Fielding (2T) J. J. Jeffrey (1T) R. H. Phillips (1T) J. P. R. Williams (4C) | |
| 1970 | 18–6 | D. J. Lloyd *J. A. Allen* | J. N. M. Frame (1T) T. G. R. Davies (1T) R. Hopkins (1T) I. Duckworth (1T) A. M. Jorden (3C) | B. Jones (1T) J. A. Allen (1T) |
| 1971 | 14–20 | D. P. Rogers *R. Grove* | J. P. A. G. Janion (2T) R. E. Webb (1T) I. B. Moffatt (1C) | R. Barker (3T) D. Whibley (2PG, 1C) |
| 1972 | 16–26 | R. J. McLoughlin *G. G. Willars* | T. O. Grace (1T) M. Davies (1T) R. A. Codd (2PG, 1C) | G. G. Willars (1T) P. J. Wheeler (1T) J. A. Allen (1T) G. Adey (1T) A. G. B. Old (1C) R. Barker (2PG, 1C) |
| 1973 | 16–7 | J. S. Spencer *P. J. Wheeler* | J. J. Williams (1T) R. A. Milliken (1T) R. W. Windsor (1T) A. R. Irvine (2C) | M. J. Duggan (1T) A. G. B. Old (1PG) |
| 1974 | 43–4 | J. V. Pullin *P. J. Wheeler* | P. S. Preece (2T) D. J. Duckham (2T) W. R. Blyth (2T, 1PG, 1C) P. J. Warfield (1T) A. G. Ripley (1T) L. E. Weston (1T) I. R. McGeechan (1C) | M. J. Duggan (1T) |
| 1975 | 20–11 | C. M. H. Gibson *R. Rowell* | B. Nelmes (1T) D. Madsen (1T) D. Rollitt (1T) R. E. Wilkinson (1T, 2C) P. Bennett (2C) | R. Rowell (1T) P. Dodge (1T) M. Rose (1PG) C. G. Martin (2PG) |
| 1976 | 8–12 | I. R. McGeechan *R. Rowell* | P. J. Squires (1T) D. Burcher (1T) | P. Dodge (1T) W. H. Hare (2PG, 1C) |

East Midland Counties R.F.U.

MOBBS' MEMORIAL MATCH

# EAST MIDLANDS

v.

# BARBARIANS

FRANKLIN'S GARDENS, NORTHAMPTON
THURSDAY, MARCH 1st, 1956
Kick-off 3.30 p.m.

## OFFICIAL PROGRAMME

## BARBARIANS v EAST MIDLANDS 1921–1976

The strong ties between the Barbarians and Midlands rugby were consolidated with the establishment of the Mobbs Memorial Match on 10 February 1921, the Barbarians' only annual meeting with a county side. The fixture was created as a tribute to the great Northampton, East Midlands, England and Barbarian centre-threequarter Edgar Mobbs, who was killed during World War I. The character of this remarkable man and the circumstances which led to the formation of the annual match in his memory are recounted elsewhere. Suffice to say that there could be no more appropriate recognition of Mobbs's services to rugby football and to his fellow men.

The first Thursday in March is now the regular occasion for this highlight in the Midlands rugby calendar. The Barbarians have won the majority of the forty-nine matches played, but the combined talents of the counties of Northamptonshire, Bedfordshire and Huntingdonshire have, nevertheless, frequently thwarted the most illustrious Barbarian fifteens. Basically, the East Midlands have been a strong county team when the Northampton club, and latterly Bedford too, have been powerful. With the captaincy of the Counties' side falling upon such famous names as Eric Coley, B.C.Gadney, Don White, Lew Cannell, Ian Laughland, Ron Jacobs, Pat Briggs and 'Budge' Rogers, this fixture has never been easy for the Barbarians. The appearance of the East Midlands in five County Championship finals, including winning the title twice, is further testimony to the recurring strength of rugby in this area during these years. At both Goldington Road and Franklin's Gardens there have been many magnificent, close-fought tussles — only once or twice has it been a carefree springtime frolic for the Baa-Baas!

## SUMMARY OF MATCHES

**Played: 49    Won: 34    Lost: 13    Drawn: 2**
**Points for: 856    Points against: 552**

Average points for Barbarians per game: 17.5
Average points for East Midlands per game: 11.3
Total tries for Barbarians: 196
Average Barbarian tries per match: 4

First win:                February 1921 (19–14)
First East Midlands win:  1925 (13–20)
Biggest win: 1974 (40–7) (8T & 4C)
Biggest defeat: 1969 (3–23) (4T, 2PG, 1DG, 1C)
Longest run of victories:  1954–1961 inclusive (8 matches)
Longest run of defeats:    1931–1932 (2 matches)
                           1936–1937 (2 matches)
                           1964–1965 (2 matches)
                           1968–1969 (2 matches)

Most tries for a Barbarian in a match: S. Williams (4T, 1939), DI.Bebb (4T, 1961)
Most tries for an East Midland player in one match: G. T. Robertson (3T, 1969)
Most points for a Barbarian in one match: W. Wooller 15 (1T, 6C) 1933
Most points for an East Midland player in one match: B. Page 10 (2PG, 2C) 1970

## MEMORABLE MOMENTS AND MATCHES

The tradition of the Mobbs Memorial Match grew from strange beginnings. 'Unprecedented Incident at Northampton' ran the headlines of the report in the local paper of the first match in 1921. Adrian Stoop, the renowned Harlequin and England halfback was the referee. He whistled for no-side after only sixty-eight minutes play, and, following strong protests from the spectators which drew the referee's attention to his error, Stoop requested the players to return to the field some minutes later, to play out full-time! But the Barbarians' win by thirty-five points in a splendid match did set an auspicious precedent for future encounters.

In 1923 the Barbarians fielded a distinguished back division that included Forsyth, Aitken and McQueen, the Scottish internationals, and Jacot, Seager and V.G.Davies, renowned in English rugby. But as is the Barbarians wont, they produced an unheralded 'man of the match' in F.W.Layman. Emile de Lissa confessed afterwards that he had never seen Layman before, but Tommy Lawton, the Oxford University and Blackheath player and later Australian international, had suggested him for inclusion on the evidence of his performances in the 'Varsity team. Layman scored two and made one of the four Barbarian tries. But at a time when Oxford could boast that incomparable threequarter line of Wallace, Macpherson, Aitken, and Smith, Layman was never to win a Blue, though Northampton were pleased to have such a strong running winger in the club team.

In 1925, nine Northampton players, five from Bedford and one Harlequin, under the captaincy of Eric Coley, made up the first East Midlands side to defeat the Barbarians. Tommy Vile, the former Welsh international player, led the traditional wreath-laying ceremony at the memorial to Mobbs in Northampton's Market Square in the morning, and later refereed the match. Four tries and a drop goal to three tries was the margin of East Midlands' victory – clearly they were taking advantage of the fact that Emile de Lissa's ill-health had prevented him, for the first time, from attending the match.

The most interesting feature of 1927 was not so much the presence of many famous players in the two sides, but the fact that the Mobbs match was used as an experiment. With the permission of the Rugby Football Union, a new law, suggested by New Zealand, was played – namely that there should be no kicking into touch outside the 'twenty-five' line. In fact, with the exception of the suggestion of an alternative penalty to a line-out from touch at the point where the kicker kicked the ball and the option of a scrummage ten yards from the spot instead, this is the present-day law – though it was not finally introduced, as 'the Australian dispensation', until the 1968–69 season! But those forty years earlier the experimental law did not unduly impress, although the correspondent of *The Times*, O.L.'Ginger' Owen, shrewdly remarked:

> 'Unfortunately for those who were more interested in the experiment than in the course of a splendidly sporting game, the new rule played a very unimportant, almost insignificant part. On a reasonably fine day this match is always fast and open – it is traditionally so. No one would dream of closing up the game . . . It is of course, a game to win but it is equally so a pleasant game to lose. The real test of the rule would come in a local "Derby", or in conditions such as those at Dublin last Saturday . . . That the Rugby Union should have encouraged the experiment suggests that Bolshevist, rather than reactionary, will be the adjective most applied to them in the near future.'

Another view was expressed by Frank Mitchell:

> 'To be perfectly frank, the operation of the new rule did not impress the majority of the onlookers. It may be that the players were unused to it, for there was much looking around and hesitancy. In many cases it worked unfairly, for a full-back all alone outside his own twenty-five could not do anything for his side with certainty and might just as well have allowed himself to be tackled in possession as risk kicking into the middle of the field. It would be unfair to condemn an innovation on one trial. We must see more of it.'

What a pity that it was forty-one years before we did!

Incidentally, in the East Midlands side of that year, 1927, was J.C.Binyon of Northampton, the sole remaining playing representative of that brave company of young athletes who marched out of Northampton Barracks with Edgar Mobbs in September, 1914.

There was additional interest too, concerning the game two years later, but for a different reason. With the kick-off postponed until a quarter-past four to enable a larger crowd to attend the match after a day's work, the Mobbs fixture was billed as a 'Semi-Official Trial' and 'The Last England Trial'. England had previously beaten Wales and France, but had lost to Ireland at Twickenham, and much interest surrounded the selection for the Calcutta Cup match ten days later at Murrayfield. Three members of the England selection committee attended to watch the Baa-Baas – 'Bim' Baxter, Vice-Admiral Percy Royds, and John 'The Prophet' Daniell – all three Barbarians of the 1890s and, incidentally, all three Presidents of the RFU. It was an immensely strong Barbarian fifteen, on paper. The side was captained at scrum-half by the 'Mighty Atom', Arthur Young, at five feet four inches; it also included Carl Aarvold, H.P.Jacob, A.L.Novis and H.C.C.Laird in the backs; and Henry Rew, David Turquand-Young, Doug Prentice and Herbert Price, all England caps, in the pack. But it was not a good day for the selectors. The match ended in an 8–8 draw, with East Midlands deserving of victory – yet again served magnificently by their pack in which Eric Coley, W.H.Weston, A.D.Matthews, T.Harris and A.N.Roncoroni were outstanding. As one scribe reported:

> 'On the evidence of the day there are forwards in the East Midlands who might with advantage replace some of those who showed up so badly against Ireland. . . . For the Barbarians there was no obvious reason why this man or that should displace someone or other in the next international.'

It may be significant that Scotland won the Calcutta Cup later that month, and in doing so clinched the Championship!

In the early thirties, the East Midlands were very much a thorn in the flesh of the Barbarians. While the Baa-Baas were enjoying their triumphant run of success in South Wales, unbeaten between 1931 and 1935 inclusive, the East Midlands too were enjoying some vintage years, culminating in their County Championship title in 1934. In 1931 an all-England international back division, under the captaincy of Carl Aarvold, was beaten five points to three. In 1932, as the Rugby Football Annual of the following year reported, snow had been falling an hour before a very late kick-off, leaving the turf treacherous:

> 'Unfortunately for the Barbarians, although Spong and Key at half-back once or twice showed what they could do, and Spong and Ford worked a fine try, among the forwards only Wickett, Troop and Dunkley showed up well in the loose.'

But again it was the combined efficiency of Harris, captain, Weston, Coley and Roncoroni that gave East Midlands the edge up front, resulting in a win by four tries to three. Two years later Aarvold and W.H.Weston were the opposing captains in a thrilling game, which built up to a dramatic climax with sixteen points scored in the last fifteen minutes. The Barbarians should have learned that a powerful pack was a prime essential, but apart from the front row of Beamish, Nicholson and Skym, there was still not sufficient strength up front to counter the formidable and entire Northampton eight that was to contest, and win, the County Championship final of 1934, eight days later. In addition to the old hands of the previous three seasons the Midlanders now included Ray Longland, and in the backs, despite the absence of Bernard Gadney at scrum-half, there was the guiding influence of Charles Slow of Leicester and John Tallent, the Blackheathen. The scratch Barbarian

*The Barbarian XV which lost to the East Midlands, 11 points to 8, in 1934. While the Baa-Baas were enjoying their most successful period ever in South Wales, winning twenty-one consecutive matches on Easter Tour between 1930 and 1936, the strength of Midlands rugby at that time resulted in three defeats at the hands of East Midlands, and one at Leicester, during these six years.*
Back row: *G.S.Waller, N.Compton, P.Cranmer, E.S.Nicholson.* Middle row: *H.L.G.Hughes, A.Key, J.P.Reidy, C.E.St J.Beamish, G.W.Parker, J.E.Gieson, W.J.Leather, H.A.Haigh Smith.* Front row: *R.A.Gerrard, P.E.Dunkley, C.D.Aarvold (captain), L.A.Booth, A.Skym.*

pack did well indeed to retain parity in face of the Midlanders, half of whose pack was made up of internationals. But in the last quarter the strain of the effort told, as the fine Northampton pack wore down the opposition to finish with a fine burst — two tries were scored, by their fast winger A.R.Charlton and by centre J.H.Treen, in reply to an early try by Key and a brilliant finale by Peter Cranmer who swept through the whole Midlands defence for a try under the posts. Thus eleven points to eight was the victory for the East Midlands in 1934.

But who could have anticipated a crushing Barbarian win, eight tries to one, the following season against much the same side? It was strengthened, too, by the presence of scrum-half and captain Bernard Gadney. Strangely it was Gadney who was to stem a tide of two Barbarian defeats, when he returned as Baa-Baa skipper in 1938, the first in a sequence of six wins. The last of these, and the third of the post World War II years, was in 1949 when, under Haydn Tanner, the Barbarians provided 'rugby fare fit for the gods', as Pat Marshall described it, continuing:

'If only games were like this, open, spirited, thrilling, crammed with all that is best in football, the Rugby Union would never glance uneasily towards the spectre of Rugby League . . .'

G.Evans, Kendall-Carpenter and Steele-Bodger excelled in the loose play, J.R.C.Matthews and J.A.Gwilliam in the set-pieces, and in the backs Haydn Tanner was in superb form, sending out a perfect service to a talented back division that included Ken Jones and W.B.Holmes. But the brightest star in the firmament, amongst the fourteen Barbarian internationals, was Bleddyn Williams, who as J.P.Jorden described it:

'. . . weaved his way past four of five defenders to score his first try and beat two more with his side-step to gain a second.'

But although tries by Ken Jones, Jack Gwilliam, Martin Jackson (the only non-international) and T.Darby, and three conversions by W.B.Holmes, gave the Barbarians a formidable total of twenty-four points, they could not claim all the honours – for a try by Don White and a drop goal and conversion by little Tom Gray brought the East Midlands back into contention when trailing 19–0. It was a memorable occasion too for eighteen-year-old Wellingborough Grammar schoolboy, J.P.Hyde, who brought off some spectacular tackles on his illustrious Welsh opposing wing, K.J.Jones. 'A great prospect for England' the press suggested, and Hyde was duly capped the following season.

Don White, one of the great names in the history of East Midlands rugby, was in his third of nine years' captaincy of the Counties side when he led them to victory over Jack Kyle's Barbarian fifteen in 1953, another era of successful County Championship rugby for the Midlands side. They had won the title for the second time in

*The Barbarian team for the Mobbs Memorial Match at Northampton, in 1950. East Midlands won 5 points to 3.*
*Back row: C.H.Gadney (referee), P.B.C.Moore, H.D.Small, S.J.Atkins, J.R.C.Matthews, J.H.Steeds, J.C.Dawson, G.Williams, B.Boobbyer. Middle row: G.M.Budge, I.Preece, J.McG.K.Kendall-Carpenter (captain), C.W.Drummond, G.H.Sullivan. On ground: R.Macdonald, P.W.Sykes.*

their history in 1951, and when they came up against the Barbarians two years later they were once more involved in the final, again under the leadership of Don White. On this occasion they were confronted by an exciting array of Barbarian players. The pack was made up of the Irish front row – Roe, O'Neill and Anderson; the England back-row – Lewis, Kendall-Carpenter and Wilson; with S.J.Adkins of Coventry and the Cambridge captain P.J.F.Wheeler in the second row. The back division was Ian King, W.P.C.Davies, Jeff Butterfield, Alun Thomas, H.Morris, Jack Kyle and Ken Spence. Even without Cannell, involved in a Hospital Cup semi-final, the East Midlands gave an astonishing display, though with the usual advantage of being a well-organised and drilled team. Ron Jacobs, R.C.Hawkes, P.S.Collingridge and White were at the hub of a magnificent forward display, with the two Bedford halves, Haynes and Fletcher, in inspired mood. Fletcher scored an early try, Haynes converted it and also dropped a goal. The score remained 8–0 with twelve minutes left to play, then the Barbarians, through Thomas, Davies and Kendall-Carpenter broke clear with a final pass from Davies giving Lewis the try. Eight points to five, and the last ten minutes were full of dramatic incident – but a great defensive effort, led by Don White, kept the visitors at bay and East Midlands hung on for a great win. The home team had to wait nine years for another.

In 1956, the big crowd witnessed a brilliant exhibition of open, attacking play by the Barbarians, despite losing O'Reilly through injury at half-time. With Vic Roberts moving to the wing, and 'Sandy' Sanders transferring from prop to flank with similar dexterity, the Barbarians continued to more than hold their own in the second half. Under the leadership of the newly-capped Irishman, Jimmy Ritchie, they scored seven tries altogether. With an effective half-back partnership between Jeeps and Mike Smith, and the Cardiff centre Gordon Wells in quite brilliant form, Arthur Smith had a 'field-day' on the wing, making the most of the overlap situation that the inside backs had created, resulting in three superb tries. Jacobs, Collingridge and Coley in the East Midlands pack, and Ian Coutts and Cannell, the captain, displaying some beautifully balanced running and sudden acceleration at centre, kept the Midlands in the hunt. But even with the advantage of the extra man in the second half there was no denying the Barbarian brilliance on that occasion.

The Mobbs Memorial matches of the early sixties brought a succession of thoroughly entertaining games. In 1960, twelve tries, seven to five in the Barbarians' favour, testified to an adventurous afternoon's rugby but, as Vivian Jenkins reported:

> 'A dozen tries was a positive riot of scoring by modern standards, and it might be inferred that the game was a frolic pure and simple. In fact, it was nothing of the sort, for though there was always a deliriously reckless air about it all, there was ever purpose behind it, and some remarkably good rugby was the result. Attack was all – the spice that seasoned the dish – and the closeness of the contest may be judged from the fact that until the Barbarians scored their last try the difference had never been more than three points.'

It was significant too, that the referee for the game was Gwyn Walters, who always had a happy knack of knowing how to let a game flow within the bounds of the laws of the game. Three tries for winger C.Elliott of Langholm, two for Malcolm Phillips, and one each for M.G.Culliton and M.J.Price were all but matched by five for the East Midlands – by White, Gibson, Smith, Jackson and Hyde. The only marginal superiority for the Barbarians lay in the pack where captain David Marques excelled in the lines-out, and Wilcock on the flank gave a class exhibition of open-side play.

The 1961 match was the day of Swansea's Dewi Bebb. The previous four years had produced thirty-four tries, and now there were to be a further nine. With Onllwyn

*Mobbs Memorial Match, 1969; Mick Molloy is tackled by East Midlander Bob Taylor. Taylor and his captain that day, Pat Briggs (on the left of the picture), were key figures in bringing about occasional Barbarian defeats, and a sequence of hard-fought matches, in the late sixties and early seventies. Molloy is flanked by fellow Barbarians John Jeffrey and Roger Young.*

Brace playing the scheming role at the base of the scrum, Haydn Mainwaring once again bewildering all as to how Wales had failed thus far to award him a cap, and Ray Prosser, Bryn Meredith, John Leleu and Brian Price revelling in the heavy going, there was a strong Welsh element in this fine victory. But it was the opportunism and spirit of Dewi Bebb's running, which brought him a record four tries, that left its mark on the occasion.

For the East Midlands, the newly capped 'Budge' Rogers was at his best as a devastating tackler, while the final appearance of Don White left all to wonder how the East Midlands could ever manage without him. Interesting too was the fact, whether coincidental or not, that two days after this match, Brace and Prosser were brought back into the Welsh team — just as earlier in the season the Irish selectors had followed the Barbarian example of moving M.G.Culliton from second row to wing-forward. As if to further corroborate the helpful influence of the Barbarians, the uncapped Ronnie Cowan, a Selkirk player and normally a centre, was on the wing in the Mobbs match, the position in which he gained his first international selection against France at the end of the season.

The sequence of Barbarian victories was broken the following year by the usual impressive performance of the East Midlands pack, with new penetration apparent in the back division. Ashby and Hawkins, the Wasps pair, showed up well in opposition to the Welshmen O'Connor and David Watkins, and with Ian Laughland, the new captain, marshalling his troops, partnered in the centre with Bob Leslie, there was ample opportunity for winger Martin Underwood to impress the England selectors present. A good win for the East Midlands resulted, in a game which may also be remembered by some for the Scottish air played on bugles, melodiously piercing the

| BARBARIANS | | | Referee:<br>Mr.<br>Gwynn Walters | EAST MIDLANDS | | |
|---|---|---|---|---|---|---|
| 15 J. G. WILLCOX | ... | Oxford University | FULL BACKS | I J. SMITH ... | ... ... | Bedford |
| | | | THREEQUARTERS | | | |
| /14 J. M. RANSON | ... ... | Rosslyn Park | Wing | 5 J. EBSWORTH | ... ... | Northampton |
| 13 M. S. PHILLIPS | ... ... | ... Flyde | Centre | 4 I. H. P. LAUGHLAND (capt.) | . London Scottish | |
| ✓12 D. K. JONES | ... ... | Llanelly | Centre | 3 R. LESLIE... | ... ... | Northampton |
| 11 J. R. C. YOUNG | ... | Harlequins | Wing | 2 B. K. WILLIAMS | ... ... | Bedford |
| | | | HALF-BACKS | | | |
| ✓10 T. B. RICHARDS | ... | ... London Welsh | Stand-off | 6 F. E. J. HAWKINS ... | ... | ... Wasps |
| 9 S. J. S. CLARKE | ... | Cambridge University | Scrum | 7 R. C. ASHBY | ... ... | ... Wasps |
| | | | FORWARDS | | | |
| ✓ 1 K. D. JONES | ... ... | ... Cardiff | | 8 R. A. LOVELL | ... ... | Bedford |
| 2 H. O. GODWIN | ... ... | Coventry | | 9 B. McCARTHY | ... ... | Bedford |
| ✓ 3 R. J. McLOUGHLIN | ... | Gosforth | | 10 C. R. JACOBS | ... ... | Northampton |
| 4 K. A. ROWLANDS | ... ... | ... Cardiff | | 11 J. TRUSS ... | ... ... | Cheltenham |
| 5 J. E. OWEN | ... ... | Coventry | | 12 A. SOUTHWELL | ... ... | Northampton |
| 6 A. PASK ... | ... ... | Abertillery | | 13 A. R. TURNELL | ... ... | Northampton |
| 8 D. G. PERRY | ... ... | Bedford | | 14 D. COLEY | ... ... | Bedford |
| 7 H. J. MORGAN (captain) | ... | Abertillery | | 15 D. P. ROGERS | ... ... | Bedford |

*Teams for the Mobbs Memorial Match 1963 – a unique occasion, since the game was played at Rich-mond, due to frost in the Midlands. The match was a thrilling one, with a record (at that time) forty-four points scored. The Barbarians won 23–21, in a game of nine tries.*

pervading gloom of the pre-match entertainment, and the intrusion of a frolicsome dog who provided additional difficulties for the Barbarians in the last desperate minutes of the match.

The encounter of 1963 was exceptional for two reasons. It was the first Mobbs match to be played outside the Midlands, and a rare visit of the Barbarians to London. Continued frost had made the club grounds in the Heartland unplayable, whereas Richmond was fit, and indeed sunny, for the rearranged fixture on the Thursday. It provided, too, a record total for the match of forty-four points, including nine tries yet again, and a Barbarian victory by only two points. As captain, Haydn Morgan set a splendid example of running and passing. There was a battle royal between the centres, Malcolm Phillips on one side, Ian Laughland on the other, which was a dress-rehearsal for the imminent Calcutta Cup match. But Phillips and his partner D.Ken Jones had the edge on this occasion, each scoring a try, with the other three coming from John Ranson, Bert Godwin, whose performance helped him back into the England side to play Scotland, and Morgan, the skipper.

On a bitterly cold afternoon the following season, the East Midlands back row inspired the home team's win. Well though Coley and Rogers played, the real hero was Bob Taylor who crowned a distinguished display on the blind-side with two tries. Ian Laughland also played 'a blinder' – as Brigadier Glyn Hughes wrote to Jock Wemyss: 'I have never seen Laughland play better.'

One unusual feature of the match was the appearance of two prop-forwards as captains of the day, two highly distinguished internationals and each in turn famous Barbarians – David Rollo and Ron Jacobs.

The alternation of win and defeat continued throughout the sixties, though under Pat Briggs, and through the consistent try-scoring feats of Glenn Robertson, the East Midlands ended the decade with a flourish, winning convincingly in both 1968 and 1969. Narrow Barbarian victories, the tenseness of which I remember only too clearly, ushered in the 1970s. The prevalence of errors in these matches, coming as they did towards the end of the international season, and the seemingly inability of the players to play relaxed rugby, may have been evidence of the increasing pressures on internationals. With the new decade it seemed that additional commitments were mushrooming — at club level, squad sessions galore, county matches, regional trials. All of this added up to the fact that by March, top players had, and have, already enjoyed, or suffered, a very long season.

However, the record points-tally of thirty-two by the Barbarians in 1973 does not lend weight to that argument, though perhaps the catalogue of injuries in the match does. The seventeen-point margin of the Barbarian win owed much to the fact that the East Midlands had by this time lost the nucleus of their formidable pack of earlier years — only the evergreen David Powell remained. Three tries for Andy Ripley and further scores by Tom David, John Bevan (later injured), and Peter Preece, with four conversions by Ray Codd (whose kicking had won the match for the Barbarians the previous year) led to a huge lead. But with injuries taking their toll — the Barbarians were finally left with thirteen players — the East Midlands retaliated with three second-half tries.

Similarly the Barbarians were in command the following season, and the margin of victory was a record forty points to seven, eight tries to one. Perhaps even more remarkable than the points-total was the fact that Peter Wheeler created a new Barbarian record by becoming the first hooker to score three tries in a match. In 1976 the Barbarian back row of Slattery, Biggar and Gareth Jenkins were in total charge of the loose ball — the vital factor that in the end provided the backs with almost a surfeit of good possession. It was, however, a pleasing change, in current top representative rugby, to see wingers scoring tries. David McKay scored a hat-trick and Gordon Wood a brace.

As was mentioned at the outset, the might of the East Midlands is directly related to the strength at the time of the Northampton and Bedford clubs. The fact that currently neither Bedford nor 'The Saints' are enjoying vintage years is, one can be sure, only a passing phase. In no way should a short sequence of results in the last few years be allowed to hide the fact that the Mobbs Memorial Match has provided over fifty-five years a match which the Midlands rugby fraternity and the Barbarians alike have long cherished. There is no doubt that they will continue to do so.

## BARBARIANS v EAST MIDLANDS

| YEAR | SCORE | CAPTAINS BARBARIANS/ EAST MIDLANDS | SCORERS FOR | AGAINST |
|---|---|---|---|---|
| 1921 | 19–14 | R. H. King A. G. Bull | A. W. L. Row (2T) A. M. David (2T) B. L. Jacot (1T) H. B. T. Wakelam (2C) | H. Jones (1T) J. Elton (1T) H. F. Nailer (1T) R. Friend (1T) A. E. Luck (1C) |
| 1923 | 14–3 | J. C. Seager C. P. Tebbitt | F. W. Layman (2T) B. L. Jacot (1T) G. G. Aitken (1T, 1C) | W. J. Gibbs (1T) |
| 1924 | 15–3 | T. Lawton | T. Lawton (1T) J. C. Hubbard (1T) G. A. C. Hamilton (1T) P. W. Lawrie (1T) I. S. Smith (1T) | N. B. Larby (1T) |
| 1925 | 13–20 | G. G. Aitken | P. S. Douty (1T) D. C. Cumming (1T) G. T. E. Cockerill (1T) F. Dearden (2C) | M. A. McCanlis (1T) W. Dodgson (1DG, 1T) R. Jones (1T) L. H. Nicholson (1T) R. Vaughan (2C) |
| 1926 | 21–7 | W. E. Tucker | B. R. Turnbull (1T) Rowe Harding (1T) O. R. Fulljames (1T) C. S. Barlow (1T) T. E. S. Francis (1T, 1C) J. C. Hubbard (2C) | L. H. Nicholson (1T) J. Millward (1DG) |
| 1927 | 24–11 | F. W. R. Douglas R. Jones | W. Alexander (2T) W. E. Tucker (1T) W. H. Sobey (1T) O. R. Fulljames (1C) Windsor H. Lewis (1DG) | N. B. Larby (1T) A. R. Alston (1T) L. Mayes (1T) R. Vaughan (1C) |
| 1928 | 8–4 | A. F. Blakiston | J. A. Roberts (1T) R. F. Kelly (1T) F. D. Prentice (1C) | F. Birch (1DG) |
| 1929 | 8–8 | A. T. Young | A. L. Novis (1T, 1C) R. W. Smeddle (1T) | L. Mayes (1T) W. H. Weston (1T) T. Harris (1C) |
| 1930 | 22–6 | F. D. Prentice E. Coley | C. C. Tanner (3T) J. S. R. Reeve (2T) P. W. P. Brook (1T) F. D. Prentice (1C) J. W. Forrest (1C) | W. H. Weston (1T) R. Vaughan (1PG) |
| 1931 | 15–21 | C. D. Aarvold | W. E. Tucker (1T) J. W. Forrest (1T) P. D. Howard (1T) B. H. Black (3C) | R. C. Brumwell (2T) W. H. Weston (1T) F. Holmes (1T) A. C. B. Forge (1T) C. H. Williams (3C) |
| 1932 | 9–12 | J. W. Forrest T. Harris | D. St Clair Ford (2T) H. J. F. Lane (1T) | J. G. Cook (2T) N. A. York (1T) W. H. Weston (1T) |

| | | CAPTAINS | SCORERS | |
| | | BARBARIANS/ | | |
| YEAR | SCORE | EAST MIDLANDS | FOR | AGAINST |
|---|---|---|---|---|
| 1933 | 30–11 | F. L. Williams<br>W. H. Weston | S. S. C. Meikle (2T)<br>W. Wooller (1T, 1C)<br>D. T. Kemp (1T)<br>A. C. Harrison (1T) | V. Watkins (2T)<br>E. Coley (1T)<br>J. H. Treen (1C) |
| 1934 | 8–11 | C. D. Aarvold<br>W. H. Weston | A. Key (1T)<br>P. Cranmer (1T)<br>G. W. Parker (1C) | A. R. Chorlton (2T)<br>J. H. Treen (1T, 1C) |
| 1935 | 32–8 | P. E. Dunkley<br>B. C. Gadney | P. Cranmer (2T)<br>F. L. Williams (1T)<br>J. R. Auty (1T)<br>P. E. Dunkley (1T)<br>G. F. Dean (1T)<br>P. C. Hordern (1T)<br>J. W. Forrest (1T, 2C)<br>R. A. Buckingham (2C) | W. H. Weston (1T)<br>R. A. Baillon (1PG, 1C) |
| 1936 | 12–14 | P. E. Dunkley<br>B. C. Gadney | M. M. Walford (1T)<br>R. Bolton (1T)<br>N. G. S. Johnston (1T)<br>E. A. Styles (1T) | D. L. K. Milman (1T)<br>B. C. Gadney (1T)<br>J. A. Tallent (1T)<br>T. D. Thevenard (1T)<br>R. G. Hurrell (1C) |
| 1937 | 3–13 | J. R. Evans<br>W. H. Weston | A. Obolensky (1T) | V. J. Lyttle (1T)<br>G. S. Sturtridge (1T)<br>J. O'B. Power (1T)<br>J. G. Cook (2C) |
| 1938 | 8–7 | B. C. Gadney | A. M. Rees (1T)<br>G. W. Parker (1C)<br>C. E. St. J. Beamish (1T) | V. J. Lyttle (1T)<br>R. O. Baillon (1DG) |
| 1939 | 23–11 | R. M. Marshall<br>J. G. Cook | S. Williams (4T)<br>W. Penman (2C)<br>T. A. Kemp (1DG)<br>J. S. Moll (1T) | A. E. Brookes (1T)<br>W. Fallowfield (1T)<br>T. W. Cranfield (1PG, 1C) |
| 1940–1945 | | WAR YEARS | | |
| 1946 | 20–6 | H. Tanner<br>M. M. Henderson | F. G. Edwards (3T)<br>D. L. Marriott (2T)<br>C. G. Gilthorpe (1T, 1C) | B. J. B. Hazel (2T) |
| April 1947 | 20–8 | B. H. Travers<br>T. W. Cranfield | D. D. Valentine (2T)<br>E. Strathdee (1T)<br>W. B. Cleaver (1T)<br>F. H. Coutts (1T)<br>D. D. Valentine (1PG, 1C) | E. R. Knapp (1T)<br>D. J. W. Bridge (1T)<br>T. W. Cranfield (1C) |
| 1948 | 13–11 | R. H. G. Weighill<br>W. R. Hamp | F. H. Coutts (1T)<br>I. Preece (1T)<br>R. Uren (2C, 1PG) | D. F. White (1T)<br>E. R. Knapp (1T)<br>T. Gray (1C, 1PG) |

| YEAR | SCORE | CAPTAINS BARBARIANS/ EAST MIDLANDS | SCORERS FOR | AGAINST |
|---|---|---|---|---|
| 1949 | 24–11 | H. Tanner<br>*R. G. Furbank* | B. L. Williams (2T)<br>J. A. Gwilliam (1T)<br>W. M. Jackson (1T)<br>T. Danby (1T)<br>K. J. Jones (1T)<br>W. B. Holmes (3C) | D. F. White (1T)<br>T. Gray (1PG, 1DG, 1C) |
| 1950 | 3–5 | J. McG. Kendall-<br>Carpenter<br>*T. Gray* | G. Williams (1T) | N. Bailey (1T)<br>T. Gray (1C) |
| 1951 | 9–5 | P. B. C. Moore<br>*D. F. White* | J. W. McKay (2T)<br>J. D. Robins (1PG) | D. F. White (1T)<br>R. N. Haynes (1C) |
| 1952 | 9–3 | J. Matthews<br>*D. F. White* | J. Butterfield (2T)<br>J. A. Gregory (1T) | J. F. Bance (1T) |
| 1953 | 5–8 | J. W. Kyle<br>*D. F. White* | A. O. Lewis (1T)<br>I. King (1C) | F. M. Fletcher (1T)<br>R. H. Haynes (1DG, 1C) |
| 1954 | 26–8 | B. L. Williams<br>*D. F. White* | J. Butterfield (2T)<br>M. C. Thomas (1T)<br>J. Gardiner (1T)<br>F. E. Anderson (1T)<br>B. L. Williams (1T)<br>J. C. Marshall (4C) | A. C. Towell (1T)<br>D. F. White (1PG, 1C) |
| 1955 | 17–3 | D. S. Wilson<br>*D. F. White* | P. G. Johnstone (1T)<br>P. H. Ryan (1T)<br>N. A. Labuschagne (1T)<br>J. E. Williams (1T)<br>P. G. Johnstone (1C)<br>J. S. Ritchie (1PG) | F. Brookman (1PG) |
| 1956 | 25–11 | J. S. Ritchie<br>*L. B. Cannell* | A. R. Smith (3T, 2C)<br>R. K. G. MacEwen (1T)<br>J. S. Ritchie (1T)<br>A. J. F. O'Reilly (1T)<br>D. L. Sanders (1T) | P. S. Collingridge (2T)<br>D. F. White (1T, 1C) |
| 1957 | 24–14 | P. G. Yarranton<br>*D. F. White* | A. R. Smith (2T)<br>A. J. Herbert (1T)<br>R. W. D. Marques (1T)<br>A. Robson (1T)<br>G. T. Wells (1T)<br>D. G. S. Baker (3C) | P. Haddon (1T)<br>A. R. Turnell (1T)<br>L. Rowe (1T)<br>S. H. Wilcock (1T)<br>D. F. White (1C) |
| 1958 | 16–14 | A. C. Pedlow<br>*D. F. White* | A. C. Pedlow (1T)<br>N. S. Bruce (1T)<br>H. J. Morgan (1T)<br>G. H. Waddell (1T)<br>B. R. Loveday (2C) | L. C. Rowe (1T, 1DG)<br>M. G. Allison (1DG)<br>T. O'Connor (1T)<br>D. F. White (1C) |
| 1959 | 21–8 | R. W. T. Chisholm<br>*D. F. White* | W. M. Patterson (2T)<br>C. Elliot (1T)<br>J. Collins (1T)<br>J. Faull (1T, 1C)<br>G. W. Hastings (2C) | T. J. O'Connor (1T)<br>J. G. G. Hetherington<br>(1DG)<br>D. F. White (1C) |

| YEAR | SCORE | CAPTAINS BARBARIANS/ EAST MIDLANDS | SCORERS FOR | AGAINST |
|------|-------|------------------------------------|-------------|---------|
| 1960 | 25–17 | R. W. D. Marques *D. F. White* | C. Elliot (3T) M. S. Phillips (2T) M. G. Culliton (1T) M. J. Price (1T) C. Elliot (1C) H. Stevens (1C) | D. F. White (1T, 1C) J. M. Gibson (1T) R. G. Smith (1T) P. Jackson (1T) J. P. Hyde (1T) |
| 1961 | 32–9 | H. J. Mainwaring *C. R. Jacobs* | D. I. Bebb (4T) W. M. Patterson (2T) B. V. Meredith (1T) H. J. Mainwaring (4C, 1PG) | D. F. White (1T, 1PG) C. Daniels (1T) |
| 1962 | 11–19 | J. Roberts *I. H. P. Laughland* | J. M. Dee (1T) A. C. B. Hurst (1T) E. N. Olsen (1T) R. W. Hosen (1C) | B. K. Williams (1T) R. Wilkins (1T) A. M. Underwood (1T) D. P. Rogers (1T) F. E. J. Hawkins (1DG) D. Coley (2C) |
| 1963 | 23–21 | H. J. Morgan *I. H. P. Laughland* | H. J. Morgan (1T) H. Godwin (1T) M. S. Phillips (1T) D. K. Jones (1T) J. M. Ransom (1T) J. G. Willcox (4C) | J. Truss (2T) B. K. Williams (1T) I. H. P. Laughland (1T) D. C. Coley (3C, 1PG) |
| 1964 | 11–13 | D. M. D. Rollo *C. R. Jacobs* | J. M. Ransom (1T) P. J. Ford (1PG) D. G. Perry (1T) A. J. Priday (1C) | R. B. Taylor (2T) R. Leslie (1T) D. C. Coley (2C, 1PG) |
| 1965 | 10–15 | H. Godwin *C. R. Jacobs* | D. M. Rollitt (1T) W. J. Morris (1T) G. H. Cole (2C) | R. B. Taylor (1T) I. H. P. Laughland (1T) R. D. Turnell (1T) B. Page (3C) |
| 1966 | 19–9 | D. M. D. Rollo *C. R. Jacobs* | D. J. Whyte (2T) D. M. D. Rollo (1T) P. B. Golding (2PG, 2C) | R. L. K. Jolliffe (1T) P. D. Briggs (1DG, 1PG) |
| 1967 | 14–14 | N. H. Brophy *D. P. Rogers* | W. Hullin (1T) T. G. Arthur (1T) A. C. B. Hurst (1T) B. John (1DG) P. B. Golding (1C) | R. B. Taylor (1T) R. C. Turnell (1T) A. G. Biggar (1T) K. F. Savage (1T) K. J. Taylor (1C) |
| 1968 | 6–19 | C. H. Norris *P. D. Briggs* | D. H. Prout (1T) I. Duckworth (1T) | G. T. Robertson (2T) P. J. Sweet (1T) J. R. Cooley (1T) R. Barker (1T) P. D. Briggs (2C) |
| 1969 | 3–23 | R. M. Young *P. D. Briggs* | D. J. Duckworth (1T) | G. T. Robertson (3T) K. V. Allen (1T) K. Taylor (2PG, 1C) P. D. Briggs (1DG) |

| YEAR | SCORE | CAPTAINS BARBARIANS/ EAST MIDLANDS | SCORERS FOR | AGAINST |
|------|-------|-----------------------------|-------------|---------|
| 1970 | 26–22 | A. M. Davies<br>*P. D. Briggs* | A. K. Morgan (2T)<br>C. S. Hogg (1T)<br>C. S. Wardlow (1T)<br>A. G. Biggar (1T)<br>B. J. O'Driscoll (4C, 1PG) | B. Waite (1T)<br>B. J. V. Oldham (1T)<br>P. Sweet (1T)<br>P. F. Duffy (1T)<br>B. Page (2PG, 2C) |
| 1971 | 18–14 | S. J. Dawes<br>*D. P. Rogers* | P. Dixon (1T)<br>M. P. Bulpitt (1T)<br>A. L. Bucknall (1T)<br>R. Hiller (3PG) | N. Boutt (1T)<br>J. P. Cooley (1T)<br>A. J. Folwell (1T)<br>B. Page (1PG, 1C) |
| 1972 | 22–17 | D. J. Lloyd<br>*D. L. Powell* | A. G. Ripley (1T)<br>W. C. C. Steele (1T)<br>J. P. A. G. Janion (1T)<br>R. A. Codd (2PG, 2C) | P. Sweet (1T)<br>J. Mawle (1T)<br>R. B. Taylor (1T)<br>B. Page (1PG, 1C) |
| 1973 | 32–15 | R. A. Codd<br>*M. Roger* | A. G. Ripley (3T)<br>T. P. David (1T)<br>J. C. Bevan (1T)<br>P. S. Preece (1T)<br>R. A. Codd (4C) | A. Jessop (1T)<br>M. Roper (1T)<br>K. Parker (1T)<br>K. Allen (1PG) |
| 1974 | 40–7 | I. R. McGeechan<br>*B. Keen* | P. J. Wheeler (3T)<br>K. Smith (2T, 1C)<br>L. G. Dick (1T)<br>I. R. McGeechan (1T)<br>J. J. Moloney (1T)<br>A. J. Martin (3C) | R. Demming (1T)<br>B. Page (1DG) |
| 1975 | 12–9 | R. C. Shell<br>*N. H. Manning* | A. G. Ripley (1T)<br>T. P. David (1T)<br>A. J. Martin (1C)<br>W. R. Blyth (1C) | K. Parker (1T)<br>R. Pebody (1C)<br>B. Page (1PG) |
| 1976 | 36–10 | I. R. McGeechan<br>*G. N. Phillips* | D. J. McKay (3T)<br>G. E. Wood (2T)<br>G. Jenkins (1T)<br>C. W. Ralston (1T)<br>K. M. Bushell (4C) | K. Parker (1T)<br>I. K. George (2PG) |

# Chapter 9

# MATCHES AGAINST MAJOR INTERNATIONAL TOURING TEAMS

## 1. BARBARIANS v AUSTRALIA 1948
31 January 1948 at Cardiff Arms Park

Barbarians 9 (3T) Australia 6 (1PG,1T)
**Barbarians:** R.F.Trott; M.F.Turner, B.L.Williams, W.B.Cleaver. C.B.Holmes; T.A.Kemp, H.Tanner (captain); H.Walker, K.D.Mullen, I.C.Henderson, J.Mycock, W.E.Tamplin, W.I.D.Elliot, S.V.Perry, M.R.Steele-Bodger
**Australia:** B.J.Piper; A.E.J.Tonkin, T.Allan (captain), M.J.Howell, J.W.T.MacBride; E.G.Broad, C.T.Burke; E.Tweedale, W.L.Dawson, N.Shehadie, P.A.Hardcastle, G.M.Cooke, D.H.Keller, A.J.Buchan, C.J.Windon.
**Referee:** A.S.Bean (Sunderland)

It was a dream come true for some, though not all, of the Barbarian committee that a meeting between the Barbarians and a major touring team should become a reality. Yet it was chance rather than design that determined that the match between the oldest touring club and the Third Wallabies should take place. It was an event that

*Barbarians v Australia 1948.*
Back row: *F.Trott, K.D.Mullen, I.C.Henderson, M.F.Turner, W.I.D.Elliot, S.V.Perry, W.E.Tamplin, H.Walker, C.B.Holmes.* Middle row: *J.Mycock, H.Tanner (captain), H.A.Haigh-Smith, E.de Lissa, H.L.Glyn Hughes, T.A.Kemp, B.L.Williams.* On ground: *W.B.Cleaver, M.R.Steele-Bodger.*
*Despite the fact that this was certainly the oldest Barbarian team to play in an important match, Haydn Tanner's fifteen gave a magnificent display. The play of the Barbarian halves — Tanner himself and Tommy Kemp, the classical style straight running fly-half — was an outstanding teature.*

*The first programme for a match between the Barbarians and an overseas touring team.*

**CARDIFF ARMS PARK**

SATURDAY, JAN. 31st, 1948

# BARBARIANS

*versus*

# AUSTRALIA

**Official Programme**

*Price* **6d.**

*Ra Cornish*

was to be unique for several reasons, but which was not without its problems for the Barbarians. The captain of the day, the brilliant Welsh scrum-half Haydn Tanner, explains:

> 'The Barbarians, under the leadership and guidance of de Lissa and Haigh-Smith, had resisted all attempts to increase the number of games the club played in any one season. Whether this was a correct policy could be argued, but there is no getting away from the fact that when a Barbarian team stepped on to the field, it was consistently representative of the finest Barbarian traditions. Nor at any time did the Barbarians wish to be classified as "The British Touring Team" – or what is now known as "The Lions". Therefore, in 1948, when the Barbarians were approached to play an extra game against the Australians, at the end of their tour, it must have been a difficult decision to take.'

Two reasons were put forward for the creation of this additional game; first, that more money was required to meet the increasing expenses of a touring side. Secondly, the Australians, already planning to return home via the Atlantic route on account of shipping problems, had accordingly expressed a wish to travel via Canada, playing several exhibition matches in British Columbia in an effort to stimulate the game of rugby football in that land. It was that second reason that decided the issue in favour of the Barbarian game being arranged.

The Four Home Union officials met in Edinburgh and invited the Barbarians to select a strong side to oppose the Wallabies. But where should the game be played? Since it was primarily a 'fund-raising exercise' for the Australians, Cardiff Arms Park was chosen as the place which would guarantee a 'full house'. The next problem for the Barbarian Committee was the selection of an appropriate team and, as Haydn Tanner recalls, that also meant a break with the Baa-Baas' tradition:

'We even held a selection meeting, after the England v Wales game at Twickenham, with those not being able to be present allowed to write in their teams. The absentees were not denied their "rights", as if that was at all possible knowing the characters! What confusion! It was emphasised that it had to be a Barbarian Team and not one representing the UK.'

In spite of the problems a side was chosen, but that was not an end to the un- usual proceedings:

'A practice session was held on the Friday afternoon – something unheard of in the history of the Barbarians. Anyone who has been associated with the Barbarians will realise that with players old and new, committee and camp followers, drawn from the four countries, the permutations of theories and tactics were unlimited. One of the more memorable "suggestions" was that because of Micky Steele-Bodger's lack of height, he should position himself in front of the line-out and not at the back. Neither the player nor I was impressed and the normal positioning was adopted. There was great conjecture before the game as to whether the Barbarians would adopt their normal style of play or "tighten it up". Contrary to popular opinion, there was no agreement between Trevor Allan, who captained Australia in the absence of Bill McLean, and myself as to the type of game we would play. There was plenty of movement and Barbarian-style handling, to such an extent that Tommy Kemp complained bitterly in the first half when a Barba- rian kicked for touch. The result was a thoroughly enjoyable match, but how we heaved a sigh of relief when the final whistle went.'

The Barbarian Fifteen that took the field in that first memorable encounter with an international touring team included six internationals from England, five from Wales, two from Scotland and one from Ireland, with the Blackheath winger Martin Turner, as the only uncapped player, initiating that pleasing tradition for most of the future 'touring side' matches.

For the crowd of 45,000 the match proved to be a great spectacle. The Barba- rians, with the wind in their favour, scored first. Tanner fed C.B.Holmes, the Olympic sprinter, on the blind side from a loose-scrum and the winger kicked infield. Micky Steele-Bodger, terrier-like, chased the loose ball as it rolled towards the Wallabies' goal-line, controlled it with his feet and followed through to gain the try. Haydn Tanner was injured in the move and briefly left the field, with Billy Cleaver moving up to scrum-half. Tanner returned and the game became increasingly exciting as the Wallabies matched the adventurous style of the Baa-Baas in a manner that brought tremendous appreciation from the crowd. Before the half-time whistle, Australia equalised. Mullen was penalised for 'foot-up' at the scrum, and A.E.J.Tonkin, the Wallaby right-wing, kicked a fine penalty goal from the touch-line, bouncing the ball off the cross-bar. Then, just on the interval, Tommy Kemp set Bleddyn Williams racing away, and the 'prince of centre threequarters' side-stepped, weaved and carved his way through the Australian defence for almost eighty yards, but, with the crowd roaring in delight, Perry, of England, took Williams's pass only to bring down the corner flag as he crossed the goal line. The cheers died in disappointment, and half-time came with the score at three points all.

The quality of play reached still greater heights in the second half, as the Barbarians produced some magnificent moves. After ten minutes, it was Bleddyn Williams who again found the gap. Cutting through, he found his forwards up in support — first Bill Tamplin, then Perry, who handed on to Joe Mycock, before Ian Henderson, the prop-forward, gave C.B.Holmes the pass that sent him sprinting in for a magnificent try in the corner.

The third and last of the Barbarian scores was another gem, this time from a scrum just inside the Australian half. Tanner was involved at both the start and finish; he broke from the scrum, passed to Kemp, the fly-half, who fed on to Williams, from Williams to Cleaver, Cleaver back to Williams who, in turn, linked to Turner. Then just as the movement looked set to die out when the winger was held, as if from nowhere Haydn Tanner appeared outside Turner to take the final pass and score the try that crowned a brilliant game by the Welshman. But far from giving up, the Australians were spurred to greater efforts. Despite an injury to Max Howell, their centre, (Buchan moving out from the scrum) the Wallabies countered with some thrilling combined movements which, in the final minutes, were rewarded. A powerful burst by MacBride, who had moved in from the wing to centre, was supported by Broad and Allan who sent the ball out to Tonkin. He then outstripped the Barbarian defence to set the seal on a great exhibition of football. At the final whistle the crowd surged on to the field and everyone acclaimed the thirty players until all of them had departed for the changing rooms. The obvious jubilation amongst the Barbarian hierarchy that included Emile de Lissa, 'Haigho' Glyn Hughes, 'Jock' Hartley, Howard Marshall, and 'Jock' Wemyss, in the Committee Box, was entirely understandable. It was a triumphant occasion and what a precedent had been set!

'Today has been the greatest in the long history of the Barbarian Football Club' said Emile de Lissa at the after-match dinner, and it was appropriate, too, that in proposing the toast to the Australian touring team, he chose to invite Bill McLean, the injured Wallaby captain, into membership of the Barbarians. In accepting the honour, McLean replied: 'It is an honour that rugby men all over the world try to achieve and I am very proud of it.'


## 2. BARBARIANS v SOUTH AFRICA 1952
26 January 1952 at Cardiff Arms Park

Barbarians 3 (1T) South Africa 17 (2T, 1C, 3PG)
**Barbarians:** G.Williams; J.E.Woodward, B.L.Williams, L.B.Cannell, K.J.Jones; C.I.Morgan, W.R.Willis; R.V.Stirling, D.M.Davies, J.McG.K.Kendall-Carpenter, E.R.John, J.E.Nelson (captain), V.G.Roberts, J.R.G.Stephens, W.I.D.Elliot.
**South Africa:** A.C.Keevy; F.P.Marais, R.A.M. van Schoor, M.T.Lategan, J.K.Ochse; P.G.Johnstone, P.A. du Toit; F.E. van der Ryst, W.Delport, H.J.Bekker, E.Dinklemann, J.M. du Rand, S.P.Fry, H.S.V.Muller (captain), C.J. van Wyk.
**Referee:** M.J.Dowling (Ireland)

It was almost inevitable that the game to follow the 'classic' of 1948 would suffer by comparison. Furthermore, the Fourth Springboks were an exceptionally strong side. Under the captaincy of Basil Kenyon (who sadly could play only five games on tour on account of an injured eye), the South Africans had won twenty-four of their twenty-five matches, losing only to London Counties. They had beaten all four home countries, including the record victory in an official international, by 44 points to nil, against Scotland. A daunting prospect, therefore, faced the Barbarians. But, confounding those who either feared or, conversely, favoured the idea of selecting a team of players to represent the 'British Isles', whether members of the club or not,

*Barbarians v South Africa, 1952.*
Back row: *Windsor H.Lewis, H.Waddell, B.Mullan.* Standing: *W.E.Crawford, H.L.G.Hughes, W.I.D.Elliot, J.McG.K.Kendall-Carpenter, J.R.G.Stephens, E.R.John, J.E.Woodward, R.V.Stirling, M.R.Steele-Bodger, H.A.Haigh Smith.* Sitting: *G.Williams, B.L.Williams, J.E.Nelson (captain), D.M.Davies, K.J.Jones.* On ground: *L.B.Cannell, C.I.Morgan, W.R.Willis, V.G.Roberts.*

the Committee selected only established members, with no deliberate attempt to choose the fifteen players in Britain that were most likely to beat the touring side. Significantly, with Ireland playing France on the same day, Jimmy Nelson, the Ulsterman, was invited to be captain. Nelson had toured with the Lions in 1950, but did not play international rugby in 1952, being regarded as something of a veteran by that time. But Irish forwards, as we know, are everlasting, and Nelson was to be capped again in 1954! Apart from the absent Irishman, Lewis Jones was another obvious omission from the side, and he had been injured at Twickenham the previous Saturday. But although there was no shortage of talented backs, it is doubtful whether a forward combination could have been found that would have overcome the powerful Springbok pack on that January afternoon.

The match was marred by many errors, the majority of them made by the Barbarians; indeed, most of the South African points were directly attributable to Barbarian defensive lapses. Yet when Bleddyn Williams, who had performed so well against the Australians four years previously, broke through the Springbok defence early in the first half, there was little to indicate that the Barbarians were ultimately to be well beaten. Williams linked to his clubmate, Cliff Morgan, and the dashing stand-off, seeing his way to the goal line blocked, lobbed a high pass out to the right wing, J.E.Woodward. The ball finally went loose on the Springbok line, only for that great marauding back-row from Scotland, W.I.D.Elliot, to pounce on it, with the suspicion of a knock-on, for a try. Thus an early lead was established by the Barbarians, but the Springboks equalised before half-time. Marais, on the wing, kicked across field, Woodward misjudged it, and the swift but stocky 'Chum' Ochse (junior), baggy shorts and all, sped in for the try.

*F.P.Marais, the Springbok winger, brings to an end Ken Jones's strong run. But there were few real chances for the Barbarian backs, as the mighty Springbok pack dominated the forward battle.*

In the second half the Springboks gained the ascendancy and this may have been due in part to the changes which captain Hennie Muller made in his back-line. With both accredited fly-halves, Hannes Brewis and Dennis Fry, unavailable through injury, Paul Johnstone, normally a wing, began the match at out-half, a position in which he had only once before played in first class rugby three years previously for Natal against Transvaal. Johnstone did not provide the vital link in the first half, so at the interval he changed initially with Ochse on the wing, only for Muller to further

*Ernst Dinkelmann leads the Springbok drive through the line-out, but is held by Rhys Stephens. The other players, from left to right, are John Kendall-Carpenter, Rex Willis, Stephen Fry, F. van der Ryst and Tjol Lategan.*

restructure his side, moving 'Jakkals' Keevy up from full-back with Marais taking his place, Johnstone switching to the right wing and Ochse back to the left. Drastic reorganisation indeed, but it produced the desired effect. Keevy, small and agile, produced the missing spark, and was the instigator of the Springbok revival. He kicked two penalties, and having gained the lead the South Africans took control. A strong forward rush led by 'Salty' du Rand, 'Jaap' Bekker and Stephen Fry (a formidable trio indeed!), took play into the Baa-Baas' half. Muller then passed to Ochse, he slipped the ball inside to Ryk van Schoor, and there was 'Basie' van Wyk to barge over, bald head first, for the try. Johnstone added a penalty, and only the defiant efforts of the Barbarians' backs and back row in defence kept the massive Springbok forward machine at bay.

## 3. BARBARIANS v NEW ZEALAND 1954

20 February 1954 at Cardiff Arms Park

Barbarians 5 (1T, 1C) New Zealand 19 (4T, 2C, 1DG)
**Barbarians:** I.King, K.J.Jones, J.Butterfield, W.P.C.Davies, G.M.Griffiths; C.I.Morgan, W.R.Willis (captain); C.R.Jacobs, E.Evans, J.H.Smith, R.C.Hawkes, J.R.G.Stephens, R.C.C.Thomas, S.Judd, D.F.White.
**New Zealand:** R.W.H.Scott; M.J.Dixon, J.T.Fitzgerald, R.A.Jarden; B.B.J.Fitzpatrick, R.G.Bowers; K.Davis; K.L.Skinner, R.C.Hemi, H.L.White, D.O.Oliver, R.A.White, G.N.Dalzell, R.C.Stuart (captain), W.A.McCaw.
**Referee**: Ivor David (Neath)

The selection of Barbarian teams, even for the most important matches, has been managed, with rare exceptions like 1948, in a most informal way — by postal correspondence between the 'alickadoos' and, more recently, by telephone as well. The letters travelled especially thick and fast between the members of the Barbarian hierarchy in the weeks prior to the first match with the All Blacks in 1954. Haigh-Smith to 'Jock' Wemyss:

> 'I feel we ought to try and get together eight grafters who will stay down and push and get kneaded into the close work. You know the NZ hate the wing-forward, who, they contend, spoils the game. I wonder whether they would "play" if we had a gentlemen's agreement not to play "winging tactics"?.... Don't forget that Judd led the Cardiff pack who beat them and that Cardiff played to a fixed plan which Judd must know all about.... Whatever you do on Sat. week watch Stephens, Meredith, Thomas and Judd, and John if he is playing. I hear Griffiths is playing again.'

Herbert Waddell to 'Jock' Wemyss, prior to the Leicester match December 1953:

> 'The queries are Smith (J.H.Smith of Ireland) or Ron Jacobs? I think it is important we go for the two front rows that we want against the New Zealanders. At Leicester, we must get these and the line-out right. In the back row I would have Judd and Kavanagh or Elliot, if he is playing well . . .'

Micky Steele-Bodger to Haigh Smith:

> '. . . I think Ken Jones is a "must". I believe it would be a mistake to ask Cardiff to release too many players for the Leicester game, and although it would be nice to have a trial run, I do not feel we ought to pick the exact side you want for the New Zealand game. I would suggest trying out a reserve pair of half-backs, O'Meara and Regan.'

Haigh Smith to Herbert Waddell:

> ... I wrote to Don White and Eric Coley ... they both mention Jacobs, a front row Northampton forward who is a farmer. He is pretty good. As you know, Northampton are pretty hot. The only thing I am sorry about at the moment is that there is no place for Rhys Stephens, who is almost certain to be captain of Wales, but you can't get a quart of beer into a pint pot!'

Letter upon letter, agreement and disagreement, inside information, 'outside' opinions, and in the end, after much heart-searching, a Barbarian selection is made; the ultimate decision, if required, being that of the President. But in 1954, impressive a line-up though it may have been, it was not sufficient to stay the might of Bob Stuart's All Blacks. New Zealand went to Cardiff in February with defeats there already by both Cardiff and Wales. The third occasion, in the by now customary final match, was to end in triumph for the touring side — a fine game of rugby, and an outstanding display by one man above all, Bob Scott, the All Black full-back.

*Barbarians v New Zealand, 1954.*
Back row: *I.David (referee), H.L.G.Hughes, C.R.Jacobs, W.P.C.Davies, R.C.C.Thomas, S.Judd, R.C.Hawkes, J.H.Smith, M.R.Steele-Bodger, H.A.Haigh Smith.* Middle row: *K.J.Jones, J.R.G.Stephens, W.R.Willis (captain), I.King, D.F.White.* On ground: *J. Butterfield, G.M.Griffiths, C.I.Morgan, E.Evans.*

As with the preceding game against the Springboks, the Barbarian pack was never able to settle down to its task — a perennial problem for a 'scratch' eight against a team that had played twenty-seven matches together. Yet it was the Barbarians who took the lead in the first half. In an almost bewildering sequence of attack and counter-attack, all menacing, nearly all thwarted, it was Ian King, the Harrogate full-back, who, ever-ready to run, gathered a long New Zealand drop out, made for the open spaces, and speculatively kicked on down-field. Scott, the opposing full-back, slipped, Gareth Griffiths picked up and darting off one foot, then the other, side-stepped between four defenders for a brilliant try. King converted and the Barbarians led five-nil after twenty-eight minutes' play.

All the remaining points in the match came from the All Blacks. Bob Scott, gathering a misdirected kick by Stephens, dropped a goal from forty yards to make it 5-3

*A memorable end to a great occasion: Barbarians, All Blacks, and referee link hands for* Now is the Hour. *Clem Thomas has the match ball safely stowed away! Left to right: R.C.Stuart (New Zealand captain), Ivor David (referee), R.C.C.Thomas, Kevin Skinner and Ian King.*

at half-time — a score line that in no way reflected the thrills and excitement of forty minutes' play that delighted the crowd. The second half was characterised by the All Blacks in the ascendant. High kicks from the base of the scrum by Keith Davis paid dividends when the scrum-half followed up his own lofted punt to beat the defence for the first try. Ron Jarden kicked the conversion, and then ten minutes later converted his own try, after the brave Barbarian defence of Jeff Butterfield and W.P.C.Davies had been outflanked by the incursion of Bob Scott into the line. Time and again it was Scott who made the clean breaks, in a majestic full-back display. But he would be the first to admit that such a commanding performance could not have been achieved without the authority up front of the All Black pack — notably inspired by R.A. 'Tiny' White, who ruled the line-out and dominated the loose. Davis made a second try, the All Blacks' third, this time for Maurice Dixon on the wing, after a brilliant blind side break. Then in fitting style a fourth was scored by White, after Dixon and Bill McCaw had set him up for his powerful thrust to the line. It was a great day for White, it was even more of a triumph for Bob Scott — and to think that the Aucklander Scott had announced his retirement from international rugby back in 1951!

But perhaps the lasting memory of that day, for Scott and for everyone present in Cardiff, will be of the scenes at the end of the match; the 60,000 crowd in a spontaneous massed farewell to the All Blacks, lending their voices first to *Auld Lang Syne* as both teams linked hands in the middle of the Arms Park, and then to the old Maori folk song *Haera Ra* ('Now is the Hour') as the hero of the All Blacks, Bob Scott, and his captain, Bob Stuart, were hoisted high on the shoulders of the Barbarian players as they left the field. What a marvellous way for two great All Blacks to end their international careers.

### 4. BARBARIANS v AUSTRALIA 1958
22 February 1958 at Cardiff Arms Park

Barbarians 11 (3T, 1C) Australia 6 (2T)
**Barbarians:** R.W.T.Chisholm; A.R.Smith, G.T.Wells, M.S.Phillips, A.J.F.O'Reilly; C.I.Morgan (captain), A.A.Mulligan; N.Shehadie, A.R.Dawson, C.R.Jacobs, R.W.D.Marques, W.R.Evans, P.G.D.Robbins, J.Faull, A.Robson.
**Australia:** T.G.Curley; A.R.Morton, R.Phelps, J.K.Lenehan, K.J.Donald; R.M.Harvey, D.M.Connor; R.A.L.Davidson (captain), R.Meadows, G.N.Vaughan, D.M.Emanuel, A.R.Miller, J.E.Thornett, N.M.Hughes, W.J.Gunter.
**Referee:** G.A.Walker (RAF)

The Fourth Wallabies' tour of 1957–58 had been a frustrating experience for the tourists by the time of their final match in Britain, against the Barbarians at Cardiff. Australia had lost all four international matches, but never by a margin greater than six points. Not surprisingly after twenty-nine games, the Wallabies had also incurred injury problems – J.A.Phipps, their most experienced centre, broke a leg early on, and three other backs, S.W.White, O.G.Fox and Arthur Simmons were all unavailable for selection for this last game. For both skipper Bob Davidson and nineteen-year-old full-back Terry Curley, it was to be the twenty-fourth appearance on tour. But just as their Wallaby predecessors had contrived to make the first Barbarians' 'international' match such a thrilling encounter, so Davidson's young and battle-weary squad managed to save their finest performance until last.

The Barbarians, under Cliff Morgan's captaincy, had a splendidly cosmopolitan side, with three Scottish, three Welsh and three Irish internationals, four from England and one from Australia. The inclusion in the Barbarians' side of Nick Shehadie,

*Barbarians v Australia, 1958.*
Back row: *R.W.T.Chisholm, C.R.Jacobs, A.J.F.O'Reilly, W.R.Evans, R.W.D.Marques, J.W.Faull, A.Robson, P.G.D.Robbins, V.G.Roberts (touch-judge).* Middle row: *N.Shehadie, A.R.Smith, C.I.Morgan, A.R.Dawson, G.T.Wells.* On ground: *M.S.Phillips, A.A.Mulligan.*

the prop forward from New South Wales, was a typically thoughtful gesture by the Committee. Shehadie was in the Australian team of 1948 that met the Baa-Baas in that first game, and now at thirty, some ten years later, he was making his sixth over-seas tour in Australian colours. Not only was he a great player and the most-capped Wallaby of the time, but he had proved himself an outstanding sporting representa-tive of his country off the field as well. Apart from the personal honour bestowed upon Shehadie, the invitation extended to him to play against his own team-mates underlined, as Vivian Jenkins pointed out at the time, an aspect of the Barbarians that was frequently overlooked:

'Since these matches between the club and touring sides from the Domin-ions were inaugurated, there has been a tendency to regard the Barbarians' team as a fully representative British Isles team in disguise. The Baa-Baas themselves have always been at pains to deny this, pointing out that no one is included who is not already a former playing member of the club. The selection of Shehadie on this occasion breaks that rule, but is also the exception that goes to prove it. It does more than that. It emphasises that membership of the Barbarians is in no way confined to players from the British Isles only.'

Eighteen years after the match of 1958, Sir Nicholas Shehadie, OBE, former Lord Mayor of Sydney, recalled in the programme of the Barbarians v Australia match of 1976, his experiences as a member of the Barbarians' team against Bob Davidson's Wallabies:

'It only seems like yesterday when "Hughie" assembled the team in the Esplanade Hotel, Penarth, and at the team meeting he said, "Today, we want to bring out the best in the Australian team and play the game in the true Barbarian spirit. Shehadie, you may purchase a team tie and Cliff Morgan, you are the captain today." No doubt, that was the best pre-match team-talk I have ever heard! It was also the only occasion that I have been a member of a winning team at Cardiff Arms Park!'

The playing surface of the Arms Park was slippery and treacherous after hours of rain before the match. So even greater credit was due to the players for producing a spectacular display of handling, open rugby. Certainly this was partly the con-sequence of a brief pre-match meeting and understanding between 'Hughie', Terry McClenaghan, the Wallabies' manager, and Bob Davidson, and an agreement to throw the ball about despite the weather. If even a third of the constant flow of ad-venturous, attacking movements had led to tries it would have been a very high-scoring game, but seldom were the moves completed — partly on account of 'scor-ing' passes falling to the ground, and partly because the muddy conditions favoured the destructive work of the back-row forward. But for all that, five tries were scored, and no one could have wished for a finer exhibition of rugby in difficult conditions.

Australia scored first, when Dave Emanuel followed up a kick-ahead from a move started by Ken Donald. Before half-time, the Barbarians drew level when Peter Robbins caught five-eighth Harvey in possession, Adam Robson, David Marques and Ron Jacobs took the loose ball on in a foot-rush, and the young Cardiff second row W.R.Evans scored the try.

Early in the second half the Barbarians took the lead. Malcolm Phillips charged down an attempted dropped goal by Lenehan, Tony O'Reilly booted the ball far down field, almost out of Curley's hands as he endeavoured to gather. The long chase after it was won by O'Reilly, who fly-hacked on once more, only to slip, but Phillips tore past him, tapped the ball over the line and scored. The Barbarians' third try was initiated by a break out of defence by Cliff Morgan. O'Reilly then hoisted the

*Australia's captain, Bob Davidson, charges through from a line-out as Barbarian hooker Ronnie Dawson makes a good tackle.*

ball high and deep into the Wallabies' twenty-five; Curley in defence, and O'Reilly chasing, collided, the ball went loose and Ronnie Dawson kicked on to follow up and score under the posts. John Faull converted the try.

The final score of the match was thought by many to be one of the best of the Wallabies' tour. Ken Donald, on the left wing for Australia, sprinted after a well-placed diagonal kick by Harvey, gathered the ball at speed, cut sharply back inside and dived over the line as the cover defence threatened to envelop him. Thus it was eleven points to six, the margin of victory for the Barbarians.

But the details of the scores tell little of the game; the unorthodox brilliance of Cliff Morgan's running, his virtuoso display of fly-half skills (that owed much to the sure handling and shrewd tactical variation of play by Andy Mulligan), those dancing and darting runs, the sustained long arcing runs outside the wing-forwards but inside the centres, the contrasting staccato stab-like bursts of acceleration that bewildered and bemused. Then there was Tony O'Reilly, restlessly seeking involvement and finding it to good effect; and Peter Robbins, the quite outstanding wing-forward. Ubiquitous, the scourge of five-eighth Harvey and, indeed, the whole Australian back division, Robbins was the destroyer and coverer supreme, but a creative force as well – first to the breakdown and transformer of defence into attack.

Up front there was the solidity of Marques and Evans, the control of Jacobs, Dawson and Shehadie, not only in the set-piece where they won four tight heads to two, but also in the loose. There this unique triumvirate exhibited a rare facility for mastery of the ball with the feet. None showed up better for Australia than twenty-one-year-old winger Ken Donald, who gave Arthur Smith a testing time, and the 'babe' of the side, Terry Curley, who capped a magnificent tour with his twenty-fourth almost faultless display.

But it was not a match of individuals. It was a team effort on both sides that created a magnificent spectacle of cut and thrust, that had the Cardiff crowd applauding both fifteens' attacking efforts, and that finally aroused the fifty thousand present, almost by way of expressing their appreciation, to sing together *Auld Lang Syne* and *Waltzing Matilda*, as old warriors Davidson and Shehadie were chaired from the field. By the end of the celebration dinner that night, Bob Davidson had been invited to join Shehadie in the membership of the Barbarian club.

## 5. BARBARIANS v SOUTH AFRICA 1961
4 February 1961 at Cardiff Arms Park

Barbarians 6 (2T) South Africa 0

**Barbarians:** H.J.Mainwaring, A.J.F.O'Reilly, H.M.Roberts, B.J.Jones, J.R.C.Young; R.A.W.Sharp, W.R.Watkins; B.G.M.Wood, A.R.Dawson (captain), S.Millar, W.R.Evans, B.Price, M.G.Culliton, W.G.D.Morgan, H.J.Morgan.

**South Africa:** L.G.Wilson; B.P. van Zyl, J.P.Engelbrecht, J.L.Gainsford, M.J.G.Antelme; D.A.Stewart, P. de W.Uys; S.P.Kuhn, G.F.Malan, J.L.Myburgh, G.H. van Zyl, A.S.Malan (captain), P.J. van Zyl, H.J.M.Pelser, D.J.Hopwood.

**Referee:** M.F.Turner (London Society)

For the Barbarians in 1961 there was the 'Springbok Head' and the 'Mainwaring tackle'; for South Africa, the heartbreak of a first defeat in the thirtieth and last match of their tour. When Ferdie Bergh handed over to Brigadier Glyn Hughes the traditional trophy, given by South African touring teams to their first conquerors, the touring team's manager masked his keen disappointment with an impressively generous tribute to the Barbarians on their victory. All earlier indignation concerning Mr Bergh's suggestion, while in Dublin, that the Barbarians match should be a 'gala affair' with the teams mixed up, was forgotten. The manager had put forward the idea of integrating the sides at a time when Springbok illnesses and injuries had reached alarming proportions, and indeed the unavailability of certain key players was to dog South Africa to the last. The Springboks made five changes from the side originally selected for the Barbarians match — notably having to replace prop-forward Piet du Toit and Johan Claassen, their renowned second-row, both suffering from flu. The Springboks were forced to reorganise their back division too, since Mannetjies Roux and Ian Kirkpatrick both had to cry off; Michel Antelme and B.P. van Zyl took their places. Van Zyl had come out as replacement on tour for Hennie van Zyl, who had returned home on the tragic death of his father, killed by lightning. It was generally felt, and the game seemed to prove, that the Springbok management erred in playing winger Jannie Engelbrecht in the centre, alongside Gainsford, when the obvious choice was Dave Stewart, who had been moved from his normal position to play at stand-off. With Stewart in the centre, South Africa could have included Keith Oxlee, and his goal-kicking ability alone might have changed the outcome of the game: after all, no team should risk taking the field without a dependable goal-kicker. The Barbarians had their late changes too, with Brian Jones replacing C.A.H.Davies, Billy Watkins for Andy Mulligan and Haydn Mainwaring for Terry Davies.

The pitch was porridge-like, a condition that used to characterise the 'bog' of Cardiff Arms Park. Nevertheless the Springboks, who had not always been favourably received by the press or the public, felt obliged to play entertaining rugby. Their invincible run, from their first match at Brighton through to their final match, twenty-nine games later (all wins apart from a draw against the Midlands at Leicester), had not always produced open, spectacular rugby. Not that that is a matter for complaint: indeed, it merely serves to bring them greater credit for endeavouring to join in the spirit of the occasion by trying to play Barbarian-style rugby in their final match, with an unbeaten record at stake. One could not blame them if, in hindsight, they regretted their decision to play a fluid style of game – but such regrets were certainly never expressed in public. It was ironic that the Barbarians themselves did not exactly indulge in a carefree 'run-it-at-all-costs' type of game on this occasion.

*Barbarians v South Africa, 1961.*
Back row: *M.F.Turner (referee), J.R.C.Young, H.M.Roberts, S.Millar, B.Price, H.J.Mainwaring, R.A.W.Sharp, W.G.D.Morgan, M.G.Culliton.* Middle row: *B.G.M.Wood, W.R.Evans, H.Waddell, A.R.Dawson (captain), H.L.Glyn Hughes, A.J.F.O'Reilly, M.R.Steele-Bodger, H.J.Morgan, V.G.Roberts (touch-judge).* On ground: *B.J.Jones, W.R.Watkins.*

The lasting memories of the match rest with the performance of Haydn Mainwaring, a substitute for Terry Davies. The burly 14st 4lb full-back, a player of all positions, was hardly thought at the time to be in the mould of a 'Barbarian' type of full-back. But he produced two, not one, heroic tackles that in all probability saved the Barbarians from defeat. The first was the one that has become a part of Barbarian folklore. Avril Malan, the South African captain, had burst through from the line-out and broken clear with the way to the goal-line open to him, bar the covering Mainwaring. Vivian Jenkins reported what happened next:

'Full thirty yards he covered, like a galloping Goliath, until the crash occurred. Malan weighs fifteen stone, Mainwaring, fourteen and a quarter, and when the two met there was a thud like a comet burying itself into earth, and it was Malan, hit with the full force of Mainwaring's shoulder, who hurtled backwards and sideways into touch, to remain semi-conscious for at least a couple of minutes.'

Although Malan recovered to continue the game, he was sadly unable to be present at the match dinner because of the after-effects of that shattering tackle, when he was awarded the insignia of honorary membership of the Barbarians, by Brigadier Glyn Hughes.

*The best remembered moment of the glorious Barbarian victory over South Africa in 1961. Avril Malan, the Springbok captain, lies prostrate in the Arms Park mud following the shattering, but try-saving, tackle on him by the Barbarians' full-back Haydn Mainwaring. He, number 15, can be observed retiring from the scene of the incident. But, in the best traditions of rugby football, Haydn Mainwaring was to be seen at the end of the match, together with Brian Jones, chairing Malan from the field of play.*

The second tackle by Mainwaring was later in the game, when Michel Antelme, the elusive Springbok wing, was similarly clear with only the full-back to beat. Like Malan before him, Antelme was brought to earth, and the Barbarians were saved. With Haydn Mainwaring's example, and the back row of Gerry Culliton and the two Monmouthshire Morgans, Derek of England, Haydn of Wales, very much to the fore, the Barbarians were able to hang-on to a six-point lead in a tempestuous second half. It was the Morgans, too, who had given the Baa-Baas the vital scores – with a try by Derek in the eleventh minute, after he'd charged down an attempted clearance by scrum-half Uys, and another by Haydn, sixteen minutes later. When Uys failed to gather a loose ball at the end of the line-out close to the Springbok line, Morgan H.J. pounced on the mistake and crossed over for the second try.

A disallowed try by Fanie Kuhn, from a disputed forward pass by Martin Pelser, and a late defiant burst by Gainsford, which almost brought a score, tell of a courageous fighting effort from the Springboks. But under the inspired leadership of Ireland's Ronnie Dawson, and with an unbending display of defiance from the all-Irish front row, allied to a magnificent effort by the whole pack, the Barbarians held out. Ironically, with the Barbarians, through half-backs Watkins and Sharp kicking back to the forwards, and the Springboks gallantly endeavouring to attack through their threequarters in which only John Gainsford appeared to excel, it was as though each side was playing to win by employing the other team's normal brand of rugby. It was a rousing contest, especially with the Welsh crowd of sixty thousand giving full voice to *Cwm Rhondda* and *Guide Me O Thou Great Jehova* in the final minutes. A remarkable and emotional climax when the final whistle blew was the hoisting aloft of Avril Malan on Barbarian shoulders – and it was pleasing to observe that one of those to bear Malan from the field was none other than Haydn Mainwaring.

## 6. BARBARIANS v NEW ZEALAND 1964
15 February 1964 at Cardiff Arms Park

Barbarians 3 (1DG) New Zealand 36 (8T, 6C)
**Barbarians**: S.Wilson; S.J.Watkins, M.S.Phillips, M.K.Flynn, C.P.Simpson; R.A.W.Sharp, S.J.S.Clarke; L.J.Cunningham, A.R.Dawson (captain), I.J.Clarke, E.Jones, B.Price, M.G.Culliton, A.E.I.Pask, D.P.Rogers
**New Zealand**: D.B.Clarke; M.J.Dick, P.F.Little, D.A.Arnold, R.W.Caulton; B.A.Watt; C.R.Laidlaw; W.J.Whineray (captain), D.Young, K.F.Gray, A.J.Stewart, C.E.Meads, D.J.Graham, K.R.Tremain, W.J.Nathan
**Referee**: D.G.Walters (Wales)

The All Blacks of 1963–64 under Wilson Whineray had as fine a pack of forwards as was ever seen in Britain. It must have been somewhat extraordinary when players such as Waka Nathan, Brian Lochore and Stan Meads had to fight for places in the international teams. There was already a great wealth of experience amongst the forwards before the touring side set foot in Britain; Colin Meads, Wilson Whineray, Dennis Young, John Graham and Kel Tremain had 271 appearances as All Blacks between them. By the time New Zealand came to Cardiff for the final game they had won twenty-eight of their thirty matches, losing only to Newport and drawing with Scotland. However, the record of the Fifth All Blacks was not the reason for the Barbarians' decision to select one of the tourists to play for them against his own New Zealand team. As with the Wallaby Shehadie in 1958, Ian Clarke was making his second tour to Britain – in fact he was the only All Black who had visited these shores before. It was, therefore, an appropriate gesture that the Barbarians should include Ian Clarke, again demonstrating in a practical way the worldwide membership of the Baa-Baas. It was also an honour for a great servant of the rugby game, who had been overshadowed in the preceding year or two by the phenomenal kicking feats of his younger brother, Don.

*Barbarians v New Zealand, 1964.*
*Back row: P.Yarranton (touch-judge), S.Wilson, L.J.Cunningham, D.P.Rogers, M.G.Culliton, A.E.J.Pask, B.E.V.Price, E.Jones, D.Gwynne Walters (referee). Middle row: S.J.Watkins, H.Waddell, A.R.Dawson (captain), H.L.G.Hughes, R.A.W.Sharp, M.R.Steele-Bodger, C.P.Simpson. On ground: M.K.Flynn, I.J.Clarke, S.J.S.Clarke, M.S.Phillips.*

*Two great All Blacks, Colin Meads and Waka Nathan, watch closely as Chris Laidlaw takes the ball from the line-out. Budge Rogers, for the Barbarians, is already off in search of a tackle!*

Ian remembers well the moment when Frank Kilby, the New Zealand manager, informed him of the invitation to play for the Baa-Baas. Since Whineray and Ken Gray had already been selected as the All Blacks' props, he jumped at the idea, thrilled to accept. He travelled from Porthcawl to Penarth on the Thursday to join the Barbarians, and took part in the training run-outs under Ronnie Dawson. No doubt Clarke was in a position to anticipate the beating that the Barbarians were to receive, though even he could scarcely have expected such a superlative All Black display. Yet, interestingly, Clarke still regards the 1956 New Zealand eight that beat the Springboks in New Zealand as a slightly superior pack – physically stronger and more accomplished in line-out play. Of the match at Cardiff in 1964, the New Zealand prop-forward recalls vividly:

'a hell of a lot of ball chasing in the second half and brilliant combined handling which swept the Barbarians aside like straws in the wind'.

The Baa-Baas selected fifteen included the uncapped RMA Sandhurst cadet Colin Simpson and Eric Jones the Penarth captain, who had never even been a Welsh trials reserve but who consistently shone in the annual Good Friday match against the Baa-Baas. Mike Gibson was originally selected at stand-off, while still uncapped, to partner his Cambridge scrum-half Simon Clarke; but on account of Ireland's reluctance to release him from their own international preparations, Gibson was replaced by Richard Sharp. It was not to prove a happy day for the Wasps and England player, nor was it for many in the black and white jerseys, hard though captain Ronnie Dawson tried to keep his team in contention in his remarkable third appearance in these 'international' games.

It is strange to recall that the Barbarians scored first – even more remarkable is that it was Ian Clarke, the New Zealand prop, who earned their only points. Some hilarity was evident in the crowd when Clarke called a 'fair catch' from his brother's drop-out on the All Black twenty-five, and promptly signalled to referee Gwynne Walters his intention to drop for goal. What few people knew was that Clarke senior was an accomplished kicker – he practised often with brother Don, was frequently goal-kicker in junior grade rugby in New Zealand, and twice before had dropped

*Wilson Whineray, the All Blacks' captain, being chaired from the field at the end of the match in which his last-minute try set the seal on a magnificent victory.*

goals in club matches at home. On this occasion, ten yards in from touch and forty-five yards out, the ball sailed between the posts, and the laughter turned to resounding cheers of appreciation — as E.W.Swanton wittily remarked, it should have been recorded as an 'own goal'.

From then until half-time, when the score was 6–3 to the All Blacks, there was no real evidence of the impending onslaught. Graham caught Sharp in possession early on and Arnold set up the try for Tremain. Meads soon added a second score, but not until seven minutes into the second half did the floodgates open. Graham and Nathan each in turn seized on defensive lapses by Simon Clarke for two tries that turned the whole pattern of the match. A combined move of forwards and backs across the field, and then back again for Dick to score, Nathan added his second try. Then the irrepressible Meads and Graham linked up with Caulton who raced in for the seventh try. The eighth and final try was the stuff of which fairytales are made. With the All Blacks again uniting in one irresistible force, as happened so often in the second half, the ball reached the centre, Paul Little, who looked certain to pass to the support on his outside. But in a moment of inspired judgement, or maybe divine guidance, he chose instead to commit the defending tackler and pass inside to none other than Wilson Whineray. Whineray had one man between himself and the goal line – Malcolm Phillips, the Barbarian centre – and not full-back Stewart Wilson as widely reported. How could Phillips have expected the classiest of dummies that was to follow from the hands of the All Black prop-forward and captain? Whineray, with the flair of a Barry John, held on to the ball as his arms swung, as if to pass outside, then with a hint of a sidestep raced on an angle to score the try. It was the perfect ending to a grand finale, the last try of the tour and the first for him, in his final appearance in All Black colours in Britain.

The Cardiff crowds had lent their voices in tribute to many preceding touring sides at the Arms Park. Never was there a more fitting reaction from this appreciative and knowledgeable crowd than the mass rendering from 58,000 people of *For he's a jolly good fellow* as Whineray walked back at the end of a personal triumph – not only in this particular game, but as a magnificent leader of a great and popular tour.

## 7. BARBARIANS v AUSTRALIA 1967
28 January 1967 at Cardiff Arms Park

Barbarians 11 (1T, 1C, 1PG, 1PT) Australia 17 (5T, 1C)
**Barbarians:** S.Wilson; S.J.Watkins, T.G.R.Davies, F.P.K.Bresnihan, P.B.Glover; D.Watkins, R.M.Young; N.Suddon, K.W.Kennedy, A.B.Carmichael, B.Price, W.J.McBride, N.A.Murphy (captain), J.W.Telfer, J.P.Fisher
**Australia:** J.K.Lenehan; E.S.Boyce, R.J.Marks, J.E.Brass, R.Webb; P.F.Hawthorne, K.W.Catchpole; J.E.Thornett (captain), P.G.Johnson, A.R.Miller, R.G.Teitzel, M.Purcell, G.V.Davis, J.F.O'Gorman, J.Guerassimoff
**Referee:** R.W.Gilliland (Ireland)

No overseas touring team visiting Britain has ever combined such a poor record in provincial matches with such a favourable record in the internationals, as the Fifth Wallabies. Victories over Wales and England were the fine achievements of a touring team of generally mediocre ability. The fact that Australia were capable of winning internationals but equally of losing 'easy' provincial games reflected the fact, as pertinent then as it is now, that the Wallabies had insufficient depth of talent in their touring party to create a good overall record. The best fifteen players could not play in every match. The successes in the internationals, the close results against Ireland and Scotland and the fine victory over the Barbarians spoke, too, of the outstanding attributes of their half-backs, Ken Catchpole and Phil Hawthorne. The genius of Catchpole, his speed of action, his ability behind a beaten pack to transform scrappily-won possession in the loose or the set piece into 'good ball' for his fly-half, his unerringly fast service, and telling breaks from the base of the scrum, make him – in my opinion – as great a player as any scrum-half I have seen.

The Barbarian fifteen was a young side under the captaincy of Noel Murphy junior, the senior player with thirty-three caps, and one of five Irishmen in the side. Twenty-two-year-old 'Sandy' Carmichael was the only uncapped player, another example of the Barbarians' ability to recognise future great internationals at an early stage of their careers. Murphy recalls the preparation for the match:

'Herbert Waddell reminded me of the heavy defeat the Barbarians had suffered three years previously, and the importance of keeping faith with the Welsh public. I made this the theme of my pre-match talk. The Barbarians are held together by a mighty tradition and can call upon some of the world's finest players, but around that time, before the present coaching influence, there was always the element of luck whether or not they blended together as an outstanding team. In the past with the challenge of playing the unbeaten Springboks, it might have been easier to make the adrenalin flow, but the '66–67 Wallabies did not offer the same interest. Yet they were a gay, attractive team remembered later for audacious victories over Wales and England rather than their thirteen defeats. Everyone, therefore, expected the final match to provide a game of rich movement. Unfortunately, the ground was muddy – typical of the Arms Park in those days. This created a problem as the need to win was always paramount when I played rugby, but I realised, too, the importance of attempting to do this in the style of the Barbarians.'

*Barbarians v Australia, 1967.*
Back row: *G.Windsor Lewis (touch-judge), K.W.Kennedy, J.P.Fisher, A.B.Carmichael, W.J.McBride, B.Price, J.W.Telfer, N.Suddon, S.J.Watkins.* Middle row: *S.Wilson, T.G.R.Davies, N.A.A.Murphy (captain), F.P.K.Bresnihan, D.Watkins.* On ground: *P.B.Glover, R.M.Young.*

In fact, it was the Australians who rose the better above the limitations imposed by the morass of a ground, to score five tries and beat the Barbarians for the first time. Hawthorne began the scoring, when, head down, he shot through a gap in the defence to score after Dick Webb had set up the position near the corner flag. Jim Lenehan played the attacking full-back role, making the extra man in the line to give an overlap for Boyce to score the second try in the corner.

At half-time the scoreline was 6–0, but the Barbarians' efforts were soon rewarded. Kennedy rounded off a good forward drive with a try, and Stewart Wilson put the scores level with a penalty. O'Gorman countered to put Australia back in front and then came the moment in the game which, but for the Wallabies' resilience, might have turned events in the Barbarians' favour. Noel Murphy fly-kicked ahead from near halfway, to send the ball within a couple of yards of the goal line.

Stuart Watkins gave chase, and reached the ball just as Lenehan, the Australian full-back, arrived. Watkins tapped the ball inwards to wrong-foot Lenehan, then kicked it on again, but in so doing was impeded by the full-back as the ball ran dead. The referee, R.W.Gilliland, had no hesitation in awarding the Barbarians a penalty try.

Noel Murphy still feels that this may have been a trifle harsh on Australia, since it appeared to him that Watkins and Lenehan had been involved in a straightforward collision. But the final outcome was not affected. The decision may in fact have brought the Wallabies a firmer resolve to win — for their best rugby came in the last ten minutes. As Uel Titley of *The Times* reported the closing minutes:

'The Australians erupted and effervesced and switched, and all at breakneck speed in a fashion that gave Lenehan ample scope for atonement. He was concerned in an abortive thrust by Webb and cut out a successful one for Boyce, converting this try with a brilliant kick. Finally, Webb was over and so was the tour — rightly, in a blaze of glory.'

*Waltzing Matilda* rebounded round the Arms Park stands, Noel Murphy and Phil Hawthorne raised John Thornett shoulder high, and the traditional valedictory songs were struck up by the band. As Noel Murphy recalls:

'Although I was disappointed at losing the game, I can sincerely say I was pleased for John. He was an outstanding sportsman whom I would have been proud to play with.'

Thornett was the man, you may remember, who had the courage to drop himself from the four internationals of that tour when displeased with his own form. There was some consolation for him in the end including honorary Barbarian membership.

## 8. BARBARIANS v NEW ZEALAND 1967
16 December 1967 at Twickenham

Barbarians 6 (1T, 1DG) New Zealand 11 (2T, 1C, 1DG)
**Barbarians:** S.Wilson (captain); W.K.Jones, R.H.Lloyd, T.G.R.Davies, R.E.Webb; B.John, G.Edwards; C.H.Norris, F.A.Laidlaw, A.L.Horton, M.Wiltshire, P.J.Larter, D.Grant, G.A.Sherriff, R.B.Taylor
**New Zealand:** W.F.McCormick; M.J.Dick, W.L.Davis, I.R.Macrae, A.G.Steel; E.W.Kirton, C.R.Laidlaw; B.L.Muller, B.E.McLeod, K.F.Gray, S.C.Strahan, C.E.Meads, K.R.Tremain, B.J.Lochore (captain), W.J.Nathan
**Referee:** Meirion Joseph (Wales)

'The worst team New Zealand has ever fielded' was how one New Zealand rugby writer summed up the ability of the Second All Blacks of 1924–25 *before* they left for Europe. A few months later C.G.Porter's side returned home with a record that read quite simply: played 32, won 32! Forty-three years later, no one had any doubts that the Sixth All Blacks were anything but a very strong touring party. In fact they were to share the distinction with the 1924 side of going back to New Zealand from Britain and France unbeaten — though the Sixth All Blacks played fifteen matches, not thirty-two, and drew once, with East Wales. But not only did they have an invincible record, the 1967 All Blacks scored almost three hundred points during the very tough fixture list of their short tour, which included four internationals, though no games in Ireland because of the outbreak of 'foot and mouth' disease in England.

Under Brian Lochore, the Sixth All Blacks were a superbly disciplined side, with typical New Zealand dedication allied to complete mastery of the basic skills of the game. Their pack was mighty indeed but, in addition, there was a refreshing fluidity in their overall style of play. Never though, was the character of the side put to a more severe test than in the concluding match of the tour against the Barbarians at Twickenham. From the *Haka* to *Auld Lang Syne* it was a dramatic, pulsating final game; a match that had everything: but only by chance did it even take place.

As the visit of the Sixth All Blacks was originally planned as a tour of only sixteen matches, the customary final fixture with the Baa-Baas could not be included. But when the fixtures in Ireland were cancelled, it was hurriedly decided that the Barbarians' match should be reinstated and played at Twickenham. Thus it was even more of a special occasion for the Barbarians, since only twice before — in the Middlesex Sevens of 1934 (which they won), and in the game the following year against London — had the nomadic Baa-Baas set foot on the Twickenham turf. Cardiff had been very much the 'spiritual' home of the Barbarians. But although the setting for the customary tourists' farewell match was new, the match itself was in the finest Barbarian tradition.

*Barbarians v New Zealand, 1967.*
Back row: *M.F.Turner (touch-judge), R.H.Lloyd, M.Wiltshire, G.A.Sherriff, P.J.Larter, R.B.Taylor, D.Grant, A.L.Horton, R.E.Webb, M.Joseph (referee), W.K.M.Jones (touch-judge).* Front row: *W.K.Jones, G.O.Edwards, C.H.Norris, S.Wilson (captain), T.G.R.Davies, B.John, F.A.L.Laidlaw.*

The Barbarians were hopeful that the inclusion of Keri Jones, Gerald Davies, Barry John and Gareth Edwards would lead to a repeat of the inspired back-play they had exhibited for East Wales in the drawn match with the All Blacks at Cardiff. As the New Zealand manager Charles Saxton had said at the time:

> 'Those Welsh backs were quite the best unit we have met — they ran with the ball on every conceivable occasion.'

On the second occasion they were again tantalisingly close to bringing about an All Blacks' defeat. Had there been anything approaching good possession up front, the Barbarians might even have won. A magnificent dropped goal of forty-five yards by Stewart Wilson, after Laidlaw missed his touch kick, was countered by another from the boot of Earl Kirton following a line-out deflection by Strahan. Yet the 3–3 scoreline at half-time definitely flattered the Barbarians. Their pack was beaten comprehensively for possession, notably in the lines-out where Strahan, Meads and Gray excelled, but more especially in the rucks, in which the work of Nathan and Lochore was that of men inspired, with the other six hardly less effective. It was fortunate for the Barbarians that although Chris Laidlaw was in fine form at scrum-half,

*Gray, Muller, Strahan, Lochore (partly obscured) and Tremain seal off Meads in the classic All Black fashion, as he prepares to pass back to Laidlaw.*

his outside backs frequently mishandled and let slip good attacking chances. But credit too must be given to the Barbarians for sheer guts and determination — the tackling of Derek Grant (a late replacement for Pringle Fisher, the original captain) and Bob Taylor was particularly ferocious. The rest of the pack, though taking a physical pounding, stuck manfully to their task. Behind them the young partnership of Edwards and John contrived to make the best of what opportunities came their way.

One of those characteristic, perfect diagonal kicks to the corner by Barry John finally set up the try for Bob Lloyd which put the Barbarians ahead early in the second half. It was a noteworthy feat by Lloyd, who 'kept his cool', gathered the loose ball as the defence got into a tangle, and scored by the corner flag. So the Harlequin scored his fourth try against the tourists — and he was the only Englishman to cross the All Blacks' line on the whole tour. Wilson's conversion attempt failed, as did five penalty attempts by him during the game, two of his longest efforts rebounding off an upright.

The Barbarians now defended and counter-attacked with the utmost gallantry, as the All Blacks risked all in a final onslaught. For twenty minutes the Barbarians held out, but in the end no one could deny the justice of the All Blacks' victory. With one minute of ordinary time left, just when every one of the 40,000 crowd was praying that the final whistle would be blown, the All Blacks launched another desperate attack. From a ruck deep in the Barbarians' half, the All Blacks moved the ball right. 'Stainless' Steel looked all set to burst his way through the defence as he tore into the line from the blind-side wing, when a fine covering tackle checked his run — but the breach had been made, and Steel managed to feed the ball to MacRae for the burly centre to touch down wide out. The scores were level. McCormick missed the conversion — the Barbarians surely were saved. But the final drama had not yet been played out; there was still injury-time to run. Again the black shirts were seen to move remorselessly upfield. Then came a fatal lapse by Stewart Wilson, a moment's error that marred a fine display by the full-back. In trying to clear under pressure, from inside the twenty-five, his kick, away from his pack, tragically failed to find touch. The ball was seized on instead by Brian Lochore; he found the ever-probing Kirton in support on his left to take it on, and with only Keri Jones left in defence, Steel was poised on the overlap. Kirton passed neatly to Steel, and the left-winger raced over to score unopposed, so clinching the match. Fergie McCormick, appropriately as one of the outstanding figures in this match and on the whole tour, added the conversion to bring his points tally to one hundred with the final kick of the game.

The traditional farewell songs, with Lochore and Meads borne aloft, set the seal on a marvellous occasion, a game which for pure drama and emotion in its closing minutes will be difficult to surpass.

## 9. BARBARIANS v SOUTH AFRICA 1970
31 January 1970 at Twickenham

Barbarians 12 (3T, 1PG), South Africa 21 (3T, 3C, 1PG, 1DG)
**Barbarians:** J.P.R.Williams; A.T.A.Duggan, J.S.Spencer, C.M.H.Gibson, D.J.Duckham; B.John, G.O.Edwards (captain); K.E.Fairbrother, F.A.L.Laidlaw, D.B.Llewellyn, A.M.Davis, I.S.Gallacher, J.J.Jeffrey, R.J.Arneil, T.M.Davies.
**South Africa:** H.O.de Villiers; S.H.Nomis, O.A.Roux, J.P.van der Merwe, A.E.van der Watt; M.J.Lawless, D.J.de Villiers (captain), J.F.K.Marais, C.H.Cockrell, J.L.Mybrugh, F.C.H.du Preez, I.J.de Klerk, P.J.F.Greyling, J.H.Ellis, M.W.Jennings.
**Referee:** Air Commodore G.C.Lamb, CBE, AFC, (RAF)

For Brigadier Glyn Hughes, it was an emotional moment when he raised his glass in the toast to the South African rugby touring team on 31 January 1970. The toast came at the end of the celebration dinner at the Savoy Hotel which followed the match between the Barbarians and the Springboks. A few moments before, the final words of his speech in tribute to the visiting team had been received with loud acclaim — when he said that politics had no place in the realms of amateur sport, that a rugby player should be free to play with whom and against whomsoever he chose, and that no one had the right to interfere with sporting rugby relations with South Africa. His sense of outrage at the events which had marred the Springbok tour of 1969–70 must have been even keener than that of most rugby men, since Hughie was himself born in South Africa.

But he must also have been proud of the dignity, restraint and good manners that the young South Africans had shown in the face of the most testing provocation. The taunts, the darts, the tin-tacks, the smoke-bombs, were never used by the tourists as an excuse for their disappointing playing record, the worst ever for South Africa in Britain. But the pressure upon the Springboks was not solely created by the overt demonstrations and open hostility. Additional pressures were the need for players to remain almost 'cooped up' in their hotels for security's sake, to suffer threatening telephone calls in their rooms, to endure bomb hoaxes, to arrive at grounds hours before kick-off and sit around in changing rooms for interminable periods and even, on the morning of the England international, to experience an attempted hijack of the team bus. I mention all this to stress the unpleasantness of the burden that Dawie de Villiers' Springboks had to bear for the duration of the tour. It was all the more to their credit, therefore, that the Sixth Springboks were able to produce their finest rugby in the twenty-fifth and final game of the tour. Yet, political

*Barbarians v South Africa, 1970.*
Back row: *R.P.Burrell (touch-judge), J.J.Jeffrey, R.J.Arneil, K.E.Fairbrother, T.M.Davies, A.M.Davis, D.B.Llewelyn, D.J.Duckham, M.G.Molloy (sub), Air Cdr. G.C.Lamb (referee), M.Joseph (touch-judge).* Middle row: *I.S.Gallacher, A.T.A.Duggan, C.M.H.Gibson, G.O.Edwards (captain), F.A.L.Laidlaw, J.S.Spencer, J.P.R.Williams.* Front row: *N.C.Starmer-Smith (sub), J.V.Pullin (sub), B.John, C.M.Telfer (sub).*

interference and protest disregarded, the side was not one of the Springbok greatest. The successes of British teams against them certainly destroyed the aura of near-invincibility which, prior to this tour, had surrounded South African rugby.

For once, the Barbarians were able to field the fifteen that was originally selected. Stuart Gallacher was the only uncapped player, and he was one of eight in the side that had toured South Africa with the Barbarians the previous summer. Incidentally, this was the first occasion on which substitutes were nominated for a Barbarian match in Britain, and three of the four replacements – Pullin, Starmer-Smith and Telfer – had also taken part on the South African tour, Molloy being the exception.

In many respects the game consisted of two quite distinct halves. The Barbarians began in great style, overcoming the usual disharmony of a scratch side to such an extent that the Springboks were made to look the team of 'strangers'. The home pack capitalised on their initial superiority, and after seven minutes a strike against the head by Laidlaw set up Edwards for a blind-side break, and the inside pass brought Rodger Arneil the first try. Three minutes later Gareth Edwards made the initial gap, after a well-won ruck, and this time fed the ball to Duckham on the blind-side wing. Dave Duckham then scored one of his greatest tries: fully sixty yards he covered, his fair hair streaming as he raced up the left touchline before stepping inside full-back H.O.de Villiers to score brilliantly. Such a wonderful start for the Baa-Baas put the crowd in high spirits.

But slowly the Springbok forward machine was finding its rhythm. 'Frik' du Preez, in his record seventy-second Springbok appearance, 'Moff' Myburgh, one of the toughest and certainly the heaviest, at eighteen stone, of South African props, Hannes Marais, another hardened international prop, and, perhaps above all, Jan Ellis, in one of his finest ever performances, reacted to the challenge. It was Ellis who scored first, after both forwards and backs had handled in the best Springbok style, Dawie de Villiers took over from 'H.O.' as kicker, the full-back having missed four early penalty chances, and converted from wide out. Back came the Barbarians,

Mike Gibson and Gareth Edwards chair a
jubilant Dawie de Villiers, the Springbok
captain, from the field at Twickenham. In
this game the South Africans produced
the finest rugby of their whole tour, to
beat the Barbarians 21 points to 12.

Spencer seared through the Springbok defence, and fed the scoring pass to 'Dixie'
Duggan. A penalty by the Springbok captain just before half-time reduced the Baa-
Baas' lead to one point. That was the last time the Barbarians were in front.

In the second half the Springboks produced some of the greatest rugby of their
tour. With their forwards dominant in the tight and loose play, and Dawie de Villiers
in devastating form behind them, points were bound to result. Mike Lawless
dropped a goal from the first of several tight-head heels and Andy van der Watt
scored a fine try. But fittingly South Africa's finest moment came from Jan Ellis. His
second try followed a pick up in the loose and an extraordinary run for a
sixteen-stone flanker, that included two dummies and a final jink that beat
J.P.R.Williams. With a further successful conversion from his captain, the match
was won. Gibson, Duggan and Spencer almost contrived to pull back some points
after a fine move, but Spencer put a foot in touch as he made for the corner. Some
consolation came as Keith Fairbrother scored in diving over from the ensuing line-
out but it was 21–12 to the Springboks at the final whistle.

The tourists had certainly saved their best rugby till last. On this occasion not
even the orange smoke- and flour-bombs, tin-tacks or chanting could distract them
– they, unlike the Barbarians, had seen it all so often before. Gibson and Edwards
chaired a beaming Dawie de Villiers from the field. But the best gesture of all came
at the dinner later that day, when the Barbarians' President not only made the touring captain an honorary Barbarian member as was customary, but also, in a break
with precedent, presented a Barbarian monogram to each of the Springboks,
thoughtfully including the unfortunate four who had returned home earlier in the
tour because of injury.

## 10. BARBARIANS v NEW ZEALAND 1973
27 January 1973 at Cardiff Arms Park

Barbarians 23 (4T, 2C, 1PG) New Zealand 11 (2T, 1PG)
**Barbarians:** J.P.R.Williams; D.J.Duckham, S.J.Dawes (captain), C.M.H.Gibson, J.C.Bevan; P.Bennett, G.O.Edwards, R.J.McLoughlin, J.V.Pullin, A.B.Carmichael, W.J.McBride, R.M.Wilkinson, T.P.David, J.F.Slattery, D.L.Quinnell
**New Zealand:** J.F.Karam; B.G.Williams, B.J.Robertson, I.A.Hurst, G.B.Batty; R.E.Burgess, S.M.Going (replacement G.L.Colling); G.J.Whiting, R.A.Urlich, K.K.Lambert, H.H.MacDonald, P.J.Whiting, A.I.Scown, A.J.Wyllie, I.A.Kirkpatrick (captain)
**Referee:** G.Domercq (FRF)

That try; that match! There can be scarcely anyone in the world who enjoys rugby football, that has not heard of, or seen, the game between the Barbarians and the Seventh All Blacks. In print, on film and on television, the match has been re-played many thousand of times in all corners of the earth. As a model for the modern game, the Barbarians v All Blacks 1973 represented the acme of achievement, illustrating the heights that could be reached in playing rugby. The match set such a high standard of excellence that it will forever be a yardstick by which games of rugby union football will be judged. It was not, however, an 'international'.

When the Barbarians team was announced, no denials would ever have persuaded Ian Kirkpatrick's All Blacks that the twenty-eighth and final match of their tour was anything more or less than the British Lions against New Zealand. To them it appeared initially to be a fifth Test match, a virtual continuation of the Lions series of 1971. There was more than just a nucleus of that exceptional side led by John Dawes to a first ever success against the All Blacks. As it so happened, 27 January 1973 also gave the crowd in Cardiff the opportunity to understand exactly why the British Isles touring team of 1971 had returned home with such a proud record.

*Barbarians v New Zealand, 1973.*
Back row: *E.M.Lewis (touch-judge), G.Windsor Lewis, J.V.Pullin, W.J.McBride, R.M.Wilkinson, D.L.Quinnell, A.B.Carmichael, D.J.Duckham, G.Domercq (referee), D.O.Spyer (touch-judge).* Middle row: *G.O.Edwards, C.M.H.Gibson, H.L.Glyn Hughes, S.J.Dawes (captain), H.Waddell, J.Bevan, R.J.McLoughlin.* Front row: *J.F.Slattery, T.O.David, P.Bennett, J.P.R.Williams. A famous team on a famous occasion.*

Key moments in the most famous Barbarian try of all time: (i) John Dawes, with Derek Quinnell in support, continues the counter-attack, begun by Phil Bennett just two minutes into the match and ten yards from the Barbarian goal-line. (ii) Dawes commits Syd Going and then passes inside to Tom David with Gareth Edwards, the eventual try-scorer, closing up behind Quinnell. (iii) David rides the tackle and passes back out to Quinnell and he in turn passed on in the direction of John Bevan, but it was Gareth Edwards who took it at speed, to score surely the greatest ever Barbarian try.

But whatever assumptions may have been made before the game, and after, by the All Blacks, the press and the rugby public, the team was not the British Lions of 1971, it was the Barbarians of 1973. For a start the match came eighteen months after the end of the Lions' tour. John Dawes returned from semi-retirement to lead the side, and the team (though admittedly not as originally selected) included three players, two of them uncapped, who had not even been to New Zealand. Only two of the pack that had contested three of the four Test matches against New Zealand on that tour were present. I think these factors would have been accorded greater significance had the 'Lions' lost! The unanswerable question is, of course, that had the cover of the programme for the game read 'British Isles v New Zealand', would we have witnessed the same quality and style of rugby football? Perhaps, we may have from the Barbarians' players, but it is a moot point as to whether or not the All Blacks, in a 'Test', would have entered so much into the spirit of the occasion as they did for this particular game. Had the final match for the Seventh All Blacks been against the Lions, would they have risked changing their pattern of play, which had, unspectacularly but effectively, brought them an unbeaten record in the four internationals? Maybe not. But 'what might have been' matters little. What is important is that whatever thoughts anyone may have had about the meeting of these two teams, both, in almost equal measure, contributed to a game of rugby that will always be hailed as a 'classic' exhibition of football.

John Dawes's Barbarian fifteen, when originally selected, included the whole of the British Lions' back division, with the exception of Barry John. With 'King' John no longer playing, heir to his throne Phil Bennett was Gareth Edwards's partner. The pack bore little resemblance to the first eight that played in the Test matches in New Zealand – only John Pullin, Mervyn Davies and Willie John McBride had played in all four, while Derek Quinnell and Fergus Slattery, who had each played in one, were the only other Test match representatives.

There were three changes from the side first chosen – Barry Llewellyn withdrew because of a knee cartilage injury, being replaced by Sandy Carmichael. Both the Davies's were forced to cry off on the morning of the match – Gerald on account of hamstring trouble, and Mervyn because of a heavy cold. John Bevan was called up as winger, and Tom David was Mervyn Davies's replacement, Quinnell transferring to number eight with David on the flank. Thus there were twelve of the 1971 Lions party in the final fifteen. David became the second uncapped player in the team, along with Bob Wilkinson, a twenty-two-year-old undergraduate, whose performance for Cambridge University against the All Blacks early in the tour had encouraged the Barbarian Committee to make a bold and surprise selection.

The All Blacks included all but Sutherland and Norton of the team that drew the last international against Ireland. It had been a further uninspiring performance by New Zealand. A plethora of dour rugby, to which could be added 'l'affaire Murdoch', the 'Mafia', and a reputation as hardly the most friendly of teams, meant that many people were more than happy to see the All Blacks well beaten in their last match. Beforehand, the crowd had grounds for hoping a Barbarian win might be possible, but what no one could have foreseen was the manner and magnificence of the victory when it came.

The pattern of the game was set in the opening exchanges, with the Barbarians playing towards the River Taff end. Scarcely had the crowd settled into their seats than Phil Bennett, after only two minutes play, ran back deep into his own twenty-five to gather a cross-kick from Bryan Williams. He turned, and perhaps with Carwyn James' pre-match words 'play your natural game' still fresh in his mind, he opted to attack out of defence. In a flash, almost dancing over the turf, he sidestepped Ian Hurst, and then left first Kirkpatrick, next Urlich, grasping at thin air behind him. From Bennett the ball went to John Williams, and the full-back, half-held, linked on the swivel with John Pullin. In other circumstances the England hooker might have put in a safe clearance to touch, but not on this occasion. Pullin found Dawes in close support and moving at speed, the Baa-Baas' skipper accelerated up the left touch-line and with a dummy that bemused the All Black cover, raced up to the half-way line. John Dawes, with Quinnell tracking him hard, cleverly committed Syd Going before passing inside to Tom David. The pace of the movement was unrelenting. As David was tackled, the Llanelli player's power and good sense made him a vital link in the chain. He rode the tackle, and, using one arm to push down the defender, clenched the ball in his other large hand and passed round the would-be tackler to Derek Quinnell, the emergency number eight, who had John Bevan outside him near the touchline. The winger was the player for whom Quinnell aimed the pass, but as he released the ball, Gareth Edwards, who had made up a tremendous amount of ground, came bursting through at top speed to 'intercept', sprint past the remnants of the All Black cover and round off the ninety-yard move with a full tilt dive – for a try near the left hand corner flag. The crescendo of noise that had built up from Bennett's first inspired counter-attack finally broke into thunderous and uninhibited applause and ecstatic shouts, to hail a try that was the consequence of one of the finest combined moves ever seen on the rugby field.

Anyone who thought that such a score might have made the rest of the match an anti-climax, soon had their fears allayed. Such a miracle beginning only served to inspire and give confidence to the Barbarians, who produced a first half of unqualified magnificence. First there followed a penalty from Bennett, then a converted try for Slattery, after Edwards had hounded Going at an All Black scrum in their own twenty-five. Finally, with the scavenging Slattery catching fly-half Burgess in possession, Quinnell picked up and linked with Dawes; he passed on to John Bevan, who cut inside Bryan Williams and raced in for the third try. Thus it was 17–0 at half-time, and the All Blacks were on the threshold of complete annihilation. Neither does the scoreline tell all – for in those first forty minutes the Barbarians' running had been outstanding. David Duckham, perhaps above all, had thrilled the crowd with his sudden bursts, bewildering sidesteps and long-striding accelerating runs from deep counter-attack positions. But the fact that both Duckham and Bevan received such a plentiful supply of ball reflected the way the scratch pack had quickly settled into a harmonious unit, as did the manner in which Edwards and Bennett provided such swift and instant service for those exemplary midfield distributors, Dawes and Gibson. The Barbarian magic was essentially a triumph of skill over rudimentary power.

Their pride injured, the All Blacks came back with a vengeance in the second-half. A crooked scrum-feed by Edwards brought Karam, and New Zealand, the encouragement of an early penalty. With Peter Whiting winning (literally!) the lion's share of the line-out, the All Blacks began to force their way back into the match. For a while the Baa-Baas looked vulnerable. After a brilliant pick-up by Burgess of a weak pass from the limping Syd Going, Bryan Williams came into the line from the blind-side wing, together with full-back Jo Karam, to create the overlap for Grant Batty. With twinkling feet and thighs working like pistons, he scored the first All Black try. But Going, a doubtful starter for the match, was clearly suffering from his injured ankle; to no one's surprise, with twenty minutes left he was replaced by Lin Colling. Colling was always the better passer of the ball, and his service brought greater fluency to the All Blacks' back division.

The petulant Batty and the more amenable Tom David had a slight skirmish, after a marginally late tackle by the flanker – a kind of David and Goliath confrontation, but the other way round. It ended with an amusing and self-disciplined ruffle of Batty's hair by the huge Llanelli man, but as a result the incident brought will o' the wisp winger Batty plenty of booing for the rest of the game. But New Zealand were still challenging. When Hurst, the centre, gathered a loose ball midfield after a tackle on Robertson, his deliberate, or accidentally-angled kick bounced perfectly for Batty who, as quick as an electric spark, chipped over the head of J.P.R., darted round him, gathered again and with a defiant, almost cocky little gesture, planted the ball down for a clever try. That made the score 17–11 – another goal would bring the All Blacks level.

But the pace of the game had by this time begun to take effect on the players' stamina. All the greater credit was therefore due to the non-touring side, in that they were able to withstand the All Blacks resurgence and come back again to clinch the match with another spectacular try in the last quarter of an hour. For that reason, and also because, quite incredibly, every single Barbarian player handled the ball in the ninety seconds of movement that led to it, the try by John Williams ranks almost equal in greatness to the one that started the match. In its final stages, a missed touch-line clearance by Colling was fielded by Duckham who counter-attacked. He ran and jinked diagonally up field at full speed, leaving the All Blacks trailing in his wake like some bewildered sheep. Quinnell, as ever, was close in support, Dawes continued the move, Williams took it further, then Gibson dodged a tackle and fed to Slattery; finally the combination of brilliant support play by players of all the home countries was completed by J.P.R.Williams, who hurled himself over in the right-hand corner for the decisive try. For the capacity crowd, it was seventh heaven. The cheering only abated briefly, to allow Phil Bennett to concentrate his efforts on the conversion attempt. A kick worthy of the try that brought it was the dream-like ending to an unforgettable game of rugby.

The crowd, still singing and applauding, enveloped the pitch and continued to hail their heroes long after the last of them had fought their way through to the dressing-rooms. Thirty-one players had produced a spectacle that was a triumph for rugby. But no one should forget the remarkable judgement and skill of the referee, Georges Domercq, who in his self-effacing and friendly style, made a notable contribution. John Dawes naturally recalls the match with great pleasure. He reflects:

'It was a tremendously enjoyable game to play in with both sides playing quality, not carefree, rugby. The All Blacks' contribution was excellent and their pressure at the start of the second half needed the sternest defence.'

So what were the principal reasons for the Barbarian victory?

'The attitude of the players involved was one of determination to win by playing the game our way. Then, the nucleus of the team was the 1971 Lions, and all the confidence of that side was recaptured in the build-up to the game itself. Thirdly, Phil Bennett had the skill and flair to play a Barry John type of rôle at fly-half, and finally there was the ability of the side to "hang-on" in the period immediately after half-time when we were subjected to a great deal of pressure. Although the game will be remembered for the unrelenting sequence of attack and counter-attack, one of the most significant factors in the match, and one which was similarly a cornerstone in building the success of the 1971 Lions, was the team's ability to withstand remorseless All Black pressure, absorb it and then fight back.'

Although there have been many outstanding matches in the thirty seasons since the Barbarians first played the touring sides, there is almost unanimous agreement that the 1973 match was the finest exhibition of rugby of them all. It was especially pleasing that both President Brigadier Glyn Hughes and his trusty friend and long time Barbarian colleague, Jock Wemyss, lived just long enough to witness one of their club's greatest triumphs.

## 11. BARBARIANS v NEW ZEALAND 1974
30 November 1974 at Twickenham

Barbarians 13 (1T, 3PG) New Zealand 13 (2T, 1C, 1PG)
**Barbarians:** A.R.Irvine; T.G.R.Davies, P.J.Warfield, P.S.Preece, D.J.Duckham; J.D.Bevan, G.O.Edwards; J.McLauchlan, R.W.Windsor, F.E.Cotton, W.J.McBride (captain), G.L.Brown, R.M.Uttley, T.M.Davies, J.F.Slattery.
**New Zealand:** J.F.Karam; B.G.Williams, B.J.Robertson, I.Hurst, G.B.Batty; D.J.Robertson, S.M.Going; K.K.Lambert, R.W.Norton, K.J.Tanner, P.J.Whiting, H.H.MacDonald, I.A.Kirkpatrick, A.R.Leslie (captain), K.W.Stewart.
**Referee:** G.Domercq (FRF)

If 1973 bore some relation to a reunion of the British Lions of 1971, the following year was very definitely a regrouping of the pack of Lions that triumphed in South Africa in 1974. The whole Test match eight, with Willie John McBride as captain, was chosen to represent the Barbarians for their encounter against New Zealand. Having selected the pack, and trusting to the fitness of Gordon Brown, who was still recovering from a broken hand suffered in South Africa, the Committee endeavoured to get away completely from a Lions' choice in the threequarter line – by including only Edwards and Irvine of the Lions' back division. John Bevan of Aberavon was included as the traditional uncapped player. In the New Zealand side, there were ten players who had taken part in the 'classic' of 1973, including the whole of the back division bar Duncan Robertson.

The New Zealanders' short, eight-match tour was a part of Ireland's centenary celebrations. The All Blacks improved with every game, beating each of the Irish provinces before undertaking a most formidable sequence of opponents, in so brief a space of time. First, there was a full international against Ireland, followed by a meeting with a Welsh XV – Wales in all but name – only four days later. Finally there was the Barbarian match, to make three international-calibre games in the space of eight days. It will be forever to the credit of the All Blacks, and their captain

*Barbarians v New Zealand, 1974.*
Back row: *J.F.Slattery, A.R.Irvine, F.E.Cotton, T.M.Davies, R.M.Uttley, G.L.Brown, P.J.Warfield, D.J.Duckham.* Middle row: *T.G.R.Davies, J.McLauchlan, W.J.McBride, G.O.Edwards, P.S.Preece.* On ground: *J.D.Bevan, R.W.Windsor.*

*The try by Mervyn Davies which enabled the Barbarians to draw with the All Blacks in 1974, in the closing minutes of the game: Mervyn Davies seized on a loose ball, and clasping it in one hand he lunged through, and round, Andy Leslie, the All Blacks captain, to plant the ball over the goal line for the equalising score. It would have been an injustice to the All Blacks if Andy Irvine's conversion attempt from wide out had been successful.*

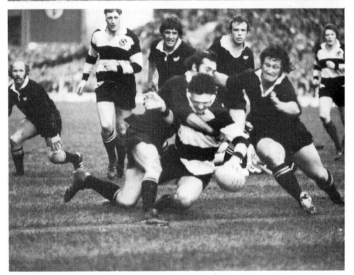

Andy Leslie in particular, that not only did they end this arduous tour unbeaten, but also brightened the off-field image of New Zealand rugby, that had become tarnished during the previous visit of the Seventh All Blacks. The 1974 touring team was very popular.

There is no doubt that the All Blacks can count themselves unlucky that they did not win at Twickenham. They certainly deserved to do so. The Barbarians' performance was not impressive. They never gained any real command up front until the closing minutes, and were unable to launch the kind of attack that the 70,000 crowd had come to see. The Barbarian wingers, Davies and Duckham, scarcely received a pass all afternoon — hardly in the best of Barbarian traditions! In fact there was little evidence of the style of Barbarian rugby which Tony O'Reilly in the match programme referred to as 'a willingness to take risks'.

An early obstruction on John Bevan brought a fine fifty-yard penalty goal by Andy Irvine, but the Barbarian lead was shortlived. Gradually, the All Black forwards asserted themselves. Peter Whiting, despite a nagging shoulder injury, dominated the line-out; while he, MacDonald, and Kirkpatrick won the close quarter duels, with the usual impressive All Black rucking and tenacity in the loose in which Leslie and Ken Stewart also excelled. Karam kicked a penalty goal when Irvine held on to the ball too long and, inevitably, after a long-continued assault, the first try was scored. Gerald Davies attempted, in one of the few moments of Barbarian ambition, to run the ball out of defence, but was held. The All Blacks drove up field, from one ruck to the next; Going almost went over, and Andy Leslie finally did so. The only remarkable thing about the try was that it took so long in coming – for the half-time score, 7–3 to New Zealand, did not in any way fairly reflect the balance of play.

Early in the second half, Irvine kicked a second penalty after a late tackle by Karam on McLauchlan. But the All Blacks, undaunted, were the team to show some enterprise and initiative thereafter, not the Barbarians. Had the New Zealand mid-field backs matched up to the performance of their pack they might, with justification, have taken a commanding lead. But Irvine put the Barbarians in front with another fine penalty kick – his kicking, seemingly, was the Barbarians' only potent weapon.

Summoning still more effort, the All Blacks countered again. Going broke off from the scrum heel, set up one ruck and then another, before Batty, now in the scrum-half position behind the ruck, produced a kick of the kind that had almost succeeded in the preceding match against Wales. He spotted Bryan Williams unmarked and some distance away from Dave Duckham, close to the far right-hand touch-line, and then placed a diagonal kick with such pinpoint accuracy to his wing partner that Williams simply picked up the ball and scored a try which Karam converted. The Barbarians, however, saved their best effort for the last five minutes: for once they attacked from their own twenty-five. Irvine ran well, making the overlap outside Gerald Davies, and then hoisted a high cross-kick in-field. The bounce beat the All Black defenders, and as the Barbarian forwards piled in on the loose ball, it popped up just right for Mervyn Davies. In characteristic style, he seemed to stretch his 6ft 4½in frame still further and, with the ball held in his mighty one-handed grasp, lunged through the last line of defence Andy Leslie, and planted it down for the try that brought the scores level. Though a fine score, it would have been an injustice to the All Blacks if Andy Irvine's injury-time conversion attempt had been successful. As it was, Mervyn Davies's brilliant effort had really denied the All Blacks the victory they had earned.

While there may have been some disappointment at the Baa-Baas' performance, there were glowing tributes to Andy Leslie's men. The All Blacks had come through a unique challenge to an international touring team with great success on the field but, perhaps more important in the long term, they had been equally triumphant in ensuring that future touring teams from New Zealand would, once again, be warmly received in Britain as ambassadors of a great rugby nation.

## 12. BARBARIANS v AUSTRALIA 1976
24 January 1976 at Cardiff Arms Park

Barbarians 19 (3T, 2C, 1PG) Australia 7 (1T, 1PG)
**Barbarians:** A.R.Irvine; T.G.R.Davies, R.W.R.Gravell, C.M.H.Gibson, J.J.Williams; P.Bennett, G.O.Edwards; F.M.D.Knill, P.J.Wheeler, A.B.Carmichael, G.L.Brown, A.J.Martin, J.F.Slattery, T.P.Evans, T.M.Davies (captain).

**Australia:** J.C.Hindmarsh; J.R.Ryan, R.D.L'Estrange, G.A.Shaw (captain), L.E.Monaghan (replacement, W.A.McKid); L.J.Weatherstone, R.G.Hauser, J.E.C.Meadows, C.M.Carberry, R.Graham, G.Fay, R.A.Smith, G.K.Pearse, A.A.Shaw, M.E.Loane (replacement D.W.Hillhouse).
**Referee:** G.Domercq (FRF)

*Barbarians v Australia, 1976.*
Back row: *A.H.Ensor (repl), D.F.Madsen (repl), D.B.Williams (repl), F.M.D.Knill, T.P.Evans, A.J.Martin, G.L.Brown, A.R.Irvine, R.M.Wilkinson (repl), B.G.Nelmes (repl), I.R.McGeechan (repl), G.Domercq (referee), M.S.Lewis (touch-judge), G.Windsor Lewis.* Middle row: *G.A.Ferguson, D.Jones (touch-judge), J.F.Slattery, T.G.R.Davies, T.M.Davies (captain), H.Waddell, C.M.H.Gibson, A.B.Carmichael, G.O.Edwards.* Front row: *P.J.Wheeler, P.Bennett, J.J.Williams, R.W.R.Gravell.*

Since 1973, there has inevitably been the burden of comparison of each and every Barbarian performance with that majestic game against the All Blacks. Not surprisingly, no match has been able to live up to that exceptional occasion. As Herbert Waddell, the President, said before the 1976 game:

> 'Such matches occur once in a generation, but there are fine players capable of great things in both the Barbarian and Australian teams this year, who can provide entertainment and good rugby.'

Nick Shehadie, who had been part of that very first match between the Baa-Baas and the Third Wallabies back in 1948, was fittingly invited to write in the programme of this game, some 28 years later. He admitted to having sat spellbound, complete with Barbarian blazer and tie, before a television set in Australia to watch the 1973 epic. He suggested, with a touch of envy and nostalgia, that the players would once again in 1976:

> '. . . be privileged, as they walk out on to this hallowed ground, to hear the beautiful singing in an atmosphere never to be emulated anywhere in the world.'

The Barbarians were indeed back in Cardiff, but however much the players and public may have willed it, the rugby entertainment could never approach the spectacle that had preceded it three years before.

There was a very strong Welsh representation in the Barbarian side to face Australia — nine in all — with J.J.Williams a late replacement for Peter Squires, who had broken his arm, and Andy Irvine coming in for J.P.R.Williams who had a facial injury. Gareth Edwards was making a record fifth successive appearance; Gerald Davies, who had first appeared in 1967, was playing for the fourth time; and Mervyn Davies was chosen as the sixth Welshman to captain the Barbarians in this special game. England, incidentally, have still to provide a captain for this match.

Yet, although they recognised the obvious strengths of the Barbarian fifteen, the Wallabies were still hopeful that they could repeat the victory of 1967. Despite having lost three internationals, and the services of their outstanding captain, John Hipwell, midway through their tour, there was an air of confidence in Wallaby ranks after their win over Ireland and Gwent in the previous week. Certainly the warmth of the reception accorded to the Australians when they took the field before the game could scarcely have been more encouraging, though the crowd's tribute to the touring party was somewhat spoiled by the appearance of the Barbarians in this farewell gesture by the whole Australian squad. Unfortunately, there was to be little joy for either the Wallabies or the Cardiff crowd on this occasion.

Strangely, the Barbarian back division never seemed to 'click'. Plenty of good possession was squandered early on, especially by Gareth Edwards whose kicking was far more in evidence, and, by his own standards much less accurate, than usual. As if in sympathy, the rest of the backs' play left much to be desired; flair and inspiration was missing from the start. J.J.Williams, who had scored a magnificent hat-trick of tries for Wales against Australia, and Gerald Davies, made the best of what few opportunities came their way. An uninspiring first half was opened by a penalty goal by Jim Hindmarsh, after the Barbarian front row had been penalised. Only occasional movements of adventure by Gibson and Bennett brightened the play. The Wallabies stayed in contention with some very effective mauling and sound defence, in which Mark Loane excelled, although early in the second half he was injured and forced to leave the fray. There was a good try by Bennett before half-time – the fly-half linked to Irvine who passed on to Williams, and when the winger was held ten yards short of the corner he managed to feed back inside to Bennett, who ran over unopposed. So at the interval it was 4–3 . . . and the crowd continued to wait for the game to come truly alive in the second half.

Unfortunately, they waited in vain. Australia regained the lead when the burly John Ryan (who, with fellow-wingers Paddy Batch and Laurie Monaghan, had been a very effective force on tour) took a high pass from Pearse, after Hindmarsh had joined the line, to set up the attack. Pearse fed the ball on to Ryan, who burst through Irvine's attempted tackle and scored.

The Barbarians were thus raised to greater efforts, and the industrious Peter Wheeler (who had achieved notoriety by scoring a record hat-trick of tries as a hooker for the Baa-Baas against the East Midlands the previous year) gathered a loose ball, after Trefor Evans had made ground from the back of a line-out, to force his way over for a try. Gerald Davies and J.J.Williams provided some occasional moments that excited the crowd, but in general the Barbarian sallies were spasmodic and fleeting. Bennett added a penalty goal, and then in the dying moments of the game, J.J.Williams, with an unobserved knock-on, took advantage of the Australians' hesitancy as they checked expecting the whistle, to sprint away in a wide arc to outflank the remaining cover and run round under the posts. Bennett's conversion completed the scoring.

Not even the sadly-contrived finale, with the band attempting to lead the farewell singing, could mask the disappointment of both the players and the spectators at the end of the game.

# Chapter 10

# BARBARIANS ABROAD

## *The New Zealand Barbarians*

The 'Little Baa-Baas', as they style themselves in New Zealand in deference to their older brothers in Britain, are a flourishing club. They owe their foundation to Hugh McLean, who, while touring as a wing-forward with the 1935 All Blacks, learned from a chance meeting at a match dinner with Emile de Lissa all about the style and enjoyment of the Barbarian club. That conversation with de Lissa planted the idea in H.F.McLean's mind of forming a counterpart club in New Zealand. With the help of his great friend and fellow All Black, Ronald Bush, he set about putting the idea into practice. In 1938, H.F.McLean's XV played a charity match at a small town, Thames, on the Firth of Thames in North Island, New Zealand. The weekend was a great success, support for such a side committed to playing open, enjoyable rugby seemed to be in evidence, and within a year the first New Zealand Barbarian side met Auckland. The Baa-Baas won by playing running rugby, and it was clear that Auckland Province welcomed the advent of the new club.

The war years, however, held up the development of the infant club — most of the playing members joined the Services, and travelled overseas. Tragically, three of their most renowned players — Bill Carson, a double All Black, George Hart, and Cyril Pepper, a 1935 All Black — lost their lives. So on the resumption of its activities after the war, the club instituted the Carson-Hart-Pepper Barbarian Shield, in memory of these three, to be presented for the best sportsmanship in the annual primary schools' tournament in Auckland. By 1947 the Little Baa-Baas were playing again with many famous names to be numbered in their ranks — Bob Scott, Freddie Allen, Eric Boggs, and several others of the 1949 All Blacks.

The club went into the country districts to play two or three matches a year, and built up a close liaison with the secondary schools. At schools level, the usual pattern of the game was to play fifteen-minute spells; then each Baa-Baa would give a short session of coaching and advice to his opposite number, and then the game resumed. This style of instruction made a great impact on the schoolboy players. At the same time the policy of encouraging young players developed, and promising talent was included in Barbarian teams. Ron Jarden, a great All Black wing-threequarter of the fifties, Bryan Fitzpatrick and Peter Jones of the 1953 All Blacks, were all helped on their way to international recognition and selection by appearing in Barbarian colours. But not everything worked in the Baa-Baas' favour. The bright adventurous style of the young Barbarian club did much to proliferate the idea outside the confines of Auckland, and six or seven other clubs were formed on similar lines elsewhere in the country.

The New Zealand Rugby Union became concerned about this development, especially as some matches took the free-running, open, carefree style to an absurd, even farcical extreme. Some British Lions of 1966 took part in one such game prior to the Fourth Test against the All Blacks. The Little Baa-Baas determined, as a result, that tighter control and authority was needed to prevent the members from losing sight of the purpose and original aims of the club, which were the same as its parent body. Younger men were welcomed as committee members, and Wilson Whineray became a highly-respected club captain. More recently still, Arthur Hughes and George Nelson were instrumental in putting the club's social well-being on a firmer footing. They bought premises, to be established as Barbarian headquarters – a small house backing on to Eden Park. The members, under the President at that time, Jack Bourke, turned the cottage into club rooms by their own efforts. Amidst collections of ties and jerseys and plaques which decorate the walls, members may call in to meet friends on the way to a match, or for a purely social gathering mid-week.

The New Zealand Barbarians have always enjoyed recognition by the parent body – the 'Big Baa-Baas' – largely achieved through the good offices of Bob Scott, and Hugh McLean's brother Terry, the renowned rugby journalist. Mrs Haigh-Smith even designed the club badge, with the Four Home Union crests on one side, and the silver fern on the other. The club tie, two white lambs gambolling on a maroon and red background, was devised by Hugh McLean, and the jersey is of similar design. The New Zealand Barbarians' Club, now thirty-nine years old, has a membership of about two hundred and seventy. They play varied fixtures, largely within Auckland, in which province they enjoy a high standing. With the valued membership of such great All Black players as Ian Kirkpatrick and Andy Leslie, and with Wilson Whineray as President, the Little Baa-Baas are flourishing. But they will always hold in the highest regard and admiration the senior Baa-Baas, who still represent the ideal towards which the New Zealand Barbarian Football Club will continue to strive.

## The South African Barbarians

The South African Barbarian Rugby Football Club was founded in 1960, with similar objects and aims as the parent club in Britain. What prompted the establishment of the club at that particular time was the fact that many small clubs, of an unofficial kind, were starting up in some of the provincial unions as invitation sides, playing carefree rugby outside the confines of the normal club structure. The idea was first mooted in Natal, and at the inaugural meeting were Harry Stacey, then the Natal Rugby Union President, his successor Basil Medway, Peter Taylor, Leo Smithers, Nic Labuschagne and Isaac van Heerden – all names well known in worldwide rugby circles. The intention of the new club was to follow the principles of the British Barbarians, in this case taking an exciting brand of rugby to the smaller unions. The 'senior' Barbarian club, in the person of Brigadier Glyn Hughes, gave the new off-shoot its blessing, and Frank Mellish was appointed the first President with Harry Stacey as Chairman.

Their first match was an auspicious occasion, played in Durban on 1 September 1960. The South African Barbarian team was composed of Springbok and All Black players who had just completed the Test series of that year. Avril Malan was the captain with Wilson Whineray his right-hand man. The opponents were Natal, a very strong province at that time, including Keith Oxlee, Roy Dryburgh, Nic Labuschagne, Trix Truter, Ormond Taylor, Lappies Labuschagne, Koos Bahlman and Brian Irvine. There were eighteen internationals on the field of play. The Baa-Baas were leading 11–5 at half-time, but Natal finally won 18–11.

Despite the promising beginnings, the South African Barbarians have been bedevilled by problems almost from the start. Although early matches were played against several of the provincial teams, including Western Province, Northern Transvaal and Rhodesia, the original idea of an Easter tour never got off the ground. Easter was far too early in the South African season; and at the season's end, provincial teams and players were inevitably tied up with Currie Cup matches. The Barbarians did not wish to be confined to Natal players, but had difficulty in getting players from other provincial unions who seemed to fear an intrusion into their own affairs.

Match programmes from two Barbarian tours of South Africa. In 1958 Western Transvaal became the first provincial team to beat the visiting 'cavemen'! In 1969, in a unique encounter, the South African Barbarians beat the touring Barbarians 23–11, in Port Elizabeth.

Neither was the South African Rugby Board's enthusiasm any greater than that of the provincial bodies. This lack became positive antagonism, when on one occasion several Springbok players appeared at a pre-Test gathering in Barbarian blazers rather than those bearing the national emblem. There was a practical problem, too, of distance — the difficulty of inviting players from so far afield within the country, although this was necessary in order to maintain the standard and variation of selection. In addition there was already a growing 'threat' in the Transvaal — a club of similar character, the Quaggas. There was scarcely room for both.

Despite the setbacks and the practical problems, the Barbarians struggled on. In 1969, the 'original' Barbarians met the South African Barbarians on the former's six-match tour of Southern Africa. In a unique encounter in Port Elizabeth, the home players deservedly won 23–11. But in terms of major events, that match may have been the South African club's swansong. The increasing strength and better organisation of the Quaggas, together with the absence of any real encouragement from the governing bodies of South African rugby, brought a decline in the club's fortunes. The match with the British Lions in 1974 was essentially a Quaggas affair. Discussions between the two clubs' chairmen, Pat Lyster and Chick Henderson, led to some sort of agreement and amalgamation between the two clubs, so that when the All Blacks toured in 1976 they met a combined Quaggas–Barbarians team.

The future position at the time of writing is still one of uncertainty. Basil Medway, one of the founder members, feels that there is still a rôle for the South African Barbarians — probably, though, in continued partnership with the stronger, and seemingly more viable, Quaggas.

## The Overseas Tours
## CANADA 1957
**Tour Record: Played 6    Won 6    Points for 227    Points against 23**

| | |
|---|---|
| 27 April v Ontario XV | Won 47–3 |
| 30 April v Ontario XV | Won 52–0 |
| 4 May v British Columbia XV | Won 19–6 |
| 8 May v British Columbia XV | Won 51–8 |
| 11 May v British Columbia XV | Won 17–3 |
| 14 May v Quebec XV | Won 41–3 |

**Players**: *Backs*: T.J.Davies, A.J.F.O'Reilly, J.E.Woodward, G.M.Griffiths, G.T.Wells, P.H.Thompson, C.I.Morgan, D.G.S.Baker, A.F.Dorward, A.A.Mulligan *Forwards:* E.Evans, R.Roe, C.R.Jacobs, G.W.Hastings, R.H.Williams, R.W.D.Marques, E.J.S.Michie, J.T.Greenwood, A.Robson, T.E.Reid
**Manager**: H.L.Glyn Hughes

In rugby terms, the 1957 tour was purely a 'missionary' one. But as a first venture abroad the visit was as resounding a success as it was an enjoyable experience for those taking part. For Robin Roe, it was especially memorable:

> 'On the Canadian tour of 1957, I met my wife at 0900 hours on the Saturday, proposed marriage the following Sunday, 10pm, and we married four months later. In rugby language I think that was one against the head!'

Eric Evans recalls the pleasure of that tour too:

> 'We had a fabulous time in Canada, entertained as we were in regal style on a millionaire's yacht. The girls were so exquisite I made no moves and kept strictly to polite conversation. As I said to one of them: "I haven't put a foot wrong, have I?" "No", she said, "why not?" My other outstanding memory is of Tony O'Reilly. How he ever became so famous in industry I'll never understand, because on tour I had to act as nursemaid for him, watch his kit, his keys, his baggage, and get him everywhere on time. In spite of my endeavours he nonetheless achieved a "classic". During the tour he had his twenty-first birthday and we bought his present, organised his party and waited for Tony. And waited and waited. I couldn't win!'

In fact, the birthday party was one of the social highlights of the tour – by the very great kindness of Mr and Mrs Edward Gibson, it was held in their magnificent home in West Vancouver.

On the playing front, perhaps the most remarkable achievement was that of A.F.Dorward, the international scrum-half, who showed his versatility in the final game, scoring three times as a winger outside O'Reilly.

## SOUTH AFRICA 1958
**Tour Record: Played 6    Won 2    Drawn 1    Lost 3    Points for 109    Points against 76**

| | |
|---|---|
| 10 May v Transvaal | Drew 17–17 |
| 14 May v Western Transvaal | Lost 3–11 |
| 18 May v Western Province | Lost 8–9 |
| 21 May v Northern Transvaal | Won 13–9 |
| 24 May v Combined Transvaal | Lost 16–18 |
| 28 May v East Africa | Won 52–12 |

**Players:** *Backs:* T.E.Davies, R.W.T.Chisholm, A.J.F.O'Reilly, C.Pedlow. M.C.Thomas, B.J.Jones, A.R.Smith, G.T.Wells, C.I.Morgan, G.H.Waddell, A.A.Mulligan, R.E.G.Jeeps *Forwards:* W.R.Evans, C.R.Jacobs, H.Morgan, H.T.McLeod, R.W.Marques, R.H.Davies, A.R.Dawson, S.H.Wilcock, J.Greenwood, A.Ashcroft, R.H.Williams, N.S.Bruce, G.M.Hastings
**Manager:** H.L.Glyn Hughes   **Asst Manager:** H.Waddell

In marked contrast with the tour the previous year, the Barbarians encountered formidable opposition during their five matches in South Africa. Their greatest triumph was, perhaps, in beating the holders of the Currie Cup, Northern Transvaal. But how close they came to conquering the might of the combined forces of all the Northern Provincial teams in the final climactic game — but for the accidental intervention of a press photographer preventing Tony O'Reilly scoring his try behind the posts, and Arthur Smith dropping the ball when about to score, the Barbarians might deservedly have won. As it was, the Barbarian rugby both in victory and defeat brought them the greatest tributes. The pack, often out-weighted, were magnificent in holding the renowned might of the South African forwards. Behind the scrum the mainspring of attack was Cliff Morgan, captivating the crowds once more as he had done when with the Lions in 1955. Andy Mulligan, with Jeeps prevented by illness from playing more than one game, came through a tough schedule with credit. The polished play of Arthur Smith and the powerful running of Tony O'Reilly on the wings (and also for O'Reilly in the centre) continually excited and thrilled. Nor is it surprising that this Barbarian tour party was as popular off the field as they were on it. A great tour, as Herbert Waddell said at the time:

> 'We could hardly have had five more exciting matches in South Africa than those.'

## SOUTH AFRICA 1969
**Tour Record: Played 6    Won 3    Lost 3    Points for 124    Points against 101**

| | |
|---|---|
| 10 May v Quaggas | Won 29– 3 |
| 14 May v Natal | Lost 14–16 |
| 17 May v SA Barbarians | Lost 11–23 |
| 21 May v Southern Universities | Lost 14–16 |
| 24 May v South African Country Districts | Won 32–22 |
| 26 May v Rhodesia | Won 24–21 |

**Players:** *Backs:* B.J.O'Driscoll, R.E.Webb, C.D.Saville, D.J.Duckham, A.G.Biggar, A.T.A.Duggan, C.M.Telfer, B.J.McGann, W.Hullin, N.C.Starmer-Smith   *Forwards:* N.Suddon, J.P.O'Shea, J.V.Pullin, F.A.L.Laidlaw, K.E.Fairbrother, W.J.Morris, G.F.Bayles, I.S.Gallacher, J.Jeffrey, D.P.Rogers, R.J.Arneil, M.L.Hipwell, R.B.Taylor
**Manager:** H.L.Glyn Hughes   **Asst Manager & Hon. Sec:** G.Windsor-Lewis
**Asst Hon. Sec & Treasurer:** G.A.Ferguson

Despite motions tabled by the Labour Party in the House of Commons, the Barbarians went ahead with their tour to South Africa, emphatic that politics should be kept out of sport. As with the preceding visit, the 1969 tour was an outstanding success, and a wonderful experience for those taking part. As the official report of the tour stated:

> 'Every match should have been won, two were lost by the smallest of margins, a conversion. Our losses could have been attributed to our efforts to play completely open Barbarian football and being guilty of poor handling on occasions in vulnerable positions.'

There was also a shortage of dependable place-kickers. Without doubt the greatest triumph was against the most powerful team, the South African Country Districts, which included — among other Springboks — Dawie de Villiers, their captain, Pete Visagie, Jan Ellis and Hannes Marais. Moreover the victory was achieved with only seven forwards for the whole of the second half, when Budge Rogers left the field with concussion. The hospitality, generosity and kindness of the South African hosts was quite magnificent — and despite enjoying social events to the full, and being hampered by many injuries, the Barbarians did reciprocate by proving to be a very popular touring side.

## CANADA 1976

**Tour Record: Played 8    Won 8    Points for 414    Points against 45**

| | |
|---|---|
| 29 May v New England | Won 40–12 |
| 31 May v BATS | Won 28– 7 |
| 2 June v British Columbia | Won 34–15 |
| 5 June v Alberta | Won 56– 4 |
| 8 June v Saskatchewan | Won 76– 0 |
| 12 June v Canada | Won 29– 4 |
| 15 June v Quebec | Won 75– 3 |
| 17 June v Atlantic All Stars | Won 76– 0 |

**Players:** *Backs:* A.R.Irvine, K.M.Bushell, B.Patrick, D.Shedden, J.J.Williams, D.J.McKay, S.Fenwick, R.W.R.Gravell, D.A.Cooke, P.Bennett, G.Davies, A.J.Lawson, D.B.Williams, *Forwards:* A.C.Carmichael, M.Knill, P.Llewellyn, D.Madsen, P.Wheeler, A.Tomes, G.Wheel, J.Watkins, G.Adey, A.Alexander, M.A.Biggar, G.Jenkins, A.Neary
**Manager:** H.Waddell **Asst Manager:** G.Windsor-Lewis **Asst Hon. Sec:** G.A.Ferguson

Two matches in the Boston Bicentennial Tournament, and six matches in Canada, made up the Barbarians' second tour to North America. Unhappily, in rugby-playing terms, the games proved little, perhaps only serving to emphasise the gulf that still remains between the standard of rugby in Britain and the New World. Seventy-five tries in eight matches must be some sort of a touring team record; sixteen tries in one match is certainly a Barbarian try-scoring record. The two totals of seventy-six points are also the highest score by the Barbarians ever in a match. But those statistics do not really count for much. For the Barbarians, the tour was a rugby frolic despite the extremely busy schedule. The opposition were very disappointing in their performances — for the Canadians it was a chastening experience. Even so, their welcome was no less warm than it had been some nine years before.

# PRESIDENTS SINCE CARPMAEL

EMILE DE LISSA – The Second President

'A Moses and Aaron, and something more besides'.       O.L.Owen, 1933

'There is no more popular figure in Rugger than "Old Emile" and next year the Barbarians will miss that old familiar figure in that old familiar grey tweed suit, holding the touch flag, and pausing after each score to mark it down on the back of an envelope, and advancing at half-time to give his views, which are so deadly accurate. Perhaps he will be missed most of all at the dinner after the matches, when he sallies forth every now and then from his perch at the head of the long table to calm the noise or vocal efforts of some members of the team. He is a great and charming personality, and few men are better capable of handling thirty cheery rugby footballers.'
I.M.B.Stuart, Ireland and Barbarians, October 1928

Emile Ernest Vere de Lissa, second President of the Barbarians, was born in Sydney, Australia in the same year as the RFU was founded, and the first ever international played – 1871. He was for a time educated at Sydney Grammar School, until his family moved to England when he was about eleven; there his schooling continued at University College School. He was a member of Blackheath, but never a player of great renown. His own rugby career scarcely extended beyond his school-days, at the end of which a foot injury, and a long overseas sojourn in Germany, really put paid to his active involvement. However he was often to be seen as a first-class referee, and always to be seen on the touch-line for both Blackheath and the Barbarians. He was well known in his younger days as a top-class croquet player; he won the Croquet Association Silver Medal in 1909, and in 1923 was one of the selected ten leading players to contest the Beddow Cup. But his love of rugby, and support for the Blackheath club, brought him into contact with their secretary, W.P.Carpmael, with whom he developed a strong friendship.

On the Easter Tour of 1901 de Lissa first became a Barbarian camp-follower, as an unelected – but requested – assistant to Carpmael. Soon he became one of the first 'alickadoos'. In 1905 Emile was elected full member and Honorary Secretary in succession to 'Jock' Hartley – and so a happy administrative partnership with Carpmael was ensured. The founder still guided the club's fortunes, but Emile de Lissa became increasingly more than just Carpmael's right-hand man. He held the post of Secretary until 1913, was Honorary Treasurer from 1914–1924, both Secretary and Treasurer in 1924–25, and Honorary Treasurer again from 1925–1928. On retiring from that office he was elected Vice-President in 1928 and succeeded to the Presidency on Carpmael's death in 1936 until he died aged eighty-four on 16 August, 1955. Those are the bare facts of his service to the Barbarians, but they tell little of his endearing personality and wise council during his fifty years as a rare non-playing member.

During his years of office Emile was not only an able organiser but a shrewd diplomat. There were crises which demanded tact – for example problems

Emile de Lissa – The
Second President.
Above: Emile's long
association with the
Barbarians began with the
Easter Tour of 1901, and
ended in 1955, during which
time he served the club as
Secretary, Treasurer, Vice-
President and finally, for
twenty years, as President in
succession to his friend
Percy Carpmael. Right:
'Emile' with E.H.D.Sewell, a
well-known rugby writer of
the time, at Richmond
Athletic Ground. For sixteen
years de Lissa presided over
the many sporting activities
that took place there, as its
secretary.

especially in South Wales concerning guarantees, playing dates, and rough play.
Matches with Swansea were suspended in 1906 and 1907, and again with Newport in 1923 and 1924, and there was trouble, too, with Cardiff after a filthy game
in 1925. Despite the enormous popularity of these fixtures, the Barbarians were not
exactly in the strongest of bargaining positions with the South Wales clubs during
de Lissa's pre-Presidential years. The Barbarians' first victory over Swansea did not
come until 1923, there was only one victory over Newport between 1893 and
1926 and only two wins at Cardiff between 1900 and 1920. But whatever the
problems may have been, de Lissa's diplomacy smoothed things over.

These Welsh fixtures have been played, except during the war, every year since.
Emile's guidance and encouragement, in happy co-operation with Haigh-Smith,
brought a new era of playing success to the Baa-Baas between the wars, without in
any way compromising the sheer enjoyment, the style of play or unique character of
the touring club. He was still at the hub of affairs when the Barbarians enjoyed
unparalleled triumphs on the field — culminating in an unbroken sequence of
twenty-two victories over Welsh clubs between 1930 and 1936. He appreciated
that for the special image of the Barbarians to be maintained, victory must be more
common than defeat. As *The Times* obituary related, his conduct of operations on
the Easter tour of South Wales quickly spread his name and fame. In his own quiet
but forceful way he won the respect and confidence of everyone, from the most

doughty of Welsh veterans — whether official or player — to the liveliest member of the Barbarian party. It was often remarked that 'only Emile could do it', and probably that was true in the old rowdy days. It was reckoned too, that if you wanted to hear all about:

'Welsh club footer in its own "midden", Emile de Lissa will tell you the whole story, A to Z and back again.'

And quite an authority he must have become, missing only one Easter Tour in the first half of the twentieth century — and that through illness in 1939. In 1929, at the second Barbarian reunion dinner at the Park Lane Hotel, Brigadier-General Philip Maud, one of the great Barbarians of early years (he played for the club some twenty-four times in the 1890s), presented Emile with a huge silver salver engraved with the names of three hundred Baa-Baas who had been associated with him.

Another treasured moment was to follow almost twenty years later, in 1948. When Emile took his place at the head of the table for the dinner that followed the first-ever fixture with a Dominion touring team, the Third Wallabies at Cardiff, during the proceedings he presented, as President of the Club, the Barbarian insignia and honorary membership to the Australian captain, Bill McLean.

In addition to his Barbarian duties, Emile was secretary to the United Hospitals for thirteen years, and between 1932 and 1948 was a highly popular figure as secretary at the Richmond Athletic Ground, presiding over all the cricket, tennis and rugby activities that took place there. Apart from the home fixtures of Richmond and London Scottish, de Lissa made the Athletic Ground a rugby centre, with county championship matches, schoolboy international games, and the Hospitals Cup.

Emile was a rugby man if ever there was one. During his reign, the Barbarians' club song was not the only one to resound raucously round the dining-room at the Esplanade. There was also another, dedicated to a great Barbarian:

'Hurrah for Emile, Emile is the man,
Hurrah for Emile on the table he shall stand,
He really is a daisy, he drives the ladies crazy,
Ein, zwei, drei, vier, Emile's going to buy us beer,
Hurrah for Emile, he's a grand old man.'

## JACK HAIGH-SMITH — The Third President

'Haigho' was President of the Barbarians for only a few weeks. The death of Emile de Lissa in August 1955 after a long period of increasing ill-health was sad and sudden; but it did not produce the profound shock that was felt on the death in hospital of H.A. Haigh-Smith in October of that same year, at the age of seventy-one. 'Haigho' had been an outstanding Barbarian from his election as a playing member to the club on the Easter tour of 1913, through a thirty-year period of office as Honorary Secretary, to his tragically brief term as the club President. All had hoped and expected that this vital and popular leader would have been able to guide the destiny of the Barbarians for at least another decade.

Haigh-Smith was educated at that renowned rugby stronghold, Marlborough, which with Rugby School was very much in the forefront as a nursery for future internationals. Haigh was captain of football, and became a fine all-round sportsman, playing rugby for Blackheath and the Trojans, and representing Hampshire not only at rugby but also cricket and hockey. He wore the Barbarian shirt as a tough prop-forward on three occasions but became renowned above all as an outstanding organiser and administrator. He was Honorary Secretary and sole selector for Hampshire between 1925 and 1937, during which time his side won the County

*Jack Haigh-Smith — The Third President.*
*Sadly, 'Haigho's' term of presidency lasted for only a few weeks before his death in 1955. He had previously given devoted service as Barbarian Honorary Secretary for more than thirty years.*

Championship twice in 1933 and 1936. He was also, for a term, the Hampshire President. He was the Hampshire representative on the RFU Committee until the time of his death, and a member of the Four Home Union Tours Committee. In 1938 he was assistant manager of the British Lions tour of South Africa, a tour run by Barbarian alickadoos since Major B.C.Hartley, an earlier Barbarian Honorary Secretary, was manager of Sammy Walker's Lions side — a tour which ended with a glorious victory in the third and final Test match.

At Twickenham Haigh-Smith was a familiar figure, since he touch-judged every international there between 1930 and 1949. Then, during World War II, when Twickenham, like many other major rugby grounds, was requisitioned for Civil Defence and Services use, Haigh-Smith (with the co-operation of J.C.Hartley and Emile de Lissa) was instrumental in organising the Red Cross and Service Internationals at the Richmond Athletic Ground. These charity matches helped to maintain the game at a high standard even during the war years. Significantly, too, the 'Barbarian-organised' fixture between the French Services and a British Empire side in 1945 paved the way to a resumption of international matches with France, with whom rugby relations had been severed in 1931. It was 'Haigho' again, who, with the remarkable Leicester Secretary Eric Thorneloe, arranged seven Barbarian matches with Midlands and 'Thorneloe's' Fifteens between 1940 and 1944. Not only did these matches provide some outstanding rugby in those lean, sporting years, but also raised large sums of money for Services charities.

It was of course for his service to the Barbarians that 'Haigho' will principally be remembered. In company with his predecessors he was a firm administrator and as Brigadier Glyn Hughes put it:

'. . . his main anxiety always was to uphold the traditions and standards of the club and woe betide anyone who let the side down.'

## BRIGADIER H.L.GLYN HUGHES – The Fourth President

Perhaps the greatest strength of the Barbarian Football Club has been its ability to provide a succession of ideal Presidents. 'Cometh the hour, cometh the man' has certainly been true for the Baa-Baas, for when the club suffered the shock of the sudden death of Haigh-Smith in his first few weeks of Presidency, there was a natural successor on hand to take over. 'Hughie', like his predecessors, personified the Barbarians; the perpetuation of the club's status and popularity was if anything enhanced during his eighteen years as their leader. He died aged eighty-one, quite suddenly, but peacefully, following the Scotland versus Argentina match in Edinburgh on 24 November 1973, after a life characterised by great achievement in medical, military, and educational, as well as rugby, spheres. He was a man of immense courage, unbounded energy, single-mindedness of purpose, and certainly not one to suffer fools gladly. Yet he combined an endearing personality with touching modesty, never less at ease than when being persuaded to talk about himself.

Hugh Llewellyn Glyn Hughes was born on 25 July 1892 and spent the first two years of his life in South Africa, a country for which he always held a great affection, and with which he was adamant that sporting links should be maintained. At Epsom College he was captain of the fifteen and his loyalty to his old school endured his life through, culminating in long and valuable service on Epsom's board of governors. Not surprisingly, Epsom has a continuing strong and successful rugby tradition! It also has a distinct medical bias (it was originally the Royal Medical College). Since Glyn Hughes's father was a doctor it was, as so often is the pattern in medical families, like father, like son. At University College Hospital, he was both scholar and prize-winner, qualifying in 1915.

His war service that followed, as a medical officer with the Wiltshire Regiment and the Grenadier Guards, was meritorious indeed. He was awarded the DSO as a subaltern on 25 August 1916, and within a year had been awarded a Bar to that medal for subsequent acts of conspicuous gallantry: the citation in *The Times* read:

> 'Temp. Capt. Hugh Llewellyn Glyn Hughes DSO RAMC. On four separate days he showed an utter contempt for danger when collecting and tending the wounded under heavy shell fire.'

In addition he gained the Military Cross, *Croix de Guerre avec palme,* was several times Mentioned in Despatches, and suffered serious wounds on three occasions – an amazing record of gallantry, of which exploits, as his obituary in *The Lancet* recorded: '. . . he could not easily be induced to speak.'

When World War II broke out he was forty-seven, a Lieutenant in the Army reserve. He was mobilised in 1939 and sent to France with the Fifth Division. He was promoted Brigadier, to become DDMS to the Eighth Corps and the Second Army, becoming Chief Medical Officer in the advance and the first MO to enter Belsen. He took on the responsibility for the care of the inmates and the cleaning up of the camp. This task, together with his many extraordinary feats, led to his being awarded the American Legion of Merit, the Order of St John of Jerusalem and more Mentions in Despatches. The Jewish people especially will long revere his name, and at the end of the war he gave evidence at the Nazi War Criminal Trials at Luneberg, describing his encounter with the concentration camp commandant, Kramer, and the conditions which had confronted him on entering Belsen Camp. He insisted on giving his evidence while standing to attention, for some nine and a half hours.

To this glorious record in the last year of the war a second Bar was added to his DSO, won during the attempt to relieve Arnhem from the South. It was some thirty years after he had won his first medal. Finally, on appointment as Vice-Director of Medical Services, BAOR, in 1945, he was awarded a CBE. His next posting was as

Commandant of the RAMC Depot at Aldershot, and it was not coincidental, I am sure, that under his command the Depot won the Army Rugby Cup for the first time.

Between the wars Hughie had enjoyed his career as a general practitioner at Moretonhampstead in Devon, visiting patients on Dartmoor — on horseback it is told. Later he practised in Kensington, keeping closer contact with his rugby flock.

At the end of World War II he retired from the Army to become the first senior administrative medical officer of the South East Metropolitan Hospital Board at the start of the National Health Service, and, as in his service days, he was very much the leader. Again, as *The Lancet* recorded:

'His striking appearance — a piercing eye amid strong features — and his capacity for quick and confident decision made him a natural leader, commanding loyalty and respect from subordinates. Off the games field it might be said that he was not a good team man, and he certainly did not take too kindly to the slow tempo of deliberation in committee ... He loved action, and if it didn't come to him he sought it.'

At sixty-five, Glyn Hughes took on a new role, as director of the Peckham Health Centre, a position he held for ten years; and he and his second wife, Thelma, involved themselves in the development of the Royal College of General Practitioners.

He was, for a time, an honorary physician to the Queen, president of the Harveian Society and the Casualties Union, and Medical Officer to the British Red Cross Society. He was a keen golfer, and a member of the Royal and Ancient Golf Club. Indeed his enthusiasm for the Barbarian Easter Sunday golf tournament could only be exceeded by Herbert Waddell. In plus-fours, and always with his own set of clubs, he strode the Penarth links for almost sixty years. All this and rugby besides.

Glyn Hughes played his first match for the Barbarians at Penarth on the 1913 tour, whilst still a promising hooker at UCH. It was quite a tough invitation for the young Hughes, even though the Barbarian party included such as E.R.Mobbs, J.M.B.Scott (captain), Tommy Vile and C.H.Pillman at half-back, W.S.D.Craven, J.H.C.Lindesay and C.M.Usher in the forwards. They lost to Penarth, Cardiff and Swansea in the three South Wales matches! Hughie did not end up on the winning side many times on those Easter tours of his playing days — in fact it was not until his eleventh game for the Barbarians, the match with Penarth in 1922, that he came off the field victorious! That must be something of a record.

The Easter tour of 1913 was to be the first of nine successive tours and twenty matches for the club of which he was to become President forty-two years later. In addition he became a staunch Blackheath club member, captain of United Hospitals, and while in the west country he captained Exeter and represented Devon before returning to London, Blackheath, Middlesex and London Counties. Despite a paucity of wins with the Barbarians he did manage to score a try against Penarth in 1923.

But if successes on the field were infrequent in his playing era, the crowds of ten, twelve and fifteen thousand at the Welsh club grounds testified to the Barbarians' popularity, though their performances were not always the showpiece that the spectators had come to expect. But no doubt adequate recompense for any disappointments on the field was made in the after match festivities.

Once Hughie's playing days were over, he became a Barbarian 'alickadoo'. In 1928 he was unanimously elected to the Treasurer's post on the retirement of Emile de Lissa, and the latter's elevation to the new position of Vice-President. Hughie remained in that office until his death forty-five years later. In his eighteen years of Presidency he led the club from the front, so to speak, not only at home but on three overseas tours. It was at the age of eighty-one that Hughie last visited Wales at Easter, his sixtieth anniversary visit with the Baa-Baas. Still flushed with pride over the incredible game between the Baa-Baas and the All Blacks of 1973, his final tour

*Brigadier H.L. Glyn Hughes – The Fourth President*
'Hughie' was a man of great achievement and rare modesty. As a Barbarian he made the first of his twenty playing appearances on the Easter Tour of 1913. Forty-two years later he became President, and led the club for eighteen years, both at home and on three overseas tours.

was a memorable and glorious farewell. The players certainly did their part, winning all four matches to make it a clean sweep for only the third time in twenty-five years.

The most delightful gesture was made at Newport, where the Barbarians notched up an incredible sixty points for the biggest ever total in the Club's history; with a touching sense of occasion, John Spencer, captain of the day and John Gray, the kicker, between them ensured that the final conversion attempt in front of the posts before the 'no-side' whistle was deliberately missed, so that the points remained at the appropriate total of sixty.

The Welsh clubs, too, paid their special tribute, in presenting Hughie with a portrait of the Barbarian President, with replicas to be hung in each of their own club houses, and from Cardiff, the longest in the line of unbroken links, there was an additional presentation on the Arms Park ground of a silver ice-bucket. In those glorious sixty years, Hughie had only once missed an Easter tour, and that on account of a baby's birth demanding his medical attention at his practice in London.

Brigadier Glyn Hughes was certainly a colourful character. For him there was always a right and a wrong way of doing things — good behaviour, respectable dress (club tie and blazer), and courteousness, were qualities he expected of his club members. He was the sort of person that the new Barbarian wanted to call 'Hughie' but felt the proper way to address him was 'Brigadier', or Mr Hughes, until the more familiar title was suggested by the President himself.

In the little snug bar at The Esplanade, Hughie or Herbert Waddell would invite the reticent Barbarian for a late-night drink unless he was one of the team for the following day. There it was more than likely that one would ask for a half, not a pint.

Hughie was both a late and an early bird. He would be supping gin and tonics till the small hours, discussing the game that day, or the encounters to come, in the company of his fellow 'alickadoos' and South Walian club committee hosts. But he would be first up for breakfast, a 'constitutional' along the Marine Parade, and perhaps a round of golf at the club. He brought camaraderie to the tour, enjoying bringing players from diverse clubs and countries together in good fellowship. He ensured that no cliques developed. Yet he remained an avuncular figure, not averse to the high jinks on a Saturday night that he himself had enjoyed in his playing days, but insistent on a certain discipline, imparted with a curt word or a piercing look, that made his feelings quite clear. One knew what was expected, and if as a player, one stepped beyond the bounds, one made sure Hughie didn't find out.

It was always in Brigadier Glyn Hughes's nature to lead by example, and during his sixty years' association with the Barbarians, he made sure the club attained his own high standards, to become, like himself, a name respected and renowned world-wide.


HERBERT  WADDELL — The Fifth President

'As the fifth President in 87 years I appreciate with deep humility that I am following in the footsteps of "the great". It could be said, like Agag in the Bible, I am walking delicately!'

If one were looking for a word to describe Herbert Waddell, 'delicate' would be the least appropriate. As most recently evidenced by his remarkable recovery from illness following the 1976 Barbarian tour of Canada, 'Herbert' has the strongest of constitutions and characters. And strength of character has possibly been the outstanding common denominator amongst an illustrious succession of Barbarian Presidents. Herbert W., as he likes to sign himself, is the last of the Barbarian 'alickadoos' of a vintage era that produced his two predecessors as President, Glyn Hughes and Haigh-Smith. As shrewd a judge over many years of rugby players, as he has been of the capers of the Stock Market, Herbert Waddell's forceful but endearing personality has ensured that the Barbarian F.C. has continued to flourish as ever through a testing period in its history.

Herbert Waddell, the first Scot to hold the office of President, was educated first at Glasgow Academy, and then Fettes College between September 1915 and April 1921. Then, as now, Fettes was a renowned proving ground for first-class rugby players. Herbert was captain of Fettes in a side which included G.P.S. Macpherson and David MacMyn, both renowned Scottish internationals, and also W.B.Scott and G.D.McK. Sutherland who won university Blues. From Fettes, he went to school in France, though his rugby career was interrupted temporarily as a result of a burst appendix. Herbert Waddell returned to Glasgow and joined Glasgow Academicals and quickly became a key figure in an 'Accies' team which was enjoying an outstanding period in the club's history. Between 1921 and 1927 Glasgow Academicals was the finest side in Scotland, very seldom defeated, and in the highly respected opinion of O.L.Owen of *The Times* the best rugby team in the British Isles at that time. International honours for fly-half Waddell followed soon after his joining the Academicals and, in 1924, Bryce and Herbert Waddell were the halves when Oxford University provided the legendary Scottish threequarter line of Smith, Jacob, Macpherson and Wallace. Strange though it may seem that foursome never played together as a unit at the University, but Oxford at that time could field two complete sets of international threequarters! It was an outstandingly successful first appearance for the Oxford players and the halves, as a unit for Scotland against Wales at Inverleith, when Scotland won 35 points to 10. Herbert Waddell won fifteen caps in all, fourteen won consecutively between 1924 and 1927. The total would have been more but for a threatened ulcer and shoulder injury which kept him out of contention in 1928 and 1929, before he returned to the Scottish team for his final cap in the victory over Wales at Murrayfield in 1930. It was a very successful era in Scottish rugby; in 1925 Waddell was stand-off in the only Scottish international side to win the Grand Slam – when his half-back partner was J.B.Nelson, with the four Oxford threequarters outside him, and Dan Drysdale at full-back, with Bannerman leading the fowards. In 1926 he played in the first of the Four Home Union teams ever to win at Twickenham, when Glasgow Accies provided both half-backs Nelson and Waddell and the two centres J.C.Dykes and W.M.Simmers. The four players scored 11 out of the 17 points that brought Scotland victory, 17–9. Joint champions also, with Ireland in 1926 and 1927, this was the most triumphant period in Scotland's international history. In his fifteen internationals Herbert Waddell contributed forty-five points including seven tries, five dropped goals and two conversions. To complete a distinguished playing record, he also toured South Africa with the British Isles Rugby Touring Side in 1924.

His associations with the Barbarians began in 1924:

> 'I was first asked to go on tour by Emile, behind the stand at Twickenham, when I was feeling very depressed after we had been badly beaten by England in 1924 and this certainly helped to lift my depression. Emile, Jock and Hughie were all on the tour, which I enjoyed almost beyond expression. We had a very strong side just before the British tour to South Africa later that year, including great players like Voyce, Blakiston, Arthur Young, J.C.R.Buchanan, and three of the Oxford threequarters, Smith, Aitken and Wallace. I was naturally very nervous. I had never been to Wales; Cardiff, Swansea and Newport were just names to me!'

It was to be a most auspicious beginning; Waddell was fly-half in the side that beat Cardiff in a thrilling game 23 points to 18, with tries by himself, Ian Smith, Buchanan, Tom Voyce and A.C.Wallace. But for two missed kicks in front of goal, in the match against Swansea, when both teams scored three tries, it would have been the first unbeaten Barbarian Easter Tour.

Herbert Waddell soon became a popular figure on successive Barbarian tours, and was quickly accorded the rare honour of being elected as a playing member to the Committee in 1926, a position he has held almost every year since. In 1956 he was elected Vice-President, and in 1974 succeeded Brigadier Glyn Hughes as President. Herbert Waddell's contribution to the Barbarians has been immense; as a player and boisterous Easter tourist; as a committee member and officer; as a constructive, if at times dogmatic critic, and as a friend to many. The stories of his late-night exposition of rugby tactics, in the dining room or the snug-bar at the Esp are legion, his staccato letters to his fellow committee men concerning the merits or

*Three great Barbarians of the same vintage — from left to right, Herbert Waddell (the fifth President and the first Scot to hold that office), Brigadier Glyn Hughes, and 'Jock' Wemyss.*

otherwise of Barbarian players, or tactics that should or should not be employed, would make a fascinating book; and his resilience in surviving and latterly leading all four of the Barbarians' overseas tours is quite remarkable! It is, incidentally, a continuing source of wonder to many how the pink pages of the FT would appear together with Herbert at the breakfast table in Boston or Cape Town, Vancouver or Salisbury!

In the highest echelons of the game also, Herbert Waddell has a very distinguished record. He was elected to the Scottish Rugby Union in 1946, was a member of the International Board between 1952 and 1963, and was President of the SRU in the season 1963–64, the same year in which he was made an Honorary Vice-President of the South African Rugby Board.

To this can be added an honourable war service, in which he initially commanded the 11th Highland Light Infantry, and when the infantry changed to tanks he ultimately commanded his second battalion, the 141 RAC (The Buffs) equipped with Churchill tanks with flame-throwers, which had a magnificent record of service in France in World War II. Herbert Waddell finished the war with a Mention in Despatches and the rank of full Colonel.

Yet Herbert Waddell would, if he were allowed to, dismiss these facts and figures, that tell only little of a distinguished career, to which could be added many details of a conspicuous life in the world of high finance in Glasgow, tales of generosity and kindness, moments that characterise his incisive wit and boyish humour with sparkling eyes and unforgettable laugh. But Herbert would only ever boast of what he would call his greatest claim to fame — the fact that he was the originator of the Barbarian Sunday golf.

From 'Tottie' Carpmael to Herbert Waddell, it is the guidance of the five Presidents which has been instrumental in leading the Barbarian Football Club to its pre-eminent position in the rugby world today: It's a way they have in the Baa-Baas, and a jolly good way too!

# COMPLETE LIST OF MEMBERS

Each member's name is followed by his year of election to the Barbarians; his club at that time; and where applicable, the year of his *first* international cap and the country for which he won it. OM signifies original member, CM committee member, and any other official Barbarian capacity is shown in abbreviated form. Also included in this list are those players who were members until they were expelled on turning professional.

**Aarvold C.D.** 1927–28, Blackheath *(E 1928)* CM
**Abrahams W.K.** 1961–62, Redruth
**Adams A.A.** 1908–09, London Hosp. *(E 1910)*
**Adams C.** 1913–14, Old Wesley *(I 1908)* CM
**Adams H.C.** 1898–99, St Bart's Hosp.
**Adams P.W.** 1930–31, Harlequins
**Adamson C.Y.** 1898–99, Durham City
**Adamson J.A.** 1928–29, Blackheath
**Adey G.J.** 1975–76, Leicester *(E 1976)*
**Adkins S.J.** 1949–50, Coventry *(E 1950)*
**Agar R.D.** 1948–49, Malone *(I 1947)*
**Agnew W.C.C.** 1929–30, Stewart's Coll. FP *(S 1930)*
**Agnew W.G.** 1919–20, U. Services
**Airey D.L.** 1964–65, Birkenhead Park
**Aitken G.G.** 1922–23, L. Scottish *(S 1924)* CM
**Aitken R.** 1945–46, L. Scottish *(S 1947)*
**Albertijn P.K.** 1920–21, Guy's Hosp. *(SA 1924)*
**Alderson F.H.R.** 1890, Hartlepool R. *(E 1891)* OM, CM
**Alexander A.** 1975–76, Harlequins
**Alexander H.** 1905–06, Birkenhead Park
**Alexander H.G.** 1899–1900, Newport
**Alexander P.C.** 1932–33, Guy's Hosp.
**Alexander R.** 1935–36, NIFC *(I 1936)*
**Alexander T.P.** 1893–94, Rockcliff
**Alexander W.** 1926–27, Northern *(E 1927)*
**Allan A.E.** 1937–38, Aldershot Services
**Allan G.A.** 1921–22, Birkenhead Park
**Allan J.F.L.** 1956–57, Cambridge Univ. *(S 1957)*
**Allan J.W.** 1929–30, Melrose *(S 1927)*
**Allen A.D.** 1926–27, Richmond
**Allen F.R.** 1945–46, Linwood, Christchurch, NZ & Kiwis *(NZ 1946)*
**Allen J.A.** 1973–74, Leicester
**Allison D.F.** 1957–58, Coventry *(E 1956)*
**Allport A.** 1890, Blackheath *(E 1892)* OM
**Ames C.G.** 1895–96, Blackheath
**Anderson D.G.** 1890, L. Scottish OM
**Anderson F.E.** 1952–53, Queens Univ. *(I 1953)*
**Anderson H.J.** 1905–06, Old Wesley *(I 1903)*
**Anderson W.F.** 1972–73, Orrell *(E 1973)*
**Andrew C.W.R.** 1946–47, Glasgow Acads
**Andrews K.P.** 1966–67, Leicester
**Armstrong R.** 1922–23, Northern *(E 1925)*
**Arneil R.J.** 1965–66, Edinburgh Acads *(S 1967)*
**Arthur T.G.** 1964–65, Wasps *(E 1966)*
**Ashby R.C.** 1964–65, Wasps *(E 1966)*
**Ashcroft A.** 1957–58, Waterloo *(E 1956)*

**Ashford W.** 1896–97, Richmond *(E 1897)*
**Ashton W.B.** 1974–75, Orrell
**Askew J.G.** 1930–31, Durham City *(E 1930)*
**Aslett A.R.** 1925–26, Richmond *(E 1926)*
**Aston F.T.D.** 1891–92, Blackheath
**Aston R.L.** 1890, Blackheath *(E 1890)* OM
**Atkinson M.P.** 1913–14, London Hosp., *(CM)*
**Auty J.R.** 1934–35, Headingley *(E 1935)*

**Babrow L.** 1937–38, Guy's Hosp. & Cape Town Univ. *(SA 1937)*
**Bacchus H.W.** 1901–02, Liverpool OBs
**Backhouse H.W.** 1921–22, Blackheath, Hon. Sec.
**Bailey L.D.** 1899–1900, Richmond
**Bailey L.S.** 1934–35, Blackheath
**Baillee T.H.E.** 1915, L. Scottish
**Baiss R.S.H.** 1892–93, Blackheath
**Baker C.D.** 1892–93, Blackheath
**Baker D.G.S.** 1952–53, Oxford Univ. *(E 1955)*
**Baker E.M.** 1893–94, Moseley *(E 1895)*
**Baker E. Watkins** 1902–03, Clifton
**Baker-Jones P.E.R.** 1919–20, Newport
**Balfour R.F.A.** 1975–76, Glasgow HSFP
**Bance J.F.** 1950–51, Bedford *(E 1954)*
**Bannerman J.M.** 1928–29, Glasgow HSFP *(S 1921)*
**Banning H.B.** 1901–02, Blackheath
**Barber T.C.** 1926–27, Seghill
**Barker D.A.** 1952–53, Harlequins
**Barr R.J.** 1931–32, Leicester *(E 1932)* CM
**Barrett E.R.** 1923–24, Old Wesley
**Barry D.M.** 1970–71, Oxford Univ.
**Bartlett J.T.** 1949–50, Waterloo *(E 1951)*
**Bartlett R.M.** 1959–60, Harlequins *(E 1957)*
**Barton J.** 1966–67, Coventry *(E 1967)*
**Bassett J.A.** 1930–31, Penarth *(W 1929)*
**Bates C.F.** 1913–14, Blackheath
**Barlow C.S.** 1925–26, Rosslyn Park CM
**Barlow R.M.M.** 1925–26, Richmond
**Batty C.F.** 1915, Mill Hill School
**Baty J.A.** 1901–02, Percy Park
**Baxter J.** 1898–99, Birkenhead Park *(E 1900)* CM
**Baxter L.D.** 1970–71, Cardiff
**Bayles G.F.** 1968–69, Rosslyn Park
**Bazley R.C.** 1951–52, Waterloo *(E 1952)*
**Beamish C.E.St.J.** 1933–34, Leicester *(I 1933)*
**Beamish C.H.** 1945–46, Leicester
**Beamish G.R.** 1927–28, Leicester *(I 1925)* CM
**Beamish T.P.H.** 1900–01, Blackheath
**Beattie J.A.** 1930–31, Hawick *(S 1929)* CM

**Beattie S.H.** 1909–10, Wanderers (Dublin)
**Beatty W.J.** 1909–10, NIFC *(I 1910)*
**Beaumont W.B.** 1974–75, Fylde *(E 1975)*
**Bebb D.I.E.** 1959–60, Swansea *(W 1959)*
**Bedell-Sivright D.R.** 1902–03, W. of Scotland *(S 1900)* CM
**Bedford L.L.** 1930–31, Headingley *(E 1931)*
**Bedford T.P.** 1965–66, Oxford Univ. *(SA 1963)*
**Beeching E.** 1899–1900, Blackheath
**Beese M.C.** 1971–72, Liverpool *(E 1972)*
**Begbie R.P.G.** 1907–08, Blackheath
**Beith A.E.** 1920–21, St Bart's Hosp.
**Bekket F.** 1919–20, Guy's Hosp.
**Bell D.L.** 1974–75, Watsonians *(S 1975)*
**Bell P.J.** 1965–66, Blackheath *(E 1968)*
**Bell R.W.** 1897–98, Northern *(E 1900)*
**Bell S.P.** 1895–96, Northern, CM
**Bell W.E.** 1952–53, Collegians *(I 1953)*
**Bendall I.C.** 1928–29, Rosslyn Park
**Bennett N.O.** 1946–47, St Mary's Hosp. *(E 1947)*
**Bennett P.** 1969–70, Llanelli *(W 1969)*
**Bennett W.N.** 1974–75, Bedford *(E 1975)*
**Bennetts B.B.** 1907–08, Penzance *(E 1909)*
**Bergiers R.T.E.** 1972–73, Llanelli *(W 1972)*
**Beringer F.R.** 1952–53, Cambridge Univ.
**Berkery P.J.** 1956–57, Lansdowne *(I 1954)*
**Berridge M.J.** 1946–47, Northampton *(E 1949)*
**Berry J.T.W.** 1938–39, Leicester *(E 1939)*
**Bethell R.A.** 1946–47, Blackheath
**Bettington R.H.B.** 1924–25, St Bart's Hosp., CM
**Bevan J.D.** 1974–75, Aberavon *(W 1975)*
**Biddle F.J.** 1920–21, Guy's Hosp.
**Biggar A.G.** 1967–68, L. Scottish *(S 1969)*
**Biggar M.A.** 1974–75, L. Scottish *(S 1975)*
**Biggs C.F.** 1899–1900, Cardiff
**Biggs E.P.** 1891–92, Cardiff
**Biggs N.H.** 1893–94, Cardiff *(W 1888)*
**Biggs S.** 1893–94, Cardiff *(W 1895)*
**Bingham R.G.** 1901–02, Blackheath
**Bird D.R.J.** 1959–60, Cambridge Univ.
**Bird W.J.** 1935–36, Old Edwardians
**Birkett J.G.G.** 1907–08, Harlequins *(E 1906)*
**Bishop C.C.** 1925–26, Blackheath *(E 1927)*
**Black A.W.** 1945–46, Edinburgh Univ. *(S 1947)*
**Black B.H.** 1929–30, Blackheath *(E 1930)*
**Black M.A.** 1896–97, L. Scottish
**Black W.P.** 1947–48, Glasgow HSFP *(S 1948)*
**Blagrove H.E.C.** 1959–60, U. Services
**Blaikie C.F.** 1967–68, Heriots FP *(S 1963)*
**Blake A.B.** 1920–21, Blackheath
**Blake J.N.** 1961–62, Bristol
**Blakiston A.F.** 1919–20, Northampton *(E 1920)*
**Blanch J.W.E.** 1922–23, Harlequins
**Bleasdale T.H.** 1957–58, Leicester
**Blencowe L.C.** 1910–11, Richmond
**Block S.A.** 1931–32, Harlequins
**Blyth W.R.** 1974–75, Swansea *(W 1974)*
**Body T.M.** 1899–1900, Richmond
**Boggs E.G.** 1945–46, Ponsonby, Auckland, Kiwis & NZ *(NZ 1946)*
**Bok L.B.** 1935–36, St Mary's Hosp.
**Bole E.** 1945–46, Cambridge Univ.
**Bolesworth D.** 1945–46, Leicester
**Bolton C.A.** 1908–09, Richmond *(E 1909)*
**Bolton R.** 1930–31, Univ. Coll. *(E 1933)*
**Bonaventure M.S.** 1926–27, Blackheath *(E 1931)*
**Bond H.** 1896–97, St Bart's Hosp.

**Bonham-Carter E.** 1892–93, Blackheath *(E 1891)*
**Boobbyer B.** 1949–50, Oxford Univ. & Rosslyn Park *(E 1950)*
**Boon R.W.** 1932–33, Cardiff *(W 1930)*
**Booth L.A.** 1932–33, Headingley *(E 1933)*
**Boothman J.A.** 1952–53, St Thomas's Hosp.
**Bos F.H.ten** 1960–61, L. Scottish *(S 1959)*
**Botting I.J.** 1949–50, Oxford Univ. *(E 1950)*
**Boucher A.W.** 1894–95, Newport *(W 1892)*
**Boucher H.B.T.** 1890–91, Blackheath
**Bowcott H.M.** 1927–28, Cardiff *(W 1929)*
**Bowen I.D.** 1922–23, Edinburgh Univ.
**Boyd C.A.** 1900–01, Dublin Univ. *(I 1900)*
**Boyle C.V.** 1935–36, Dublin Univ. *(I 1936)*
**Brace D.O.** 1960–61, Llanelli *(W 1956)*
**Bradford J.D.** 1929–30, Rosslyn Park
**Bradley D.** 1927–28, Morley
**Bradshaw K.** 1965–66, Bridgend *(W 1964)*
**Bradstreet G.E.** 1913–14, Dublin Univ.
**Brady J.R.** 1956–57, CIYMS *(I 1951)*
**Brennan B.J.** 1949–50, Old Alleynians
**Brennan J.I.** 1956–57, CIYMS *(I 1957)*
**Bresnihan F.P.K.** 1965–66, UC Dublin *(I 1966)*
**Brettargh A.T.** 1898–99, Liverpool OBs *(E 1900)* CM
**Bridge D.J.W.** 1946–47, Oxford Univ.
**Briggs P.D.** 1968–69, Bedford
**Briggs R.** 1923–24, Harlequins
**Broderick J.M.** 1971–72, Coventry
**Brodie H.V.** 1925–26, Harlequins
**Bromet E.** 1891–92, St Thomas's Hosp.
**Bromet W.E.** 1891–92, Tadcaster *(E 1891)*
**Bromley L.L.** 1942–43, St Mary's Hosp.
**Brook P.W.P.** 1929–30, Harlequins *(E 1930)*
**Brooke T.J.** 1967–68, Richmond *(E 1968)*
**Brophy N.H.** 1962–63, Blackrock *(I 1957)*
**Broster L.R.** 1910–11, Blackheath CM
**Brown A.** 1900–01, Blackheath
**Brown A.A.** 1937–38, Exeter *(E 1938)*
**Brown D.I.** 1932–33, L. Scottish *(S 1933)*
**Brown G.D.M.** 1959–60, Melrose
**Brown G.L.** 1970–71, W. of Scotland *(S 1969)*
**Brown G.S.** 1909–10, U. Services *(I 1912)*
**Brown H.J.C.** 1961–62, Blackheath
**Brown L.G.** 1910–11, Blackheath *(E 1911)* CM
**Brown P.C.** 1968–69, Gala *(S 1964)*
**Brown T.W.** 1932–33, Bristol *(E 1928)*
**Browse C.H.** 1944–45, St Mary's Hosp.
**Bruce A.W.** 1945–46, Glasgow Acads *(S 1947)* CM
**Bruce N.S.** 1957–58, Blackheath *(S 1958)*
**Brumwell R.C.** 1930–31, Bedford
**Bryce R.D.H.** 1970–71, L. Scottish *(S 1973)*
**Buchanan A.B.W.** 1936–37, L. Scottish
**Buchanan J.C.R.** 1922–23, Stewart's Coll. FP *(S 1921)* CM
**Buckingham R.A.** 1934–35, Leicester *(E 1921)*
**Bucknall A.L.** 1969–70, Richmond *(E 1969)*
**Budge G.M.** 1949–50, Edinburgh Wands *(S 1950)*
**Budworth R.T.D.** 1890, Blackheath *(E 1890)* OM
**Bulger L.Q.** 1896–97, Lansdowne *(I 1896)*
**Bulkeley H.I.** 1906–07, Harlequins
**Bull A.G.** 1915, Northampton *(E 1914)*
**Bullard G.L.** 1951–52, Oxford Univ.
**Bullock H.** 1910–11, Blackheath
**Bulloch J.H.** 1898–99, Blackheath
**Bulpitt M.P.** 1969–70, Blackheath *(E 1970)*
**Bunney F.M.T.** 1926–27, Richmond
**Bunting W.L.** 1895–96, Richmond *(E 1897)*

Burcher A.C. 1946–47, Blackheath
Burcher D. 1976–77, Newport *(W 1977)*
Burdett J.C. 1912–13, Leicester
Burgess E. 1930–31, Richmond
Burgess R.B. 1913–14, Dublin Univ. *(I 1913)*
Burland D.W. 1933–34, Bristol *(E 1931)*
Burnard F.E. 1896–97, Blackheath
Burnet W.A. 1934–35, W. of Scotland *(S 1934)*
Burnett R. 1951–52, Newport *(W 1953)*
Burton H.C. 1924–25, Richmond *(E 1926)*
Burton M.A. 1971–72, Gloucester *(E 1972)*
Bushell K.M. 1975–76, Harlequins
Butcher E.G. 1915, Plymouth
Butcher W.V. 1904–05, Bristol *(E 1903)*
Butler A.G. 1936–37, Harlequins *(E 1937)*
Butterfield J. 1951–52, Northampton *(E 1953)*
Byers R.M. 1924–25, NIFC *(I 1928)*
Byrne J.F. 1897–98, Moseley *(E 1894)* CM

*Played v Leicester but not elected*
Burke W. 1915
*Membership cancelled on expulsion from RFU or joined
    Rugby League*
Brown T.W. 1933–34
Blackett G. 1962–63, Gosforth
Broatch A.R. 1962–63, Hawick
Brophy T.J. 1963–64, Liverpool
Butler B.L. 1969–70, Llanelli
Bevan J.C. 1972–73, Cardiff

Callan C.P. 1945–46, Lansdowne *(I 1947)*
Cameron A. 1954–55, Glasgow HSFP *(S 1948)*
Campaes A. 1968–69, Lourdes
Campbell D.A. 1936–37, Cambridge Univ. *(E 1937)*
Campbell E. 1920–21, Edinburgh Acads
Campbell G.D. 1910–11, U. Services
Campbell G.T. 1892–93, L. Scottish *(S 1892)*
Campbell H.H. 1947–48, L. Scottish *(S 1947)*
Campbell R.T. 1939–40, St Mary's Hosp.
Campbell Lamerton M.J. 1961–62, Halifax *(S 1961)*
Candler P.L. 1935–36, St Bart's Hosp. *(E 1935)*
Cannell L.B. 1948–49, Oxford Univ. *(E 1948)*
Capaldi B. 1966–67, Cheltenham
Carbutt W.J.O. 1920–21, Blackheath
Carey G.M. 1892–93, Blackheath *(E 1895)* CM
Carey G.V. 1908–09, Harlequins, CM
Carey W.H. 1890–91, Leicester
Carey W.J. 1894–95, Blackheath, CM
Carlton E.N. 1897–98, Blackheath
Carmichael A.B. 1965–66, W. of Scotland *(S 1967)*
Carnegie-Brown A. 1923–24, St Bart's Hosp.
Carpenter A.D. 1936–37, Gloucester *(E 1932)*
Carpmael F. 1895–96, Blackheath
Carpmael M.H. 1932–33, Blackheath
Carpmael R.H. 1892–93, Clapham Rovers
Carpmael W.P. 1890, Blackheath, OM, Hon. Sec.,
    Treas., 1st Pres.
Carris H.E. 1929–30, Old Millhillians
Carroll P.R. 1970–71, Oxford Univ.
Carson C.F. 1910–11, Blackheath
Carter E.C. 1900–01, Hartlepool R.
Cartwright V.H. 1902–03, Harlequins *(E 1903)* CM
Casement J.M. 1901–02, Blackheath
Cass E.E.E. 1924–25, Richmond
Cattell R.H.B. 1893–94, Blackheath
Cave W.T.C. 1903–04, Blackheath *(E 1905)*
Cawkwell G.L. 1946–47, Oxford Univ. *(S 1947)*

Chadwick W.O. 1937–38, Cambridge Univ.
Chaldecott R.F. 1890, Rosslyn Park, OM
Challis R.L. 1972–73, L. Scottish
Chamberlain J. 1904–05, Moseley
Champain F.H.B. 1898–99, Cheltenham
Chapman G.M. 1908–09, London Hosp., CM
Chapman K.H. 1942–43, Harlequins
Chisholm D.H. 1964–65, Melrose *(S 1964)*
Chisholm R.W.T. 1955–56, Melrose *(S 1955)*
Christopherson P. 1890, Blackheath *(E 1891)* OM
Clarke I.J. 1963–64, Waikato *(NZ 1954)*
Clarke N. 1912–13, Old Wesley, CM
Clark R.L. 1971–72, Edinburgh Wands *(S 1972)*
Clarke S.J.S. 1961–62, Blackheath *(E 1963)*
Clauss P.R. 1891–92, Oxford Univ. & Birkenhead
    Park *(S 1891)* CM
Cleaver W.B. 1946–47, Cardiff *(W 1947)*
Clements J.W. 1956–57, Old Cranleighans & U. Ser-
    vices *(E 1959)*
Clifford J. 1965–66, Swansea
Clifford J.T. 1950–51, Young Munster *(I 1949)*
Clinch J.D. 1922–23, Dublin Wands *(I 1923)*
Coates N. 1923–24, Leicester
Coates V.H.M. 1909–10, Bath *(E 1913)*
Cobb H.H. 1897–98, Rosslyn Park
Cobby W. 1900–01, Hull *(E 1900)*
Cobden D.G. 1938–39, RAF & Christchurch HSOB
    *(NZ 1937)*
Cobner T.J. 1973–74, Pontypool *(W 1974)*
Cochrane E.N.N. 1896–97, Blackheath
Cock T.A. 1899–1900, Marlborough Nomads
Cockburn H.D. 1947–48, Richmond
Cockerill G.T.E. 1924–25, Old Blues
Codd R.A. 1971–72, Rosslyn Park
Coffey J.J. 1904–05, Lansdowne *(I 1900)* CM
Coghlan G.B. 1927–28, Harlequins
Coles P. 1890, Blackheath, OM
Cole G.H. 1964–65, Coventry
Coley D.C. 1961–62, Northampton
Coley E. 1924–25, Northampton *(E 1929)*
Collard J.W. 1959–60, Headingley
Collett G.F. 1898–99, Cheltenham
Collins J. 1958–59, Aberavon *(W 1958)*
Collins M. 1953–54, Cardiff
Collins W.R. 1929–30, Rosslyn Park
Collison L.H. 1929–30, Old Millhillians
Collopy W.P. 1919–20, Bective R. *(I 1914)*
Coltart H.N. 1896–97, Lennox
Compton N. 1933–34, Wasps
Considine H.W.H. 1921–22, Richmond *(E 1925)*
Constantine C.F. 1910–11, Blackheath
Conway G.S. 1920–21, Blackheath *(E 1920)* CM
Cook D.S. 1912–13, Harlequins
Cook J.G. 1936–37, Bedford *(E 1931)*
Cook P.W. 1963–64, Richmond *(E 1965)*
Cook S. 1915, Blackheath
Cooke D.A. 1975–76, Harlequins *(E 1976)*
Cooke P. 1938–39, Richmond *(E 1939)*
Cookson G. 1900–01, Manchester
Cookson G.H.F. 1893–94, Oxford Univ.
Cooper G.K. 1923–24, St Thomas's Hosp.
Cooper M.J. 1972–73, Moseley *(E 1973)*
Cooper M.McG. 1935–36, Oxford Univ. *(S 1936)*
Cooper R.M. 1946–47, Rosslyn Park
Coopper S.F. 1901–02, Blackheath *(E 1900)*
Cope W. 1891–92, Blackheath *(W 1896)*
Coxley H.H. 1900–01, Dublin Wands *(I 1902)* CM

Dorward A.F. 1948–49, Cambridge Univ. *(S 1950)*
Douglas F.W.R. 1922–23, Richmond, CM
Douglas J. 1960–61, Stewarts Coll. FP
Douglass W.N.G. 1900–01, Monkstown
Douty P.S. 1923–24, L. Scottish *(S 1927)* CM
Dovey B.A. 1963–64, Rosslyn Park *(E 1963)*
Dove G.R. Maxwell 1909–10, Harlequins
Dowse P.R.O. 1957–58, Dublin Univ.
Doyle M.G. 1966–67, Edinburgh Wands
Druce W.G. 1893–94, Marlborough Nomads
Drummond C.W. 1947–48, Melrose *(S 1947)* CM
Dryden R.H. 1936–37, Watsonians *(S 1937)*
Drysdale D. 1922–23, Heriots FP *(S 1923)* CM
Drysdale T. 1899–1900, St George's Hosp.
du Boulay A.H. 1898–99, Blackheath
Duckham D.J. 1968–69, Coventry *(E 1969)*
Duckworth F.E. 1890–91, Blackheath
Duckworth I. 1967–68, Bath
Dudbridge L. 1915, Gloucester
Dudgeon H.W. 1897–98, Richmond *(E 1897)*
Duff P.L. 1937–38, Glasgow Acads *(S 1936)* CM
Duggan A.T.A. 1965–66, Lansdowne *(I 1964)*
Duncan R.F.H. 1920–21, Guy's Hosp. *(E 1922)*
Duncan R.T. 1890–91, Cardiff
Dunne M.J. 1932–33, Lansdowne *(I 1929)*
Dunkley F.P. 1944–45, Harlequins
Dunkley P.E. 1931–32, Harlequins *(E 1931)*
Dunlop E.E. 1939–40, St Mary's Hosp. *(A 1932)*
Dunn B.M. 1924–25, L. Welsh
Dunne M.J. 1932–33, Lansdowne
Durr J.M. 1924–25, Guy's Hosp.
Dussek E.A. 1911–12, Blackheath
Dyas R.S.V. 1894–95, L. Irish
Dyke J.C.M. 1908–09, Penarth *(W 1906)*
Dyke L.M. 1907–08, Cardiff *(W 1910)*
Dykes A.S. 1926–27, Glasgow Acads *(S 1932)*
Dykes J.C. 1924–25, Glasgow Acads. *(S 1922)*

*Joined Rugby League*
Daly J.C. 1947–48, L. Irish
Danby T. 1948–49, Harlequins
*Substitutes*
Dean F. *played as substitute v Plymouth 1904, v Exeter 1906*

Easterbrook R.F. 1892–93, L. Scottish
Eastwood P.A. 1963–64, Richmond
Eddison J.H. 1912–13, Headingley *(E 1912)*
Ede E.G. 1908–09, U. Services
Edgar C.S. 1899–1900, Birkenhead Park *(E 1901)*
Edgecombe G.J.B. 1959–60, Richmond
Edwards B.P. 1947–48, Blackheath
Edwards F.G. 1938–39, Leicester
Edwards G.O. 1967–68, Cardiff *(W 1967)*
Edwards H.O. 1936–37, Cardiff
Edwards M.G.A. 1905–06, U. Services
Ekin C. 1891–92, Middx Wands
Elders J. 1958–59, Northern
Elliot C. 1958–59, Langholm *(S 1958)*
Elliot T. 1955–56, Gala *(S 1955)*
Elliot T.G. 1970–71, Langholm *(S 1968)*
Elliot W. 1932–33, U. Services *(E 1932)*
Elliott A.E. 1894–95, St Thomas's Hosp.
Elliott E.W. 1900–01, Sunderland *(E 1901)*
Elliott H.R. 1902–03, Sunderland
Elliott J.J. 1975–76, Nottingham
Elliott W.I.D. 1945–46, Edinburgh Acads *(S 1947)*
Ellis J. 1938–39, Wakefield *(E 1939)*

Ellis R.L. 1958–59, Plymouth Albion
Embleton J.J.A. 1929–30, Old Paulines, CM
Emley E. 1890, Northern, OM
Emms D.A. 1952–53, Northampton
England D.G. 1942–43, Rosslyn Park
English M.A.F. 1957–58, Bohemians *(I 1958)*
Ensor A.H. 1972–73, Dublin Wands *(I 1973)*
Entwistle T. 1909–10, Manchester
Estcourt N.S.D. 1954–55, Blackheath *(E 1955)*
Evans A.L. 1941–42, Rosslyn Park
Evans D.L. 1906–07, Cardiff
Evans D.W. 1890–91, Cardiff *(W 1889)*
Evans E. 1946–47, Sale *(E 1948)* CM
Evans E.D. 1902–03, L. Welsh
Evans Gwyn 1948–49, Cardiff *(W 1947)*
Evans G.W. 1971–72, Coventry *(E 1972)*
Evans J.D. 1957–58, Cardiff *(W 1958)*
Evans J.R. 1935–36, Newport *(W 1934)*
Evans M.R.M. 1960–61, Wilmslow
Evans N.L. 1931–32, U. Services *(E 1932)*
Evans T.G. 1970–71, L. Welsh *(W 1970)*
Evans T.P. 1975–76, Swansea *(W 1975)*
Evans V. 1953–54, Neath *(W 1954)*
Evans W.R. 1957–58, Cardiff *(W 1958)*
Evan-Thomas C.M. 1919–20, Richmond
Evers C.P. 1898–99, Moseley
Evers G.V. 1902–03, Moseley
Evershed F. 1890, Blackheath *(E 1889)*
Eyres W.C.T. 1926–27, U. Services *(E 1927)*

Fagan A.N.D. 1891–92, RMC Sandhurst *(E 1887)*
Faithfull C.K.T. 1927–28, Harlequins *(E 1924)*
Falcon W. 1894–95, Blackheath
Falla G.C.M. 1931–32, U. Services
Farmer S. 1913–14, Leicester
Farrell J.L. 1928–29, Bective R. *(I 1926)*
Fasson F.H. 1897–98, Edinburgh Univ. *(S 1900)*
Faulkner A.G. 1974–75, Pontypool *(W 1975)*
Faull J. 1957–58, Swansea *(W 1957)*
Faviell H.L.V. 1934–35, Harlequins
Fearenside E. 1905–06, Harlequins
Fearsen A.O.M. 1897–98, L. Scottish
Fegan J.H.C. 1892–93, Blackheath *(E 1895)*
Fellows-Smith G. 1924–25, Guy's Hosp.
Fenning R.M.P. 1945–46, Bristol
Fenwick S.P. 1975–76, Bridgend *(W 1975)*
Ferguson G.A. 1961–62, Hendon, Asst Hon. Sec., Treas.
Fergusson E.A.J. 1953–54, Oxford Univ. *(S 1954)*
Fforde A.B. 1892–93, Cambridge Univ.
Field E. 1892–93, Middx Wands *(E 1893)*
Finlan J.F. 1965–66, Moseley *(E 1967)*
Finlay T. 1900–01, Rockliff
Finlayson A.A.J. 1973–74, Cardiff *(W 1974)*
Finlinson H.W. 1893–94, Blackheath *(E 1895)*
Finlinson M.E. 1901–02, Blackheath
Fisher J.L. 1907–08, Hull & ER
Fisher J.P. 1964–65, L. Scottish *(S 1963)*
Flemmer W.K. 1906–07, Blackheath
Fletcher F.M. 1948–49, Bedford
Fletcher N.C. 1898–99, OM Taylors *(E 1901)*
Flynn M.K. 1959–60, Dublin Wands *(I 1959)*
Fookes E.F. 1896–97, Sowerby Bridge *(E 1896)*
Foote A.J. 1924–25, Blackheath
Foote P. 1910–11, London Hosp.
Ford A.K. 1898–99, Rosslyn Park
Ford D. St Clair 1929–30, U. Services *(S 1930)*

Ford I.G. 1963–64, Newport
Ford P.J. 1962–63, Gloucester *(E 1964)*
Forrest J.E. 1929–30, Glasgow Acads *(S 1932)*
Forrest J.G.S. 1937–38, Cambridge Univ. *(S 1938)*
Forrest J.W. 1929–30, U. Services *(E 1930)* CM
Forrest R. 1898–99, Blackheath *(E 1899)* CM
Forsayth H.H. 1922–23, Blackheath *(S 1921)*
Forsyth I.W. 1972–73, Stewarts Coll. FP *(S 1973)*
Forward A. 1951–52, Pontypool *(W 1951)*
Foulds R.T. 1927–28, Waterloo *(E 1929)*
Fox F.H. 1890, Wellington *(E 1890)* OM
Francis T.E.S. 1924–25, Blackheath *(E 1926)*
Francomb J.S. 1898–99, Manchester
Frankcom G.P. 1964–65, Northampton *(E 1965)*
Franklin H.W.F. 1925–26, Old Blues
Franks J.G. 1897–98, Monkstown *(I 1898)* CM
Fraser G. 1900–01, Richmond *(E 1902)*
Freakes H.D. 1937–38, Oxford Univ. *(E 1938)*
Fry C.B. 1894–95, Blackheath
Fry H.A. 1942–43, Waterloo *(E 1934)*
Fulljames O.R. 1925–26, Rosslyn Park
Fyfe K.C. 1932–33, Cambridge Univ. *(S 1933)* CM

*Joined Rugby League*
French R.J. 1960–61, St Helens
Fairbrother K.E. 1968–69, Coventry
Fielding K.J. 1969–70, Moseley

Gachassin J. 1967–68, Lourdes *(F 1961)*
Gadney B.C. 1932–33, Leicester *(E 1932)* CM
Gage J.H. 1925–26, Queen's Univ. Belfast *(I 1926)*
Gaisford W.F. 1923–24, St Bart's Hosp.
Gale B.H. 1949–50, Blackheath
Galloway E.C. 1899–1900, Marlborough Nomads
Ganly J.B. 1926–27, Monkstown *(I 1927)*
Gardiner F. 1907–08, NIFC *(I 1900)*
Gardiner J. 1953–54, Coventry
Garnett H.G. 1899–1900, Liverpool
Garnons-Williams G.A. 1919–20, U. Services
Gay D.J. 1967–68, Bath *(E 1968)*
Geddes A.C. 1902–03, Edinburgh Univ.
Gedge A.S. 1890, Richmond, OM
Gedge H.T.S. 1894–95, L. Scottish *(S 1894)*
Geen W.P. 1910–11, Newport *(W 1912)*
Gemmill R. 1949–50, Glasgow HSOB *(S 1950)*
George J.T. 1946–47, Falmouth *(E 1947)*
Gerrard R.A. 1932–33, Bath *(E 1932)*
Gibb C. 1911–12, Guy's Hosp.
Gibbs G.A. 1946–47, Bristol *(E 1947)*
Gibbs R.A. 1907–08, Cardiff *(W 1906)*
Gibbs V.F. 1904–05, U. Services
Giblin L.F. 1895–96, Blackheath *(E 1896)*
Gibson C.M.H. 1963–64, Cambridge Univ. *(I 1964)*
Gibson C.O.P. 1899–1900, Northern *(E 1901)*
Gibson G.R. 1899–1900, Northern *(E 1899)*
Gibson J.C. 1962–63, US Portsmouth
Gibson T.A. 1900–01, Northern *(E 1905)*
Gibson W.R. 1892–93, Royal HSFP
Gieson J.E. 1933–34, Guy's Hosp.
Gilchrist J. 1926–27, Glasgow Acads *(S 1925)*
Giles J.L. 1937–38, Coventry *(E 1935)*
Gill A.D. 1972–73, Gala *(S 1973)*
Gillespie J.C. 1921–22, Dublin Wands *(I 1922)*
Gilthorpe C.G. 1941–42, Wasps
Gimson C. 1909–10, Leicester
Glasgow R.J.C. 1961–62, Dunfermline *(S 1962)*
Glass D.C. 1957–58, Collegians *(I 1958)*

Gloag L.G. 1948–49, Cambridge Univ. *(S 1949)*
Glover P.B. 1966–67, RAF Cranwell *(E 1967)*
Godfrey N.W. 1902–03, Moseley
Godwin H. 1958–59, Coventry *(E 1959)*
Golding P.L. 1965–66, Royal Navy
Goldring P.W. 1898–99, Lennox
Goldschmidt K.P.P. 1936–37, Trojans
Goldson C.P.B. 1932–33, Blackheath
Goodhue F.W.J. 1890, St Thomas's Hosp. *(S 1890)* OM
Goodman R.M. 1911–12, Richmond
Goold A.N. 1927–28, Liverpool
Goold J.C. 1894–95, Liverpool OBs
Gordon D.R. 1904–05, Devonport Albion
Gordon-Smith G. 1897–98, Blackheath *(E 1900)*
Gosling C.G. 1929–30, U. Services
Gotley A.L.H. 1909–10, Blackheath *(E 1910)*
Gowans J.J. 1894–95, L. Scottish *(S 1893)*
Grace T.O. 1972–73, St Mary's Coll. *(I 1972)*
Graham I.N. 1938–39, Edinburgh Acads. *(S 1939)*
Graham J. 1929–30, Kelso *(S 1926)*
Graham J.G. 1900–01, Liverpool OBs
Graham P.R.G. 1942–43, St Mary's Hosp.
Graham T.C. 1894–95, Newport *(W 1890)*
Graham-Jones J. 1941–42, St Mary's Hosp.
Grant D. 1964–65, Hawick *(S 1965)*
Grant E. 1941–42, Gisborne HSOB
Grant M.L. 1958–59, Harlequins *(S 1955)*
Grant T.O. 1961–62, Hawick *(S 1960)*
Gravell R.W.R. 1975–76, Llanelli *(W 1975)*
Graves C.R.A. 1934–35, Dublin Wands *(I 1934)* CM
Gray A.J. 1971–72, L. Welsh *(W 1968)*
Gray B.M. 1951–52, Devonport Services
Gray R.D. 1923–24, Old Wesley *(I 1923)*
Gray T. 1947–48, Northampton *(S 1950)*
Gray W.A. 1957–58, Blackheath
Gray W.R. 1890, Northumberland, OM
Greenslade D. 1961–62, Newport *(W 1962)*
Greenwood D.M. 1952–53, Halifax
Greenwood J.E. 1911–12, Richmond
Greenwood J.R.H. 1965–66, Waterloo *(E 1966)*
Greenwood J.T. 1954–55, Dunfermline *(S 1952)*
Gregory G.G. 1931–32, Bristol *(E 1931)*
Gregory J.A. 1951–52, Bristol *(E 1949)*
Grenfell C.H. 1909–10, U. Services
Grenning V. 1920–21, Blackheath
Grierson H. 1922–23, Rosslyn Park
Grieve C.F. 1938–39, Aldershot Services *(S 1935)*
Grieve R.J. 1965–66, Hawick
Grieve R.M. 1935–36, Kelso *(S 1935)*
Grieveson O. 1960–61, Headingley
Griffin L.J. 1948–49, Dublin Wands *(I 1949)*
Griffith A.L.P. 1911–12, Blackheath
Griffiths F.G. 1951–52, Sale
Griffiths G.M. 1952–53, Cardiff
Grimshaw M.N. 1967–68, Queen's Univ. Belfast
Grose L.E. 1947–48, Richmond
Gubb T.W. 1928–29, Blackheath, CM
Gunnery E.H. 1892–93, OM Taylors
Guest R.H. 1937–38, Waterloo *(E 1939)*
Gwilliam J.A. 1948–49, Cambridge Univ. *(W 1947)*
Gwynn L.H. 1894–95, Monkstown *(I 1893)*
Gwynne F.H.X. 1919–20, Blackheath

*Joined Rugby League*
Goodall K.G. 1966–67, Newcastle Univ. *(I 1967)*
Gallacher I.S. 1968–69, Llanelli *(W 1970)*
Gray J.D. 1972–73, Coventry

Haigh L. 1910–11, Manchester *(E 1910)*
Haines D.D. 1969–70, Newport
Hall I. 1970–71, Aberavon *(W 1967)*
Hall N.M. 1958–59, Richmond *(E 1947)*
Hall R.L. 1941–42, St Bart's Hosp.
Hallaran C.F.G.T. 1919–20, U. Services *(I 1921)*
Hamilton A.S. 1919–20, Headingley *(S 1914)*
Hamilton G.A.C. 1923–24, Blackheath
Hamilton-Wickes R.H. 1920–21, Harlequins *(E 1924)*
Hammett E.D.G. 1921–22, Newport *(E 1920)*
Hammond C.E.L. 1903–04, Harlequins *(E 1905)* CM
Hammond F.A.L. 1892–93, Blackheath
Hammond J. 1890, Blackheath, OM
Hammond R.J.L. 1934–35, U. Services, CM
Hamp W.R. 1947–48, Northampton
Hanbury L.F. 1899–1900, St Thomas's Hosp.
Hancock A.W. 1964–65, Northampton *(E 1965)*
Hancock E. 1890, Wiveliscombe, OM
Hancock P.F. 1890, Wiveliscombe *(E 1886)* OM
Handford F.G. 1910–11, Manchester *(E 1909)*
Hands R.H.M. 1908–09, Blackheath *(E 1910)*
Hankin G.T. 1898–99, OM Taylors
Hannaford R.C. 1970–71, Bristol *(E 1971)*
Hannen F.B. 1890, Harlequins, OM
Hanrahan C.J. 1929–30, Dolphin *(I 1926)*
Harding A.F. 1904–05, L. Welsh *(W 1902)*
Harding K. 1912–13, Blackheath
Harding Rowe 1923–24, Swansea *(W 1923)* CM
Harding V.S.J. 1958–59, Cambridge Univ. *(E 1961)*
Hardman K. 1900–01, Liverpool OBs
Hards K.C.M. 1910–11, Blackheath
Hardy E.M.P. 1949–50, Blackheath & Army *(E 1951)*
Hare W.H. 1973–74, Nottingham *(E 1974)*
Harman G.R. 1897–98, Dublin Univ. *(I 1899)*
Harris G.N.A. 1894–95, Blackheath
Harris R.F.S. 1968–69, Penryn
Harris S.W. 1919–20, Blackheath *(E 1920)*
Harrison A.C. 1930–31, Hartlepool R. *(E 1931)*
Harrison E.M. 1901–02, Guy's Hosp.
Harrison H.C. 1909–10, U. Services *(E 1909)* CM
Harrison N.S.A. 1898–99, Richmond
Harry R.C. 1932–33, U. Services
Hart A.I. 1963–64, New Brighton
Hartgill W.C. 1911–12, London Hosp.
Hartley B.C. 1900–01, Blackheath *(E 1901)* Hon. Sec.
Hartley J.C. 1895–96, Blackheath, CM
Harvey G.H. 1896–97, Blackheath
Harvey T.A. 1901–02, Dublin Univ. *(I 1900)*
Haslett L.W. 1919–20, Blackheath *(E 1926)*
Hastie A.J. 1960–61, Melrose *(S 1961)*
Hastings G.W.D. 1954–55, Gloucester *(E 1955)*
Hastings P.R.H. 1941–42, Welsh Guards
Hathorn D.McF. 1965–66, Edinburgh Wands
Hawkes R.C. 1953–54, Northampton
Hawkins F.E.J. 1964–65, Wasps
Hayward P.J. 1967–68, Blackheath
Hazel B.J.B. 1947–48, L. Scottish
Hazell D.St G. 1954–55, Leicester *(E 1955)*
Hearn R.D. 1966–67, Bedford *(E 1966)*
Hearson H.F.P. 1904–05, Richmond
Heath P.M. 1895–96, Bath
Heaton J. 1934–35, Waterloo *(E 1935)*
Hedderwick J.H. 1890, L. Scottish, OM
Hefer W.J. 1950–51, Oxford Univ.
Hegarty J.J. 1959–60, Hawick *(S 1951)*
Helder W.J.R. 1898–99, Catford Bridge

Hellier R.S. 1920–21, Old Alleynians
Helmore P. 1975–76, Penarth
Hemmerde C.L. 1919–20, Blackheath
Henderson A.P. 1946–47, Cambridge Univ. *(E 1947)*
Henderson B.C. 1962–63, Edinburgh Wands *(S 1963)*
Henderson E.M.M. 1933–34, L. Scottish
Henderson I.C. 1945–46, Edinburgh Acads *(S 1939)*
Henderson J.H. 1951–52, Oxford Univ. *(S 1953)*
Henderson J.M. 1932–33, Edinburgh Acads *(S 1933)*
Henderson M.M. 1936–37, Dunfermline *(S 1937)*
Henderson N.J. 1950–51, Queen's Univ. Belfast *(I 1949)*
Henderson R.J. 1928–29, Edinburgh Acads
Hendrickse A.J. 1967–68, Rosslyn Park
Hendry T.L. 1896–97, Clydesdale *(S 1893)*
Henley W.E. 1930–31, Blackheath
Henshaw A. 1896–97, Newport
Henshaw D.P. 1930–31, Watsonians
Hepburn D.P. 1947–48, Woodford *(S 1948)*
Heppenstall A.F. 1928–29, Old Alleynians
Herbert A.J. 1956–57, Cambridge Univ. *(E 1958)*
Herbert K.L. 1924–25, L. Scottish
Herschell E. 1905–06, Birkenhead Park
Hewitt D. 1957–58, Queen's Univ. Belfast *(I 1958)*
Hewitt W.J. 1950–51, Instonians *(I 1954)*
Hickie A.J. 1966–67, UC Dublin
Hickie D.J. 1971–72, St Mary's Coll. *(I 1971)*
Hickson J.L. 1890, Bradford *(E 1887)* OM
Higgins H.L. 1913–14, Old Edwardians
Higgins R. 1953–54, Liverpool *(E 1954)* CM
Highton J.E. 1960–61, Devonport Services
Hill A. 1969–70, Llanelli
Hill B.A. 1901–02, Blackheath *(E 1903)* CM
Hill G.P. 1960–61, Gordonians
Hill J.N. 1896–97, Harlequins
Hill R.V. 1915, Neath
Hillard R.J. 1924–25, Old Paulines *(E 1925)*
Hiller R. 1970–71, Harlequins *(E 1968)*
Hind G.R. 1909–10, Guy's Hosp. *(E 1910)*
Hinings F.W. 1907–08, Headingley
Hinshelwood A.J.W. 1964–65, Stewart's Coll. FP *(S 1966)*
Hinton W.P. 1906–07, Old Wesley *(I 1907)* CM
Hipwell J.N.B. 1975–76, NSW *(A 1968)*
Hipwell M.L. 1968–69, Terenure Coll. *(I 1962)*
Hirst G.L. 1919–20, Newport *(W 1912)*
Hoare A.H.M. 1958–59, Harlequins
Hobbs R.F.A. 1898–99, Blackheath *(E 1899)*
Hobbs R.G.S. 1929–30, Richmond *(E 1932)*
Hodgson G.T.R. 1962–63, Neath *(W 1962)*
Hodgson J.McD. 1929–30, Northern *(E 1932)*
Hodgson S.A.M. 1959–60, Durham City *(E 1960)*
Hofmeyr M.B. 1949–50, Oxford Univ. *(E 1950)* CM
Hofmeyr S.J. 1930–31, Oxford Univ.
Hogg C.S. 1969–70, Harlequins
Hole F.T.A. 1961–62, Richmond
Hollis G. 1939–40, Richmond
Holmes C.B. 1946–47, Manchester *(E 1947)*
Holmes M.A. 1949–50, Nuneaton *(E 1950)*
Holmes W.B. 1948–49, Cambridge Univ. *(E 1949)*
Honey R. 1909–10, Blackheath
Hood N.L. 1892–93, St Thomas's Hosp.
Hooper C.A. 1890–91, Middx Wands *(E 1894)* CM
Hopkins G. 1915, Leicester
Hopkins R.G. 1923–24, Blackheath
Hopley F.J.V. 1906–07, Blackheath *(E 1907)*

**Hopper L.B.** 1897–98, Liverpool
**Hopwood C.R.** 1927–28, Richmond, CM
**Horan A.K.** 1912–13, Blackheath *(I 1920)*
**Hordern P.C.** 1930–31, Newport *(E 1931)* CM
**Horrocks-Taylor J.P.** 1957–58, Cambridge Univ. *(E 1958)*
**Horsburgh G.B.** 1936–37, L. Scottish *(S 1937)*
**Horton A.L.** 1964–65, Blackheath *(E 1965)*
**Hosen R.W.** 1961–62, Northampton *(E 1963)*
**Hosken H.** 1905–06, Old Leysians
**Hosker W.** 1955–56, Birkenhead Park
**Hoskin W.W.** 1906–07, Blackheath, CM
**Hosking G.R.d'A.** 1949–50, Devonport S. *(E 1949)*
**Houston D.M.** 1920–21, L. Scottish
**Houston K.J.** 1963–64, Queen's Univ. *(I 1961)*
**Howard P.D.** 1930–31, Old Millhillians *(E 1930)*
**Howard W.G.** 1938–39, Old Birkonians
**Howard-Jones S.I.** 1935–36, Aldershot Services
**Hubbard G.C.** 1890, Blackheath *(E 1892)* OM, CM
**Hubbard J.C.** 1922–23, Blackheath *(E 1930)*
**Hudson G.A.** 1944–45, Gloucester
**Hudson P.** 1919–20, UC Hosp.
**Hughes A.** 1964–65, Newbridge
**Hughes D.** 1969–70, Newbridge *(W 1967)*
**Hughes Griff** 1901–02, Cardiff
**Hughes H.L.G.** 1912–13, Blackheath, Treas., Hon. Sec., Pres.
**Hughes K.** 1969–70, Cambridge Univ. *(W 1970)*
**Hughes N.M.** 1958–59, Blackheath *(A 1952)*
**Huins S.J.** 1925–26, Moseley
**Hullin W.G.** 1966–67, Cardiff *(W 1967)*
**Hulme F.C.** 1901–02, Birkenhead Park *(E 1903)*
**Hume J.W.G.** 1929–30, Edinburgh Wands *(S 1928)*
**Humfrey L.C.** 1894–95, Blackheath
**Humphrey S.H.G.** 1912–13, Northampton
**Humphreys R.M.** 1913–14, St Thomas's Hosp.
**Hunt E.W.F.deV.** 1928–29, Rosslyn Park *(I 1930)*
**Hunt G.W.** 1915, Leicester
**Hunt R.W.** 1891–92, Harlequins
**Hunt W.J.** 1962–63, Ebbw Vale
**Hunter W.J.** 1964–65, Hawick *(S 1964)*
**Hunter W.R.** 1961–62, CIYMS *(I 1962)*
**Hurst A.C.B.** 1959–60, Wasps *(E 1962)*
**Huskisson T.F.** 1936–37, OM Taylors *(E 1937)*
**Hutchinson F.** 1907–08, Headingley *(E 1909)*
**Hutchinson P.** 1903–04, Birkenhead Park
**Hyde J.P.** 1949–50, Northampton *(E 1950)*

**Hughes W.E.** 1900, *played but not elected*
*Joined Rugby League*
**Hopkins R.** 1970–71, Maesteg

**Ingledew H.M.** 1890, Cardiff *(W 1890)* OM
**Inglis H.M.** 1950–51, Edinburgh Acads *(S 1951)*
**Innes J.R.S.** 1945–46, Aberdeen GSFP *(S 1939)*
**Ireland J.C.H.** 1926–27, Glasgow HSOB *(S 1925)*
**Irvine A.R.** 1973–74, Heriots FP *(S 1973)*
**Irwin J.W.S.** 1938–39, NIFC *(I 1938)*

**Jacklin I.S.** 1939–40, St Mary's Hosp.
**Jackson A.R.V.** 1911–12, Dublin Wands *(I 1911)*
**Jackson B.S.** 1965–66, Broughton Park *(E 1970)*
**Jackson H.C.** 1905–06, Blackheath
**Jackson K.L.T.** 1933–34, Oxford Univ. *(S 1933)*
**Jackson R.R.** 1913–14, Liverpool
**Jackson S.H.** 1965–66, Collegians
**Jackson T.G.H.** 1945–46, L. Scottish *(S 1947)*

**Jackson W.M.** 1948–49, Harlequins
**Jacob F.** 1897–98, Richmond *(E 1897)*
**Jacob H.P.** 1922–23, Blackheath *(E 1924)*
**Jacobs C.R.** 1956–57, Northampton *(E 1956)* CM
**Jacot B.L.** 1920–21, Harlequins
**James C.R.** 1957–58, Llanelli *(W 1958)*
**Janion J.P.A.G.** 1970–71, Bedford *(E 1971)*
**Jeeps R.E.G.** 1955–56, Northampton *(E 1956)*
**Jeffrey G.L.** 1891–92, Blackheath *(E 1886)*
**Jeffrey J.J.** 1968–69, Newport *(W 1967)*
**Jenkins G.** 1975–76, Llanelli
**Jenkins H.W.** 1973–74, Llanelli
**Jenkins J.C.** 1905–06, L. Welsh *(W 1906)*
**Jenkins V.G.J.** 1932–33, Oxford Univ. *(W 1933)* CM
**Jenkins V.L.** 1972–73, Bridgend
**Jenkins W.J.** 1915, Cardiff *(W 1912)*
**Jerwood H.P.** 1947–48, Leicester
**John B.** 1966–67, Llanelli *(W 1966)*
**John C.** 1970–71, Llanelli
**John D.** 1975–76, Penarth
**John E.R.** 1950–51, Neath *(W 1950)*
**Johns C.R.** 1961–62, Redruth
**Johns N.A.** 1915, Cheltenham
**Johnson A.G.** 1929–30, Guy's Hosp.
**Johnson A.G.** 1970–71, Northampton
**Johnston A.S.** 1890, Blackheath, OM
**Johnston D.J.B.** 1943–44, St Mary's Hosp.
**Johnston W.G.S.** 1935–36, Richmond *(S 1935)*
**Johnstone P.G.** 1953–54, Oxford Univ.
**Johnstone R.D.B.** 1945–46, Wanderers & Pukekohe
**Jolliffe R.L.K.** 1963–64, Northampton
**Jolly W.A.** 1899–1900, L. Scottish
**Jones A. Vaughan** 1933–34, U. Services
**Jones B.J.** 1957–58, Newport *(W 1960)*
**Jones C.W.** 1937–38, Cardiff *(W 1934)*
**Jones D.K.** 1962–63, Llanelli *(W 1962)*
**Jones E.** 1957–58, Penarth
**Jones G.** 1957–58, Penarth
**Jones H.A.** 1951–52, Barnstaple *(E 1950)*
**Jones J.D.K.** 1898–99, Birkenhead Park
**Jones J.P. (Tuan)** 1911–12, Guy's Hosp.
**Jones J.P. (Ponty)** 1912–13, Pontypool *(W 1908)*
**Jones K.D.** 1962–63, Cardiff *(W 1960)*
**Jones K.J.** 1948–49, Newport *(W 1947)*
**Jones L.L.O.** 1970–71, Ebbw Vale
**Jones R.C.** 1919–20, Northampton
**Jones T.R.K.** 1925–26, Exeter
**Jones W.I.** 1923–24, Llanelli *(W 1925)*
**Jones-Davies T.E.** 1928–29, L. Welsh *(W 1930)*
**Jorden A.M.** 1969–70, Cambridge Univ. *(E 1970)*
**Joubert S.** 1909–10, Stellenbosch *(SA 1906)*
**Juckes R.** 1915, Blackheath
**Judd P.E.** 1962–63, Coventry *(E 1962)*
**Judd S.** 1951–52, Cardiff *(W 1953)*

*Joined Rugby League*
**Jones W.K.** 1966–67, Cardiff
**Jukes B.** 1903, v Cardiff *(substitute)*

**Kavanagh J.R.** 1951–52, UC Dublin *(I 1953)*
**Kavanagh P.** 1951–52, UC Dublin *(I 1952)*
**Keane M.I.** 1973–74, Lansdowne *(I 1974)*
**Keeffe E.** 1945–46, Sunday's Well *(I 1947)*
**Keeling J.H.** 1949–50, Army *(E 1948)*
**Keen B.W.** 1968–69, Moseley *(E 1968)*
**Keith-Roach P.D'A.** 1975–76, Rosslyn Park
**Keller D.H.** 1948–49, L. Scottish *(S 1949)* CM

Kelly G.A. 1945–46, Bedford *(E 1947)*
Kelly J.C. 1963–64, UC Dublin *(I 1962)*
Kelly R.F. 1925–26, Watsonians *(S 1927)*
Kemble W.S. 1938–39, Harlequins
Kemp D.T. 1930–31, Trojans *(E 1935)* CM
Kemp J.T. 1923–24, Blackheath
Kemp J.W.Y. 1954–55, Glasgow HSFP *(S 1954)*
Kemp T.A. 1936–37, St Mary's Hosp. *(E 1937)* CM
Kendall F.S. 1929–30, Rosslyn Park
Kendall P.D. 1899–1900, Birkenhead Park *(E 1901)* CM
Kendall-Carpenter J.McG.K. 1948–49, Oxford Univ. *(E 1949)* CM
Kendrew D.A. 1929–30, Woodford *(E 1930)*
Kennedy K.W. 1965–66, CIYMS *(I 1965)*
Kent C.P. 1974–75, Oxford Univ. *(E 1977)*
Kenyon B.J. 1951–52, Border *(SA 1949)*
Kerr C.G.C. 1921–22, Watsonians
Kerr G.C. 1897–98, Durham City *(S 1898)*
Kershaw C.A. 1919–20, U. Services *(E 1920)*
Key A. 1928–29, Old Cranleighans *(E 1930)*
Kidman G.E. 1915, Guy's Hosp.
Kiernan T.J. 1960–61, UC Cork *(I 1960)*
King I. 1951–52, Harrogate *(E 1954)* CM
King J.A. 1913–14, Headingley *(E 1911)*
King P.L.C. 1964–65, Blackheath
King Q.E.M.A. 1913–14, Blackheath *(E 1921)*
King R.H. 1919–20, Harlequins
Kingscote T.H. 1898–99, Manchester
King-Stephens A.F. 1898–99, Rosslyn Park
Kininmonth P.W. 1950–51, Richmond *(S 1949)*
Kipling J.H. 1896–97, Richmond
Kirkby E.W. 1909–10, U. Services
Kirkpatrick I.A. 1972–73, Poverty Bay *(NZ 1967)*
Kirton E.W. 1971–72, Harlequins *(NZ 1967)*
Kitching A.E. 1911–12, Blackheath
Knight R.V. 1911–12, Bedford
Knill F.M.D. 1975–76, Cardiff *(W 1976)*
Knowles T.C. 1930–31, Birkenhead Park *(E 1931)*
Knox H.N. 1922–23, Blackheath
Krige J.A. 1919–20, Guy's Hosp. *(E 1920)*
Krige P. 1919–20, Guy's Hosp.
Kyle J.W. 1947–48, Queen's Univ. Belfast *(I 1947)*
Kyrke G.V. 1903–04, Marlborough Nomads

*Joined Rugby League*
Kinnear R.M. 1926–27, *played as substitute v Penarth 1920*
Kerr J.

Laborde C.D. 1936–37, Richmond
Labuschagne N.A. 1954–55, Harlequins *(E 1953)*
Lacaze C. 1967–68, Angoulême *(F 1961)*
Lacey E.C. 1950–51, Leicester
Lacey F.H. 1912–13, Blackheath
Laidlaw F.A.L. 1962–63, Melrose *(S 1965)*
Laird H.C.C. 1927–28, Harlequins *(E 1927)*
Lambert D. 1905–06, Harlequins *(E 1907)*
Lamont R.A. 1964–65, Instonians *(I 1965)*
Lamphier C.W. 1892–93, Blackheath
Lane H.J.B. 1931–32, U. Services
Lane M.F. 1948–49, UC Cork *(I 1947)*
Lane R. 1971–72, Cardiff
Lane R.O.B. 1890, Marlborough Nomads, OM
Langrish R.W. 1931–32, L. Scottish *(S 1930)*
Lansbury J. 1971–72, Sale
Larmour S. 1913–14, Dublin Wands

Larter P.J. 1965–66, Northampton *(E 1967)*
Latter A. 1892–93, Blackheath
Lauder W. 1968–69, Neath *(S 1969)*
Laughland I.H.P. 1960–61, L. Scottish *(S 1959)* CM
Lavelle K.A.C. 1964–65, Royal Navy
Lawless A.P. 1921–22, Richmond
Lawless P.H. 1920–21, Richmond, CM
Lawrie H.S.B. 1913–14, Leicester
Lawrie P.W. 1923–24, Leicester *(E 1910)*
Lawrie S.J. 1898–99, Blackheath
Lawton T. 1921–22, Blackheath, CM
Layman F.W. 1922–23, Northampton
Leadbetter M.M. 1969–70, Broughton Park *(E 1970)*
Leadbetter V.H. 1953–54, Edinburgh Wands
Leake W.R.M. 1890, Harlequins *(E 1891)* OM
Leather W.J. 1933–34, Liverpool
Lee A.B. 1943–44, Guy's Hosp.
Lee H. 1905–06, Guy's Hosp. *(E 1907)*
Lee T.S. 1929–30, U. Services
Le Fleming J. 1891–92, Blackheath *(E 1887)*
Leith J.M.B. 1895–96, W. of Scotland
Leleu J. 1960–61, Swansea *(W 1959)*
Leslie D.G. 1974–75, Dundee HSFP *(S 1975)*
Leslie O.E.H. 1919–20, Sheffield
Leslie R.E. 1965–66, Northampton
Leslie-Jones F.A. 1896–97, Richmond *(E 1895)*
Lester H. 1902–03, Richmond
Lewis A.J.L. 1970–71, Ebbw Vale *(W 1970)*
Lewis A.O. 1952–53, Bath *(E 1952)*
Lewis B.R. 1912–13, Swansea *(W 1912)*
Lewis G. Windsor 1958–59, Cambridge Univ. *(W 1960)* Hon. Sec.
Lewis Windsor H. 1926–27, Guy's Hosp. *(W 1926)* CM
Lewis J.M.C. 1915, Cardiff *(W 1912)*
Leyland R. 1934–35, Waterloo *(E 1935)*
Liebson A.S. 1911–12, Guy's Hosp.
Lilley G.D. 1968–69, Blackheath
Lind H. 1932–33, Dunfermline *(S 1928)*
Lindesay J.H.C. 1912–13, Blackheath
Lindsay A.B. 1909–10, London Hosp. *(S 1910)*
Livesay R.O'H. 1895–96, Blackheath *(E 1898)*
Llewelyn D.B. 1969–70, Newport *(W 1970)*
Llewellyn P.D. 1972–73, Swansea *(W 1973)*
Lloyd D.J. 1964–65, Cardiff Trg. Coll. *(W 1966)*
Lloyd D.P.M. 1892–93, Llanelli
Lloyd R.H. 1967–68, Harlequins *(E 1967)*
Lloyd T.P. 1909–10, L. Welsh
Lochore B.J. 1967–68, Wairarapa *(NZ 1963)*
Lockhart J.H. Bruce 1909–10, L. Scottish *(S 1913)*
Lockyer S.H. 1906–07, Llanelli
Logan W.R. 1930–31, Edinburgh Univ. *(S 1931)*
Lohden F.C. 1892–93, Blackheath *(E 1893)*
Longland R.J. 1935–36, Northampton *(E 1932)*
Louwrens J.J. 1905–06, St Mary's Hosp.
Loveitt F.R. 1896–97, Coventry
Loveday B.R. 1957–58, Cambridge Univ.
Low E.G.L. 1957–58, Watsonians
Ludlow L.G. 1928–29, Liverpool
Lumb R. 1915, Headingley
Lumsden I.J.M. 1945–46, Watsonians *(S 1947)*
Luxmoore A.F.C.C. 1896–97, Richmond *(E 1900)*
Luyt R.E. 1939–40, Blackheath
Luya H.F. 1947–48, Headingley *(E 1948)*
Lyddon H.C. 1937–38, U. Services, CM
Lynch J.F. 1970–71, St Mary's Coll. *(I 1971)*
Lyon G.H.D'O. 1907–08, U. Services *(E 1908)*

Meredith C.C. 1953–54, Neath *(W 1953)*
Merriam L.P.B. 1919–20, Blackheath *(E 1920)* Hon. Sec.
Methuen A. 1890–91, L. Scottish *(S 1899)*
M'Gregor A. 1920–21, Pontypridd
M'Gregor D.G. 1906–07, Pontypridd *(S 1907)*
Michaelson R.C.B. 1966–67, L. Welsh *(W 1963)*
Michie E.J.S. 1955–56, L. Scottish & Army *(S 1954)*
Millar S. 1958–59, Ballymena *(I 1958)*
Miller D.G. (formerly D.G. Schultze) 1905–06, L. Scottish *(S 1905)*
Miller J.S. 1901–02, Percy Park
Millett H. 1913–14, Richmond *(E 1920)*
Milliken R.A. 1970–71, Queen's Univ. Belfast *(I 1973)*
Mills W.H. 1925–26, Old Blues
Milman D.L.K. 1935–36, Bedford *(E 1937)*
Milton C.H. 1904–05, Camborne S. of Mines *(E 1906)*
Milton J.G. 1902–03, Camborne S. of Mines *(E 1904)*
Milton N.W. 1906–07, Oxford Univ.
Minch J.B. 1915, Bective Rangers *(I 1913)*
Minns P.C. 1932–33, Blackheath
Mitchell E.H. 1898–99, Lennox
Mitchell F. 1893–94, Blackheath *(E 1895)* CM
Mitchell G.W.E. 1966–67, Edinburgh Univ. *(S 1967)*
Mitchell W.G. 1890, Richmond *(E 1890)* OM
Mobbs E.R. 1911–12, Northampton *(E 1909)* CM
Moffat I.B. 1971–72, Northampton
Moffat J. 1929–30, Edinburgh Acads.
Moffatt-Pender I.M. 1915, L. Scottish *(S 1914)*
Moll J.S. 1938–39, Blackheath
Molloy M.G. 1968–69, L. Irish *(I 1966)*
Maloney J.J. 1971–72, St Mary's Coll. *(I 1972)*
Monaghan D.L. 1910–11, Rosslyn Park
Monaghan P.J. 1907–08, Guy's Hosp.
Monypenny C.J.B. 1891–92, Bath
Moore H.B. 1913–14, Rosslyn Park
Moore P.B.C. 1949–50, Blackheath *(E 1951)*
Moore T.A.P. 1969–70, Highfield *(I 1967)*
Moore W.K.T. 1948–49, Leicester *(E 1947)*
Moran F.G. 1936–37, Clontarf *(I 1936)*
Morel T.E. 1920–21, O. Leysians
Morgan A.K. 1968–69, L. Welsh
Morgan C.H. 1956–57, Llanelli *(W 1957)*
Morgan C.I. 1950–51, Cardiff *(W 1951)*
Morgan D.R.R. 1962–63, Llanelli *(W 1962)*
Morgan D.W. 1972–73, Melville Coll. FP *(S 1973)*
Morgan E. Wayne 1903–04, Cardiff
Morgan G.J. 1934–35, Clontarf *(I 1934)*
Morgan H.J. 1957–58, Abertillery *(W 1958)*
Morgan M.E. 1938–39, Swansea *(W 1938)*
Morgan M.H. 1895–96, Cardiff
Morgan N.H. 1959–60, Newport *(W 1960)*
Morgan W.A.B. 1971–72, Bridgend
Morgan W.G. 1927–28, Swansea *(W 1927)* CM
Morgan W.G.D. 1959–60, Newcastle Medicals *(E 1960)*
Morgan W.L. 1905–06, Guy's Hosp.
Morgan W.S. 1923–24, St Bart's Hosp.
Morley A.J. 1973–74, Bristol *(E 1972)*
Morlock H.V. 1919–20, St Bart's Hosp.
Morris H. 1952–53, Cardiff *(W 1951)*
Morris S.A. 1963–64, Newton Abbot
Morris W.D. 1970–71, Neath *(W 1967)*
Morris W.J. 1964–65, Newport *(W 1965)*

Morrish W. 1913–14, Cardiff
Morrisson P.H. 1890, Northern *(E 1890)* OM
Mortimer L. 1893–94, Middx Wands
Mortimer W. 1897–98, Marlborough Nomads *(E 1899)* CM
Morton D.D. 1920–21, Lansdowne
Morton H.J.S. 1908–09, Blackheath *(E 1909)*
Moss-Blundell B.S. 1905–06, Old Alleynians
Muddiman F. 1915, Northampton
Mudge J.B. 1913–14, St Bart's Hosp.
Muir D.E. 1949–50, Heriot's FP *(S 1950)*
Mulcahy W.A. 1957–58, UC Dublin *(I 1958)*
Mullan B. 1946–47, Clontarf *(I 1947)* CM
Mullen K.D. 1946–47, Old Belvedere *(I 1947)*
Mulligan A.A. 1956–57, Cambridge Univ. *(I 1956)*
Mullins H.R. 1904–05, Guy's Hosp.
Munks W.C.O. 1961–62, Richmond
Munro P. 1902–03, L. Scottish *(S 1905)* CM
Munro W.H. 1943–44, Glasgow HSFP *(S 1947)*
Murdoch H.B. 1896–97, Rosslyn Park
Murdoch W.C.W. 1938–39, Hillhead HSFP *(S 1935)*
Murphy C.J. 1945–46, Lansdowne *(I 1939)*
Murphy J.G.W.M. 1957–58, L. Irish *(I 1952)*
Murphy N. 1929–30, Cork Const. *(I 1930)*
Murphy N.A.A. 1958–59, Cork Const. *(I 1958)*
Murray G.C. 1970–71, Harlequins
Murray J. 1965–66, UC Dublin *(I 1963)*
Murray P.F. 1930–31, Dublin Wands *(I 1927)*
Murrell A.G. 1896–97, Lennox
Mycock J. 1941–42, Harlequins *(E 1947)*

*Joined Rugby League*
Mathias R. 1971–72, Llanelli

Napier Sir J.W.L. 1924–25, Richmond
Nash D. 1961–62, Ebbw Vale *(W 1960)*
Nash J.E. 1915, Bank of England
Neale M.E. 1911–12, Bristol *(E 1912)*
Neary A. 1971–72, Broughton Park *(E 1971)*
Neave A.L.W. 1913–14, Richmond
Neely H.B. 1953–54, Blackheath
Neill J.B. 1963–64, Edinburgh Acads *(S 1963)*
Neilson G.T. 1896–97, W. of Scotland *(S 1891)*
Neilson W. 1891–92, L. Scottish *(S 1891)* CM
Nelmes B.G. 1975–76, Cardiff *(E 1975)*
Nelson J.B. 1924–25, Glasgow Acads *(S 1925)*
Nelson J.E. 1947–48, Malone *(I 1948)* CM
Nelson J.W. 1957–58, Cardiff
Nelson T.A. 1898–99, Edinburgh Acads *(S 1898)*
Neser E.E. 1919–20, Guy's Hosp.
Neser V.H. 1920–21, Blackheath
Newbigging W.E. 1891–92, Middx Wands
Newbold C.J. 1902–03, Blackheath *(E 1904)*
Newman S.C. 1946–47, Oxford Univ. *(E 1947)*
Newton A.W. 1906–07, Blackheath *(E 1907)*
Newton N.J. 1935–36, Bournemouth
Newton-Thompson C.L. 1939–40, Blackheath
Newton-Thompson J.O. 1945–46, Oxford Univ. *(E 1947)* CM
Nickalls C.P. 1898–99, Blackheath
Nicholas D.L. 1907–10, Blackheath
Nicholas P.L. 1897–98, Exeter *(E 1902)*
Nicholl C.B. 1890–91, Llanelli *(W 1891)* CM
Nicholls E. Gwyn 1926–27, Cardiff
Nicholls J.B. 1944–45, Northern Suburbs
Nicholson B.E. 1936–37, Harlequins *(E 1938)*
Nicholson E.S. 1933–34, Oxford Univ. *(E 1935)*

Norman D.J. 1926–27, Leicester *(E 1932)*
Norman R.T. 1933–34, St Thomas's Hosp.
Norman T.B.M. 1947–48, Edinburgh Univ.
Norris C.H. 1963–64, Cardiff
North E.G.H. 1891–92, Blackheath *(E 1891)*
Norton G.W. 1948–49, Bective R. *(I 1949)*
Novis A.L. 1928–29, Blackheath *(E 1929)*

Oakes R.F. 1896–97, Hartlepool R. *(E 1897)*
Oakley L.F.L. 1948–49, Bedford *(E 1951)*
Obolensky A. 1936–37, Oxford Univ. *(E 1936)*
O'Brien A. 1906–07, Blackheath
O'Brien D.J. 1947–48, L. Irish *(I 1948)*
O'Brien R.H. 1921–22, Richmond
O'Callaghan P. 1968–69, Dolphin *(I 1967)*
O'Connor A. 1961–62, Aberavon *(W 1960)*
O'Connor J.J. 1933–34, UC Cork *(I 1933)*
O'Conor R.C. 1919–20, U. Services
Odgers F.W. 1903–04, U. Services
Odgers W.B. 1901–02, Richmond
O'Donoghue P.J. 1956–57, Bective R. *(I 1955)*
O'Dowda B.F. 1897–98, Croydon
O'Driscoll B.J. 1968–69, Manchester *(I 1971)*
O'Hanlon B. 1947–48, Dolphin *(I 1947)*
Old A.G.B. 1971–72, Middlesbrough *(E 1972)*
Oldfield A.D. 1926–27, Blackheath
Olliff G.L. 1924–25, Old Paulines
Olsen E.N. 1961–62, Blackheath
O'Meara J.A. 1952–53, UC Cork *(I 1951)*
O'Neill W.A. 1952–53, UC Dublin *(I 1952)*
Onslow A.J.M. 1893–94, Blackheath
Orchard S. 1920–21, St Bart's Hosp.
O'Reilly A.J.F. 1954–55, Old Belvedere *(I 1955)*
O'Reilly F.P. 1913–14, U. Services
O'Rorke J. 1903–04, Wanderers
Orr C.E. 1892–93, W. of Scotland *(S 1887)*
Orr H.J. 1906–07, L. Scottish *(S 1903)*
Orr P.C.R. 1963–64, Richmond
Osbourn A.J. 1915, Bedford
Oscroft P.W. 1895–96, Leicester
O'Shea J.P. 1968–69, Cardiff *(W 1967)*
Ostling P.L. 1966–67, Blackheath
Oughtred B.F. 1900–01, Hartlepool R. *(E 1901)*
Owen G.D. 1954–55, Newport *(W 1955)*
Owen J.E. 1961–62, Cambridge Univ. *(E 1963)*
Owen O.L. 1954–55, Swansea
Owen W. 1911–12, Blackheath
Owen-Smith H.G. 1933-34, St Mary's *(E 1934)*

Page J.J. 1975–76, Northampton *(E 1971)*
Pailthorpe D.W. 1913–14, Rosslyn Park
Pallant J.N. 1965–66, Loughborough Colls
Pallot E.G. 1902–03, RNE College Keyham
Palmer A.C. 1908–09, London Hosp. *(E 1909)*
Palmer F.H. 1903–04, Richmond *(E 1905)*
Palmer G.V. 1924–25, Richmond *(E 1928)*
Palmer H.R. 1899–1900, Cambridge Univ.
Park J.C. 1935–36, Furness
Parke J.C. 1907–08, Monkstown *(I 1903)*
Parker G.W. 1933–34, Gloucester *(E 1938)*
Parker G.W.C. 1920–21, St Bart's Hosp.
Parker T. 1891–92, Richmond
Parsons C.G. 1906–07, Blackheath
Partridge J.E.C. 1905–06, Newport, CM
Pask A.E.I. 1961–62, Abertillery *(W 1961)*
Patrick B. 1975–76, Gosforth
Patterson W.M. 1958–59, Sale *(E 1961)*
Pavitt H.W. 1902–03, Richmond

Payne C.M. 1959–60, Oxford Univ. *(E 1964)*
Payne G.W. 1960–61, Newport *(W 1961)*
Peacock M.F. 1934–35, Richmond
Pearson T.W. 1892–93, Cardiff *(W 1891)*
Peart T.G.A.H. 1963–64, Hartlepool R. *(E 1964)*
Pearey M.A. 1956–57, Royal Navy
Pease F.E. 1890, Hartlepool R. *(E 1887)* OM
Pedlow A.C. 1955–56, Queen's Univ. *(I 1953)*
Peel H.R. 1945–46, Headingley
Pemberton H.J. 1913–14, Coventry
Penberthy R.M. 1975–76, Pontypridd
Penman W.M. 1938–39, U. Services *(S 1939)*
Percival L.J. 1891–92, Rugby *(E 1891)*
Perkins A.B. 1890, Bradford, OM
Periton H.G. 1922–23, Waterloo *(E 1925)* CM
Perry D.G. 1961–62, Bedford *(E 1963)*
Perry S.V. 1946–47, Cambridge Univ. *(E 1947)*
Phesey F.C. 1905–06, Richmond
Phillips J.R. 1955–56, Newport
Phillips M.S. 1957–58, Oxford Univ. *(E 1958)* CM
Phillips R.H. 1969–70, L. Welsh
Pickering A.S. 1906–07, Harrogate *(E 1907)*
Pickering R.D.A. 1966–67, Bradford *(E 1967)*
Pierce R. 1895–96, Liverpool *(E 1898)*
Pike V.J. 1932–33, Lansdowne *(I 1931)*
Pilkington W.N. 1897–98, Liverpool *(E 1898)*
Pillman C.H. 1909–10, Blackheath *(E 1910)* CM
Pincknay H.C. 1901–02, Blackheath
Plumbridge R.A. 1956–57, Oxford Univ.
Plummer R.C.S. 1921–22, Newport *(W 1912)*
Pocock W.A. 1911–12, Cheltenham
Pollock T.W.S. 1902–03, Liverpool
Pomathios M. 1950–51, Agen, Lyon *(F 1948)*
Poole F.O. 1892–93, Gloucester *(E 1895)*
Poole-Hughes W. 1892–93, L. Welsh
Pope E.B. 1930–31, Blackheath *(E 1931)*
Popplewell J.R.F. 1929–30, Guy's Hosp.
Portus G.V. 1907–08, Blackheath *(E 1908)*
Potter F.W. 1895–96, Bedford
Powell D.L. 1966–67, Northampton *(E 1966)*
Powell W.C. 1928–29, L. Welsh *(W 1926)*
Pratten W.E. 1926–27, Blackheath *(E 1927)*
Preece I. 1945–46, Coventry *(E 1948)*
Preece P.S. 1972–73, Coventry *(E 1972)*
Prentice F.D. 1926–27, Leicester *(E 1928)*
Prescott A.E.C. 1929–30, Harlequins
Prescott R.E. 1936–37, Harlequins *(E 1937)*
Preston F.S. 1897–98, Marlborough Nomads
Price B. 1960–61, Newport *(W 1961)*
Price G. 1974–75, Pontypool *(W 1974)*
Price H.L. 1920–21, Harlequins *(E 1922)*
Price T.W. 1945–46, Gloucester *(E 1948)*
Price V.R. 1920–21, Harlequins
Priest T.E. 1926–27, Old Alleynians
Priday A.J. 1963–64, Cardiff *(W 1958)*
Priday C.A. 1904–05, Blackheath
Prosser T.R. 1957–58, Pontypool *(W 1956)*
Prout D.H. 1967–68, Northampton *(E 1968)*
Purcell N.M. 1912–13, Lansdowne *(I 1921)*
Pullin J.V. 1965–66, Bristol *(E 1966)*
Purdy S.J. 1959–60, Rugby *(E 1962)*
Purves W.D.C.L. 1911–12, L. Scottish *(S 1912)*
Purvis F. 1901–02, Hartlepool R.
Pym J.A. 1911–12, Blackheath *(E 1912)*

*Joined Rugby League*
Price M.J. 1959–60, Pontypool *(W 1959)*
Prosser W.R. 1964–65, Newport

Quinn J.P. 1915, Dublin Univ. *(I 1910)*
Quinn J.P. 1953–54, New Brighton *(E 1954)*
Quinnell D.L. 1970–71, Llanelli *(W 1972)*

Ralston C.W. 1971–72, Richmond *(E 1971)*
Ramsay A.W. 1959–60, Old Millhillians
Ramsay A.R. 1931–32, L. Scottish
Ranson J.M. 1962–63, Rosslyn Park
Rashleigh W. 1891–92, Blackheath
Raybould W.H. 1966–67, L. Welsh *(W 1967)*
Raymond R.L. 1923–24, Blackheath
Rea C.W.W. 1970–71, Headingley *(S 1968)*
Read A.B. 1913–14, Richmond
Rees A.M. 1934–35, L. Welsh *(W 1934)*
Rees C.F.W. 1975–76, L. Welsh *(W 1974)*
Rees H. 1932–33, Blackheath *(W 1939)*
Rees H.J.C. 1941–42, Rosslyn Park
Rees J. Conway 1892–93, Llanelli, CM
Rees J. Idwal 1933–34, Swansea *(W 1934)*
Rees J.V. 1912–13, Harlequins
Reeve J.S.R. 1929–30, Harlequins *(E 1929)*
Reeve P.B. 1948–49, Old Novocastrians
Regan M. 1951–52, Liverpool *(E 1953)*
Reid N. 1912–13, Blackheath
Reid T.E. 1953–54, Garryowen *(I 1953)*
Reidy J.P. 1933–34, L. Irish
Reity F.W. 1919–20, Guy's Hosp.
Renwick J.R. 1975–76, Hawick *(S 1972)*
Rew H. 1925–26, Exeter *(E 1929)*
Reynolds F.J. 1936–37, Old Cranleighans *(E 1937)*
Reynolds G.J. 1939–40, St Mary's Hosp.
Reynolds H.P. 1892–93, Rosslyn Park
Reynolds R.U. 1937–38, Sale
Reynolds S. 1896–97, Richmond *(E 1900)*
Richards A.A. 1974–75, Fylde
Richards D. 1976–77, Swansea
Richards G.A. 1974–75, Wasps
Richards T.B. 1962–63, L. Welsh
Richardson J.V. 1923–24, Birkenhead Park *(E 1928)*
Richmond M. 1925–26, U. Services
Rigby J.C.A. 1893–94, Blackheath
Rimmer G.R. 1950–51, Waterloo *(E 1949)*
Ripley A.G. 1971–72, Rosslyn Park *(E 1972)*
Risk W.S. 1934–35, Glasgow Acads
Ritchie B.W.T. 1942–43, St Thomas's Hosp.
Ritchie J.S. 1954–55, L. Irish *(I 1956)* CM
Ritchie W.T. 1904–05, Cambridge Univ. *(S 1905)*
Ritson J.A.S. 1910–11, Northern *(E 1910)*
Robbins P.G.D. 1955–56, Oxford Univ. *(E 1956)* CM
Roberts A.B.P. 1919–20, Blackheath
Roberts A.D. 1910–11, Northern *(E 1911)*
Roberts A.F. 1902–03, Cambridge Univ.
Roberts C.S.L. 1909–10, Guy's Hosp.
Roberts E.W. 1904–05, RNE College, Keyham *(E 1901)* CM
Roberts G. 1937–38, Watsonians *(S 1938)*
Roberts G.D. 1906–07, Harlequins *(E 1907)* CM
Roberts G. Lloyd 1894–95, Cardiff
Roberts H.M. 1960–61, Cardiff *(W 1960)*
Roberts J. 1926–27, Cardiff *(W 1927)*
Roberts J.M.H. 1950–51, Harlequins
Roberts J. 1958–59, Old Millhillians *(E 1960)* CM
Roberts M.G. 1972–73, L. Welsh *(W 1971)*
Roberts V.G. 1946–47, Penryn *(E 1947)* CM
Robertshaw P. 1891–92, Bradford
Robertshaw R. 1890–91, Bradford *(E 1886)*
Robertson I. 1965–66, Watsonians *(S 1968)*
Robertson W. 1915, Edinburgh Inst. FP

Robins J.D. 1950–51, Birkenhead Park
Robinson C.O. 1896–97, Percy Park
Robinson D. 1973–74, Gosforth
Robinson E. 1952–53, Coventry *(E 1954)*
Robinson G.C. 1898–99, Percy Park *(E 1897)*
Robinson I. 1972–73, Cardiff *(W 1974)*
Robinson J.J. 1894–95, Headingley *(E 1893)*
Robson A. 1954–55, Hawick *(S 1954)*
Robson C.G. 1903–04, Blackheath
Robson M. 1929–30, Heriots FP *(E 1930)*
Roche W.J. 1921–22, UC Cork *(I 1920)*
Rodd J.A.T. 1962–63, L. Scottish *(S 1958)*
Rodgers A.K. 1973–74, Rosslyn Park
Roe R. 1950–51, Dublin Univ. *(I 1952)*
Rogers A. 1890, Moseley, OM
Rogers D.P. 1960–61, Bedford *(E 1961)* CM
Rogers J.G. 1936–37, Bedford
Rogers J.H. 1890, Moseley *(E 1890)* OM
Rogers J.M.T. 1962–63, Rosslyn Park
Rogers W.L.Y. 1903–04, Blackheath *(E 1905)*
Rolinson L.J. 1971–72, Coventry
Rollitt D.M. 1963–64, Bristol Univ. *(E 1967)*
Rollo D.M.D. 1959–60, Howe of Fife *(S 1959)*
Rougier G.R. 1920–21, Harlequins
Rosher J.B. 1915, Rosslyn Park
Rossborough P.A. 1970–71, Coventry *(E 1971)*
Ross A.R. 1910–11, Edinburgh Univ. *(S 1911)* CM
Ross J. 1901–02, L. Scottish *(S 1901)*
Ross J.A. 1926–27, L. Scottish
Ross J.E. 1913–14, Liverpool
Ross J.H. 1957–58, Malone
Ross W.Mc 1932–33, Queen's Univ. Belfast *(I 1932)*
Rosser D.W.A. 1964–65, Cambridge Univ. *(E 1965)*
Rossiter W. 1926–27, Lansdowne
Rotherham Arthur 1891–92, Richmond *(E 1898)* CM
Rottenburg H. 1898–99, L. Scottish *(S 1899)*
Roughhead W.N. 1930–31, L. Scottish *(S 1927)*
Rougier C.R. 1920–21, Harlequins
Rouillard A. 1894–95, Richmond
Row A.W.L. 1919–20, Blackheath
Rowand R. 1931–32, Glasgow HSFP *(S 1930)*
Rowlands K.A. 1961–62, Cardiff *(W 1962)*
Roy A. 1938–39, Waterloo *(S 1938)*
Royds P.M.R. 1897–98, Blackheath *(E 1898)*
Rudd E.L. 1964–65, Oxford Univ. *(E 1965)*
Russell E.S.B. 1898–99, Blackheath
Russell J. 1931–32, UC Cork *(I 1931)*
Russell J.C. 1919–20, London Hosp.
Rutherford D. 1959–60, Percy Park *(E 1960)*
Ryan P.H. 1954–55, Richmond *(E 1955)*
Ryder D.C.D. 1921–22, Blackheath

*Substitute*
Reed D. 1903
*Joined Rugby League*
Robins R.J. 1955–56, Pontypridd *(W 1953)*
Risman A.B.W. 1958–59, Manchester Univ. *(E 1959)*

Sagar J.W. 1899–1900, Castleford *(E 1901)*
Sampson H.F. 1910–11, Blackheath
Sampson R.W.F. 1938–39, L. Scottish *(S 1939)*
Sanders D.L. 1953–54, Harlequins *(E 1954)*
Sangwin R.D. 1963–64, Hull & ER *(E 1964)*
Sargant W.W. 1928–29, Old Leysians
Saunders C.J. 1951–52, Richmond
Saunders H.R. 1925–26, Blackheath

Saunders S.McK 1904–05, Guy's Hosp.
Saunders-Jacobs S.M. 1928–29, Richmond
Saville C.D. 1968–69, Blackheath
Sawyer F.W.C. 1906–07, Blackheath
Saxby L.E. 1931–32, Gloucester *(E 1932)*
Sayers H.J.M. 1934–35, Richmond *(I 1935)*
Schlund J.F.G. 1921–22, Old Alleynians
Scholfield F.B. 1910–11, Preston Grasshoppers
Schultze D.G. 1905–06, L. Scottish *(S 1905)*
Scholfield J.A. 1910–11, Preston Grasshoppers *(E 1911)*
Schute F.G. 1912–13, Dublin Univ. *(I 1913)*
Schwarz R.O. 1896–97, Richmond *(E 1899)* CM
Scotland K.J.F. 1957–58, Heriots FP *(S 1957)*
Scott A.C. 1892–93, Blackheath
Scott C.T. 1899–1900, Blackheath *(E 1900)*
Scott D.M. 1950–51, Langholm & Army *(S 1950)*
Scott E.K. 1944–45, St Mary's Hosp. *(E 1947)*
Scott G. 1893–94, Eden Wands
Scott J.M.B. 1907–08, Edinburgh Acads *(S 1907)*
Scott M.T. 1890, Northern *(E 1887)* OM
Scott T.P.L. 1962–63, Royal Navy
Scott W.M. 1890, Northern *(E 1889)* OM
Scott W.P. 1899–1900, W. of Scotland *(S 1900)* CM
Scoular J.G. 1904–05, Blackheath *(S 1905)*
Seagar J.C. 1919–20, Blackheath
Sealy J. 1897–98, Dublin Univ. *(I 1896)*
Sedgwick H.R. 1891–92, St Thomas's Hosp.
Sellar K.A. 1927–28, U. Services *(E 1927)*
Semmens L. 1947–48, Redruth
Senior E.W. 1890, St Thomas's Hosp., OM
Sever H.S. 1934–35, Sale *(E 1936)*
Shackleton J.A.P. 1964–65, L. Scottish *(S 1959)*
Shacksnovis A. 1923–24, Blackheath
Shand E.G.Loudon 1915, Old Alleynians *(S 1913)*
Shannon F. 1897–98, Bristol
Sharp R.A.W. 1959–60, Oxford Univ. *(E 1960)*
Sharrat H. 1923–24, Leicester
Shaw C. 1920–21, St Bart's Hosp.
Shaw G. 1972–73, Neath *(W 1972)*
Shaw G.D. 1943–44, Sale *(S 1935)*
Shaw J.F. 1898–99, RNE College Keyham *(E 1898)*
Shaw R.W. 1933–34, Glasgow HSFP *(S 1934)* CM
Shedden D. 1972–73, W. of Scotland *(S 1973)*
Sheehan W.B.J. 1927–28, London Hosp.
Shehadie N. 1957–58, NSW *(A 1947)*
Shell R.C. 1973–74, Aberavon *(W 1973)*
Shelswell A.H. 1919–20, Guy's Hosp.
Sherriff G.A. 1966–67, Saracens *(E 1966)*
Sherwell P.W. 1901–02, Blackheath
Sherwell W.B. 1898–99, Upper Clapton
Shirley M. 1942–43, Middx Hosp.
Shuker A.C. 1947–48, Broughton Park
Shuttleworth D.W. 1949–50, Blackheath *(E 1951)*
Sibree H.J.H. 1907–08, Harlequins *(E 1908)*
Siggins J.A.E. 1932–33, Collegians *(I 1931)*
Simmers W.M. 1928–29, Glasgow Acads *(S 1926)*
Simmons K. 1912–13, Richmond
Simpson C.P. 1892–93, Richmond
Simpson C.P. 1963–64, RMA Sandhurst *(E 1965)*
Simpson G.W. 1922–23, Heriots FP
Simpson J.W. 1893–94, Royal HSFP *(S 1893)*
Simpson T. 1902–03, Rockliffe *(E 1902)*
Skrimshire R.T. 1898–99, Newport *(W 1899)* CM
Skym A.S. 1932–33, Cardiff *(W 1928)*
Sladen G.M. 1928–29, U. Services *(E 1929)*
Slattery J.F. 1969–70, UC Dublin *(I 1970)*

Slemen M.A.C. 1973–74, Liverpool *(E 1976)*
Sloan A.T. 1920–21, Edinburgh Acads *(S 1914)*
Sloan D.A. 1949–50, Edinburgh Acads *(S 1950)*
Small H.D. 1949–50, Oxford Univ. *(E 1950)*
Smartt F.N. 1908–09, Dublin Univ. *(I 1908)*
Smeddle R.W. 1928–29, Blackheath
Smith A.R. 1898–99, L. Scottish *(S 1895)*
Smith A.R. 1954–55, Cambridge Univ. *(S 1955)*
Smith D.F. 1908–09, Richmond *(E 1910)*
Smith D.W.C. 1948–49, L. Scottish *(S 1949)*
Smith G.F. 1938–39, Blackheath
Smith G.J. 1923–24, Kelvinside Acads
Smith G.K. 1959–60, Kelso *(S 1957)*
Smith H.W. 1899–1900, Blackheath
Smith H.A. Haigh 1912–13, Trojans, Hon. Sec., Pres.
Smith I.S. 1923–24, L. Scottish *(S 1924)*
Smith J. 1964–65, Bedford
Smith J.B. 1945–46, Kaikohe *(NZ 1946)*
Smith J.H. 1951–52, Collegians *(I 1951)*
Smith J.V. 1948–49, Cambridge Univ. *(E 1950)*
Smith K. 1973–74, Roundhay *(E 1974)*
Smith Lewis 1902–03, Gloucester
Smith Lindsey 1892–93, Lennox
Smith M.W. 1899–1900, Blackheath
Smith M.A. 1968–69, L. Scottish *(S 1970)*
Smith M.J.K. 1955–56, Oxford Univ. *(E 1956)*
Smith R. 1971–72, Gloucester
Smith S.J. 1972–73, Sale *(E 1973)*
Smith S.R. 1957–58, Cambridge Univ. *(E 1959)*
Smith W.H. 1892–93, RIE College
Smuts P. 1919–20, St Bart's Hosp.
Smyth G.J.C. 1911–12, Blackheath
Smyth P.J. 1911–12, Collegians *(I 1911)*
Smyth R.S. 1901–02, Dublin Univ. *(I 1903)*
Smyth T. 1910–11, Malone *(I 1908)*
Soane F. 1891–92, Bath *(E 1893)*
Sobey W.H. 1926–27, Old Millhillians *(E 1930)*
Somerville H.R. 1930–31, Old Edwardians
Sparks C.W. 1912–13, Blackheath
Spear J.R. 1938–39, Blackheath
Spence A. 1897–98, Marlborough Nomads
Spence I.C. 1962–63, Gordonians
Spence K.M. 1951–52, Oxford Univ. *(S 1953)*
Spence P.D.B. 1924–25, Guy's Hosp.
Spencer J.S. 1968–69, Headingley *(E 1969)*
Spong R.S. 1929–30, Old Millhillians *(E 1929)*
Spray K.A.N. 1947–48, Newport
Spriggs F. 1919–20, Blackheath
Squires P.J. 1973–74, Harrogate *(E 1973)*
Stafford P.M.W. 1961–62, Oxford Univ.
Stagg P.K. 1965–66, Sale *(S 1965)*
Stanbury E. 1927–28, Plymouth Albion *(E 1926)*
Stanley C.G.J. 1926–27, Harlequins
Stanniford D. 1961–62, New Brighton
Stark K.J. 1926–27, Old Alleynians *(E 1927)*
Starmer-Smith N.C. 1966–67, Oxford Univ. *(E 1969)*
Steeds J.H. 1942–43, Middx Hosp. *(E 1949)*
Steel J. 1890, Eden Wands, OM
Steel W.B. 1892–93, Manchester
Steele J.L.F. 1922–23, Dublin Univ.
Steele W.C.C. 1970–71, Bedford *(S 1969)*
Steele-Bodger M.R. 1945–46, Cambridge Univ. *(E 1947)* Hon. Sec., Vice-Pres.
Stephen C.S.M. 1942–43, St Bart's Hosp.
Stephens J.R.G. 1947–48, Neath *(W 1947)* CM
Stephenson G.V. 1927–28, Queen's Univ. *(I 1920)*

Steven J.B. 1961–62, Madras Coll. FP
Steven R. 1961–62, Edinburgh Wands *(S 1962)*
Stevens C.B. 1969–70, Penzance *(E 1969)*
Stevens D.T. 1963–64, Blackheath
Stevens H. 1959–60, Redruth
Stevenson A.K. 1924–25, Glasgow Acads *(S 1922)*
Stevenson G.D. 1960–61, Hawick *(S 1966)*
Stevenson R. 1909–10, St Andrew's Univ. *(S 1910)*
Stewart A. 1976–77, Cambridge Univ.
Stewart C.E.B. 1965–66, Kelso *(S 1960)*
Stewart M.S. 1933–34, Stewarts FP *(S 1932)*
Stewart R.C. 1953–54, Canterbury *(NZ 1949)*
Steyn C.L. 1919–20, Guy's Hosp.
Steyn S.S.L. 1910–11, L. Scottish *(S 1911)*
Stirling F. 1899–1900, Blackheath
Stirling H.W. 1902–03, Blackheath
Stirling R.V. 1950–51, Leicester *(E 1951)*
Stoddart A.E. 1890–91, Blackheath *(E 1895)* CM
Stoddart W.B. 1893–94, Liverpool *(E 1897)*
Stoker F.O. 1893–94, Dublin Wands *(I 1886)*
Stokes A.L. 1911–12, Blackheath
Stokes G.L. 1912–13, Blackheath
Stokes M. 1959–60, Blackheath
Stone F.Le S. 1909–10, Blackheath *(E 1914)*
Stoneman B.M. 1964–65, Richmond
Stoop A.D. 1903–04, Harlequins *(E 1905)* CM
Stoop F.M. 1909–10, Harlequins *(E 1910)*
Storey T.W.P. 1890, Middx Wands, OM, CM
Stout F.M. 1896–97, Gloucester *(E 1897)* CM
Stout P.W. 1897–98, Gloucester *(E 1898)*
Stranahan J.S. 1907–08, Penarth
Strathdee E. 1946–47, Queen's Univ. Belfast *(I 1947)*
Stranach W.S. 1909–10, Harlequins
Stringer L.B. 1910–11, Guy's Hosp.
Stuart I.M.B. 1923–24, L. Irish *(I 1924)*
Stuart L.M. 1927–28, Glasgow HSFP
Styles E.A. 1934–35, Richmond
Suddon N. 1964–65, Hawick *(S 1965)*
Sugars H.S. 1904–05, Lansdowne *(I 1906)*
Sugden M. 1925–26, Dublin Wands *(I 1925)*
Sullivan G.H. 1948–49, St Mary's Hosp.
Surtees A.A. 1890, Harlequins, OM
Swanson J.C. 1942–43, Middx Hosp.
Susman W.J. 1898–99, Lennox
Sutton M.A. 1946–47, Richmond
Swaby W.P. 1896–97, Rosslyn Park
Swan M.W. 1957–58, Oxford Univ. *(S 1958)*
Swarbrick D.W. 1946–47, Oxford Univ. *(E 1947)*
Sweet-Escott R.B. 1890, Cardiff *(W 1891)* OM
Sykes A.R.V. 1915, Blackheath *(E 1914)*
Sykes F.D. 1951–52, Huddersfield *(E 1955)*
Sykes P.W. 1949–50, Wasps *(E 1948)*
Symes J. 1906–07, Marlborough Nomads
Syrett R.E. 1954–55, Wasps *(E 1958)*

*Joined Rugby League*
Sullivan J. 1920–21, Cardiff
Stone T. *(played v E. Midlands 1937 but never elected)*
Sparks B.A. 1956–57, Neath *(W 1954)*
Standing C.J. 1967–68, Bridgend

Taberer H.M. 1891–92, Richmond
Tagg E.J.B. 1908–09, U. Services
Tallent J.A. 1930–31, Blackheath *(E 1931)*
Tamplin W.E. 1947–48, Cardiff *(W 1947)*
Tandy M.O'C. 1894–95, Blackheath

Tanner C.C. 1929–30, Richmond *(E 1930)*
Tanner H. 1936–37, Swansea *(W 1935)* CM
Tarbutt P.C. 1895–96, Blackheath, CM
Tarr D.J. 1934–35, U. Services *(W 1935)*
Taylor A.R. 1939–40, Cross Keys *(W 1937)*
Taylor B. 1900–01, Rockcliff
Taylor E.G. 1928–29, L. Scottish *(S 1927)*
Taylor E.W. 1892–93, Rockcliff *(E 1892)*
Taylor G. 1900–01, Rockcliff
Taylor G. 1928–29, Waterloo
Taylor H.B.J. 1898–99, Blackheath
Taylor P.J. 1952–53, Wakefield *(E 1955)*
Taylor R.B. 1963–64, Northampton *(E 1966)*
Taylor R.C. 1950–51, Kelvinside West *(S 1951)*
Taylor W.J. 1926–27, Blackheath *(E 1928)*
Teden D.E. 1936–37, Richmond *(E 1939)*
Telfer C.M. 1968–69, Hawick *(S 1968)*
Telfer J.W. 1962–63, Melrose *(S 1964)*
Templeman B. 1959–60, Penarth
Te Water C.T. 1908–09, Richmond
Theron T.P. 1921–22, Blackheath
Thom D.A. 1932–33, L. Scottish *(S 1934)*
Thomas A. 1963–64, Newport *(W 1963)*
Thomas A.B.W. 1959–60, St Mary's Hosp.
Thomas Alun G. 1952–53, Cardiff *(W 1952)*
Thomas B. 1973–74, Llanelli
Thomas C.J. 1897–98, Newport *(W 1888)*
Thomas E.R. 1974–75, Llanelli
Thomas H.W. 1911–12, Cambridge Univ. *(W 1912)*
Thomas L.G. 1912–13, Neath
Thomas M.C. 1950–51, Devonport Services *(W 1949)*
Thomas M.G. 1919–20, St Bart's Hosp.
Thomas R.C.C. 1951–52, Swansea *(W 1949)*
Thomas T.J. 1895–96, Cardiff
Thomas T.P. 1898–99, Guy's Hosp.
Thomas Watcyn G. 1931–32, Swansea
Thomas W.A.V. 1927–28, L. Welsh
Thomas W.D. 1966–67, Llanelli *(W 1966)*
Thomas W.J. 1966–67, Cardiff *(W 1961)*
Thomas W.L. 1894–95, Newport
Thomas W.P. 1915, Cardiff
Thompson A.B. 1911–12, Northern
Thompson A.R. 1903–04, Richmond
Thompson C. 1934–35, Harlequins
Thompson C.E.K. 1900–01, Manchester
Thompson F.d'A. 1892–93, Blackheath
Thompson J. 1893–94, Rockcliff
Thompson P.H. 1955–56, Headingley *(E 1956)*
Thompson R.H. 1953–54, Instonians *(I 1952)*
Thompson R.J.C. 1899–1900, St Thomas's Hosp.
Thomson J.E. 1895–96, Blackheath
Thomson R.H. 1960–61, L. Scottish *(S 1960)*
Thorburn C.W. 1965–66, Guy's Hosp.
Thorman W.H. 1893–94, St Thomas's Hosp.
Thorne P.J. 1966–67, Blackheath
Thorneloe N.T. 1922–23, Leicester
Thornett J.E. 1966–67, NSW *(A 1955)*
Thorning P. 1961–62, Richmond
Thornton J.W. 1945–46, Gloucester
Tierney D.F. 1937–38, UC Cork *(I 1938)*
Tikoisuva P.B. 1975–76, Harlequins *(Fiji)*
Till P.H. 1945–46, Wasps
Timmins J.T. 1905–06, Bath
Tindall B.R. 1949–50, New Brighton *(E 1951)*
Tinson G.G.N. 1911–12, Blackheath
Tod B.R. 1930–31, Edinburgh Acads

Todd A.F. 1894–95, Blackheath *(E 1900)*
Todd J.W. 1949–50, Penrith
Todd W.J. 1898–99, Blackheath
Toft H.B. 1932–33, Broughton Park *(E 1936)* CM
Toga S. 1970–71, Nadi RU *(Fiji)*
Toller M.H. 1894–95, Barnstaple
Tomes A.J. 1975–76, Hawick *(S 1976)*
Torrens J.D. 1937–38, Bohemians *(I 1938)*
Tosswill L.R. 1902–03, Exeter
Townsend C.M. 1901–02, Liverpool OBs
Travers B.H. 1946–47, Oxford Univ. *(E 1947)* CM
Travers W.H. 1938–39, Newport *(W 1937)*
Treadwell W.J. 1965–66, Wasps *(E 1966)*
Tregellas T.S. 1890, Lennox, OM
Treloar T.R. 1912–13, Rosslyn Park, Hon. Sec.
Trench D.J.K. 1971–72, Rosslyn Park
Trenham F. 1913–14, Otley
Trickey A.R. 1974–75, Sale
Tripp D.O.H. 1911–12, Harlequins
Troop C.L. 1931–32, Richmond *(E 1933)*
Trott R.F. 1944–45, Penarth *(W 1948)*
Tucker J.S. 1927–28, Bristol *(E 1922)*
Tucker W.E. 1893–94, Blackheath *(E 1894)* CM
Tucker W.E. 1922–23, Blackheath *(E 1926)*
Turnbull B.R. 1925–26, Cardiff *(W 1925)*
Turnbull F.O. 1950–51, Kelso *(S 1951)*
Turner E.F. 1920–21, L. Scottish
Turner F.T. 1904–05, Richmond
Turner G.F. 1899–1900, Richmond
Turner J.W.C. 1967–68, Gala *(S 1966)*
Turner M.F. 1946–47, Blackheath *(E 1948)*
Turquand-Young D. 1925–26, Richmond *(E 1928)* CM
Tweedie G.D. 1970–71, Melrose
Twining D.O. 1906–07, Blackheath


*Joined Rugby League*
Thomas W.Haydn 1949–50, Newport


Udy Witt 1920–21, Northampton
Unwin E.J. 1934–35, Rosslyn Park *(E 1937)*
Upson J.R. 1907–08, Blackheath
Upton E.J. 1896–97, Richmond
Uren R. 1947–48, Waterloo *(E 1948)*
Urquhart J.L. 1915, Rosslyn Park
Urwin G.T. 1898–98, Blackheath
Usher C.M. 1912–13, London Scottish *(S 1912)* CM
Uttley R.M. 1972–73, Gosforth *(E 1973)*


Vallance G.P.C. 1942–43, Leicester
van der Reit E.F. 1919–20, Blackheath, CM
van Druten J. 1922–23, Dublin Univ. *(SA 1924)*
van Ryneveld C.B. 1948–49, Oxford Univ. *(E 1949)* CM
van Schalkwijk J.G. 1920–21, Guy's Hospital
van Zyl H. 1920–21, Guy's Hospital
Vassall H.H. 1906–07, Blackheath *(E 1908)*
Vaughan C.A. 1915, Rosslyn Park
Vaughan D.B. 1946–47, United Services *(E 1948)*
Venniker J.A. 1945–46, St. Mary's Hosp.
Vernon C.J. 1890, Wellington, OM
Vile T.H. 1912–13, Newport *(W 1908)*
Villepreux P. 1971–72, Toulouse *(F 1967)*
Vincent G.G. 1897–98, Bath
Vintcent A.N. 1949–50, Oxford Univ.
Voyce A.T. 1923–24, Gloucester *(E 1920)*


*Joined Rugby League*
Valentine D.D. 1946–47, Hawick *(S 1947)*


Waddell G.H. 1957–58, Devonport Services *(S 1957)*
Waddell H. 1923–24, Glasgow Acads *(S 1924)* Vice-Pres., Pres.
Wade A.L. 1905–06, L. Scottish *(S 1908)*
Wade M.R. 1958–59, Cambridge Univ. *(E 1962)*
Wade-Gery R.H. 1903–04, Marlborough Nomads
Wainwright J.W. 1928–29, Richmond
Wakefield W.W. 1925–26, Harlequins *(E 1920)*
Wakelam H.B.T. 1920–21, Harlequins
Wakers F.H. 1931–32, L. Scottish *(S 1930)*
Waldron R. 1961–62, Neath *(W 1965)*
Walford M.M. 1935–36, Oxford Univ.
Walke J.C. 1957–58, Edinburgh Acads
Walker A.W. 1930–31, Birkenhead Park *(S 1931)*
Walker G.A. 1938–39, Blackheath *(E 1939)*
Walker H. 1897–98, Old Dunelmians
Walker H. 1946–47, Coventry *(E 1947)*
Walker H.J.I. 1912–13, Blackheath
Walker P.N. 1942–43, Gloucester
Walker S. 1934–35, Instonians *(I 1934)*
Wall A.H.E. 1901–02, Guy's Hosp.
Wallace A.C. 1922–23, L. Scottish *(S 1923)*
Wallace C.R.V. 1895–96, Cardiff
Wallace Jos 1903–04, Dublin Wands *(I 1903)*
Wallace T. 1923–24, Cardiff *(I 1920)*
Wallace W.M. 1913–14, L. Scottish *(S 1913)* CM
Waller G.S. 1933–34, Cambridge Univ.
Wallis H.T. 1895–96, Blackheath
Wallis T.G. 1921–22, Dublin Wands *(I 1921)*
Walpole A. 1890, Dublin Univ. *(I 1888)* OM
Walsh J.C. 1965–66, UC Cork *(I 1960)*
Walton E.J. 1902–03, Castleford *(E 1901)*
Wandsborough L.B.R. 1913–14, U. Services
Ward H.E. 1909–10, Harlequins
Ward R.O.C. 1903–04, Harlequins
Wardlow C.S. 1968–69, Carlisle *(E 1969)*
Warfield P.J. 1974–75, Cambridge Univ. *(E 1973)*
Warr A.L. 1933–34, Oxford Univ. *(E 1934)*
Warrington-Morris A.D. 1908–09, U. Services
Waters J.A. 1932–33, Selkirk *(S 1933)* CM
Waters J.B. 1903–04, L. Scottish *(S 1904)*
Watkins J.A. 1972–73, Gloucester *(E 1972)*
Watkins J.K. 1933–34, Devonport Services *(E 1939)*
Watkins S.J. 1963–64, Newport *(W 1964)*
Watson F. Burges 1907–08, U. Services *(E 1908)*
Watson J.H.D. 1911–12, Edinburgh Acads *(E 1914)*
Watson R.W. 1942–43, St Mary's Hosp.
Watkins W.R. 1960–61, Newport *(W 1959)*
Watson W.S. 1973–74, Boroughmede FR *(S 1974)*
Watt D.E.J. 1966–67, Bristol *(E 1967)*
Weatherstone T.G. 1952–53, Stewart's FP *(S 1952)*
Weaver F.W.H. 1899–1900, Liverpool
Webb L.H. 1958–59, Bedford
Webb R.E. 1966–67, Coventry *(E 1967)*
Webster J.G. 1970–71, Moseley *(E 1972)*
Weighill R.G.H. 1944–45, Waterloo *(E 1947)* CM
Wells B.C. 1913–14, Rosslyn Park
Wells C. 1893–94, Harlequins
Wells C.M. 1891–92, Harlequins *(E 1893)* CM
Wells G.T. 1955–56, Cardiff *(W 1955)*
Wemyss A. 1923–24, Edinburgh Wands *(S 1914)* CM, Registrar & Keeper of Records
Wentworth W.C. 1894–95, Richmond

West H. 1908–09, L. Scottish
West L. 1902–03, West Hartlepool *(S 1903)*
Weston L.E. 1974–75, Rosslyn Park *(E 1972)*
Weston M.P. 1959–60, Richmond *(E 1960)* CM
Weston W.H. 1932–33, Northampton *(E 1933)*
Wheatley H.F. 1937–38, Coventry *(E 1936)*
Wheel G.A.D. 1974–75, Swansea *(W 1974)*
Wheeler D.R. 1921–22, Collegians Belfast
Wheeler J.R. 1921–22, Collegians Belfast *(I 1922)*
Wheeler P.J. 1973–74, Leicester *(E 1975)*
Wheeler P.J.F. 1952–53, Cambridge Univ.
Whetham P. 1896–97, Blackheath
Whineray W.J. 1963–64, Auckland *(NZ 1957)*
White D.F. 1949–50, Northampton *(E 1947)*
White D.M. 1962–63, Oxford Univ. *(S 1963)*
White H.J. 1915, Headingley
White J.B. 1922–23, Glasgow Acads
White J.R. 1973–74, Bristol
White N.T. 1906–07, Marlborough Nomads
Whitehead H. 1909–10, Manchester, CM
Whiteley E.C.P. 1928–29, Old Alleynians *(E 1931)*
Whiteray S.E.A. 1893–94, Cambridge Univ.
Whitfield S.R. 1925–26, Batley
Whiting P.J. 1974–75, Auckland *(NZ 1971)*
Whittaker T. 1890, Manchester, OM
Whyte D.J. 1961–62, St Andrew's Univ. *(S 1965)*
Whyte R.A.M. 1959–60, Harlequins
Wickert H.F.W. 1931–32, Rosslyn Park
Wilcock S.H. 1957–58, Oxford Univ.
Wilkins D.T. 1951–52, U. Services *(E 1951)*
Wilkins H.E.B. 1911–12, Catford Bridge
Wilkinson H. 1929–30, Halifax *(E 1929)*
Wilkinson R.M. 1971–72, Cambridge Univ. *(E 1975)*
Willcox J.G. 1961–62, Harlequins *(E 1961)*
Willett H. 1915, Bedford
Williams A.D. 1969–70, Cardiff
Williams B.L. 1944–45, Cardiff *(W 1947)* CM
Williams C.D. 1958–59, Cardiff *(W 1955)*
Williams D. 1967–68, Ebbw Vale *(W 1963)*
Williams D.B. 1974–75, Cardiff
Williams E.J.H. 1941–42, Coventry
Wiliams F.J. 1968–69, L. Welsh
Williams F.L. 1930–31, Cardiff *(W 1929)* CM
Williams G. 1949–50, L. Welsh *(W 1950)*
Williams G.E.S. 1930–31, RAF
Williams J.E. 1953–54, Old Millhillians *(E 1954)*
Williams J.F. 1905–06, L. Welsh *(W 1905)*
Williams J.J. 1973–74, Llanelli *(W 1973)*
Williams J.M. 1950–51, Penzance/Newlyn *(E 1951)*
Williams J.P.R. 1969–70, L. Welsh *(W 1969)*
Williams L.H. 1956–57, Cardiff *(W 1957)*
Williams R.F. 1915, Cardiff *(W 1912)*
Williams R.H. 1911–12, St Bart's Hosp.
Williams R.H. 1953–54, Llanelli *(W 1954)* CM
Williams R.N. 1929–30, St Bart's Hosp.
Williams W.O.G. 1954–55, Swansea *(W 1951)*
Williamson R.H. 1907–08, Blackheath *(E 1908)*
Williment M.W. 1965–66, Blackheath
Willis H. 1949–50, Cambridge Univ.
Willis W.R. 1951–52, Cardiff *(W 1950)* CM
Wilsher R. 1934–35, Bedford
Wills D. 1961–62, Wasps
Wilson C.E. 1895–96, Blackheath *(E 1898)*
Wilson D.S. 1952–53, Met. Police *(E 1953)*

Wilson G.A. 1948–49, Oxford Univ. *(S 1949)*
Wilson G.S. 1930–31, Tyldesley *(E 1929)*
Wilson F.O'B. 1908–09, U. Services
Wilson J.S. 1908–09, U. Services *(S 1908)*
Wilson K.H.S. 1945–46, L. Scottish
Wilson R.L. 1950–51, Gala *(S 1951)*
Wilson S. 1963–64, Oxford Univ. *(S 1964)*
Wilson S.E. 1892–93, Liverpool
Wilson W.C. 1907–08, Richmond *(E 1907)* CM
Wiltshire M. 1967–68, Aberavon *(W 1967)*
Windsor R.W. 1973–74, Cross Keys *(W 1973)*
Winn C.E. 1950–51, Oxford Univ. *(E 1952)*
Winn R.R. 1956–57, Northampton
Wintle T.C. 1962–63, St Mary's Hosp. *(E 1966)*
Witherby H.F. 1898–99, Blackheath
Witt C.F. 1899–1900, Rosslyn Park
Witters H.H.C. 1932–33, Blackheath *(I 1931)*
Wix R.S. 1903–04, Marlborough Wands
Wood B.G.M. 1956–57, Garryowen *(I 1954)*
Wood F. 1902–03, Cardiff
Wood G.E. 1974–75, Cambridge Univ.
Wood G.E.C. 1913–14, Blackheath
Wood G.F. 1921–22, Blackheath
Wood G.W. 1915, Leicester *(E 1914)*
Wood R.D. 1899–1900, Liverpool OBs *(E 1901)*
Wood S.G. 1900–01, Liverpool
Wood W.H. 1928–29, U. Services
Woodgate E.E. 1951–52, Paignton *(E 1952)*
Woodgate W.C. 1951–52, Paignton
Woodhouse N.A. 1909–10, U. Services *(E 1910)*
Woodruff C.G. 1950–51, Harlequins *(E 1951)*
Woods S.M.J. 1890, Blackheath *(E 1890)* CM, OM
Woodward J.E. 1951–52, Wasps *(E 1952)*
Wooller W. 1972–73, Sale *(W 1933)*
Wordsworth A.J. 1974–75, Cambridge Univ.
Wordsworth C.R. 1923–24, Harlequins
Worton J.R.B. 1925–26, Harlequins *(E 1926)*
Wrench D.F.B. 1963–64, Harlequins *(E 1964)*
Wrey W.A.B. 1904–05, RMC Sandhurst
Wright C.C.G. 1906–07, Blackheath *(E 1909)* CM
Wright I.D. 1971–72, Northampton *(E 1971)*
Wright T.P. 1954–55, Blackheath *(E 1960)*
Wynter E.C.C. 1947–48, Oxford Univ.

*Joined Rugby League*
Weatherall T. *played v Hartlepool R. 1900*
Welsh W.B. 1932–33, *played v Leicester 1932*
Williams S. 1938–39, Aberavon *(W 1939)*
Williams C.O. 1961–62, Cardiff
Watkins D. 1961–62, Newport *(W 1963)*
West B.R. 1968–69, Northampton *(E 1968)*

Yarranton P.G. 1954–55, Wasps *(E 1954)* CM
Yiend W. 1890, Hartlepool Rovers *(E 1892)* OM
Young A.T. 1920–21, Blackheath *(E 1924)* CM
Young A.W. 1942–43, St. Mary's Hosp.
Young F.S. 1898–99, Rosslyn Park
Young Gavin D. 1919–20, Harlequins
Young J.R.C. 1958–59, Oxford Univ. *(E 1958)*
Young R.M. 1965–66, Queens Univ. *(I 1965)*
Young W. 1901–02, Plymouth
Young W.B. 1937–38, Kings College Hosp. *(S 1937)*

Ziegler G.G. 1915, Richmond

# RECORD OF ALL OTHER BARBARIAN MATCHES

**ALBERTA**
**1976    Score:** 56–4    **Captain:** P. Bennett (Barbarians)
**Scorers For:** D. McKay (3T), J. J. Williams (2T), S. Fenwick (2T), A. J. Lawson (1T), M. A. Biggar (1T), A. R. Irvine (1T), G. D. Wheel (1T), P. Bennett (6C).    Against: J. Parton (1T).
**ATLANTIC ALL-STARS (CANADA)**
**1976    Score:** 76–0    **Captain:** P. Bennett (Barbarians).
**Scorers For:** D. B. Williams (3T), J. J. Williams (5T), A. R. Irvine (3T, 2C), P. Bennett (2T, 4C), A. Alexander (1T), D. Shedden (1T), A. Neary (1T).
**AUSTRALIA**
**1948    Score:** 9–6    **Captains:** H. Tanner (Barbarians), T. Allen (Australia).
**Scorers For:** M. R. Steele-Bodger (1T), C. B. Holmes (1T), H. Tanner (1T).    Against: A. E. J. Tonkin (1T, 1PG).
**1958    Score:** 11–6    **Captains:** C. I. Morgan (Barbarians), R. A. L. Davidson (Australia).
**Scorers For:** W. R. Evans (1T), M. S. Phillips (1T), A. R. Dawson (1T), J. Faull (1C).    Against: D. M. Emanuel (1T), K. J. Donald (1T).
**1967    Score:** 11–17    **Captains:** N. A. A. Murphy (Barbarians), J. E. Thornett (Australia).
**Scorers For:** K. W. Kennedy (1T), S. Watkins (1PT), S. Wilson (1PG, 1C).    Against: P. W. Hawthorne (1T), E. S. Boyce (2T), J. F. O'Gorman (1T), R. Webb (1T), J. M. K. Lenehan (1C).
**1976    Score:** 19–7    **Captains:** T. M. Davies (Barbarians), G. A. Shaw (Australia).
**Scorers For:** P. Bennett (1T), P. J. Wheeler (1T), J. J. Williams (1T), P. Bennett (2C, 1PG).    Against: J. R. Ryan (1T), J. C. Hindmarsh (1PG).
**BATH**
**1894    Score:** 14–0
**Scorers For:** M. H. Toller (2T), W. J. Carey (1T), E. M. Baker (1T), N. H. Biggs (1C).
**1896    Score:** 13–13    **Captains:** P. Maud (Barbarians), F. Soane (Bath).
**Scorers For:** R. O'H. Livesay (1T), N. H. Biggs (1T, 2C), P. Maud (1T).    Against: F. Belson (2T),F. Derrick (1T), W. F. Long (2C).
**1897    Score:** 8–3    **Captains:** F. H. R. Alderson (Barbarians), F. Soane (Bath).
**Scorers For:** F. M. Stout (1T), H. N. Cottart (1T), F. H. R. Alderson (1C).    Against: F. Soane (1T).
**BAY AREA TOURING SIDE (CALIFORNIA)**
**1976    Score:** 28–7    **Captain:** M. A. Biggar (Barbarians).
**Scorers For:** D. B. Williams (1T), D. J. McKay (1T), K. M. Bushell (4PG, 1T, 2C).
**BEDFORD**
**1894    Score:** 3–7    **Captains:** W. P. Carpmael (Barbarians), W. Rees (Bedford).
**Scorers For:** W. G. Druce (1T).    Against: G. L. Hamilton (1T), P. G. Jacob (1DG).
**BIRKENHEAD PARK**
**1899    Score:** 8–9    **Captains:** J. Baxter (Birkenhead Park).
**Scorers For:** J. D. K. Jones (2T), E. S. B. Russell (1C).    Against: H. P. Hebblethwaite (2T), E. Herschell (1T).
**BLACKHEATH**
**1934    Score:** 16–13    **Captains:** P. C. Hordern (Barbarians), B. H. Black (Blackheath).
**Scorers For:** B. T. V. Cowey (1T), W. R. Logan (1T), R. W. Shaw (1T), J. W. Forrest (2C).    Against: B. H. Black (1T), R. T. Norman (1T), B. H. Black (2C, 1PG).
**1959    Score:** 21–8    **Captains:** R. H. Williams (Barbarians), J. B. Williamson (Blackheath).
**Scorers For:** M. C. Thomas (3T), A. J. F. O'Reilly (1T), R. W. D. Marques (1T), T. E. Davies (2C), B. J. Jones (1C).    Against: K. R. F. Bearne (1T), D. L. Gudgeon (1T), R. A. van Heerden (1C).
**BRADFORD**
**1890    Score:** 6–6    **Captains:** A. E. Stoddart? (Barbarians), J. Hawcridge (Bradford).
**Scorers For:** A. E. Stoddart (1T), E. W. Senior (1T), F. H. R. Alderson (1C), G. McGregor (1C).    Against: H. Wilkinson (1T), H. Fieldhouse (1T), E. Doyle (1PG, 2C).
**1891    Score:** 0–14
**Scorers Against:** H. Wilkinson (1T), J. H. Crompton (1T), E. Dewhurst (1T), J. Dyson (1T), E. Doyle (2C).
**Oct 1965    Score:** 47–3    **Captains:** M. P. Weston (Barbarians), M. J. Bayes (Bradford).
**Scorers For:** J. Douglas (2T), D. M. Rollitt (2T), J. A. P. Shackleton (1T), A. W. Hancock (1T), C. E. B. Stewart (1T), A. J. W. Hinshelwood (1T), B. C. Henderson (1T), N. Suddon (1T), M. P. Weston (1T), T. J. Kiernan (7C).    Against: R. A. Childs (1T).

## BRITISH COLUMBIA
**4 May 1957   Score:** 19–6   **Captains:** J. T. Greenwood (Barbarians), D. Oliver (BC).
**Scorers** For: A. J. F. O'Reilly (1T), G. M. Griffiths (1T), C. I. Morgan (1T), R. W. D. Marques (1T), D. G. S. Baker (2C, 1PG).   Against: N. Henderson (2PG).
**8 May 1957   Score:** 51–8   **Captain:** J. E. Woodward (Barbarians).
**Scorers** For: A. J. F. O'Reilly (4T), G. M. Griffiths (2T), J. E. Woodward (2T), P. H. Thompson (1T), E. J. S. Michie (1T), A. Robson (1T), T. J. Davies (4C), G. W. Hastings (2C).   Against: (1T), (1C), (1PG).
**11 May 1957   Score:** 17–3   **Captain:** C. I. Morgan (Barbarians).
**Scorers** For: C. I. Morgan (2T), A. J. F. O'Reilly (1T), G. T. Wells (1T), T. J. Davies (1PG, 1C).
**1976 Score:** 34–15   **Captains:** P. Bennett (Barbarians), C. Leferre (BC).
**Scorers** For: A. Neary (1T), A. R. Irvine (1T), J. J. Williams (1T), P. J. Wheeler (1T), P. Bennett (4PG, 3C).   Against: Hindson (1T, 1C, 2PG), Wiley (1PG).

## CAMBRIDGE UNIVERSITY (Past and present)
**1972   Score:** 14–37   **Captains:** P. C. Brown (Barbarians), J. M. Howard (Cambridge University).
**Scorers** For: P. C. Brown (1T), D. J. Duckham (1T), G. W. Evans (1T), P. Villepreux (1C).   Against: W. A. Jones (1T), C. R. Williams (1T), J. R. H. Greenwood (1T), J. M. Howard (1T), R. C. O. Skinner (1T), A. M. Jorden (1PG, 3C).

## CANADA
**1962   Score:** 3–3   **Captains:** C. R. Jacobs (Barbarians), D. L. Moore (Canada).
**Scorers** For: K. J. F. Scotland (1PG).   Against: D. Burgess (1PG).
**1976   Score:** 29–4   **Captains:** P. Bennett (Barbarians), K. Wilke (Canada).
**Scorers** For: D. McKay (2T), S. Fenwick (1T), A. R. Irvine (1DG), P. Bennett (4PG, 1C).   Against: S. McTavish (1T).

## CARLISLE AND DISTRICT
**1894   Score:** 16–5   **Captains:** W. P. Carpmael (Barbarians), R. N. Burgess (Carlisle and District).
**Scorers** For: F. H. Maturin (2T), W. B. Stoddart (2T), F. Mitchell (2C).   Against: C. W. Gooch (1T), P.Westray (1C).

## CHELTENHAM
**1909   Score:** 9–3   **Captains:** G. D. Roberts (Barbarians), G. T. Unwin (Cheltenham).
**Scorers** For: H. J. S. Morton (1T), H. Martin (1T), H. West (1T).   Against: G. T. Unwin (1PG).
**1910   Score:** 8–11   **Captain:** G. Cossens (Cheltenham).
**Scorers** For: C. H. Pillman (1T), H. Martin (1T), G. D. Roberts (1C).   Against: C. Bennett (1T), H. Hughes (1T), W. A. Pocock (1T), B. Davey (1C).
**1911   Score:** 8–3   **Captain:** J. M. B. Scott (Barbarians).
**Scorers** For: L. B. Stringer (2T), C. H. Pillman (1C).   Against: B. Onslow (1T).
**1912   Score:** 10–6   **Captain:** A. R. Ross (Barbarians).
**Scorers** For: W. M. Dodds (1T), C. Gibb (1T), W. M. Dickson (2C).   Against: A. F. Burnell (1T), S.Young (1T).
**1913   Score:** 13–6   **Captain:** W. S. D. Craven (Barbarians).
**Scorers** For: B. R. Lewis (2T), C. W. Sparks (1T), A. L. Stokes (1C), G. L. Stokes (1C).   Against: W. Hall (1T), G. E. C. Wood (1T).
**1914   Score:** 19–5   **Captain:** J. E. C. Partridge (Barbarians).
**Scorers** For: C. W. Sparks (2T), L. B. R. Wansborough (1T), M. P. Atkinson (1T, 2C), R. R. Jackson (1T).   Against: H. Hughes (1PT), E. Ward (1C).

## COMBINED TRANSVAAL
**24 May 1958   Score:** 16–18   **Captains:** A. R. Smith (Barbarians), J. Claassen (Combined Transvaal).
**Scorers** For: B. J. Jones (2T), A. J. F. O'Reilly (1T), A. Ashcroft (1T), G. W. Hastings (2C).   Against: P. Baartman (1T), N. Bridger (1T), J. Prinsloo (1T), D. Dippenaar (1T), J. Buys (3C).

## CORINTHIANS
**1892   Score:** 12–14
**Scorers** For: C. A. Hooper (2T), H. M. Taberer (1T), A. S. Johnston (2C).   Against: T. Lindley (2T), C. B. Fry (1T), A. M. Walters (1T), F. M. Ingram (2C).

## COVENTRY
**1973   Score:** 30–19   **Captains:** J. S. Spencer (Barbarians), D. J. Duckham (Coventry).
**Scorers** For: T. G. R. Davies (2T), T. P. David (1T), D. B. Llewelyn (1T), R. T. E. Bergiers (1T), A. H. Ensor (2PG, 2C).   Against: D. J. Duckham (2T), B. Corless (1T), P. A. Rossborough (2C).

## DEVONPORT ALBION
**1902   Score:** 0–6   **Captain:** R. T. Skrimshire (Barbarians).
**Scorers** Against: E. J. Vivyan (1T), T. Fitzgerald (1T).
**1903   Score:** 7–0   **Captain:** R. T. Skrimshire (Barbarians).
**Scorers** For: R. T. Skrimshire (1T, 1DG).
**1904   Score:** 8–19   **Captain:** B. C. Hartley (Barbarians).
**Scorers** For: B. C. Hartley (1T), S. F. Coopper (1T), W. L. Y. Rogers (1C).   Against: W. Mills (T), B. B. Bennetts (2T), S. G. Williams (1T), R. Jackett (1T), S. H. Irvin (2C).
**1905   Score:** 3–11
**Scorers** For: N. W. Godfrey (1T).   Against: W. Spiers (1T), D. R. Gordon (1T), J. Summers (1T), E. J. Vivyan (1T).
**1906   Score:** 0–18   **Captain:** F. M. Stout (Barbarians).
**Scorers** Against: C. Marshall (1T), H. Connett (1T), S. Harvey (1T), E. J. Vivyan (1T), F. Lillicrap (3C).

**1907   Score:** 9–0   **Captain:** J. J. Coffey (Barbarians).
**Scorers** For: J. F. Williams (1T), H. H. Vassall (1T), D. Lambert (1T).
**DEVONSHIRE**
**April 1891   Score:** 11–0   **Captain:** A. E. Stoddart (Barbarians).
**Scorers** For: C. A. Hooper (2T), R. L. Aston (1T), A. E. Stoddart (1T, 3C), H. Marshall (1T).
**Dec 1891   Score:** 0–0
**DUBLIN UNIVERSITY**
**1891   Score:** 7–0
**Scorer** For: W. Neilson (2T, 1C).
**DUBLIN WANDERERS**
**1970   Score:** 30–9   **Captains:** J. S. Spencer (Barbarians), K. McGowan (Dublin Wanderers).
**Scorers** For: G. O. Edwards (2T), J. P. R. Williams (2T), T. G. Elliot (1T), T. G. R. Davies (1T), D. J. Duckham (1T), J. P. R. Williams (1PG, 3C).   Against: K. McGowan (1T), J. O'Gorman (2PG).
**EAST AFRICA**
**28 May 1958   Score:** 52–12   **Captains:** J. T. Greenwood (Barbarians), I. McLean (East Africa).
**Scorers** For: A. J. F. O'Reilly (7T), H. F. McLeod (1T, 1C), B. J. Jones (3T, 2C), G. H. Waddell (1T), M. C. Thomas (1T, 2C), A. C. Pedlow (1T).   Against: Angus (1T), Marshall (1T), T. Tory (1DG), Meintges (1PG).
**EXETER**
**1898   Score:** 0–12
**Scorers** Against: F. L. Hitt (1T), E. Hislett (1T), H. Reed (1DG, 1C).
**1907   Score:** 18–3   **Captains:** J. J. Coffey (Barbarians), E. C. Morgan (Exeter).
**Scorers** For: A. W. Newton (1T), H. H. Vassall (1T), F. W. Sawyer (1T), J. F. Williams (1T), B. MacLear (3C).   Against: G. D. Roberts (1T).
**1908   Score:** 17–11   **Captains:** J. J. Coffey (Barbarians), E. C. Morgan (Exeter).
**Scorers** For: M. E. Finlinson (2T), F. Gardiner (1T), S. F. Coopper (1T), R. H. Williamson (1T), J. J. Coffey (1C).   Against: R. Colgrave (1T), G. D. Roberts (1T, 1PG, 1C).
**FIJI**
**1970   Score:** 9–29   **Captains:** F. A. L. Laidlaw (Barbarians), S. Toga (Fiji).
**Scorers** For: J. S. Spencer (1T), D. J. Duckham (1T), J. P. R. Williams (1PG).   Against: S. Nasave (1T), J. Visei (1T), A. Racike (1T), J. Qoro (1T), I. Batibasaga (1T), I. Tuisese (1T), N. Ravouvou (1T), I. Batibasaga (4C).
**GLOUCESTER**
**1892   Score:** 9–10   **Captain:** T. Bagwell (Gloucester).
**Scorers** For: W. Neilson (2T), C. M. Wells (1T), A. S. Johnston (1C).   Against: A. Cromwell (1T), W. H. Jackson (1T, 2C).
**1900   Score:** 0–13   **Captain:** W. H. Taylor (Gloucester).
**Scorers** Against: A. H. Click (1T), C. Smith (1T), J. Lewis (1T), G. Romans (3C).
**HAMPSHIRE**
**1929   Score:** 9–5   **Captains:** G. V. Stephenson (Barbarians), D. Turquand-Young (Hampshire).
**Scorers** For: H. E. Carris (1T), A. Key (1T), H. G. Periton (1T).   Against: S. G. Collins (1T), H. C. Browne (1C).
**HARTLEPOOL ROVERS**
**1890   Score:** 9–4   **Captains:** A. E. Stoddart (Barbarians), W. Yiend (Hartlepool Rovers).
**Scorers** For: A. Allport (1T), G. M'Gregor (1T, 3C), R. L. Aston (1T).   Against: A. C. Scott (1T), T. Burt (1T), F.H.R.Alderson (1C).
**1893   Score:** 10–7   **Captains:** W. P. Carpmael (Barbarians), W. Yiend (Hartlepool Rovers).
**Scorers** For: W. H. Manfield (1T), F. D'A. Thompson (1T), S. E. Wilson (2C).   Against: C. Hodgson (1T), W. Yiend (1T), F. H. R. Alderson (1C).
**April 1895   Score:** 8–7   **Captains:** W. Neilson (Barbarians), R. F. Oakes (Hartlepool Rovers).
**Scorers** For: J. J. Gowans (1T), W. Neilson (1T), J. H. C. Fegan (1C).   Against: F. H. R. Alderson (1DG, 1PG).
**Dec 1895   Score:** 8–8   **Captains:** J. Conway Rees (Barbarians), R. F. Oakes (Hartlepool Rovers).
**Scorers** For: A. Rouillard (1T), H. T. Wallis (1T), W. Ashford (1C).   Against: D. Gilchrist (1T), R. F. Oakes (1T), J. F. Thompson (1C).
**April 1897   Score:** 14–9   **Captains:** F. H. R. Alderson (Barbarians), R. F. Oakes (Hartlepool Rovers).
**Scorers** For: R. O. Schwarz (1T), O. G. Mackie (1T), T. L. Hendry (1T), F. H. R. Alderson (1T), E. F. Fookes (1C).   Against: R. F. Oakes (2T), W. J. McSloy (1PG).
**Dec 1897   Score:** 11–0   **Captains:** P. C. Tarbutt (Barbarians), R. F. Oakes (Hartlepool Rovers).
**Scorers** For: O. G. Mackie (1T), G. C. Robinson (1T), P. C. Tarbutt (1T), J. F. Byrne (1C).
**April 1900   Score:** 5–3   **Captains:** R. W. Bell (Barbarians), C. Hodgson (Hartlepool Rovers).
**Scorers** For: H. Rottenburg (1T), J. W. Sagar (1C).   Against: J. Robinson (1T).
**Dec 1900   Score:** 4–3   **Captain:** F. Yeoman (Hartlepool Rovers).
**Scorers** For: R. S. V. Dyas (1DG).   Against: H. Francis (1T).
**April 1902   Score:** 3–3   **Captain:** A. G. Murrell (Hartlepool Rovers).
**Scorers** For: H. C. Pinckney (1T).   Against: A. B. Wales (1T).
**Oct 1965   Score:** 35–8   **Captains:** N. A. A. Murphy (Barbarians), P. O. Fitzgerald (Hartlepool Rovers).
**Scorers** For: A. J. W. Hinshelwood (2T), T. J. Brophy (2T), M. P. Weston (2T), B. C. Henderson (1T), N. A. A. Murphy (1T), J. Douglas (1T), T. J. Kiernan (3C), M. P. Weston (1C).   Against: H. Fraser (1T), P. C.

Brown (1T), S. P. Welsh (1C).

**HUDDERSFIELD**
**1891** **Score:** 2–7  **Captain:** J. Dyson (Huddersfield).
**Scorers** For: T. A. F. Crow (1T).  Against: J. Dyson (2T), J. W. Thewlis (1C).
**1893** **Score:** 9–2
**Scorers** For: F. D'A. Thompson (1T), E. Field (1DG), S. E. Wilson (1C).  Against: T. Dickenson (1T).

**LEEDS**
**1892** **Score:** 0–2
**Scorers** Against: Parfitt (1T).

**LE HAVRE**
**1900** **Score:** 41–3  **Captain:** Mason (Le Havre).
**Scorers** For: P. C. Tarbutt (4T, 1C), J. H. Bulloch (2T, 1C), T. A. Cock (1T), A. F. C. C. Luxmoore (1T), B. C. Hartley (1T, 1C), G. T. Campbell (1T, 1C), E. Beeching (1T), J. W. Sagar (1C).  Against: Bernstein (1T).

**LIVERPOOL**
**1897** **Score:** 35–0  **Captains:** W. P. Carpmael? (Barbarians), J. Graham (Liverpool).
**Scorers** For: F. A. Leslie-Jones (2T), H. T. Wallis (2T), 3T by others unknown, J. F. Byrne (7C).

**LLANELLI**
**1965** **Score:** 28–15  **Captains:** D. G. Perry (Barbarians), J. Leleu (Llanelli).
**Scorers** For: B. M. Stoneman (1T), P. E. Judd (1T), J. P. Fisher (1T), A. W. Hancock (1T), J. A. P. Shackleton (1T), M. C. M. Cormack (5C), D. H. Chisholm (1DG).  Against: B. John (1T), I. S. Gallacher (1T), D. Rogers (1T), J. Prothero (3C).
**1972** **Score:** 17–33  **Captains:** A. J. L. Lewis (Barbarians), W. D. Thomas (Llanelli).
**Scorers** For: I. G. McRae (1T), G. W. Evans (1T), L. G. Dick (1T), R. A. Codd (1PG, 1C).  Against: R. Davies (2T), A. Hill (1T), R. T. E. Bergiers (1T), D. B. Llewelyn (1T), P. Bennett (1PG, 5C).

**LONDON**
**1935** **Score:** 34–3  **Captains:** J. A. E. Siggins (Barbarians), G. J. Dean (London).
**Scorers** For: J. E. Forrest (3T), H. S. Sever (2T), H. Lind (1T), R. W. Shaw (1T), C. R. A. Graves (1T), R. W. Shaw (5C).  Against: E. A. Styles (1T).

**MELROSE**
**1976** **Score:** 47–17  **Captains:** P. Bennett (Barbarians), J. M. Sharp (Melrose).
**Scorers** For: J. J. Williams (2T), M. A. Biggar (1T), D. J. McKay (1T), A. J. Tomes (1T), G. Adey (1T), A. R. Irvine (1T, 1DG), P. Bennett (5C, 2PG).  Against: T. Bleasdale (2T), F. Calder (1T), E. R. Brown (1PG), G. R. Wood (1C).

**MIDLANDS XV & J. E. THORNELOE'S XV**
**Jan 1940**  *Cancelled owing to frost*
**March 1940** **Score:** 34–18  **Captains:** T. A. Kemp (Barbarians), J. T. W. Berry (Midlands XV & J. E. Thorneloe's XV).
**Scorers** For: R. H. Guest (3T), G. Hollis (2T), L. Babrow (1T), L. Manfield (1T), S. Walker (3C, 1PG), R. E. Prescott (2C).  Against: F. G. Edwards (2T), H. P. Jerwood (1T), A. W. Seaton (1T), C. G. Gilthorpe (3C).
**Dec 1941** **Score:** 8–3  **Captains:** R. E. Prescott (Barbarians), J. T. W. Berry (Midlands XV & J. E. Thorneloe's XV).
**Scorers** For: E. J. H. Williams (1T), H. Tanner (1T), G. W. Parker (1C).  Against: C. B. Holmes (1T).
**April 1942** **Score:** 24–11  **Captains:** T. A. Kemp (Barbarians), J. T. W. Berry (Midlands XV & J. E. Thorneloe's XV).
**Scorers** For: A. L. Evans (2T), C. L. Melville (1T), H. J. M. Sayers (1T), H. J. C. Rees (1T), H. J. M. Sayers (2C, 1PG), C. G. Gilthorpe (1C).  Against: K. James (1T), K. Biggar (1T), B. W. T. Ritchie (1PG, 1C).
**Dec 1942** **Score:** 21–17  **Captains:** R. E. Prescott (Barbarians), J. T. W. Berry (Midlands XV & J. E. Thorneloe's XV).
**Scorers** For: J. H. Steeds (1T), G. P. C. Vallance (1T), J. C. Swanson (1T), H. A. Fry (1T), W. C. W. Murdoch (1DG, 1C), W. M. Penman (1PG).  Against: H. Webber (1T), G. J. Humphrey (1T), E. Grant (1T), K. H. Chapman (2PG, 1C).
**April 1943** **Score:** 32–0  **Captains:** T. A. Kemp (Barbarians), J. T. W. Berry (Midlands XV & J. E. Thorneloe's XV).
**Scorers** For: J. C. Swanson (4T), R. W. Watson (1T), H. Tanner (1T), A. W. Young (1T), J. Heaton (2C, 1PG), R. W. Watson (1C), H. J. M. Sayers (1C).
**Dec 1943** **Score:** 42–16  **Captains:** R. J. Longland (Barbarians), J. T. W. Berry (Midlands XV & J. E. Thorneloe's XV).
**Scorers** For: G. Hollis (3T), W. H. Munro (2T), T. A. Kemp (1T), J. Heaton (1T), R. Willsher (1T), R. W. Watson (1T), G. D. Shaw (1T), J. Heaton (3C, 1DG), B. W. T. Ritchie (1C).  Against: J. C. Swanson (1T), D. W. Ballard (1T), D. M. Strathie (1T), F. W. Gilbert (1T), K. H. Chapman (1C), F. W. Gilbert (1C).
**Dec 1944** **Score:** 23–11  **Captains:** H. Tanner (Barbarians), J. Parsons (Midlands XV & J. E. Thorneloe's XV).
**Scorers** For: E. K. Scott (1T), G. A. Hudson (1T), J. B. Nicholls (1T), B. L. Williams (1T), R. G. H. Weighill (1T), H. Tanner (1T), R. F. Trott (1T), J. Heaton (1C).  Against: H. Greasley (1T), C. S. Harris (1T), N. M. Hall (1C, 1PG).

**MOSELEY**
**1974** **Score:** 22–25  **Captains:** J. F. Slattery (Barbarians), J. G. Webster (Moseley).

**Scorers** For: A. A. J. Finlayson (1T), A. J. Morley (1T), P. D. Llewellyn (1T), A. R. Irvine (1T, 1C), A. G. B. Old (2C).    Against: R. Wain (1T), J. G. Webster (1T), N. E. Horton (1T), M. J. Green (1T), M. J. Cooper (1T), S. A. Doble (1PG, 1C).

**NATAL**
**14 May 1969    Score:** 14–16    **Captains:** D. P. Rogers (Barbarians), R. Gould (Natal).
**Scorers** For: D. P. Rogers (2T), D. J. Duckham (1T), C. D. Saville (1PG, 1C).    Against: A. Donovan (1T), R. Steyn (1T), R. Gould (1T), M. Swanby (2C, 1PG).

**NEATH**
**1921    Score:** 10–12    **Captains:** H. L. G. Hughes (Barbarians), L. G. Thomas (Neath).
**Scorers** For: A. M. David (1T), C. L. Steyn (1T), C. L. Steyn (2C).    Against: W. E. Thomas (1T), E. Evans (1T), A. Hopkins (1T), W. Powell (1PG)
**1923    Score:** 5–16    **Captain:** M. P. Atkinson (Barbarians).
**Scorers** For: I. D. Bowden (1T), D. Drysdale (1C).    Against: W. Smith (2T), S. Jenkins (1T), F. Coope (1T), T. H. Francis (1DG).
**1924    Score:** 11–11    **Captain:** G. G. Aitken (Barbarians).
**Scorers** For: R. Harding (1T), I. S. Smith (1T), A. C. Wallace (1T), W. E. Crawford (1C).    Against: W. Parry (1T), G. Phillips (1T), E. Watkins (1T), I. Thomas (1C).
**1971    Score:** 12–4    **Captains:** D. L. Powell (Barbarians), D. Parker (Neath).
**Scorers** For: I. D. Wright (1T), I. G. McRae (1T), A. M. Jorden (2C).    Against: J. McAvoy (1T).

**NEW ENGLAND XV**
**1976    Score:** 40–12    **Captain:** P. Bennett (Barbarians).
**Scorers** For: A. R. Irvine (2T), D. J. McKay (1T), J. J. Williams (1T), D. A. Cooke (1T), A. G. Alexander (1T), H. Jenkins (1T), P. Bennett (6C).    Against: Collier (1T), Danforth (2PG, 1C).

**NEWPORT AND DISTRICT**
**1933    Score:** 16–10    **Captains:** H. Rew (Barbarians), W. A. Everson (Newport and District).
**Scorers** For: J. Russell (1T), C. C. Tanner (1T), P. C. Hordern (1T), B. C. Gadney (1T), G. G. Gregory (2C).    Against: Gwyn Bayliss (2T), W. A. Everson (2C).

**NEW ZEALAND**
**1954    Score:** 5–19    **Captains:** W. R. Willis (Barbarians), R. C. Stuart (New Zealand).
**Scorers** For: G. M. Griffiths (1T), I. King (1C).    Against: K. Davies (1T), R. A. Jarden (1T), M. J. Dixon (1T), R. A. White (1T), R. A. Jarden (2C), R. W. H. Scott (1DG).
**1964    Score:** 3–36    **Captains:** A. R. Dawson (Barbarians), W. J. Whineray (New Zealand).
**Scorers** For: I. J. Clarke (1GM).    Against: W. J. Nathan (2T), K. R. Tremain (1T), C. E. Meads (1T), D. J. Graham (1T), M. J. Dick (1T), R. W. Caulton (1T), W. J. Whineray (1T), D. B. Clarke (6C).
**1967    Score:** 6–11    **Captains:** S. Wilson (Barbarians), B. J. Lochore (New Zealand).
**Scorers** For: R. H. Lloyd (1T), S. Wilson (1DG).    Against: I. R. Mac Rae (1T), A. G. Steel (1T), E. W. Kirton (1DG), W. F. McCormick (1C).
**1973    Score:** 23–11    **Captains:** S. J. Dawes (Barbarians), I. A. Kirkpatrick (New Zealand).
**Scorers** For: G. Edwards (1T), J. F. Slattery (1T), J. C. Bevan (1T), J. P. R. Williams (1T), P. Bennett (1PG, 2C).    Against: G. Batty (2T), J. F. Karam (1PG).
**1974    Score:** 13–13    **Captains:** W. J. McBride (Barbarians), A. R. Leslie (New Zealand).
**Scorers** For: T. M. Davies (1T), A. R. Irvine (3PG).    Against: A. R. Leslie (1T), B. G. Williams (1T), J. F. Karam (1PG, 1C).

**NORTHERN TRANSVAAL**
**21 May 1958    Score:** 13–9    **Captains:** R. H. Williams (Barbarians), F. de Jager (Northern Transvaal).
**Scorers** For: A. J. F. O'Reilly (1T), C. I. Morgan (1T), T. J. Davies (2C, 1PG).    Against: L. Schmidt (1T), A. Ferreira (1T), A. Du Plessis (1DG).

**OLD DUNELMIANS**
**1897    Score:** 18–5    **Captains:** P. C. Tarbutt (Barbarians), H. Walker (Old Dunelmians).
**Scorers** For: P. W. Oscroft (1T), P. W. Stout (2T), J. F. Byrne (3C, 1PG).    Against: P. F. Cumberlege (1T), H. B. Fawcus (1C).

**ONTARIO**
**28 April 1957    Score:** 47–3    **Captain:** E. Evans (Barbarians).
**Scorers** For: A. J. F. O'Reilly (5T), P. H. Thompson (4T), G. T. Wells (3T), G. W. Hastings (3C), T. J. Davies (1C, 1PG).    Against: Nicholl (1T).
**30 April 1957    Score:** 52–0    **Captain:** R. Roe (Barbarians).
**Scorers** For: P. H. Thompson (2T), G. T. Wells (2T), J. E. Woodward (1T), D. G. S. Baker (1T), A. F. Dorward (1T), G. W. Hastings (1T, 5C, 5PG), R. Roe (1T).

**OXFORD UNIVERSITY (Past and Present)**
**1969    Score:** 18–16    **Captains:** W. G. Hullin (Barbarians), C. R. Laidlaw (Oxford University).
**Scorers** For: A. T. A. Duggan (1T), G. F. Bayles (1T), A. Hill (1T, 3C, 1PG).    Against: E. C. Osborne (1T), D. S. Boyle (1T), A. K. Morgan (1T), R. Hiller (2C), C. R. Laidlaw (1T).

**PERCY PARK**
**1895    Score:** 3–5    **Captain:** W. Mackay (Percy Park).
**Scorers** For: W. Ashford (1PG).    Against: G. C. Robinson (1T), W. MacKay (1C).
**1897    Score:** 20–9    **Captain:** H. Spencer (Percy Park).
**Scorers** For: R. W. Bell (1T), P. W. Stout (1T), O. G. Mackie (1T), R. F. Cumberlege (1T), P. W. Oscroft

(1T), W. E. Tucker (1T), J. F. Byrne (1C).    Against: R. A. Morland (1T), F. Stone (1T), W. Bates (1T).
**1900    Score:** 24–8
**Scorers** For: L. D. Bailey (1T), P. D. Kendall (1T), B. Oughtred (1T), R. F. Cumberlege (1T), C. S. Edgar (1T), A. F. King-Stephens (1DG), F. W. Odgers (1PG, 1C).    Against: G. C. Robinson (1T), B. S. Robson (1PG, 1C).
## PLYMOUTH
**1904    Score:** 8–26    **Captain:** F. M. Stout (Barbarians).
**Scorers** For: D. R. Bedell-Sivright (1T), F. H. Palmer (1T), F. M. Stout (1C).    Against: A. Avery (2T), T. Mills (1T), W. Beasley (1T, 2DG), W. Kressinger (1DG).
**1905    Score:** 8–15
**Scorers** For: W. V. Butcher (1T), E. W. Dillon (1T), H. F. P. Hearson (1C).    Against: W. Beasley (1T), T. Willcocks (1T), T. Mills (1T), W. Beasley (1DG), J. Peters (1C).
**1906    Score:** 6–15    **Captain:** F. M. Stout (Barbarians).
**Scorers** For: D. Lambert (2T).    Against: A. G. C. de Smidt (2T), J. Peters (1T), W. Hym (1DG), T. Mills (1C).
## QUAGGAS
**10 May 1969    Score:** 29–3    **Captains:** R. B. Taylor (Barbarians), I. Grant (Quaggas).
**Scorers** For: R. E. Webb (2T), A. T. A. Duggan (1T), A. G. Biggar (1T), M. L. Hipwell (1T), R. B. Taylor (1T). B. J. McGann (4C, 1DG).    Against: R. Bryant (1T).
## QUEBEC
**14 May 1957    Score:** 41–3    **Captain:** A. Robson (Barbarians).
**Scorers** For: A. F. Dorward (3T), A. J. F. O'Reilly (2T), P. H. Thompson (3T), G. M. Griffiths (1T), A. Robson (1T), T. J. Davies (1T, 3C), G. W. Hastings (1T).
**1976    Score:** 75–3    Captain: A. B. Carmichael (Barbarians).
**Scorers** For: D. McKay (4T), J. J. Williams (2T), D. A. Cooke (2T), A. J. A. Lawson (1T), J. Watkins (1T), B. Patrick (1T), G. Davies (2T, 10C, 1PG).    Against: Alder (1PG).
## RACING CLUB DE FRANCE
**1908    Score:** 13–0    **Captains:** J. E. C. Partridge (Barbarians), G. Lane (Racing Club de France).
**Scorers** For: J. S. Wilson (1T), P. F. McEvedy (1T), J. L. Fisher (1T), J. S. Wilson (2C).
**1910**    *Not played due to flooded ground.*
## RHODESIA
**26 May 1969    Score:** 24–21    **Captains:** J. P. O'Shea (Barbarians), R. Mundell (Rhodesia).
**Scorers** For: A. T. A. Duggan (1T), C. M. Telfer (1T), G. F. Bayles (1T), R. B. Taylor (1T), M. L. Hipwell (1T), B. J. McGann (3C, 1PG).    Against: T. Martin (1PG, 3C), R. Robertson (1T), J. Jones (3T).
## ROCKCLIFF
**1894    Score:** 0–8
**Scorers** Against: S. Anderson (1T), S. Murfitt (1T), E. W. Taylor (1C).
## RAMC (Crookham, Aldershot)
**1915    Score:** 10–3    **Captain:** E. R. Mobbs (Barbarians).
**Scorers** For: E. G. Butcher (1T), A. J. Dingle (1T), G. D. Roberts (1DG).    Against: J. C. A. Dowse (1T).
## SASKATCHEWAN
**1976    Score:** 76–0    **Captain:** P. J. Wheeler (Barbarians).
**Scorers** For: D. McKay (5T), B. Patrick (2T, 3C), G. Davies (2T, 7C), A. R. Irvine (2T), S. Fenwick (1T), F. M. D. Knill (1T), P. J. Wheeler (1T).
## SCOTTISH XV
**1970    Score:** 33–17    **Captains:** J. S. Spencer (Barbarians), F. A. L. Laidlaw (Scottish XV).
**Scorers** For: D. J. Duckham (2T), J. S. Spencer (1T), M. G. Molloy (1T), K. J. Fielding (1T), G. O. Edwards (1T), D. B. Llewelyn (1T), J. P. R. Williams (6C).    Against: T. G. Elliott (1T), P. C. Brown (4PG, 1C).
## SHOREHAM CAMP
**1914    Score:** 16–13    **Captains:** H. C. Harrison (Barbarians), E. R. Mobbs (Shoreham Camp).
**Scorers** For: L. R. Broster (1T), G. E. Kidman (1T), G. G. Ziegler (1T), H. Coverdale (2C).    Against: J. J. Lawson (1T), E. G. Butcher (2T, 2C).
## SOUTH AFRICA
**1952    Score:** 3–17    **Captains:** J. E. Nelson (Barbarians), H. S. V. Muller (South Africa).
**Scorers** For: W. I. D. Elliot (1T).    Against: J. K. Ochse (1T), C. J. van Wyk (1T), A. C. Keevy (2PG, 1C), P. G. Johnstone (1PG).
**1961    Score:** 6–0    **Captains:** A. R. Dawson (Barbarians), A. S. Malan (South Africa).
**Scorers** For: W. G. D. Morgan (1T), H. J. Morgan (1T).
**1970    Score:** 12–21    **Captains:** G. O. Edwards (Barbarians), D. J. de Villiers (South Africa).
**Scorers** For: R. J. Arneil (1T), D. J. Duckham (1T), A. T. A. Duggan (1T), K. E. Fairbrother (1T).    Against: J. H. Ellis (2T), A. E. van der Watt (1T), M. J. Lawless (1DG), D. J. de Villiers (1PG, 3C).
## SOUTH AFRICAN BARBARIANS
**17 May 1969    Score:** 11–23    **Captains:** W. G. Hullin (Barbarians), G. Carelse (South African Barbarians).
**Scorers** For: J. P. O'Shea (1T), I. S. Gallacher (1T), B. J. McGann (1PG), C. D. Saville (1C).    Against: K. Meiring (2T), W. Stapelberg (1T), G. Nortje (1T), C. Luther (3PG, 1C).
## SOUTH AFRICAN COUNTRY DISTRICTS
**24 May 1969    Score:** 32–22    **Captains:** F. A. L. Laidlaw (Barbarians), D. J. de Villiers (South African Country Districts).

**Scorers** For: A. T. A. Duggan (2T), A. G. Biggar (1T), C. Telfer (1T), F. A. L. Laidlaw (1T), B. J. McGann (2PG, 3C), C. D. Saville (1PG, 1C).    Against: K. Koorts (1T), J. Joubert (1T), P. Visagie (2PG, 2C, 1DG), M. Roux (1PG).

**SOUTH AFRICAN SERVICES**
**1915    Score:** 9–3    **Captains:** H. C. Harrison (Barbarians), H. E. Turnley (South African Services).
**Scorers** For: W. P. Thomas (2T), R. V. Hill (1T).    Against: F. Janion (1T).

**SOUTHERN UNIVERSITIES** (South Africa)
**21 May 1969    Score:** 14–16 .    **Captains:** R. B. Taylor (Barbarians), I. McCallum (Southern Universities).
**Scorers** For: W. Hullin (1T), R. B. Taylor (1T), J. Jeffrey (1T), B. J. McGann (1PG, 1C).    Against: H. de Vos (1T), S. Hillock (1T), I. McCallum (2PG, 2C).

**SOUTH SHIELDS**
**1895    Score:** 27–5    **Captain:** P. Maud (Barbarians).
**Scorers** For: C. G. Ames (2T), J. Conway Rees (2T), H. T. Wallis (1T), F. Mitchell (1T), E. M. Baker (1T), F. Mitchell (3C).    Against: W. G. Baty (1T), W. E. Kassell (1C).

**STADE FRANÇAIS**
**1899    Score:** 33–0    **Captain:** M. Moulu (Stade Français).
**Scorers** For: R. O. Schwarz (3T), W. B. Sherwell (2T), F. S. Young (1T), C. Dixon (1T), J. F. Byrne (6C).

**SWINTON**
**1891    Score:** 0–9
**Scorers** Against: J. Valentine (3T), J. T. Haslam (1C).

**TRANSVAAL**
**10 May 1958    Score:** 17–17    **Captains:** C. I. Morgan (Barbarians), G. van Tander (Transvaal).
**Scorers** For: A. R. Smith (3T), A. J. F. O'Reilly (2T), T. J. Davies (1C).    Against: J. Kaminer (1T), J. Nel (1T), J. Prinsloo (1T), M. Gericke (1T), M. Pelser (1T), J. Buys (1C).

**ULSTER**
**1957    Score:** 14–11    **Captains:** J. T. Greenwood (Barbarians), J. W. Kyle (Ulster).
**Scorers** For: W. A. Gray (1T), J. C. Walker (1T), G. H. Waddell (1T), C. R. James (1DG), D. F. Allison (1C).    Against: N. C. Hamilton (2T) J. I. Brennan (1T), D. Hewitt (1C).

**WALES**
**1915    Score:** 26–10    **Captains:** E. R. Mobbs (Barbarians), J. Alban Davies (Wales).
**Scorers** For: J. P. Quinn (2T), A. G. Bull (1T), J. B. Minch (1T), A. K. Horan (1T), J. G. G. Birkett (1T), E. G. Butcher (2C), G. D. Roberts (2C).    Against: B. R. Lewis (1T), I. T. Davies (1T), J. M. C. Lewis (1DG).

**WASPS**
**1967    Score:** 36–8    **Captains:** P. E. Judd (Barbarians), D. W. A. Rosser (Wasps).
**Scorers** For: T. G. R. Davies (3T), W. K. Jones (2T), R. E. Webb (1T), C. J. Standing (1T), J. Barton (1T), B. M. Stoneman (1T), D. T. Deans (1T), S. Wilson (2C), B. M. Stoneman (1C).    Against: G. Wyman (1T), F. E. J. Hawkins (1T), D. W. A. Rosser (1C).

**WEST HARTLEPOOL**
**1902    Score:** 4–25    **Captain:** J. T. Taylor (West Hartlepool).
**Scorers** For: R. W. Poole (1DG).    Against: J. Emmerson (2T), F. Spence (1T), J. T. Taylor (3DG), J. Emmerson (2C).

**WEST OF ENGLAND**
**1896    Score:** 0–0
**1898    Score:** 0–14
**Scorers** Against: F. Goulding (1T), E. W. Baker (2T), R. G. Parsons (1T), J. Oates (1C).

**WESTERN PROVINCE**
**18 May 1958    Score:** 8–9    **Captains:** C. I. Morgan (Barbarians), J. A. J. Pickard (Western Province).
**Scorers** For: A. J. F. O'Reilly (1T), S. H. Wilcock (1T), T. J. Davies (1C).    Against: F. Coetzee (2PG), J. Nel (1DG).

**WESTERN TRANSVAAL**
**14 May 1958    Score:** 3–11    **Captains:** R. W. D. Marques (Barbarians), J. T. Claassen (Western Transvaal).
**Scorers** For: J. T. Greenwood (1T).    Against: D. Putter (1T), J. Claassen (1T), C. Meyer (1C, 1DG).